Call to Mission and Perceptions of Proselytism

Call to Mission and Perceptions of Proselytism

A Reader for a Global Conversation

Compiled and Edited by
JOHN BAXTER-BROWN

Foreword by
LARRY MILLER

PICKWICK Publications • Eugene, Oregon

CALL TO MISSION AND PERCEPTIONS OF PROSELYTISM
A Reader for a Global Conversation

Copyright © 2022 Wipf and Stock Publishers. All rights reserved. Except for brief quotations in critical publications or reviews, no part of this book may be reproduced in any manner without prior written permission from the publisher. Write: Permissions, Wipf and Stock Publishers, 199 W. 8th Ave., Suite 3, Eugene, OR 97401.

Pickwick Publications
An Imprint of Wipf and Stock Publishers
199 W. 8th Ave., Suite 3
Eugene, OR 97401

www.wipfandstock.com

PAPERBACK ISBN: 978-1-5326-5877-8
HARDCOVER ISBN: 978-1-5326-5878-5
EBOOK ISBN: 978-1-5326-5879-2

Cataloguing-in-Publication data:

Names: Baxter-Brown, John, editor. | Miller, Larry, foreword.

Title: Call to mission and perceptions of proselytism : a reader for a global conversation / edited by John Baxter-Brown ; foreword by Larry Miller.

Description: Eugene, OR : Pickwick Publications, 2022 | Includes bibliographical references and index(es).

Identifiers: ISBN 978-1-5326-5877-8 (paperback) | ISBN 978-1-5326-5878-5 (hardcover) | ISBN 978-1-5326-5879-2 (ebook)

Subjects: LCSH: Missions. | Evangelistic work.

Classification: BV2061.3 .C34 2022 (print) | BV2061.3 .C34 (ebook)

APRIL 8, 2022

This volume is dedicated to
my family—Pippa, Katie, and Rosie—
and to my colleagues and friends on MTAG, the Mission Theology
Advisory Group

but also to those millions of people who seek to follow Jesus
and share the Good News,
sometimes doing so incredibly well
and sometimes making mistakes out of their enthusiasm.
Let us have more enthusiasm
and more wisdom and sensitivity.

Contents

Foreword by Larry Miller | xi
Preface | xiii
Acknowledgments | xv
Abbreviations | xvii

Part 1: SETTING THE SCENE

  1.1 Mission and Proselytism: Themes and Issues | 3
    —John Baxter-Brown

  1.2 Proselytism or Evangelism? | 14
    Evangelical Review of Theology 26.4 (2002) 337–53
    —Cecil Stalnaker | 14

  1.3 Christian Understandings of Proselytism | 24
    International Bulletin of Missionary Research 23.1 (1999) 8–14
    —David A. Kerr | 24

  1.4 UN Declarations | 39

Part 2: STATEMENTS AND REPORTS FROM CHRISTIAN BODIES

  Introduction | 49

  2.1 Second Vatican Council | 51
    RCC 1965

    Ad Gentes | 53

    Dignitatis Humanae | 58

  2.2 Common Witness and Proselytism (A Study Document) | 66

  2.3 Stuttgart Consultation | 78
    WCC/CWME 1987

  2.4 Orthodox Advisory Group to WCC/CWME | 81

Orthodox/CWME

2.5 Mission in Christ's Way: Your Will Be Done | 84
CWME World Conference on Mission and Evangelism
San Antonio 1989

2.6 Proselytism, Sects, and Pastoral Challenges: Middle East Council of Churches | 86
Unit on Faith and Unity 1989

2.7 The Balamand Declaration: Uniatism, Method of Union of the Past, and the Present Search for Full Communion | 93
RCC/Orthodox 1993

2.8 The Challenge of Proselytism and the Calling to Common Witness: A Study Document of the Joint Working Group | 104
WCC/RCC 1995

2.9 Evangelization, Proselytism, and Common Witness: The Report from the Fourth Phase of the International Dialogue 1990–1997 between the Roman Catholic Church and some Classical Pentecostal Churches and Leaders | 117
RCC/Pentecostal 1997

2.10 Towards Common Witness: A Call to Adopt Responsible Relationships in Mission and to Renounce Proselytism | 133
WCC 1997

2.11 Statement on Religious Liberty, Evangelism, and Proselytism | 146
Seventh-Day Adventist Statement 2000

2.12 Communicating the Message: Common Witness/Evangelism/Proselytism | 148
WCC 2001

2.13 Church, Evangelization, and the Bonds of *Koinonia:* A Report of the International Consultation between the Catholic Church and the World Evangelical Alliance (1993–2002) | 154

2.14 Proselytism Policy Statement: A Paper from the Micah Network Disaster Management Working Group, South Asia | 158
Micah Network 2007

2.15 Lausanne Movement Documents | 162

2.16 Christian Witness in a Multi-Religious World: Recommendations for Conduct | 182
WCC/RCC/WEA 2011

2.17 Together Towards Life | 189
    WCC/CWME 2013

2.18 Orthodox Perspectives | 193
    Orthodox

2.19 Common Declaration of His Holiness Francis
    and His Holiness Tawadros II | 199
    RCC/Coptic Orthodox 2017

Part 3 ARTICLES BY INDIVIDUAL COMMENTATORS

3.1 Fishing in the Neighbor's Pond: Mission and Proselytism
    in Eastern Europe | 207
    International Bulletin of Missionary Research 20.1 (1996) 26–31
    —Miroslav Volf

3.2 Mission and Proselytism: A Middle East Perspective | 222
    International Bulletin of Missionary Research 20.1 (1996) 12–16, 18–22
    —David A. Kerr

3.3 Mission and the Issue of Proselytism | 243
    International Bulletin of Missionary Research 20.1 (1996) 2–8
    —Cecil M. Robeck Jr.

3.4 Mission, Evangelism, and Proselytism in Christianity: Mainline Conceptions as Reflected in Church Documents | 259
    Emory International Law Review 12 (1998) 563–650
    —Joel A. Nichols

3.5 Proselytism in a Central and Eastern European Perspective | 289
    Journal of European Baptist Studies 8.2 (2008) 18–36
    —Darrell Jackson

3.6 An Evangelical View of Proselytism | 308
    Prepared for and Authorized by the Department for Theological Concerns of the World Evangelical Alliance, December 1, 2018
    —Elmer Thiessen and Thomas Schirrmacher

3.7 Christian Witness and Proselytism (Some Initial Thoughts after the Panorthodox Council) | 321
    —Petros Vassiliadis

Bibliography | 327
Subject Index | 347
Scripture Index | 361

Foreword

THE STORY OF THIS *Reader* is rooted in the Second Global Gathering of the Global Christian Forum (Manado, Indonesia, October 2011). Its path has been long and occasionally winding. So it is with special gratitude for the result and appreciation for all those involved in producing it that I commend the book to you.

At that 2011 Gathering, participants called on the Forum to move forward in providing "space" for global conversations on challenges churches worldwide should address together, especially when they are not in agreement with one another. Consultation with the widest possible spectrum of church leadership in 2012 identified two priority issues for such conversation: (1) the growing phenomenon of discrimination, persecution, and martyrdom of Christians, and (2) the common call to mission mixed with problematic perceptions of proselytism—the sort of proselytism sometimes referred to pejoratively as "sheep-stealing."

In full collaboration with four main Forum participant bodies—The Catholic Church (Pontifical Council for Promoting Christian Unity), the Pentecostal World Fellowship, the World Council of Churches, the World Evangelical Alliance—the Forum convened a series of working group meetings and consultations during the following years. The culmination of the conversation on discrimination, persecution and martyrdom was a global consultation held in Tirana, Albania, in November 2015.[1] On the matter of proselytism, the more "church-dividing" of the two issues, there have also been a number of meetings and consultations, from which and for which this *Reader* has already emerged even though the conversation has not yet concluded.

While the leadership of all Forum participant bodies agree that the church is called to mission and evangelism, powerful emotions and deep wounds remain widely manifest, rooted in experiences, perceptions, or

1. See Beek and Miller, *Discrimination, Persecution, Martyrdom*.

accusations of proselytism between churches. After extensive consultation and careful consideration, the GCF Committee decided in 2013 to convene a global conversation in response to this "challenge." The Catholic Church (PCPCU), the Pentecostal World Fellowship, the World Council of Churches, and the World Evangelical Alliance each named representatives to the Working Group responsible for the development, implementation, and oversight of the initiative.

This Working Group met for the first time in September 2014 (Strasbourg) and developed an initial plan. It met next in November 2015 (Geneva), when it appointed three task groups to develop specific components of the initiative. The task groups and the Working Group met again in October 2016 (Rome). In June 2017 a larger consultation was held in Accra, Ghana, with participation of practitioners and leaders from across the full scope of Christian traditions and from around the world. At present, the global conversation continues, with a conclusion anticipated in late 2018 or 2019.

This *Reader*, edited and compiled by John Baxter-Brown, a member of the Working Group, is one outcome of these many meetings. It has had the input from the entire Working Group and from many others. It is a unique book that gathers in one volume the most significant texts, documents, and statements from multi-lateral, bi-lateral or denominational discussions on the difficult topic of proselytism between Christian traditions. The history of these texts shows careful work by many Christians over the decades who have wrestled with the issues and sought a way forward for their churches so as to overcome divisions and to witness to the unity Christians have in Jesus Christ.

I hope that this *Reader* will encourage these conversations to continue in truthfulness, gentleness, love, healing, and common mission.

Larry Miller
Secretary, Global Christian Forum (January 2012–June 2018)
Strasbourg, July 2018

Preface

THIS READER IS THE product of myriad conversations, consultations, prayers, and debates over many decades. Many people have contributed to these various activities, offering their wisdom and reflections as well as—at times—their pain and frustration, for the topic of proselytism touches some very pertinent and painful issues. The following documents give life to some of these discussions and emotions.

The various contributions to this volume have been written and complied in different contexts. This shows in the language and styles used. Some are formal, others less so; some are couched in theological language; some reflect the policies and positions of Christian bodies and Churches, others the opinions of the authors alone. But all reveal something of the passion and commitment of Christians to mission and evangelism, and all highlight some of the crucial obstacles to Christian unity facing those who claim to follow Jesus in these early years of the twenty-first century.

I have tried to allow the authors and drafters of the different documents to keep their own voice. The only editing I have done is by way of shortening some of the longer contributions, to include only the relevant sections. Thus, some papers use American spelling and others UK spelling; there are different approaches to grammar and punctuation, and to the use of inclusive language; some papers have been translated from their original language into English (usually by their drafters), and this can be observed at times. These different characteristics each contribute to the overarching narrative that can be discerned in this volume.

It is a narrative of *world Christianity*. Perceptions of proselytism are not limited to a specific geopolitical or theological context. Every Church and tradition is impacted by the issue. There is an *historical dimension* to the topic, and understanding the past may—*just may*—help unlock a better future. The story is of *ecumenical encounters* between those who have (in the distant and more recent past) actively persecuted one another. But above all (if I may speak personally), the narrative is a *missionary story* as different traditions and streams within the global Christian community wrestle with one of the core purposes of the Church: the task, entrusted to us by Jesus Himself, of world mission and evangelization.

If this volume can contribute to more evangelism and better evangelism, then I shall be pleased.

John Baxter-Brown
Salisbury, England, August 2019

Acknowledgments

THE FOLLOWING INDIVIDUALS HAVE all contributed to this volume through engaging with the GCF Working Group and consultations: Femi Adeleye, Kim Cain, Andrzej Choromanski, Catherine Clifford, Rosalee Velloso Ewell, Coorilos Mor Geevarghese, Wesley Granberg-Michaelson, Mikhail Goundiaev, Arto Hämäläinen, Kathryn Johnson, Jooseop Keum, Nicta Lubaale, Larry Miller, Magali Moreno, Cecil M. Robeck, Thomas Schirrmacher, Richard Van Houton, Petros Vassiliadis, Katalina Tahaafe Williams, and Dominic Yeo.

The following copyright holders have generously granted permission for the reproduction of their intellectual property:

IBTS Centre Amsterdam

Lausanne Movement

Libreria Editrice Vaticana

Micah Network

Middle East Council of Churches

Joel Nichols

Pontifical Council for Promoting Christian Unity

Sage Publications and International Bulletin of Missionary Research

Seventh-Day Adventist Church

Elmer Thiessen, Mark Oxbrow, and Tim Grass

The United Nations

Petros Vassiliadis

World Council of Churches

World Evangelical Alliance, Department for Theological Concerns

I owe a debt of gratitude to Rev Dr Larry Miller and the entire Working Group for their advice and guidance, and especially to my family, Pippa, Katie, and Rosie, for their patient endurance.

Any errors or mistakes are, of course, my personal responsibility.

Abbreviations

CPC	Classical Pentecostal Churches
CWME	Commission on World Mission and Evangelism
GCF	Global Christian Forum
IRM	International Review of Mission
JWG	Joint Working Group
MECC	Middle East Council of Churches
NRM	New Religious Movements
PCID	Pontifical Council for Interreligious Dialogue
PCPCU	Pontifical Council for Promoting Christian Unity
RCC	Roman Catholic Church
ROC	Russian Orthodox Church
WCC	World Council of Churches
WEA	World Evangelical Alliance

Part 1

SETTING THE SCENE

1.1

Mission and Proselytism

Themes and Issues

John Baxter-Brown

Evangelism is the queen of all Christian ministries. It is the one dedicated to making the Triune God's Good News known to all the world through the words, deeds and character of God's people.[1] It is an outward-looking ministry, facing into the world that is loved by God and yet wounded and broken by sin.

The Church's very existence is both a result of evangelism and God's chosen tool for evangelism. She is called to be salt and light in the world if she is to be faithful to her calling of love and obedience towards God. There is an urgency and necessity for the Church to embrace her responsibility before God such that the whole world is invited to participate in the life and love of God.

Throughout Christian history, the Church has endeavored to find how best to be faithful to her calling to mission and evangelism. Not always has she been successful and too often even the best of intentions led to hurt and pain, and caused disrepute to the gospel. In the twentieth century there were many expressions of concern and growth in the ways the Christian traditions thought about mission. In 1910 was the famous Edinburgh World Missions Conference. It produced two "messages" calling the Church to mission and

---

1. I should declare upfront that my primary vocation is that of an evangelist and secondly as a theologian. Thus, I may be accused of approaching the issue of *proselytism* from this perspective. I am more than happy to acknowledge this.

evangelism, as well as leading to the founding of the International Missionary Council (IMC, now known as CWME, and part of the World Council of Churches). The Anglican Church produced a report on "the Evangelistic work of the Church" in 1919. There followed a series of IMC world missionary conferences; the rise of the Pentecostal and charismatic movements; the formation of the Lausanne Committee for World Evangelization (now called the Lausanne Movement); Papal encyclicals and other documents, and in 2016, the Holy and Great Council of the Orthodox Church produced *The Mission of the Orthodox Church in Today's World*. During the twentieth century, there was a rapid demographic shift in world Christianity, from the North Atlantic (Europe and North America) to the developing countries of the majority world.

And yet . . . even "while leadership of all participant bodies [of the Global Christian Forum] agree that the church is called to mission and evangelism, powerful emotions and deep wounds rooted in experiences, perceptions, or accusations of proselytism between churches—understood popularly as the 'stealing of sheep' from one Christian body by another Christian body—are widely manifest."[2]

This book, which is primarily concerned with proselytism from a theological perspective, is itself part of the initiative of the Four Pillars of the GCF to explore the issue of proselytism.[3] It is a multi-layered issue within the global Christian community, with complex inter-connecting themes which can play out differently in varying contexts. However, the subject is of significant interest beyond the boundaries of the Christian community as it raises legal, ethical, and political concerns as well as theological and methodological ones. Thus, both Christian and secular bodies have addressed the issue from within their areas of competence. For example, this book includes an edited version of a long article from the *Emory International Law Review*, as well as theological and ethical reflections drawn from the main Christian traditions.

---

2. Quoted from *"Call to Mission and Perceptions of Proselytism": A Global Conversation*, the Global Christian Forum's memo, outlining an initiative to "convene a global conversation on this theme and to do so in cooperation with other global bodies. The Catholic Church (Pontifical Council for Promoting Christian Unity), the Pentecostal World Fellowship, the World Council of Churches, and the World Evangelical Alliance have joined with the GCF in this initiative."

3. The "Four Pillars" are the Pentecostal World Fellowship (PWF), the Pontifical Council for Promoting Christian Unity (PCPCU), the World Council of Churches (WCC), and the World Evangelical Alliance (WEA).

THE LEGAL AND POLITICAL INTERSECTION

There are several reasons why the intersection with law and politics is important.

Firstly, and most obviously, we all live in societies that are governed by law (however it is formulated and administered). As such governments have the power to shape and change the cultural and legal framework of their societies (for good or ill), and this includes creating, defining and imposing boundaries around the religious life of its citizens. Thus, when governments enact such legislation, or act in such a way as to enforce policies on religious practice, there will usually be direct implications for adherents of religion. These may be beneficial—or detrimental.

Secondly, religious belief and behaviour are often closely associated with national and cultural identity. National Churches, for example, can be custodians of national culture (to varying degrees). The national Churches from the former Soviet-bloc countries of Eastern Europe and the Middle East, subjected to many years of oppressive, foreign rule, make this claim with some justification. The religious tradition, as cultural guardian, may therefore be deeply valued and the boundaries between religious and cultural institution may be difficult to define. Changing one's religious affiliation and loyalty can be perceived as a denunciation of one's national citizenship.[4] This is a sociological aspect, but intersects with the legal one as well.

Thirdly, human rights, especially those rights connected to religious freedoms and expressions, create an international framework in which the issue of proselytism comes into sharp focus. For example, Stahnke notes that "all major international human rights documents recognize the right to freedom of religion, which includes not only the freedom to hold religious beliefs but also the freedom to manifest those beliefs."[5] However, "while the freedom to hold beliefs is considered to be absolute, i.e., not subject to limitation by the State, the freedom to manifest beliefs is subject to valid limitations."[6] The State, therefore, can impose restrictions upon the practice of faith which is especially relevant when so-called "anti-conversion" laws are applied.[7] In theory, the development of national legal frameworks

---

4. Paul does claim that Christians are "citizens of heaven" (Phil 3:20). One of the accusations against the first Christians was that they claimed "there is another king—Jesus" (Acts 17:7). Thus, there is a theological and biblical case for arguing that becoming a follower of Jesus requires a change in citizenship-allegiance, but this is a theological argument and not directly relevant to the cultural discussion above.

5. Stahnke, "Proselytism and the Freedom to Change Religion," 269.

6. Stahnke, "Proselytism and the Freedom to Change Religion," 270.

7. See, for example, Law Library of Congress, "State Anti-Conversion Laws in

should protect the rights all interested parties; in practice, it is questionable if this is achieved.

Fourthly, and closely connected to the previous point, there are competing "rights" within the issue of proselytism. Variables exist within this "rights" context. Stahnke expresses it well: "The problem lies in finding the proper balance between the freedom to proselytize and the multitude of rights, duties, and interests of religious groups, individuals, and the state that may conflict with that freedom."[8] These arise either because of different interpretations of the UN framework, or because the rights themselves create tensions. For example, the rights of minority religious groups and of individuals may at times compete one against the other, or the rights to freedom of expression and propagation of one's religious beliefs may conflict with the rights to privacy. Such conflicts are rightly addressed through the judiciary since they pertain to law.

Finally, it is important to consider the competencies involved in this intersection. Modern states are not (usually) theocracies. Rather, they are governed through statues, and the appropriate competencies for developing the legislative framework and interpreting them lie with government and the judiciary. As such, whilst Church leaders and theologians may have necessary perspectives to share, the legal side of this issue is not theological, and the theological dimension is not legal. It is essential that both narratives interact in wholesome and suitable ways, but it also vital that there is appropriate distance between these differing competencies.

THEOLOGY AND MISSION

Several significant theological themes emerge from the documents collected together in this volume.

Evangelism and Mission

Proselytism only arises in the context of evangelism and mission. If there were no Christians participating in evangelism, there would be no issue.[9] From this one perspective—that there are Christians passionate about their faith and making efforts to share it with others—the whole debate about

---

India"; SAHRDC, "Anti-Conversion Laws."

8. Stahnke, "Proselytism and the Freedom to Change Religion," 250–51.

9. This volume is concerned primarily with *intra-Christian* contexts and not with recruitment by cults and sects or with inter-religious mission.

what counts as proselytism and what does not can be seen as arising from an encouraging phenomenon. The desire to share the Good News about Jesus and the kingdom of God with other people is a positive sign that God, through the Holy Spirit, continues to be active in the world today. It is a sign that Christians are attempting to fulfil the various pre- and post-resurrection commissions of our Lord, Jesus Christ; that Christians, motivated by love, wish to tell others the story of Jesus, God incarnate, through their words, deeds and character, and wish to invite other people to share in their joy and salvation. No follower of Jesus should object to such ideals.

However, quickly we come across the complications of what counts as appropriate practice, purity of purpose, depth of empathy, transparency of theology and the integrity of ethics. The zeal of the evangelizer or proselytizer is rarely in doubt, but these other dimensions are the basis for most accusations of proselytism—and all of them are intimately associated with the practice and theology of mission and evangelism.

Practice refers to the methods adopted by the evangelizer (or proselytizer).

Empathy concerns the ability of the missionary to understand and appreciate the culture in which they are working, and especially the context in which any existing Christian community find themselves.

Theology here means the various doctrinal understandings of the faith, especially those of soteriology, ecclesiology, and missiology.

Ethics involves reflection upon all the above in the light of the values of the kingdom of God.

Language and Definitions

Proselytism itself is an emotionally-laden term. This was not always the case, but in modern usage the term has come to carry a pejorative meaning.[10] However, there remains a lack of clarity about the precise meaning of the term such that "one person's evangelization is another person's proselytism."[11] Several papers in this volume highlight this issue, with some writers wishing to keep the historical and honorable meaning of the word *proselytism*; others believe that the common understanding of "sheep stealing" is now so widespread that it is impossible to maintain positive usage. However, nearly all Churches and commentators agree that there are unethical practices that are detrimental to Christian unity and strategically counter-productive and

---

10. See sections 1.2 and 3.9 in this volume. See also Penner, "Proselytism"; Barrington-Ward, "Prosleytism."

11. Haughey, "Complex Accusation of Sheep-Stealing." See also section 2.9 (93).

they are done by others not themselves! A healthy dose of self-examination (and undoubtedly, repentance) is called for, probably by all parties.

What might be hailed as appropriate methodology in mission and evangelism in one tradition can easily be perceived as aggressive proselytizing from within a different part of the Christian community. Thus, of central importance in any discussion is a need to be clear about definitions, but herein lies a second dilemma: which language? Do we begin to draw upon legal concepts, including the narratives of human rights and religious liberty? Or would sociology provide better tools for thinking about social anthropology and social group loyalties? Or moral philosophy? Or theology, drawing upon doctrines of ecclesiology, soteriology, the *missio Dei*, or upon the core practice of evangelization, and so forth? Is there a way of discussing intra-Christian proselytism without bringing in charged allegations against fellow-believers, or—in contrast—without being defensive or protectionist? These are difficult issues to address for they touch upon the core issue of self-identity for many Christian bodies.

These questions logically point to a second issue: *authority*.

AUTHORITY AND POWER

Within this book there are two dimensions to this theme.

This volume is a modest collection of statements and essays about proselytism: it is not intended to be a comprehensive compilation. Rather I seek to illustrate a breadth of Christian traditions and interpretations. Some of the statements presented are formal: they arose from a long and structured process by Christian bodies and are intended to carry the weight of the Church or organization; others are a summary of a process, a record of conversations and discussions distilled into a document: these lack the formal authority of the Churches or bodies involved but nonetheless reflect the formal positions adopted. Other papers are the views of scholars. These papers lack formal, structured authority completely, for their authority rests upon the wisdom of the author and the quality of their content: they carry weight only insofar as the arguments and positions presented are persuasive.

However, the issue of authority within the proselytism discussion plays out in an altogether more pronounced way. *By whose authority does a missionary or evangeliser act?* Many of the formal papers refer to the obligation to evangelize laid upon the Churches by Jesus. For example, The Holy and Great Council of the Orthodox Church stated:

> The conveyance of the Gospel's message according to the last commandant of Christ, "Go therefore and make disciples of all

nations, baptizing them in the name of the Father and of the Son and of the Holy Spirit, teaching them to observe all that I have commanded you" (Matt 28:19) is the diachronic mission of the Church.[12]

This text—among other commissioning texts in the Gospels and the book of Acts (and elsewhere throughout Scripture)—are presumed to give due authority to the Church, and therefore to Christians, to go to *all* nations. The Christian claims direct authority from Jesus Christ, mediated through the Scriptures, not only to go, but to make disciples, and to teach and baptize. The logic is straight forwards: *if* all authority on earth has been given to Jesus, and Jesus commands the missionary to go, then the missionary is authorized by Jesus himself: nowhere is off limits, for there are no boundaries on earth given by Jesus in the text. Thus, the missionary may go anywhere and if any earthly (or ecclesial?) authority that attempts to inhibit the missionary's journey is acting—not simply without God's authority—but *against* it.

However, hidden away within this logic are at least two contentious issues. Firstly, there is both a personal and corporate dimension to the Christian faith, with various Churches and traditions giving different weight to each, at times including a nationalistic understanding to the corporate dimension. There are times where this power balance is at best precarious. Western exegetes will tend towards a personal or individualistic interpretation of the text. An alternative perspective sees Christ commissioning *a group* of people, not eleven individuals. The institution of the Church, it is argued, is the body duly authorized to go, through its commissioned representatives; authority resides within the collective group—the Church—and not with the individual missionaries. Secondly, the stated purpose is to make disciples. However, defining what genuine discipleship is remains contested among Christian traditions except in the broadest sense. Whilst Matthew records Jesus as saying disciples are "to obey everything that I have commanded you" (28:20), the moral and spiritual teaching referred to has been interpreted in various ways. What is the situation then, when one ecclesial body claims that members of another ecclesial body are *not* disciples, or that there is a level of dysfunctionality with the discipleship in the other group? By what authority are such judgements made?

In one post-resurrection commissioning text, Jesus promises the disciples, "You will receive power when the Holy Spirit comes on you; and you

---

12. HGCOC, "Mission of the Orthodox Church in Today's World" (see section 2.18). Many other traditions and Churches make reference to Matthew 28 as a justification for mission and evangelism.

will be my witnesses in Jerusalem, and in all Judea and Samaria, and to the ends of the earth" (Acts 1:8). Jesus again imposes no geographical or ethnic limitations upon the disciples' missionary work. Rather, he promises that they will be empowered in their witness by the Holy Spirit. There is no indication that the power Jesus refers to is political, military or economic, but rather this power is directly linked to the Trinity in the person of the Spirit.

Proselytism is an abuse of power, whereas wholesome, holistic evangelism is an application of God's power into individual lives and social contexts for God's glory and the building up of God's church. However, discerning the difference between the varying types of power, its ethical use and abuse, may require a complex judgement because different Churches and Christian traditions have different sensitivities regarding what is the appropriate use of authority and power. Depending upon one's perception, one group may believe that they are practicing ethical evangelism, whereas another group may see the same activity as harmful proselytism. The latter group may feel threatened, whereas the former group may feel that ecclesial (and/ or political and civil) power is being used against them.

This leads to a third major theme.

ECCLESIOLOGY

The different Christian traditions have unique characteristics and their understanding of ecclesiology has substantial implications for the issue of proselytism. This is particularly acute when linked to doctrines of salvation and the associated sociological consideration of who is saved—that is, who is understood to be part of the Christian community and who is excluded. For the more sacramental traditions baptism is paramount: if someone is baptized, then they are part of the Christian community. However, the younger traditions (such as the evangelical and Pentecostal ones) generally assert that the process of becoming part of the Christian community is intrinsically associated with personal commitment to certain doctrines, and therefore baptism, whilst an important public witness of their inward faith, does not confer salvation. Only faith does that. Thus, there are different understandings of how a person becomes part of the Christian community and of the nature of salvation and how it is granted.

Likewise, the levels of expected behaviour of members of the Christian community vary among the different traditions, with (generally) the younger churches placing significant emphasis on personal piety and individual witness compared to the older traditions which place greater emphasis upon attending corporate, public worship and partaking of the sacraments. This is not an either/or polarity: rather it is a question of emphasis. However, the strength of emphasis is at times significant, and has led to border conflicts about who is *in* and *out* of the church. Soteriology has become a major point of dissension within the Christian community, with some traditions not accepting, and sometimes completely rejecting, the legitimacy of other traditions. For example, many traditions have made exclusivist claims regarding salvation, claiming that it is only their own adherents who are truly saved; members of other traditions are therefore, at best, second class Christians (if they are Christians at all).

These conflicts also exist *within* the same traditions, whether based on doctrine, praxis, theological and philosophical commitments, or the celebration of specific liturgies. One specific application of this conflict is in the use of terms such as *nominal Christians*, sometimes also called *functional atheism*. This refers to people who attend church, or claim to be Christians, but their attendance or claims appear to have no impact on their lifestyles: their moral attitudes and behaviour are not shaped by the faith, and their doctrinal understanding is limited or non-existent. The term could refer to people who might go to church for baptism or a wedding, but who otherwise are not involved at all in the daily life of the Church. In effect, they are not followers of Jesus except in name only, despite allegiance to a local congregation; church attendance is perhaps a cultural imperative rather than a witness to an internal reality. Is evangelism among such people necessary and legitimate, or is it proselytism? Does it not show a pastoral concern for their growth in the faith, and concern for their well-being?

When ecclesiology, soteriology and politics coincide the issue of proselytism becomes particularly acute. Serious challenges and misunderstandings arise in contexts where canonical territory shapes the identity of the church, and especially when the church has a function of carrying ethnic or national cultural history. This is compounded when infant baptism is viewed as a sacrament through which the child is saved. Former countries oppressed under the Soviet empire provide many examples of where national, mainly Orthodox, Churches survived decades of extreme persecution and began to regain their strength and national identity after the collapse of communism. Simultaneously Western missionaries saw the fall of the Soviet Union as providing a gateway to new mission fields and poured resources into the newly independent countries and Russia herself. This created fertile ground for inter-church friction and accusations of proselytism.[13]

---

13. See Jackson, *Canonical Territory and National Security*.

RELIGIOUS LIBERTY

The UN Universal Declaration of Human Rights states:

> Everyone has the right to freedom of thought, conscience and religion; this right includes freedom to change his religion or belief, and freedom, either alone or in community with others and in public or private, to manifest his religion or belief in teaching, practice, worship, and observance.[14]

The theme of religious freedom appears numerous times within this volume.[15] It is central to the entire controversy, weaving throughout the discussions and bringing into focus many of the sub-themes. Such freedom cannot exist where force, coercion, inducements, *etc.* undermine its very basis. This can be particularly acute in different regions of the world, and especially in contexts where political power is used to remove religious liberty. This theme also appears in contexts where a person decides to "change" their allegiance from one Christian tradition to another. Questions such as, has the person been given ample time to make an informed choice? Who decides what sort of time is necessary and what that freedom of choice looks like?

CHRISTIAN UNITY

Proselytism is a major stumbling block on the path to Christian unity and is, therefore, one of the most pressing issues facing the global Christian community. The current controversy has emerged as a result of several missiological, cultural, and political factors. These include a renewed commitment to evangelization within the Christian traditions, the bloody history of European and world wars in the last century, mass human migration and globalization; continuing ethnic and religious persecution, ideological extremism, political instability, economic hardship and inequality and environmental devastation. In this changing global context, Christians are more exposed to one another with an increasing diversity of the Christian population in many local contexts. Such exposure opens churches to possibilities of both positive and negative interactions with other Christians—and with people of other faiths or no faith at all. It is, therefore, paramount that there be serious considerations about the character of the Church's witness, and about how we, as Christians, learn to lay aside all forms of competition and

---

14. UN, *Universal Declaration of Human Rights* 18.
15. For example, see sections 2.3, 8, 9; 3.4 in this volume.

rivalry. Instead, we are called to support one another through prayer and the mutual sharing of resources, and to develop new models of collaboration and joint witness.

1.2

Proselytism or Evangelism?

CECIL STALNAKER

Evangelical Review of Theology 26.4 (2002) 337–53[1]

Editor's Introduction

I AM INCLUDING AN *exerpt from Stalnaker's article from 2002. He introduces the article by noting how the term is "problematic" in the current context. Stalnaker provides a helpful sketch of the biblical and cultural history of the term "proselytism," from pre-exilic through to post-Constantinian times, placing the issue within an historical framework. It is this section (339) that I reproduce here by way of background to the rest of the volume. However, contemporary usage of the term is predominantly negative, as Stalnaker argues later in the article (but not reproduced here).*

BIBLICAL AND HISTORICAL OVERVIEW OF PROSELYTISM

INITIALLY, PROSELYTISM WAS AN internal affair. In other words, proselytism occurred within the confines of Palestine. Yet, in time, proselytism outstretched its borders as well-meaning Jews would traverse the sea and land

---

1. Reproduced with kind permission of the Department for Theological Concerns of World Evangelical Alliance.

to make proselytes. Proselytism appears differently prior to and after the exile.

Pre-Exhilic Proselytism

The concept of proselytism originates in the Old Testament and is tied to the Hebrew word, *ger*, meaning a foreigner or sojourner. In Ezekiel 14:7, the New American Standard Bible translates this word as "immigrant." Such immigrants would "attach themselves to the house of Jacob" (Isa 14:1). This word *ger* is translated in the LXX as "proselyte."

In the book of Genesis the notion of proselytism appears (Gen 15:13; 23:4). Early on, the Lord God declared to Abraham that his descendants would be enslaved "strangers" or proselytes in the foreign land of Egypt (Gen 15:13). In fact, due to the Israelites' own personal experience as strangers, they were able to empathize with foreigners in their own land (Exod 23:9). Here, the term applied initially to both Israelites and non-Israelites. In his intensive study of the proselyte Richard DeRidder Based explains: "The rabbis taught that Abraham was the first proselyte, and that he made converts and brought them under the wings of the Shekinah,"[2] and that the "persons whom Abraham and Sarah had *gotten* in Haran (Gen 12:5) were said to be people whom they had converted from idolatry."[3]

Biblically, Israel had specific obligations towards the *ger*. First, God had warned it several times to "not wrong" or "oppress" them (Exod 22:21; Deut 24:14; Jer 7:6; 22:3; Zech 7:10) nor to turn them aside (Mal 3:5). Unfortunately, the rulers of Israel violated this at certain times (Ezek 22:7, 29). On the contrary, they were to treat them according to Leviticus 19:34, the "stranger who resides with you shall be to you as the native among you, and you shall love him as yourself." They were to provide for the proselytes by permitting them to glean from the fruits of their fields (Lev 19:10), by giving them food and clothing (Deut 10:18–19), and even part of their tithes (Deut 26:12). Concerning worship, they were not to be hindered if they worshipped the true God of Israel (Num 15:14). The *ger* were considered to be among the needy strata of society along with orphans and widows (Deut 14:29).

Not only were there obligations on the part of Israel towards the proselyte, but stipulations were made for these converts as well. Regarding worship, they were obligated just as were the Israelites. For instance, they were to observe the Feast of the Unleavened Bread (Exod 12:19), the Feast of

---

2. DeRidder, *Discipling the Nations*, 26.
3. DeRidder, *Discipling the Nations*, 27.

Weeks (Deut 16:10–11), the Sabbath (Exod 20:10; Deut 5:14), and the day of Atonement (Lev 16:29–30). They were to stay clear of false worship by not offering sacrifices to pagan gods (Lev 20:2) and were warned against blasphemy against Yahweh (Lev 24:16; Num 15:30). Because they had attached themselves to the house of Jacob (Isa 14:1), they were to fulfill their spiritual obligations to the Lord just as were the Jewish faithful.

The *ger* had many of the same rights as the native Israelites, including access to the cities of refuge (Num 35:15) and to a just trial (Deut 1:16; 24:17; 27:19). Most importantly, they were permitted to learn from and fear the Lord (Deut 31:12) and to enter into the covenant with him just as were the naturally born Israelites (Deut 29:11–12).

Beyond the period of the patriarchs and the exodus, the *ger* are seen participating in the worship of the true Lord with the nation of Israel (Josh 8:33–35; 2 Chr 30:25). In referring to the building of the Temple, it is implied that foreigners were also engaged in its construction (1 Chr 22:2).

In general, the expression *ger* in the Old Testament identifies those who did not actually have Jewish blood. They were outsiders who had come on their own initiative into the confines of Judaism and who had aligned themselves with Israel and its faith in the true living God. In other words, there was a type of internal proselytism taking place as outsiders were coming into the midst of Israel.

The expression "proselyte" had both religious and sociological connotations. It was a term used to describe the assimilation of the foreigner into the Semitic community, that is, to identify a resident alien within the boundaries of Israel (Exod 12:49; Deut 5:14; 31:12). But because the foreigner had to worship the God of Israel, it is impossible to separate the political and cultural spheres from the religious.

Israelites were to be the people of God. In Exodus 19:15–16, God confirms to the nation the nature of the life he would have Israel live in these words: "And you shall be to me a kingdom of priests and a holy nation." This expression calls attention to the universal priestly status of Israel and refers to Israel, as being set apart for God's possession and service. "It is here that Israel's missionary role became explicit. . . . The whole nation was to function on behalf of the kingdom of God in a mediatorial role in relation to the nations."[4] Israel was to play a priestly role in the midst of the peoples of the world. Israel would become the recipient of God's mercy and justice, and in turn, would attempt to live as the people of God, demonstrating his grace, mercy, justice, and liberating power. "As the priest is a mediator between God and man, so Israel was called to be the vehicle of the knowledge

---

4. Kaiser, "Israel's Missionary Call," 13.

and salvation of God to the nations of the earth."[5] Thus, the reality of being "a kingdom of priests and a holy nation" would also have its effect on the proselytes, those living within the nation of Israel.

At Sinai the Lord God had laid down basic legislation regarding the proselyte, which indeed related to the fulfilment of mission to the world. DeRidder states that "when the *ger* assumed all the group obligations—ethnic, social, and religious—the proselyte became a full-fledged member of the congregation of Israel and the descendants were legally indistinguishable from other Israelites. In Joshua 8:33 the *ger* is described as being 'part of Israel.'"[6]

Some would say that the translation "stranger" for the Hebrew *ger* is an unfortunate one because the proselyte "was a guest, a resident alien, under the protection of the law of the land."[7] When foreigners fully accepted the true faith of Israel, they became in essence Israelites and had the same privileges, rights, and commitments as native Israelites. The proselyte was considered to be of the true faith, participating in the covenant promises of the Lord. The non-Israelites could share in salvation through obedience of faith in God just as the Israelites did. Becoming a proselyte was an act of conversion.

Although the term "proselyte" does not occur in reference to the Moabite Ruth, it is evident that the notion of conversion occurs. Ruth returns to Judah with her mother-in-law Naomi and meets Boaz. Taking an interest in her work in the fields and her plight, he said to her: "May the Lord reward your work, and your wages be full from the Lord, the God of Israel, under whose wings you have come to seek refuge" (Ruth 2:12). The latter part of the phrase is most likely a reference to Ruth when she committed herself to Yahweh, abandoning Chemosh, the god of the Moabites. She sought protection and comfort from God.[8] Not only was she looking to the Lord as her protector but in seeking refuge she was identifying herself with Israel. In essence, she was converting to Judaism.

According to 2 Kings 5:15–19, Naaman, a foreigner, was a Syrian convert to the worship of Israel's true God. The term *ger* is used also to express the pilgrimage of the faithful in 1 Chronicles 29:15 and Psalms 39:12; 119:19. These proselytes were not gathered by any missionary zeal on the part of Israel. Rather, they, themselves, approached Israel and were seeking the one true God.

---

5. Keil and Delitzch, *Pentateuch*, 98.
6. DeRidder, *Discipling the Nations*, 44.
7. DeRidder, *Discipling the Nations*, 46.
8. Block, *Judges, Ruth*, 664.

Earlier in the history of Israel, thousands of foreigners came to Israel on their own initiative. Prior to the exile, great numbers of aliens joined their ranks. Later on, according to the census of Solomon, foreigners in Israel's midst numbered 153,600 (2 Chr 2:17). The *ger* was looked upon as more or less a permanent resident of Israel and basically accepted in the society.

Examination of the lives of the prophets leads one to conclude that they did not go forth and make proselytes. The message of the prophet varied. Sometimes it was disciplinary in nature; at other times it concerned the future. In reality, "the central concern of the prophets was to communicate to Israel what it meant to be Israel."[9] It was the ministry of the prophet to remind the nation of her election, an election that has a testimony among the other nations, for her choosing was not for personal privilege but for service.

When the nation did not heed her responsibilities the Lord God would raise up his prophetic messenger. The prophets attempted to call the nation back to her covenant, back to being a "kingdom of priests and a holy nation." Why? Their ministry was a witness to and emphasized the fact that Israel's mission in the world was to bring the nations to the knowledge of the true God. The prophets, for the most part, directed their ministries to the nation of Israel itself. However, a few of the primarily pre-exilic prophets, Obadiah, Jonah, and Nahum, headed toward the non-Israelite nations to proclaim God's message. But on the whole the prophet focused on the nation of Israel.

Israel was not, for the most part, called to cross national boundaries to make proselytes, but she was to be a blessing to the world of nations. Dr. George Peters states Israel's responsibility in the following manner: "Israel, by living a life in the presence and fear of the Lord, was to experience the fullness of the blessings of God. In this way they were to startle the nations to attention, arouse their inquiry, and draw them like a magnet to Jerusalem and to the Lord."[10] Foreigners would come to Israel and conversion to the faith of Israel would occur, resulting in proselytes.

Proselytism was a natural consequence of Israel's being a light to the nations. The *ger* referred to the individual who would come voluntarily to Israel, adopt its religion, and become Yahweh's worshiper. They were in essence converts to Judaism, having joined themselves to the Lord God from other nations. To be completely incorporated into religious union with God's people and become a proselyte, they had to be circumcised. DeRidder comments: "A careful reading of the Old Testament legislation concerning circumcision leads to the conclusion that this rite was intended to mean

---

9. Bruggemann, *Tradition for Crisis*, 25.
10. Peters, *Biblical Theology of Missons*, 21.

the incorporation of the person into a special relationship to God."[11] In essence this indicated entrance into the redemptive covenant of God. So, in a real sense, a religious meaning was attached to the Old Testament term "proselyte."

The fact that foreigners came into the fold of Israel is interesting because, with the major exception of a few minor prophets, Jonah being one, we do not find the mission of crossing geographical and cultural barriers to take the message of Yahweh to those who know nothing about the Lord God. However, the Old Testament does not ignore this issue. The concept of reaching out to other nations is inherent in its revelation for the concept of universality in reference to salvation pervades the entire Old Testament. God the Father manifests his missionary nature in the Old Testament.

Dr. George Peters very clearly states:

> The Old Testament does not contain missions; it is itself "missions" in the world. Like a lonely voice in the wilderness the Old Testament boldly proclaims revelational, ethical, monotheism in protest to Greek, Egyptian, and early Indian heathenism—the multitudinous systems of surrounding polytheism and incipient philosophical Eastern monism.[12]

Johannes Blauw also declares that "long before the missionary movement as an act of witness of the Christian Church started, Israel itself was engaged in missionary work."[13]

Post-Exilic Proselytism

The true sense of the word "proselyte" took on the notion of convert later on, especially during the Babylonian exile. It was with the Exile that the attitude and outlook of Israel undertook a drastic change. Judaism began to take on a more centripetal sense, an aggressive missionary spirit during the post-exilic period.

With the deportations, Jews could be found scattered throughout the Persian empire. After the sixth century BC, most of the Israelites lived outside of Palestine. Assyria, Babylonia, and Egypt became homes to many of the Jews. As time passed, it has been estimated that one-third of the population of Alexandria was Jewish. All commercial centers in Asia

---

11. DeRidder, *Discipling the Nations*, 29.
12. Peters, *Biblical Theology of Missions*, 129.
13. Blauw, *Missionary Nature of the Church*, 54.

Minor, Macedonia, Greece, or the Aegean area had Jewish residents.[14] J. Klausner maintains that the major portion of the three million Jews living in the Diaspora were proselytes.[15] Wherever the Jews went they took with them their monotheistic faith. It was during this postexilic time that many non-Israelites were drawn to the Jewish faith and assimilated into it. In other words, proselytism was taking place outside of Israel's geographical borders—an external proselytism was prominent.

It was really during the Inter-Testamental period that the term "proselyte" took on a new meaning. An intensive missionary movement began in the Hellenistic Jewish Diaspora. In time proselytism became quite common. Many Jews aggressively propagated Judaism. The use of the Greek language in the LXX made it easier to proselytize the Greeks.

The desire to proselytize did not stop with the Greeks, but continued well into the Roman world. Before the birth of Christ, many of the Jews settled in Rome and were so intense in their zeal to proselytize that the Roman authorities expelled many of their leaders. Some showed their discontent with this proselytizing spirit. Horace wrote: "If you won't come willingly, we shall act like the Jews and force you to."[16] Exposing some of the cruel side of proselytism, the Jewish historian, Josephus, maintains that Ituraeans were forced to convert to Judaism by Aristobulus[17] and that a Roman centurion was forced to accept circumcision in order to live.[18] Prior to Christianity, Judaism had made abundant proselytes. In almost every corner of the biblical world Jewish customs and moral virtues were adhered to by its followers, namely, Jewish proselytes. In summary, the activity of direct proselytism at this time is well attested. Some have summarized it in the following manner:

> With the conquests of Alexander, the wars between Egypt and Syria, the struggle under the Maccabees, the expansion of the Roman empire, the Jews became more widely known, and their power to proselytize increased. They had suffered for their religion in the persecution of Antiochus, and the spirit of martyrdom was followed naturally by propagandism. Their monotheism was rigid and unbending. Scattered through the East and West, a marvel and a portent, wondered at and alternatively, attracting and repelling, they presented, in an age of

---

14. Feinberg, "Proselyte," 906.
15. Klausner cited in Danker, "Proselyte, Proselytism," 426.
16. Horace quoted in DeRidder, *Discipling the Nations*, 94.
17. Josephus, *Life and Works of Flavius Josephus*, article XIII, 9, 3.
18. Josephus cited in Mclintock and Strong, "Proselyte," 659.

shattered creeds and corroding doubts, the spectacle of faith, not least a dogma, which remained unshaken.[19]

In the New Testament era, there is considerable evidence that the activity of proselytism was carried out among the Gentiles in the early part of the first century. For instance, the Jews prepared extensive literature to win over converts to Judaism.

The Greek New Testament uses the word for proselyte, *proselutos*, only four times (Matt 23:15; Acts 2:10; 6:5; 13:43). In three of the four occurrences it maintains a neutral or positive connotation.

In the Judaism of Palestine, the *ger* always referred to the pagan who made the conversion from paganism to Judaism. Male proselyte candidates were required to undergo circumcision, a purifying bath, and an offering of sacrifice in the Temple at Jerusalem. Female proselyte candidates submitted to the latter two requirements. Woman proselytes outnumbered men converts.[20]

Referring to the one negative occurrence in Matthew 23, Jesus makes reference to Palestinian proselytism. He condemns the teachers of the law and the Pharisees by pronouncing seven curses or woes on them (vv. 13–33). The second woe concerns the subject of proselytism. The scribes and Pharisees were winning non-Israelites to their own position. The New Testament scholar D. A. Carson believes that the "converts in view . . . are not converts to Judaism but to Pharisaism."[21] In any case, they were scouring the empire to make converts. It is interesting to see that Jesus did not criticize nor condemn them for making proselytes but for making them "sons of hell." Carson adds, "The Pharisees teaching locked them into a theological frame that left no room for Jesus the Messiah and therefore no possibility of entering the messianic kingdom."[22] Jesus did condemn the fact that their proselytizing efforts were leading people to eternal damnation. The word "proselyte," and this is important, is never employed in reference to a convert to Christ.

Having dealt with the negative use in Matthew, let us look at its employment in the book of Acts as it reveals some additional information regarding the proselyte. Acts 2:10 shows that proselytes who had come from geographical boundaries beyond Jerusalem made up part of the apostle Peter's audience at Pentecost. In using the expression "Jews and proselytes" Luke is distinguishing between the national group of Jews and non-birth

19. Mclintock and Strong, "Proselyte," 658.
20. Bruce, *New Testament History*, 147, 156.
21. Carson, *Matthew*, 478.
22. Carson, *Matthew*, 479.

Jews. He called for them to repent and be baptized in the name of Jesus Christ. Because they continued to go to the Temple and synagogue after their conversion (Acts 2:46; 3:1; 14:1; 21:26), Heideman, says that "there is no indication that they are expected to change their community identity."[23] However, this is understandable because the need for the true church to distinguish itself from Judaism had not yet arisen.

Acts 6:5 speaks of "Nicolas, a proselyte from Antioch." He was not born a Jew but a pagan. He was appointed as one of the original deacons in the early church. Philip baptized an Ethiopian proselyte or God-fearer who was travelling to Jerusalem to worship (Acts 8:27–39). Many of the proselytes followed Paul and Barnabas, committing their lives to the gospel (Acts 13:43). These devout Jewish converts left Judaism to follow the ways of Jesus Christ.

The term "proselyte" does not occur in the writings of Paul. However, he does desire that his own Jewish brethren experience true salvation through the Messiah, Jesus Christ. He states, "My heart's desire and my prayer to God for them is for their salvation" (Rom 10:1). Although proselytism does not occur in the ministry of Paul, converts to Christ do occur. Multitudes of Jews converted to Christ during Paul's ministry.

In the New Testament, the term "proselytism" never occurs in reference to Christianity. Neither Paul nor the other apostles viewed their ministry of evangelism and church planting as proselytism. Their activity in proclaiming the gospel was never done in order to build their own kingdom. They had no desire to enlarge their borders nor increase their numbers for their own sake. Paul says that his ministry did not come "from error or impurity or by way of deceit" (1 Thess 2:3). Paul did want to proclaim the gospel and see the kingdom of God advance. His motive was to give to all the world the great redemptive truths of the gospel which is rooted in Jesus Christ. This was his passion and his plea, that East and West would be evangelized, not proselytized.

So the new followers of Christ *were not considered to be proselytized but evangelized*, even though they actually changed religious commitment from Judaism to Christ. Many of these individuals were actually Jewish proselytes who became followers of Christ. So, religious change was quite common in the New Testament era, from paganism to Judaism, and to Christianity.

In addition, the issue of people changing from one branch of Christianity to another was non-existent.

The call to conversion in the New Testament is, of course, a call to follow Jesus Christ. Some individuals would, therefore, say that it is not a call

---

23. Heideman, "Proselytism, Mission, and the Bible," 11.

to change one's Christian community. However, it is also evident that other Christian communities did not exist at that period of time.

In Judaism, the proselytism of Gentiles continued late into the first century AD. Some Jewish Christians still attended the Synagogues until as late as 90 AD when it became unbearable for them to do so. Jewish anti-Christian propaganda attempted to exclude Christian participation in worship at the synagogue.[24]

Proselytism was looked upon positively by Judaism. Rabbis were often zealous for converts. The very large number of favorable references in the Talmud and Mishnah towards the true proselytes shows how eager the Jews were to acquire them.[25] In fact, some rabbis "were provoked when they saw a country or province that had produced few proselytes."[26] It may be concluded that many rabbis approved of proselytizing and encouraged it. They even used the patriarchs and other great historical figures as examples to follow in their making of proselytes.[27]

Some contend that the proselytizing efforts by the Jews continued even after 478 AD when the Theodosian Code was published, which threatened those who were circumcised with the death penalty.[28] Eventually Roman laws were created to abort the proselytizing efforts of Jews towards Gentiles. Some Jews were even exiled from Rome for proselytizing activities.[29]

---

24. Parks, *Conflict of the Church and Synagogue*, 61–79, cited in DeRidder, *Discipling the Nations*, 73.
25. DeRidder, *Discipling the Nations*, 93.
26. Braude, *Jewish Proselytizing*, 18–19.
27. DeRidder, *Discipling the Nations*, 101.
28. Simon, *Verus Israel*, 315–55; Jeremias, *Jesus' Promise to the Nations*, 11–12.
29. DeRidder, *Discipling the Nations*, 120.

1.3

Christian Understandings of Proselytism

DAVID A. KERR

International Bulletin of Missionary Research 23.1 (1999) 8–14.[1]

Editor's Introduction

KERR'S ARTICLE GIVES A *more recent overview of the issue, tracing recent developments in dialogue and the perceptions that different Christian traditions hold. At the time of writing the article, "David A. Kerr [was] Professor of Christianity in the Non-Western World at the University of Edinburgh and Director of the center of the same name. He was formerly a professor in Hartford Seminary, Connecticut, where he directed the Macdonald Center for the Study of Islam and Christian-Muslim Relations."*

LIKE THE CHAMELEON, PROSELYTISM displays itself in many shades of color. The word has different nuances in individual languages and among languages. Importantly from the point of view of this article, it is used variously among different sectors' of the Christian church. It refers both to the transfer of allegiance from one religion to another and to the transfer of allegiance between churches. Attitudes to proselytism are conditioned by political, social, and cultural considerations, and responses vary from one church to

---

1. Reprinted with permission of the *International Bulletin of Mission Research*, which is owned by the Overseas Ministries Study Center and published by Sage Publications.

another, from one culture to another. I attempt here to clarify some of the issues, particularly as they have emerged in Christian thinking through the second half of the twentieth century. I argue that the hard-sought consensus that has emerged within the ecumenical movement needs to extend itself further to include new global realities of Christianity.[2]

To begin with English linguistic definitions, the Shorter Oxford English Dictionary considers "proselytism" simply as a synonym of "conversion." Derived from the Latin *proselytus* and the Greek *proselytos*, the proselyte is "one who has come to a place"—that is, a newcomer or convert. Use of the term in English literature displays both positive and negative characteristics. For Shakespeare, the proselyte's power of attraction was an evocative metaphor of female beauty; thus, of Perdita, he wrote: "This is a creature, would she begin a sect, might quench the zeal of all professors else; make proselytes of who she but bid follow."[3]

By the eighteenth century, however, Enlightenment literature identified proselytism with intolerance. The leading philosopher of the Enlightenment in Scotland, David Hume, criticized an opponent for "his zeal for proselytism that he stopped not at toleration or equality."[4] Edmund Burke vented his dislike of the French Revolution in the carping criticism that "the spirit of proselytism attends this spirit of fanaticism."[5]

Reflecting this negative nuancing of meaning, Webster's Dictionary of Synonyms draws a plain distinction between conversion and proselytism: the former denotes "a sincere and voluntary change of belief," whereas the latter implies "an act or process of inducing someone to convert to another faith." In current ecumenical usage, this American English meaning prevails, coercive inducement being the attribute of proselytism that differentiates it from conversion.[6]

---

2. This article is adapted from a lecture given at the Tantur International Conference on Religion and Culture, Jerusalem, May 31–June 4, 1998. The conference theme was "Religious Freedom and Proselytism."

3. Shakespeare, *Winter's Tale*, act 5, scene 1.

4. Hume, *From the Invasion of Julius Caesar*, 256. [Editor's note: Hume is commenting on the last Roman Catholic King of England, James II, saying, "And such was his zeal for proselytism, that whatever he might at first have intended, he plainly stopped not at toleration and equality; He confined all power, encouragement and favor, to the catholics: Converts from interest would soon have multiplied upon him."]

5. Burke, *Reflections on the Revolution in France*, 228.

6. This is not to suggest that international English always uses the word negatively. International lawyers at the Tantur Conference used "proselytism" as a neutral term meaning "conversion." A study of the use of the term in other languages would be instructive.

BIBLICAL PERSPECTIVES

The proselyte is a familiar figure in both the Hebrew Scriptures and the New Testament. The Greek *proselytos* was used in the Septuagint to translate the Hebrew *ger*, the "stranger" who sojourned in the land of Israel. The Deuteronomist taught that the proselyte-stranger (*ger*) was to be honored among the Jews, who had themselves been strangers (*gerim*) in Egypt (Deut 10:19). The bulk of Talmudic literature welcomes the proselyte into the full fellowship of Israel, subject to the requirements of circumcision, baptism, and the offering of sacrifice. Jesus criticized what he deemed the Pharisaic tendency of making the proselyte a slave to the law (Matt 23:15). From this it may be inferred that the matter of how a proselyte should be incorporated into Israel was a matter of controversy in Jesus' time. New Testament references to Jewish proselytes among the first Christians indicate that they were welcome members of the early church (Acts 2:10; 6:5; 13:43).[7] The postbiblical histories of both Judaism and Christianity continued to honor the proselyte until more recent times, when, roughly speaking from the eighteenth century, the term came to have the negative connotations we have noted in English literary usage. The present writer would speculate that the roots of the negative interpretation of proselytism as the overzealous or coercive expression of religion lie contextually both in post-Enlightenment ideas of freedom of conscience and in secular reactions to the rise of the modern Western Christian missionary movement in the colonial era. The Bible, however, shows that the proselyte was not viewed negatively in Scripture and that Jesus defended the proselyte from the legalistic tendency of institutional religion.

CURRENT DEFINITIONS: ROMAN CATHOLIC

The Second Vatican Council's "Constitution on the Sacred Liturgy" (1963) affirms that the call to conversion is one of the fundamental tasks of the church. To this end "the Church announces the good news of salvation to those who do not believe, so that all men may know the true God and Jesus Christ whom He has sent, and may repent and mend their ways." Equally, "to believers also the Church must ever preach faith and repentance."[8] Conversion is therefore understood as a process: it begins with an initial turning in faith to God in Christ and continues throughout a believer's Christian

---

7. For fuller discussion of the biblical material, see Heideman, "Proselytism, Mission, and the Bible," 10–12.

8. Vatican II, *Sacrosanctum Concilium* (Abbott, *Documents of Vatican II*, 142).

life. Conversion in this sense is "a spiritual journey."[9] In relation to this journey, "the Church strictly forbids forcing anyone to embrace the faith, or alluring or enticing people by unworthy techniques."[10]

With sensitivity to the ambiguities of the word, the Second Vatican Council's documents do not use the term "proselytism." But the distinction between conversion as a sincere act of faith and as a result of coercive manipulation is clearly maintained. Moreover, it is given substantial theological and philosophical exposition in the "Declaration on Religious Freedom" (1965), which propounds the case for religious freedom on grounds of divine intent, human right, and civic duty. The case against coercive proselytism is equally clear:

> The human person has the right to religious freedom. This freedom means that all men are to be immune from coercion on the part of individuals or of social groups or of any human power, in such wise as in matters of religion no one is to be forced to act in a manner contrary to his own beliefs, whether privately or publicly, whether alone or in association with others.[11]

In affirming sincere conversion as a right of religious freedom, and in rejecting proselytism as the infringement of such freedom, the Second Vatican Council mainly addresses the church's relations with other religions. These are addressed in the "Declaration on the Relationship of the Church to Non-Christian Religions," more commonly referred to by its Latin title, *Nostra aetate*. In this document the church states that "[it] rejects nothing which is true and holy in these religions" and calls for "dialogue and co-operation" with them "to acknowledge, preserve and promote the spiritual and moral goods found among these men, as well as the values of their society and culture."[12]

Conversion and dialogue are thus placed side by side. If the inherent tension is not resolved theologically, a modus vivendi is at least implied: conversion as an inalienable expression of religious freedom should be understood as ongoing spiritual journey; interreligious dialogue is an important part of this journey in which partners affirm their common spiritual and human values. In both respects proselytism is rejected.

---

9. Vatican II, *Ad Gentes* (Abbott, *Documents of Vatican II*, 600).
10. Vatican II, *Ad Gentes* (Abbott, *Documents of Vatican II*, 600).
11. Vatican II, *Dignitatis Humanae* (Abbott, *Documents of Vatican II*, 678–79).
12. Vatican II, *Nostra Aetatei* (Abbott, *Documents of Vatican II*, 662–63).

EASTERN AND ORIENTAL ORTHODOX

Among the Eastern[13] and Oriental[14] Orthodox Churches, proselytism refers primarily to interchurch relations—that is, relations between non-Orthodox and Orthodox churches. This view is based on their self-understanding as churches that exercise their ecclesiastical authority within the geographic domain of the people, or nation, whose evangelization was and continues to be the responsibility of the national church. Each Orthodox Church is autocephalous, or self-governing, within its own canonical territory. Recalling the earliest mode of Christian evangelization, whereby an apostle-missionary preached the Gospel among his own people and initiated a process by which the whole nation was Christianized through its leaders, its people, and its culture, the concept of canonical territory denotes the inseparable identity of people, culture, land, and church. This is what it means for the church to be local, or indigenized, in the national life of a people.

Within this strongly ethnic identity of people and church, the Orthodox regard as illegitimate any attempt by other churches or religious groups to convert members of an Orthodox church away from Orthodoxy. This is tantamount to proselytism, whether the means are foul or fair. The Russian Orthodox Church thus defines proselytism as the active or passive encouraging of members of a given ethnic or national group to join a religion, denomination, or sect that is not historically rooted in that ethnic group or nationality.

Orthodox sensitivities regarding this understanding of proselytism arise from their historical experience of being the object of Catholic and Protestant strategies of conversion. A statement by the Armenian Catholicos Karekin[15] in respect of the Oriental Orthodox applies equally to the Eastern Orthodox: "they underwent the hard experience of being exposed to the proselytizing policies of the Roman Church and, later, the Protestant Missionary Societies of various kinds."[16]

---

13. That is, the autocephalous, "national" Orthodox Churches that accept the credal definitions of the seven ecumenical councils (Nicaea I to Nicaea II [325–787]) and recognize the Ecumenical Patriarchate of Constantinople as their *primus inter pares*.

14. That is, the churches that accept the credal definitions of the first three ecumenical councils (Nicaea I to Ephesus [325–431]) but developed separately from the Council of Chalcedon (451). They are the Armenian Apostolic Church, the Coptic Orthodox Church, the Ethiopian Orthodox Church, the Syrian Orthodox Church, and the Malankara Orthodox Syrian Church (India).

15. Supreme Patriarch-Catholicos of All Armenians and spiritual leader of the Armenian Apostolic Church

16. Sarkissian, *Witness of the Oriental Orthodox Churches*, 41.

CATHOLIC-ORTHODOX RELATIONS

In order to understand Orthodox sensitivity to proselytism, it is necessary to introduce a brief historical excursus in explanation of problems to which Catholicos Karekin refers. The historical problem goes back to the rift between Rome and Constantinople in 1054 and the subsequent failure of the fifteenth-century Council of Ferrara-Florence (1437–1439) to reunite the church. Rome thereafter developed an alternative strategy for reunion that aimed at the conversion of both the Eastern and the Oriental Orthodox to Roman doctrine and allegiance. Medieval Catholic missions, led initially by the Franciscans and later by the Jesuits, persuaded groups within these churches to declare their union with Rome as Eastern Catholic Churches. The persuasive powers of these Catholic missions was backed by the educational and economic opportunities they offered and by the diplomatic patronage of the emerging European states. As a result, to each Eastern and Oriental Orthodox Church a Catholic equivalent was created.[17] They are known collectively as Eastern Catholic Churches, their rites of origin (liturgy and canon law) being formally upheld within their obedience to the Holy See, albeit historically with a heavy dose of Latinization—a trend that has been reversed since the Second Vatican Council. Rome claimed them as the firstfruits of a reunited church and referred to them in the Second Vatican Council as part of "the divinely revealed and undivided heritage of the universal Church."[18]

What Rome celebrated as reunion by way of conversion, the Eastern and Oriental Orthodox Churches view disparagingly as "Uniatism," which for them was coterminous with Catholic proselytizing incursions into their canonical territories. Rome stood accused of treating Orthodox lands as *term missionis*—land open for mission.

Only in the present decade has this problem been effectively addressed.[19] In 1990 a joint Catholic-Orthodox commission on theological

---

17. From the Assyrian Church of the East was created the Chaldean (Assyrian) Catholic Church (1553) and the Syro-Malabar Catholic Church (1599); from the Oriental Orthodox Church—the Syrian Catholic Church (1663), the Coptic Catholic Church (1741), the Armenian Catholic Church (1742), and the Ethiopian Catholic Church (1839); from the Eastern Orthodox Churches—the Ruthenian (Polish) and Hungarian Catholic Churches (1595), the Romanian Catholic Church (1701), the Melkite (Greek) Catholic Church (1724), the Greek Catholic Church (1860), and the Ukrainian Catholic Church (1596).

18. Vatican II, *Orientalium Ecclesiarum* (Abbott, *Documents of Vatican II*, 373).

19. Rapprochement between the Catholic and Eastern Orthodox Churches began at the Second Vatican Council and was symbolized by the historic meeting of Pope Paul VI and Ecumenical Patriarch Athenagoras (Constantinople) in Jerusalem (1965),

dialogue published Statement on the Subject of Uniatism, which agrees that Uniatism no longer provides a model or method for Catholic-Orthodox rapprochement. Further deliberations resulted in the Balamand Statement (Lebanon) of 1993, "Uniatism, Method of Union of the Past, and the Present Search for Full Communion."[20]

Accepting that the Eastern Catholic Churches may remain part of the Catholic communion, with "the right to exist and act in response to the spiritual needs of their faithful," the Balamand Statement (see section 2.7 in this volume) sets out ecclesiological principles for a new relationship between the Catholic and Orthodox churches. Henceforth they commit themselves to recognizing each other as "sister churches." They agree that neither church can claim exclusively to profess the full apostolic faith and therefore join in shared responsibility, as sisters, "for maintaining the Church of God in fidelity to the divine purpose, most especially in what concerns unity." Rome agrees to end its "missionary apostolate" toward the Orthodox churches and declares that its "pastoral activity . . . no longer aims at having the faithful of one Church pass over to the other; that is to say, it no longer aims at proselytizing among the Orthodox." While recognizing that the Eastern Catholics have an integral role to play in preparing for eventual Catholic-Orthodox reunion, it was agreed that such reunion would not be modeled on the institution of Uniatism.

The Eastern Catholic Churches will continue to exist under the canonical jurisdictions of their respective patriarchs, while accepting the spiritual primacy of the patriarch of Rome; at the same time, they will continue to follow the liturgical, theological, and spiritual traditions of their Orthodox "sister" churches. But—to quote a recent Orthodox-Catholic consultation in the United States—"in the negative sense of the term, 'Uniatism,' which in the spirit of the Orthodox is identified with proselytism, is rejected by the Balamand Statement . . . as a method for the conversion of Orthodox Christians and making them members of the Catholic Church."[21]

PROTESTANT-ORTHODOX RELATIONS

Nineteenth-century Protestant encounter with Orthodoxy largely replicated the medieval Catholic pattern, although with a very different understanding

---

where they committed themselves in mutual forgiveness to search for reconciliation between their two churches. See Paul VI and Athenagoras, "Common Declaration," in Kinnamon and Cope, *Ecumenical Movement*, 145–46.

20. JIC, "Uniatism, Method of Union of the Past."
21. "Rapport de Balamand," 5–12.

of the nature of Christian faith and the church. With their emphases on the authority of the Bible over ecclesiastical institution, on direct personal faith in Jesus Christ mediated through Scripture, and on the priesthood of all believers replacing the clerical authority of a centralized church, Protestant missions inevitably clashed with the Orthodox churches.[22] From the perspective of their evangelical faith, Protestants tended to regard Orthodox as "nominal" Christians whom they wished to convert into "Christians of the heart."

Taking the example of the American Board of Commissioners for Foreign Missions (ABCFM), which began sending evangelical missionaries from New England to the Middle East in the 1820s, a clear transition of policy is evident. The initial aim was to inject a biblically based evangelical spirit into the Orthodox churches:

> Not to subvert them; not to pull them down and build anew. It is to reform them; to revive among them . . . the knowledge and spirit of the Gospel. . . . It is not part of our object to introduce Congregationalism or Presbyterianism among them. . . . We are content that their present ecclesiastical organization should remain, provided the knowledge and spirit of the Gospel can be revived under it.

In the face of strong resistance from the indigenous churches (Orthodox and Eastern Catholic) and at the urging of its own missionaries and their early converts, ABCFM revised its policy. There was no alternative, it argued, but "the restoration of pre-Constantinian and primitive (Pauline) Christianity . . . [by] the formation not only of exemplary individuals in their midst [i.e., among Orthodox/Eastern Catholics] but of exemplary communities as well." Rufus Anderson acknowledged that "this admission of converts into a church, without regard to their previous ecclesiastical relations, was a practical ignoring of the old church organizations in that region. It was so understood, and the spirit of opposition and persecution was roused to the utmost."[23]

This is but a particular instance of the general practice of Anglican, Lutheran, and Reformed churches in nineteenth-century Turkey, Syria-Palestine, and Egypt. Evangelical attitudes to the Orthodox churches varied from

---

22. The same was true of the Protestant-Eastern Catholic encounter. The nineteenth-century conflict was most intense between Protestant missionaries and the Maronite Church (the largest Eastern Catholic Church, for which there is no Orthodox equivalent) in Lebanon. The first Maronite convert to Protestantism, As'ad Shidyaq, was imprisoned by the Maronite patriarch and died in jail (ca. 1823).

23. Anderson, *History of the Missions*, 1:47. For a full account of the ABCFM mission in Lebanon, see Badr, "Mission to 'Nominal Christians.'"

Anglican appreciation of episcopal succession to Reformed impatience with perceived liturgical atrophy. But the result of their missions was the same: the creation of new evangelical churches throughout the Middle East.[24]

Western implants as they originally were, these churches have integrated themselves culturally and to a degree politically in the Middle East. This has facilitated far-reaching discussion about ways of resolving the historical legacy of proselytism within the Middle East Council of Churches (MECC)—the most inclusive regional ecumenical council in the world, with Orthodox (Eastern and Oriental), Catholic (Latin and Eastern), and Protestant members. In an MECC study document entitled *Proselytism, Sects, and Pastoral Challenges* (1989, see section 2.7 in this volume), representatives of these churches agreed in defining proselytism as "a practice that involves attempts aimed at attracting Christians from a particular church or religious group, leading to their alienation from their church of origin." Criticized for being at variance with biblical teaching and human rights, proselytism is seen to be rooted psychologically in "individual and group egotism," socially in "feelings of cultural, political and economic superiority," and institutionally in "an overtrust in one's own methods and programmes."[25] The document is particularly insightful in identifying "unconscious" forms of proselytism: for example, within mixed marriages and in religious education. In its conclusion it calls for "a pastoral agreement" among MECC members for the resolution of historical and contemporary problems of proselytism, the way to such agreement being through "a dialogue of love."

The then MECC general secretary, Gabriel Habib (Eastern Orthodox), wrote an open letter to North American evangelicals in which he argued that it is only through such dialogue of love that Christians of different traditions can learn to listen to one another in mutual openness to mutual correction and mutual enrichment.[26] The most constructive response to this letter is to be seen in the development of a group known as Evangelicals for Middle East Understanding (EMEU), which provided a forum for renewed discussion between Western evangelical missions and the MECC member churches. The EMEU director, Donald Wagner, has called this "a new day

---

24. These churches included the National Evangelical Synod of Syria and Lebanon (from 1823), the Anglican (originally Anglican-Lutheran) bishopric of Jerusalem (1841), the Union of Armenian Evangelical Churches in the Near East (1846), the Coptic Evangelical Church (1853), the Evangelical Church of Iran (1855), the Evangelical Church of Sudan (1900), and the Presbyterian Church in the Sudan (1902).

25. See section 2.7 in this volume (para. 6–11). For further elaboration, see Sabra, "Proselytism, Evangelism, and Ecumenism."

26. See Habib, "Renewal, Unity, and Witness."

in mission . . . [in which] we [North American evangelicals] must strive to become authentic partners with the churches in the Middle East."[27]

THE ECUMENICAL CONSENSUS

These specific examples of bilateral agreements to end intra-Christian proselytism need to be seen within a wider framework of discussions that have taken place between the World Council of Churches (WCC) and the Vatican. As a result of intra-Protestant tensions in the early years of the WCC, a working party was established after the Evanston General Assembly (1954), which wrote "Christian Witness, Proselytism, and Religious Liberty."[28] This was perhaps the first document to draw the distinction between authentic Christian witness and proselytism. The New Delhi General Assembly (1961) affirmed the distinction, in so doing, paving the way for Orthodox participation in the WCC. The 1960s saw a further widening of the discussion to include Roman Catholics, and a definitive agreement was reached by the Joint Working Group between the Roman Catholic Church and the WCC in 1970, entitled "Common Witness and Proselytism: A Study Document."[29]

Its discussion of proselytism includes both interreligious and intra-Christian dimensions. "Christian witness, to those who have not yet received or responded to the announcement of the Gospel or to those who are already Christians, should have certain qualities, in order to avoid being corrupted in its exercise, thus becoming proselytism." The document outlines the New Testament qualities that mark genuinely Christian witness: love of one's neighbor; seeking the glory of God rather than the prestige of one's own community; empowerment by the Holy Spirit; respect for the free will and dignity of all, including the right to refuse the Gospel; freedom from any form of coercion that impedes people from witnessing to their own convictions. Specific forms of coercion to be avoided include physical coercion, moral constraint, or psychological pressure; temporal or material benefits offered in exchange for religious adherence; exploitation of the weak and uneducated; legal, social, economic, or political pressure, especially when aimed to prevent members of a religious minority from exercising their right of religious freedom; and unjust and uncharitable characterization of the beliefs and practices of another religion.

27. Wagner, *Anxious for Armageddon*, 181–82.
28. WCC, "Christian Witness, Proselytism, and Religious Liberty." See section 2.1 in this volume.
29. JWG, "Common Witness and Proselytism." See also Kinnamon and Cope, *Ecumenical Movement*, 351–53.

On the issue of specifically intra-Christian relations, the document urges that missionary action should always be carried out in an ecumenical spirit of cooperation between churches. While affirming that one church has legitimate freedom to exercise its missionary effort where another church is already established, it encourages cooperation, common witness, and fraternal assistance and rejects the competitive spirit that seeks to enhance the power and privilege of one church over another.

In terms of missionary encounter with other religions, the WCC has repeatedly affirmed that the Church has a mission, and it cannot be otherwise. At the same time, it accepts self-critically that Christian witness has often been distorted by coercive proselytism—conscious and unconscious, overt and subtle. Two later WCC documents deal with this aspect in greater detail. The first, dealing with Christian-Jewish relations, states: "Such rejection of proselytism, and such advocacy of respect for the integrity and the identity of all persons and all communities of faith are urgent in relation to the Jews, especially those who live as minorities among Christians. Steps toward assuring non-coercive practices are of highest importance. In dialogue ways should be found for the exchange of concerns, perceptions, and safeguards in these matters."[30] The second, dealing with Christian-Muslim relations, affirms that "missionary activity is integral to Christian discipleship" but recommends that "Christians explore new ways of witnessing to Christ in words and deeds, for instance, through living Christ-like lives and by demonstrating that Christianity is, like Islam, concerned with the whole of life."[31]

POLITICAL DIMENSIONS

The ecumenical consensus treats proselytism as a religious question that needs to be addressed through dialogue (1) between churches and other religions in terms of interreligious aspects of proselytism, and (2) between churches in terms of intra-Christian dimensions of the problem. Significant as the ecumenical achievement has been, the consensus is limited to the conciliar groups that give it consent. It cannot and does not bind nonconciliar groups, Christian or other, who continue to exercise their own understanding of missionary activity, irrespective of potential proselytizing

---

30. "Authentic Christian Witness," in WCC, *Ecumenical Considerations on Jewish-Christian Dialogue*, section 4.3.

31. "On Understanding Islam and Muslims," in WCC, *Ecumenical Considerations on Christian-Muslim Relations*, section 2.

consequences. The right freely to propagate one's religion is given priority over all else.

The missionary activity of such nonconciliar groups has been nowhere more evident than in the Russian Federation and other post-Communist eastern European states during much of the 1990s. As part of the perestroika reform of the former Soviet Union, the 1990 Law on Freedom of Worship marked a radical departure from traditional Soviet restrictions on religion: freedom of religion and belief was guaranteed; all religious communities in the USSR were placed on an equal footing; foreign religious groups were accorded equal protection under the law; and the free exercise of missionary activity was permitted, subject only to basic principles of constitutional order. This wholesale removal of former barriers against religious activity opened the door to an avalanche of foreign missionary activity, predominantly by North American evangelical (nonconciliar) groups and new religious movements.[32]

The ensuing confrontation between these groups and the Russian Orthodox Church exposed the clash of values that the ecumenical consensus had sought to reconcile:[33] the individual right to propagate one's faith, and a church's collective right to preserve and extend the faith among its people, within its culture. The Moscow Patriarchate's perception of the problem was candidly expressed in the following terms: "Many Protestants do not even consider the Orthodox Church to be a proper church but regard it as a dangerous phenomenon in religious life."[34]

In consort with Communist and nationalist groupings, the church pressed for a new law on religion.[35] Amid much internal controversy and international criticism, the Russian Duma passed the Law of Freedom of Conscience and Religious Organizations in September 1997. The preamble acknowledges "the special contribution of Orthodoxy to the history of Russia and the development of Russia's spirituality and culture," thereby distinguishing Orthodoxy's status in relation to the Russian state from that of other religions—Christianity,[36] Islam, Buddhism, and Judaism—which are associated with Russian peoples. The law requires the legal registration of all religious organizations. To qualify as Russian, a religious organization

32. For the latter, the author is indebted to Federov, "New Religious Movements."
33. Berman, "Religious Rights in Russia," 301–3.
34. Metropolitan Kirill of Kaliningrad and Smolensk, head of foreign affairs, Moscow Patriarchate, quoted in *Nezavisimaya Gazeta*, November 28, 1996. For reference and translation, the author is indebted to Luchterhandt, "Religous Freedom and Proselytism in Russia and Eastern Europe."
35. See Ellis, *Russian Orthodox Church*, 157ff.
36. Here "Christianity" refers to non-Orthodox churches.

must have been established in Russia for more than fifty years at the time of registration; all others are by definition foreign and subject to a gradation of restrictions depending on whether they have been in Russia for less than fifty or less than fifteen years at the time of registration. While the law makes no reference to proselytism, its catalog of forbidden activities effectively proscribes any form of religious propaganda that would impinge on the Orthodox Church.

The 1997 Russian law represents the most restrictive legal/political response to what is perceived as intra-Christian proselytizing missionary activity. In terms of interreligious proselytism, it is well known that several Islamic states have taken legal measures to prohibit or severely restrict foreign (specifically Christian) missionary activity within their borders. As early as 1977 Israel also introduced what is commonly known as an anti-mission law that makes any inducement to change religion an offense punishable by five years' imprisonment. This law has never yet been enforced, but pressure has recently increased for legislation to prohibit any form of preaching or writing that could be deemed to solicit a person to change his or her religion. A private member's bill to this effect was brought before the Knesset in 1996 by two members, Gafni and Zvili. Faced with domestic and international criticism, the bill's promoters reportedly met with representatives of Christian organizations in Israel and agreed to drop the bill in return for a cessation of missionary activities in Israel.[37]

INTERNATIONAL LAW

The examples given in the previous section illustrate that where the ecumenical consensus on proselytism is disregarded, states are resorting to national law to stem the tide of what they perceive as illegitimate missionary activity. The Russian law and similar legislation invite criticism that they contravene article 18 of the 1948 *Universal Declaration of Human Rights*, which affirms "the right to freedom of thought, conscience and religion," adding that "this right includes freedom to change [one's] religion or belief."[38] Those who support legal constraints on missionary activity, however, appeal to the 1966 International Covenant on Civil and Political Rights, which reaffirms

---

37. See *Ha'aretz*, March 31, 1998. The author is indebted for the reference and translation to Hirsch, "Freedom of Proselytism."

38. For the full text, see UN, *Universal Declaration of Human Rights*. Professor Johan van der Vyver, for example, makes the following criticism: "Values that are upheld by virtue of state-imposed coercion instead of personal conviction or individual persuasion forfeit their ethical quality" (Vyver, "Religious Freedom and Proselytism").

the fight of religious freedom but significantly reinterprets the 1948 declaration's right to change religion by stating that "this right shall include freedom to have or to adopt a religion or belief of [one's] choice." At the same time, the covenant specifically prohibits coercion: "No one shall be subject to coercion which would impair his freedom to have or to adopt a religion or belief of his choice."[39] A third instrument of international law, the 1981 Declaration on the Elimination of All Forms of Intolerance and Discrimination based on Religion or Belief, makes no reference to the right to change or adopt a religion, simply stating that one has the right "to have a religion or whatever belief of one's choice," reiterating that this choice must not be impaired by any form of coercion.[40]

The force of these statements seems to indicate that "the focus of international law has shifted from an emphasis on the freedom to change a religion to an emphasis on the freedom to retain a religion."[41] Freedom to change a religion remains a right in international law but needs to be set in balance with the freedom to maintain a religion—a principle that has been strongly argued by Muslim member states of the United Nations.[42]

CONCLUSION

The value of the ecumenical consensus that has been outlined in this article is precisely that it seeks to mediate between the two competing freedoms guaranteed in international law. Its commitment to the right of witness/mission entails, as a corollary, the right to change one's religion. In rejecting unethical (coercive) forms of witness as proselytism, it calls for discernment regarding the integrity of other churches, and indeed other religions, within God's purposes for humankind and human society. It appeals to dialogue rather than legislation as the way of discernment and encourages partners from different traditions to be willing to listen to one another in mutual openness, ready to accept mutual correction as well as receive mutual enrichment.

To continue to be effective, however, this dialogue must extend to include as partners those movements of Christian growth that established churches are inclined to rebuke as proselytizers. This must embrace, for

39. Dickson, "United Nations and the Freedom of Religion."
40. Lerner, "Final Text of the UN Declaration."
41. Hirsch, "Freedom of Proselytism," 445.
42. Mayer, *Islam and Human Rights*. For differing Muslim views, see the contributions of Roger Garaudy and Abdallahi Ahmed An-Na'im in Küng and Moltmann, *Ethics of World Religions and Human Rights*, 46–69.

example, the charismatic and neo-Pentecostal churches in Latin America, which the pope [John Paul II] caricatured as "rapacious wolves" in his opening address to the 1992 Conference of Latin American Bishops,[43] and the phenomenon of African Independent Churches, which he likewise condemned at the opening of the Conference of African Bishops for being "unyielding fundamentalist or aggressive proselytizing."[44]

These examples are not merely incidental to the concluding argument of this study. They represent regions where, in many respects, Christianity is showing its greatest vitality at the close of the twentieth century. Research into both African Independent Churches and Latin American neo-Pentecostalism illustrates their significance as indigenizing movements that are sowing the seeds of the Gospel in new cultural soils. The new plants are proving hugely attractive to peoples who are estranged by the alien culture of most historic mission churches in non-Western societies. As Shakespeare said of Perdita, the indigenous movements have the power to "quench the zeal of all professors else." If, as seems probable, these radically indigenized transformations of the Christian faith predict important new trends in global Christianity of the twenty-first century, historic churches cannot simply dismiss them with the charge of "proselytism."

The understandings of proselytism discussed in this article amount to the assault by one religious group against the territorial, ecclesiological, or faith integrity of another—an unethical way of engaging in interreligious relations, and particularly hurtful in terms of intra-Christian relations. But progress toward resolving this problem so far reflects a status quo, the product of centuries of Orthodox, Catholic, and Protestant hegemony over Christianity in its historic forms. The challenge for the future is for the current ecumenical consensus to open itself to the possibility that the Spirit of God, which Christians believe brings human communities into ever-new understandings of the presence and action of God in Christ, is moving in transformative ways among Christians who have little or no stake in traditional forms of Western ecclesiology. "Newcomers" they may be, but in giving honor to the proselyte, the early church showed its capacity to embrace new experience. To require non-Western Christians to conform to Western criteria of what it is to be "church," and to condemn as proselytism what may be faith-renewing workings of the Holy Spirit, is to imitate the ancient Danish king of England, Canute, who vainly tried to set his throne against a rising tide.

---

43. John Paul II, "Opening Address," 326.
44. John Paul II, "Evangelizing Mission of the Church in Africa," 665–84.

1.4

UN Declarations

Editor's Introduction

Here I list three relevant Declarations from the United Nations that have a direct or indirect application to the issue of proselytism and freedom of religion. These are important background documents, but there is a large volume of secondary material that relates to their application and interpretation (issues which are beyond the scope and competency of this Reader).

The first document is the Universal Declaration of Human Rights (UDHR). It is "a milestone document in the history of human rights. Drafted by representatives with different legal and cultural backgrounds from all regions of the world, it set out, for the first time, fundamental human rights to be universally protected. The Declaration was adopted by the UN General Assembly in Paris on December 10, 1948, during its 183rd plenary meeting."[1] The significant article is 18, reproduced below with 19 and 20. The latter two are relevant by implication.

The second document is the International Covenant on Civil and Political Rights (ICCPR), adopted in December 1966. Articles 18 and 19 are reproduced below, along with 27.

The third document is the Declaration on the Elimination of All Forms of Intolerance and of Discrimination Based on Religion or Belief. This document is dated November 1981. I reproduce all the articles, but not the Preamble.[2]

---

1. OHCHR, "Universal Declaration of Human Rights."
2. These, and other UN documents, can be accessed online (www.ohchr.org).

UNIVERSAL DECLARATION OF HUMAN RIGHTS

From *The Universal Declaration of Human Rights*, by the UN General Assembly, ©1948 United Nations. Reprinted with the permission of the United Nations.

Article 18

Everyone has the right to freedom of thought, conscience and religion; this right includes freedom to change his religion or belief, and freedom, either alone or in community with others and in public or private, to manifest his religion or belief in teaching, practice, worship and observance.

Article 19

Everyone has the right to freedom of opinion and expression; this right includes freedom to hold opinions without interference and to seek, receive and impart information and ideas through any media and regardless of frontiers.

Article 20

1. Everyone has the right to freedom of peaceful assembly and association.
2. No one may be compelled to belong to an association.

INTERNATIONAL COVENANT ON CIVIL AND POLITICAL RIGHTS

From *The International Covenant on Civil and Political Rights*, by UN General Assembly, ©1966 United Nations. Reprinted with the permission of the United Nations.

Article 18

1. Everyone shall have the right to freedom of thought, conscience and religion. This right shall include freedom to have or to adopt a religion or belief of his choice, and freedom, either individually or in community with others and in public or private, to manifest his religion or belief in worship, observance, practice and teaching.
2. No one shall be subject to coercion which would impair his freedom to have or to adopt a religion or belief of his choice.
3. Freedom to manifest one's religion or beliefs may be subject only to such limitations as are prescribed by law and are necessary to protect public safety, order, health, or morals or the fundamental rights and freedoms of others.
4. The States Parties to the present Covenant undertake to have respect for the liberty of parents and, when applicable, legal guardians to ensure the religious and moral education of their children in conformity with their own convictions.

Article 19

1. Everyone shall have the right to hold opinions without interference.
2. Everyone shall have the right to freedom of expression; this right shall include freedom to seek, receive and impart information and ideas of all kinds, regardless of frontiers, either orally, in writing or in print, in the form of art, or through any other media of his choice.
3. The exercise of the rights provided for in paragraph 2 of this article carries with it special duties and responsibilities. It may therefore be subject to certain restrictions, but these shall only be such as are provided by law and are necessary:

(a) For respect of the rights or reputations of others;

(b) For the protection of national security or of public order, or of public health or morals. . . .

Article 27

In those States in which ethnic, religious or linguistic minorities exist, persons belonging to such minorities shall not be denied the right, in community with the other members of their group, to enjoy their own culture, to profess and practice their own religion, or to use their own language.

DECLARATION ON THE ELIMINATION OF ALL FORMS OF INTOLERANCE AND OF DISCRIMINATION BASED ON RELIGION OR BELIEF

From *Declaration on the Elimination of All Forms of Intolerance and of Discrimination Based on Religion or Belief,* by UN General Assembly, ©1981 United Nations. Reprinted with the permission of the United Nations.

Article 1

1. Everyone shall have the right to freedom of thought, conscience and religion. This right shall include freedom to have a religion or whatever belief of his choice, and freedom, either individually or in community with others and in public or private, to manifest his religion or belief in worship, observance, practice and teaching.
2. No one shall be subject to coercion which would impair his freedom to have a religion or belief of his choice.
3. Freedom to manifest one's religion or beliefs may be subject only to such limitations as are prescribed by law and are necessary to protect public safety, order, health or morals or the fundamental rights and freedoms of others.

Article 2

1. No one shall be subject to discrimination by any State, institution, group of persons, or person on grounds of religion or other beliefs.
2. For the purposes of the present Declaration, the expression "intolerance and discrimination based on religion or belief" means any distinction, exclusion, restriction or preference based on religion or belief and having as its purpose or as its effect nullification or impairment of the recognition, enjoyment or exercise of human rights and fundamental freedoms on an equal basis.

Article 3

Discrimination between human beings on grounds of religion or belief constitutes an affront to human dignity and a disavowal of the principles of the Charter of the United Nations, and shall be condemned as a violation of the human rights and fundamental freedoms proclaimed in the Universal Declaration of Human Rights and enunciated in detail in the International Covenants on Human Rights, and as an obstacle to friendly and peaceful relations between nations.

Article 4

1. All States shall take effective measures to prevent and eliminate discrimination on the grounds of religion or belief in the recognition, exercise and enjoyment of human rights and fundamental freedoms in all fields of civil, economic, political, social and cultural life.

2. All States shall make all efforts to enact or rescind legislation where necessary to prohibit any such discrimination, and to take all appropriate measures to combat intolerance on the grounds of religion or other beliefs in this matter.

Article 5

1. The parents or, as the case may be, the legal guardians of the child have the right to organize the life within the family in accordance with their religion or belief and bearing in mind the moral education in which they believe the child should be brought up.

2. Every child shall enjoy the right to have access to education in the matter of religion or belief in accordance with the wishes of his parents or, as the case may be, legal guardians, and shall not be compelled to receive teaching on religion or belief against the wishes of his parents or legal guardians, the best interests of the child being the guiding principle.

3. The child shall be protected from any form of discrimination on the ground of religion or belief. He shall be brought up in a spirit of understanding, tolerance, friendship among peoples, peace and universal brotherhood, respect for freedom of religion or belief of others, and in full consciousness that his energy and talents should be devoted to the service of his fellow men.

4. In the case of a child who is not under the care either of his parents or of legal guardians, due account shall be taken of their expressed wishes or of any other proof of their wishes in the matter of religion or belief, the best interests of the child being the guiding principle.

5. Practices of a religion or beliefs in which a child is brought up must not be injurious to his physical or mental health or to his full development, taking into account article 1, paragraph 3, of the present Declaration.

Article 6

In accordance with article 1 of the present Declaration, and subject to the provisions of article 1, paragraph 3, the right to freedom of thought, conscience, religion or belief shall include, inter alia, the following freedoms:

(a) To worship or assemble in connexion with a religion or belief, and to establish and maintain places for these purposes;

(b) To establish and maintain appropriate charitable or humanitarian institutions;

(c) To make, acquire and use to an adequate extent the necessary articles and materials related to the rites or customs of a religion or belief;

(d) To write, issue and disseminate relevant publications in these areas;

(e) To teach a religion or belief in places suitable for these purposes;

(f) To solicit and receive voluntary financial and other from individuals and institutions;

(g) To train, appoint, elect or designate by succession appropriate leaders called for by the requirements and standards of any religion or belief;

(h) To observe days of rest and to celebrate holidays and ceremonies in accordance with the precepts of one's religion or belief;

(i) To establish and maintain communications with individuals and communities in matters of religion and belief at the national and international levels.

Article 7

The rights and freedoms set forth in the present Declaration shall be accorded in national legislation in such a manner that everyone shall be able to avail himself of such rights and freedoms in practice.

Article 8

Nothing in the present Declaration shall be construed as restricting or derogating from any right defined in the Universal Declaration of Human Rights and the International Covenants on Human Rights.

Part 2

STATEMENTS AND REPORTS FROM CHRISTIAN BODIES

Part 2 Introduction

ALL THE DOCUMENTS REPRODUCED in part 2 represent Churches or Christian movements. They have different levels of authority, with some reflecting formal policy positions of their drafters' bodies whilst others are more descriptive of a breadth of views. They are presented roughly in chronological order with the one exception of the Lausanne Movement: I have collated relevant extracts from Lausanne documents together for this volume.

The section begins with documents from Vatican II in 1965. However, proselytism has been a significant issue across the Christian community for much longer. As early as 1920 there has been the acknowledgement that proselytism was a major hindrance to Christian unity. In the words of the Ecumenical Patriarch:

> *First*, we consider as necessary and indispensable the removal and abolition of all the mutual mistrust and bitterness between the different churches which arise from the tendency of some of them to entice and proselytize adherents of other confessions. For nobody ignores what is unfortunately happening today in many places, disturbing the internal peace of the churches. . . . So many troubles and sufferings are caused by other Christians and great hatred and enmity are aroused, with such insignificant results, by this tendency of some to proselytize and entice the followers of other Christian confessions.[1]

This quote illustrates the pain that proselytism caused and causes. There are concrete historical events that lie behind this plea for unity, based on geopolitical changes that occurred in the interwar years in Europe and the Middle East, but also upon misplaced missionary zeal. Germanos V, the Ecumenical Patriarch, went on to make suggestions as to how to overcome the "great hatred and enmity," yet it took many more years before his recommendations saw much fruit.

1. "Patriarchal and Synodical Encyclical of 1920."

Thus, it is against the background of geopolitics and global wars, the rise of post-war attempts to limit further violence (for example, through the UN and the EU), and developments in inter-church relations (as evidenced in Edinburgh 1910, the 1920 Encyclical, the establishment of the WCC in 1948, the re-establishment of the WEA in 1951 and Vatican II in 1965) that the controversy surrounding proselytism is addressed.

This book is another very modest step forwards in this slow history.

2.1

Second Vatican Council[1]

- *Ad Gentes* [Decree on Missionary Activity]
- *Dignitatis Humanae* [Declaration on Religious Freedom]

RCC 1965

Editor's Introduction

THESE DOCUMENTS ARE FROM the Roman Catholic Church. Both arise out of the Second Vatican Council held between 1962 and 1965. It is hard to overstate the dramatic impact that Vatican II has had upon the RCC—and on the Churches more widely. This is particularly true regarding Catholic approaches to mission and missiology.[2] Whilst neither of these documents use the word "proselytism," both use language and concepts that are pertinent to the issue. I reproduce only these relevant portions below.

The Decree[3] on the Mission Activity of the Church, usually called "Ad Gentes," after its first two words in Latin (meaning "to the nations"), was published by Vatican II on December 7, 1965. It consists of a Preface followed by six chapters (Principles of Doctrine; Mission Work Itself; Particular Churches; Missionaries; Planning Missionary Activity, and Cooperation) with a short Conclusion. Paragraph 13 is the most relevant regarding proselytism. It is

---

1. Vatican II documents reproduced here with kind permission of Libreria Editrice Vaticana.

2. See, for example, Bevans, "Mission at the Second Vatican Council," and, from a broader historical perspective, Schreiter, "Changes in Roman Catholic Attitudes."

3. Vatican II published three types of official documents—in order of authority—*Constitutions* (of which there were four), *Decrees* (nine), and *Declarations* (three).

reproduced below within the context of the first two articles of chapter 2, "Mission Work Itself."

Dignitatis Humanae, "Declaration on Religious Freedom on the Right of the Person and of Communities to Social and Civil Freedom in Matters Religious," was published on the same date. It is a document of fifteen numbered paragraphs. Paragraphs 2, 4, and 10 are particularly relevant, but I have reproduced much of the document.

Both documents are referred to in subsequent Catholic reflection on mission, so, for example, "The Attitude of the Church towards the Followers of Other Religions,"[4] states: "In this process of conversion, the law of conscience is sovereign, because 'no one must be constrained to act against his conscience, nor ought he to be impeded in acting according to his conscience, especially in religious matters' (DH 3)."[5]

---

4. Secretariat for Non-Christians, "Attitude of the Church."
5. Secretariat for Non-Christians, "Attitude of the Church," para. 38.

Ad Gentes

II. MISSION WORK ITSELF

10. THE CHURCH, SENT by Christ to reveal and to communicate the love of God to all men and nations, is aware that there still remains a gigantic missionary task for her to accomplish. For the Gospel message has not yet, or hardly yet, been heard by two million human beings (and their number is increasing daily), who are formed into large and distinct groups by permanent cultural ties, by ancient religious traditions, and by firm bonds of social necessity. Some of these men are followers of one of the great religions, but others remain strangers to the very knowledge of God, while still others expressly deny His existence, and sometimes even attack it. The Church, in order to be able to offer all of them the mystery of salvation and the life brought by God, must implant herself into these groups for the same motive which led Christ to bind Himself, in virtue of His Incarnation, to certain social and cultural conditions of those human beings among whom He dwelt.

Article 1. Christian Witness

11. The Church must be present in these groups through her children, who dwell among them or who are sent to them. For all Christians, wherever they live, are bound to show forth, by the example of their lives and by the witness of the word, that new man put on at baptism and that power of the Holy Spirit by which they have been strengthened at Conformation. Thus other men, observing their good works, can glorify the Father (cf. Matt 5:16) and can perceive more fully the real meaning of human life and the universal bond of the community of mankind.

In order that they may be able to bear more fruitful witness to Christ, let them be joined to those men by esteem and love; let them acknowledge themselves to be members of the group of men among whom they live; let them share in cultural and social life by the various undertakings and enterprises of human living; let them be familiar with their national and religious traditions; let them gladly and reverently lay bare the seeds of the Word which lie hidden among their fellows. At the same time, however, let them look to the profound changes which are taking place among nations, and let them exert themselves to keep modern man, intent as he is on the science and technology of today's world from becoming a stranger to things divine; rather, let them awaken in him a yearning for that truth and charity which God has revealed. Even as Christ Himself searched the hearts of men, and led them to divine light, so also His disciples, profoundly penetrated by the Spirit of Christ, should show the people among whom they live, and should converse with them, that they themselves may learn by sincere and patient dialogue what treasures a generous God has distributed among the nations of the earth. But at the same time, let them try to furbish these treasures, set them free, and bring them under the dominion of God their Savior.

12. The presence of the Christian faithful in these human groups should be inspired by that charity with which God has loved us, and with which He wills that we should love one another (cf. 1 John 4:11). Christian charity truly extends to all, without distinction of race, creed, or social condition: it looks for neither gain nor gratitude. For as God loved us with an unselfish love, so also the faithful should in their charity care for the human person himself, loving him with the same affection with which God sought out man. Just as Christ, then, went about all the towns and villages, curing every kind of disease and infirmity as a sign that the kingdom of God had come (cf. Matt 9:35ff; Acts 10:38), so also the Church, through her children, is one with men of every condition, but especially with the poor and the afflicted. For them, she gladly spends and is spent (cf. 2 Cor 12:15), sharing in their joys and sorrows, knowing of their longings and problems, suffering with them in death's anxieties. To those in quest of peace, she wishes to answer in fraternal dialogue, bearing them the peace and the light of the Gospel.

Let Christians labor and collaborate with others in rightly regulating the affairs of social and economic life. With special care, let them devote themselves to the education of children and young people by means of different kinds of schools, which should be considered not only as the most excellent means of forming and developing Christian youth, but also as a valuable public service, especially in the developing nations, working toward the uplifting of human dignity, and toward better living conditions. Furthermore, let them take part in the strivings of those peoples who, waging war on famine, ignorance, and disease, are struggling to better their way of life and to secure peace in the world. In this activity, the faithful should be eager to offer prudent aid to projects sponsored by public and private organizations, by governments, by various Christian communities, and even by non-Christian religions.

However, the Church has no desire at all to intrude itself into the government of the earthly city. It claims no other authority than that of ministering to men with the help of God, in a spirit of charity and faithful service (cf. Matt 20:26; 23:11).

Closely united with men in their life and work, Christ's disciples hope to render to others true witness of Christ, and to work for their salvation, even where they are not able to announce Christ fully. For they are not seeking a mere material progress and prosperity for men, but are promoting their dignity and brotherly union, teaching those religious and moral truths which Christ illumined with His light; and in this way, they are gradually opening up a fuller approach to God. Thus they help men to attain to salvation by love for God and neighbor, and the mystery of Christ begins to shine forth, in which there appears the new man, created according to God (cf. Eph 4:24), and in which the charity of God is revealed.

Article 2. Preaching the Gospel and Gathering Together the People of God

13. Wherever God opens a door of speech for proclaiming the mystery of Christ (cf. Col 4:3), there is announced to all men (cf. Mark 16:15; 1 Cor 9:15; Rom 10:14) with confidence and constancy (cf. Acts 4:13, 29, 31; 9:27, 28; 13:46; 14:3; 19:8; 26:26; 28:31; 1 Thess 2:2; 2 Cor 3:12; 7:4; Phil 1:20; Eph 3:12; 6:19, 20) the living God, and He Whom He has sent for the salvation of all, Jesus Christ (cf. 1 Thess 1:9–10; 1 Cor 1:18–21; Gal 1:31; Acts 14:15–17, 17:22–31), in order that non-Christians, when the Holy Spirit opens their heart (cf. Acts 16:14), may believe and be freely converted to the Lord, that they may cleave sincerely to Him Who, being the "way, the truth, and the life" (John 14:6), fulfills all their spiritual expectations, and even infinitely surpasses them.

This conversion must be taken as an initial one, yet sufficient to make a man realize that he has been snatched away from sin and led into the mystery of God's love, who called him to enter into a personal relationship with Him in Christ. For, by the workings of divine grace, the new convert sets out on a spiritual journey, by means of which, already sharing through faith in the mystery of Christ's Death and Resurrection, he passes from the old man to the new one, perfected in Christ (cf. Col 3:5–10; Eph 4:20–24). This bringing with it a progressive change of outlook and morals, must become evident with its social consequences, and must be gradually developed during the time of the catechumenate. Since the Lord he believes in is a sign of contradiction (cf. Luke 2:34; Matt 10:34–39), the convert often experiences an abrupt breaking off of human ties, but he also tastes the joy which God gives without measure (cf. 1 Thess 1:6).

The Church strictly forbids forcing anyone to embrace the Faith, or alluring or enticing people by worrisome wiles. By the same token, she also strongly insists on this right, that no one be frightened away from the Faith by unjust vexations on the part of others.[1]

In accord with the Church's ancient custom, the convert's motives should be looked into, and if necessary, purified.

14. Those who, through the Church, have accepted from God a belief in Christ are admitted to the catechumenate by liturgical rites. The catechumenate is not a mere expounding of doctrines and precepts, but a training period in the whole Christian life, and an apprenticeship duty drawn out, during which disciples are joined to Christ their Teacher. Therefore, catechumens should be properly instructed in the mystery of salvation and in the practice of Gospel morality, and by sacred rites which are to be held at successive intervals, they should be introduced into the life of faith, of liturgy, and of love, which is led by the People of God.

Then, when the sacraments of Christian initiation have freed them from the power of darkness (cf. Col 1:13), having died with Christ been buried with Him and risen together with Him (cf. Rom 6:4–11; Col 2:12–13; 1 Pet 3:21–22; Mark 16:16), they receive the Spirit (cf. 1 Thess 3:5–7; Acts 8:14–17) of adoption of sons and celebrate the remembrance of the Lord's death and resurrection together with the whole People of God.

It is to be desired that the liturgy of the Lenten and Paschal seasons should be restored in such a way as to dispose the hearts of the catechumens to celebrate the Easter mystery at whose solemn ceremonies they are reborn to Christ through baptism.

But this Christian initiation in the catechumenate should be taken care of not only by catechists or priests, but by the entire community of the faithful, so that right from the outset the catechumens may feel that they belong to the people of God. And since the life of the Church is an apostolic one, the catechumens also should learn to cooperate wholeheartedly, by the witness of their lives and by the profession of their faith, in the spread of the Gospel and in the building up of the Church.

---

1. The original footnote refers to Vatican II, *Dignitatis Humanae* 2, 4, 10; *Gaudium et Spes*.

Finally, the juridical status of catechumens should be clearly defined in the new code of Canon law. For since they are joined to the Church, they are already of the household of Christ, and not seldom they are already leading a life of faith, hope, and charity.

Dignitatis Humanae

1. A SENSE OF the dignity of the human person has been impressing itself more and more deeply on the consciousness of contemporary man, and the demand is increasingly made that men should act on their own judgment, enjoying and making use of a responsible freedom, not driven by coercion but motivated by a sense of duty. The demand is likewise made that constitutional limits should be set to the powers of government, in order that there may be no encroachment on the rightful freedom of the person and of associations. This demand for freedom in human society chiefly regards the quest for the values proper to the human spirit. It regards, in the first place, the free exercise of religion in society. This Vatican Council takes careful note of these desires in the minds of men. It proposes to declare them to be greatly in accord with truth and justice. To this end, it searches into the sacred tradition and doctrine of the Church-the treasury out of which the Church continually brings forth new things that are in harmony with the things that are old.

First, the council professes its belief that God Himself has made known to mankind the way in which men are to serve Him, and thus be saved in Christ and come to blessedness. We believe that this one true religion subsists in the Catholic and Apostolic Church, to which the Lord Jesus committed the duty of spreading it abroad among all men. Thus He spoke to the Apostles: "Go, therefore, and make disciples of all nations, baptizing them in the name of the Father and of the Son and of the Holy Spirit, teaching them to observe all things whatsoever I have enjoined upon you" (Matt 28:19–20). On their part, all men are bound to seek the truth, especially in what concerns God and His Church, and to embrace the truth they come to know, and to hold fast to it.

This Vatican Council likewise professes its belief that it is upon the human conscience that these obligations fall and exert their binding force.

The truth cannot impose itself except by virtue of its own truth, as it makes its entrance into the mind at once quietly and with power.

Religious freedom, in turn, which men demand as necessary to fulfill their duty to worship God, has to do with immunity from coercion in civil society. Therefore it leaves untouched traditional Catholic doctrine on the moral duty of men and societies toward the true religion and toward the one Church of Christ.

Over and above all this, the council intends to develop the doctrine of recent popes on the inviolable rights of the human person and the constitutional order of society.

2. This Vatican Council declares that the human person has a right to religious freedom. This freedom means that all men are to be immune from coercion on the part of individuals or of social groups and of any human power, in such wise that no one is to be forced to act in a manner contrary to his own beliefs, whether privately or publicly, whether alone or in association with others, within due limits.

The council further declares that the right to religious freedom has its foundation in the very dignity of the human person as this dignity is known through the revealed word of God and by reason itself. This right of the human person to religious freedom is to be recognized in the constitutional law whereby society is governed and thus it is to become a civil right.

It is in accordance with their dignity as persons—that is, beings endowed with reason and free will and therefore privileged to bear personal responsibility—that all men should be at once impelled by nature and also bound by a moral obligation to seek the truth, especially religious truth. They are also bound to adhere to the truth, once it is known, and to order their whole lives in accord with the demands of truth. However, men cannot discharge these obligations in a manner in keeping with their own nature unless they enjoy immunity from external coercion as well as psychological freedom. Therefore the right to religious freedom has its foundation not in the subjective disposition of the person, but in his very nature. In consequence, the right to this immunity continues to exist even in those who do not live up to their obligation of seeking the truth and adhering to it and the exercise of this right is not to be impeded, provided that just public order be observed.

3. Further light is shed on the subject if one considers that the highest norm of human life is the divine law—eternal, objective and universal—whereby God orders, directs and governs the entire universe and all the ways of the human community by a plan conceived in wisdom and love. Man has been made by God to participate in this law, with the result that, under the gentle disposition of divine Providence, he can come to perceive

ever more fully the truth that is unchanging. Wherefore every man has the duty, and therefore the right, to seek the truth in matters religious in order that he may with prudence form for himself right and true judgments of conscience, under use of all suitable means.

Truth, however, is to be sought after in a manner proper to the dignity of the human person and his social nature. The inquiry is to be free, carried on with the aid of teaching or instruction, communication and dialogue, in the course of which men explain to one another the truth they have discovered, or think they have discovered, in order thus to assist one another in the quest for truth.

Moreover, as the truth is discovered, it is by a personal assent that men are to adhere to it.

On his part, man perceives and acknowledges the imperatives of the divine law through the mediation of conscience. In all his activity a man is bound to follow his conscience in order that he may come to God, the end and purpose of life. It follows that he is not to be forced to act in a manner contrary to his conscience. Nor, on the other hand, is he to be restrained from acting in accordance with his conscience, especially in matters religious. The reason is that the exercise of religion, of its very nature, consists before all else in those internal, voluntary and free acts whereby man sets the course of his life directly toward God. No merely human power can either command or prohibit acts of this kind. The social nature of man, however, itself requires that he should give external expression to his internal acts of religion: that he should share with others in matters religious; that he should profess his religion in community. Injury therefore is done to the human person and to the very order established by God for human life, if the free exercise of religion is denied in society, provided just public order is observed.

There is a further consideration. The religious acts whereby men, in private and in public and out of a sense of personal conviction, direct their lives to God transcend by their very nature the order of terrestrial and temporal affairs. Government therefore ought indeed to take account of the religious life of the citizenry and show it favor, since the function of government is to make provision for the common welfare. However, it would clearly transgress the limits set to its power, were it to presume to command or inhibit acts that are religious.

4. The freedom or immunity from coercion in matters religious which is the endowment of persons as individuals is also to be recognized as their right when they act in community. Religious communities are a requirement of the social nature both of man and of religion itself.

Provided the just demands of public order are observed, religious communities rightfully claim freedom in order that they may govern themselves according to their own norms, honor the Supreme Being in public worship, assist their members in the practice of the religious life, strengthen them by instruction, and promote institutions in which they may join together for the purpose of ordering their own lives in accordance with their religious principles.

Religious communities also have the right not to be hindered, either by legal measures or by administrative action on the part of government, in the selection, training, appointment, and transferral of their own ministers, in communicating with religious authorities and communities abroad, in erecting buildings for religious purposes, and in the acquisition and use of suitable funds or properties.

Religious communities also have the right not to be hindered in their public teaching and witness to their faith, whether by the spoken or by the written word. However, in spreading religious faith and in introducing religious practices everyone ought at all times to refrain from any manner of action which might seem to carry a hint of coercion or of a kind of persuasion that would be dishonorable or unworthy, especially when dealing with poor or uneducated people. Such a manner of action would have to be considered an abuse of one's right and a violation of the right of others.

In addition, it comes within the meaning of religious freedom that religious communities should not be prohibited from freely undertaking to show the special value of their doctrine in what concerns the organization of society and the inspiration of the whole of human activity. Finally, the social nature of man and the very nature of religion afford the foundation of the right of men freely to hold meetings and to establish educational, cultural, charitable and social organizations, under the impulse of their own religious sense.

5. . . . [Concerning family life and religious freedom.]

6. . . . [Concerning religious freedom and government.]

Finally, government is to see to it that equality of citizens before the law, which is itself an element of the common good, is never violated, whether openly or covertly, for religious reasons. Nor is there to be discrimination among citizens.

It follows that a wrong is done when government imposes upon its people, by force or fear or other means, the profession or repudiation of any religion, or when it hinders men from joining or leaving a religious community. All the more is it a violation of the will of God and of the sacred rights of the person and the family of nations when force is brought to bear in any way in order to destroy or repress religion, either in the whole of mankind or in a particular country or in a definite community.

7. . . . [Concerning religious freedom within human society.]

8. . . . [Concerning people "acting on their own judgement."]

9. . . . [Concerning the basis for religious freedom in human reason and divine revelation.]

10. It is one of the major tenets of Catholic doctrine that man's response to God in faith must be free: no one therefore is to be forced to embrace the Christian faith against his own will. This doctrine is contained in the word of God and it was constantly proclaimed by the Fathers of the Church. The act of faith is of its very nature a free act. Man, redeemed by Christ the Savior and through Christ Jesus called to be God's adopted son, cannot give his adherence to God revealing Himself unless, under the drawing of the Father, he offers to God the reasonable and free submission of faith. It is therefore completely in accord with the nature of faith that in matters religious every manner of coercion on the part of men should be excluded. In consequence, the principle of religious freedom makes no small contribution to the creation of an environment in which men can without hindrance be invited to the Christian faith, embrace it of their own free will, and profess it effectively in their whole manner of life.

11. God calls men to serve Him in spirit and in truth, hence they are bound in conscience but they stand under no compulsion. God has regard for the dignity of the human person whom He Himself created and man is to be guided by his own judgment and he is to enjoy freedom. This truth appears at its height in Christ Jesus, in whom God manifested Himself and His ways with men. Christ is at once our Master and our Lord and also meek and humble of heart. In attracting and inviting His disciples He used patience. He wrought miracles to illuminate His teaching and to establish its truth, but His intention was to rouse faith in His hearers and to confirm them in faith, not to exert coercion upon them. He did indeed denounce the unbelief of some who listened to Him, but He left vengeance to God in expectation of the day of judgment. When He sent His Apostles into the world, He said to them: "He who believes and is baptized will be saved. He who does not believe will be condemned" (Mark 16:16). But He Himself, noting that the cockle had been sown amid the wheat, gave orders that both should be allowed to grow until the harvest time, which will come at the end of the world. He refused to be a political messiah, ruling by force: He preferred to call Himself the Son of Man, who came "to serve and to give his

life as a ransom for the many" (Mark 10:45). He showed Himself the perfect servant of God, who "does not break the bruised reed nor extinguish the smoking flax" (Matt 12:20).

He acknowledged the power of government and its rights, when He commanded that tribute be given to Caesar: but He gave clear warning that the higher rights of God are to be kept inviolate: "Render to Caesar the things that are Caesar's and to God the things that are God's" (Matt 22:21). In the end, when He completed on the cross the work of redemption whereby He achieved salvation and true freedom for men, He brought His revelation to completion. For He bore witness to the truth, but He refused to impose the truth by force on those who spoke against it. Not by force of blows does His rule assert its claims. It is established by witnessing to the truth and by hearing the truth, and it extends its dominion by the love whereby Christ, lifted up on the cross, draws all men to Himself.

Taught by the word and example of Christ, the Apostles followed the same way. From the very origins of the Church the disciples of Christ strove to convert men to faith in Christ as the Lord; not, however, by the use of coercion or of devices unworthy of the Gospel, but by the power, above all, of the word of God. Steadfastly they proclaimed to all the plan of God our Savior, "who wills that all men should be saved and come to the acknowledgment of the truth" (1 Tim 2:4). At the same time, however, they showed respect for those of weaker stuff, even though they were in error, and thus they made it plain that "each one of us is to render to God an account of himself" (Rom 14:12), and for that reason is bound to obey his conscience. Like Christ Himself, the Apostles were unceasingly bent upon bearing witness to the truth of God, and they showed the fullest measure of boldness in "speaking the word with confidence" (Acts 4:31) before the people and their rulers. With a firm faith they held that the Gospel is indeed the power of God unto salvation for all who believe. Therefore they rejected all "carnal weapons: they followed the example of the gentleness and respectfulness of Christ and they preached the word of God in the full confidence that there was resident in this word itself a divine power able to destroy all the forces arrayed against God and bring men to faith in Christ and to His service. As the Master, so too the Apostles recognized legitimate civil authority. "For there is no power except from God," the Apostle teaches, and thereafter commands: "Let everyone be subject to higher authorities. . . . He who resists authority resists God's ordinance" (Rom 13:1–5). At the same time, however, they did not hesitate to speak out against governing powers which set themselves in opposition to the holy will of God: "It is necessary to obey God rather than men" (Acts 5:29). This is the way along which the martyrs and other faithful have walked through all ages and over all the earth.

12. In faithfulness therefore to the truth of the Gospel, the Church is following the way of Christ and the apostles when she recognizes and gives support to the principle of religious freedom as befitting the dignity of man and as being in accord with divine revelation. Throughout the ages the Church has kept safe and handed on the doctrine received from the Master and from the apostles. In the life of the People of God, as it has made its pilgrim way through the vicissitudes of human history, there has at times appeared a way of acting that was hardly in accord with the spirit of the Gospel or even opposed to it. Nevertheless, the doctrine of the Church that no one is to be coerced into faith has always stood firm.

Thus the leaven of the Gospel has long been about its quiet work in the minds of men, and to it is due in great measure the fact that in the course of time men have come more widely to recognize their dignity as persons, and the conviction has grown stronger that the person in society is to be kept free from all manner of coercion in matters religious.

13. . . . [Concerning religious freedom and the life and practice of the Roman Catholic Church.]

14. In order to be faithful to the divine command, "teach all nations" (Matt 28:19–20), the Catholic Church must work with all urgency and concern "that the word of God be spread abroad and glorified" (2 Thess 3:1). Hence the Church earnestly begs of its children that, "first of all, supplications, prayers, petitions, acts of thanksgiving be made for all men. . . . For this is good and agreeable in the sight of God our Savior, who wills that all men be saved and come to the knowledge of the truth" (1 Tim 2:1–4). In the formation of their consciences, the Christian faithful ought carefully to attend to the sacred and certain doctrine of the Church. For the Church is, by the will of Christ, the teacher of the truth. It is her duty to give utterance to, and authoritatively to teach, that truth which is Christ Himself, and also to declare and confirm by her authority those principles of the moral order which have their origins in human nature itself. Furthermore, let Christians walk in wisdom in the face of those outside, "in the Holy Spirit, in unaffected love, in the word of truth" (2 Cor 6:6–7), and let them be about their task of spreading the light of life with all confidence and apostolic courage, even to the shedding of their blood.

The disciple is bound by a grave obligation toward Christ, his Master, ever more fully to understand the truth received from Him, faithfully to proclaim it, and vigorously to defend it, never—be it understood—having recourse to means that are incompatible with the spirit of the Gospel. At the same time, the charity of Christ urges him to love and have prudence and patience in his dealings with those who are in error or in ignorance with regard to the faith. All is to be taken into account—the Christian duty to Christ, the life-giving word which must be proclaimed, the rights of the human person, and the measure of grace granted by God through Christ to men who are invited freely to accept and profess the faith.

15. The fact is that men of the present day want to be able freely to profess their religion in private and in public. Indeed, religious freedom has already been declared to be a civil right in most constitutions, and it is solemnly recognized in international documents. The further fact is that forms of government still exist under which, even though freedom of religious worship receives constitutional recognition, the powers of government are engaged in the effort to deter citizens from the profession of religion and to make life very difficult and dangerous for religious communities.

This council greets with joy the first of these two facts as among the signs of the times. With sorrow, however, it denounces the other fact, as only to be deplored. The council exhorts Catholics, and it directs a plea to all men, most carefully to consider how greatly necessary religious freedom is, especially in the present condition of the human family. All nations are coming into even closer unity. Men of different cultures and religions are being brought together in closer relationships. There is a growing consciousness of the personal responsibility that every man has. All this is evident. Consequently, in order that relationships of peace and harmony be established and maintained within the whole of mankind, it is necessary that religious freedom be everywhere provided with an effective constitutional guarantee and that respect be shown for the high duty and right of man freely to lead his religious life in society.

May the God and Father of all grant that the human family, through careful observance of the principle of religious freedom in society, may be brought by the grace of Christ and the power of the Holy Spirit to the sublime and unending and "glorious freedom of the sons of God" (Rom 8:21).

2.2

Common Witness and Proselytism (A Study Document)[1]

Editor's Introduction

THIS IS A ROMAN Catholic Church and World Council of Churches document dated January 1, 1971. This document is described as a *"Documentary Supplement—Joint Working Group between the Roman Catholic Church and the World Council of Churches Third Official Report."* The Joint Working Group was established in 1965. In the First Report proselytism was identified as an issue that the JWG could consider, and the decision was made during the Second phase of the dialogues to study the issue in more depth during the Third phase. This document is the result of that study process: as such it is the first official RCC/WCC comment on the issue of proselytism. The excerpt below is Appendix II of the Report.[2]

THE FOLLOWING DOCUMENT, PREPARED by a Joint Theological Commission, was received by the Joint Working Group between the Roman Catholic Church and the World Council of Churches at its meeting in May, 1970, which recommended it for publication.

The document was elaborated by the commission on the initiative of the Joint Working Group. The commission held two full meetings (in Arnoldshain, Germany, in 1968, and in Zagork, USSR, in 1969). Various subsequent drafts were submitted to a wide group of consultants. The text being presented now has been formulated in the light of comments received.

---

1. Reproduced with kind permission of PCPCU and the WCC.
2. For the full document, see JWG, "Third Offical Report."

The Joint Working Group, having examined it, recommends to its parent bodies that it be offered to the Churches as a study document for their consideration. Although there may not be complete agreement on everything contained in the document, it represents a wide area of consensus on the subject of common witness and proselytism which may guide the Churches in their mutual relations.

It is, therefore, suggested that the Churches in the same area study it together. The further examination of the theme of common witness will inevitably demand a fuller development of, and agreement on, the content of the witness Christians are bound to give to Christ and his Gospel.

INTRODUCTION

1. Unity in witness and witness in unity. This is the will of Christ for his people. The Lord has called all his disciples to be witnesses to him and his Gospel, to the ends of the earth (cf. Acts 1:8), and he has promised to be with them always, to the close of his age (Matt 28:20). But for centuries. in their efforts to fulfil this mission. Christian Communions have borne the burden of divisions, even differing about the meaning of the one Gospel. They have not been a clear sign of the one and holy people, so it has been hard for the world to believe (John 13:35; 17:21).

2. Today, moved by the Holy Spirit, the various Christian Communions are seeking to restore the unity they have lost, in the hope that one day, when they are fully renewed and united in faith and charity, they may be better able to glorify God by bringing home to the whole world the hope of the coming kingdom. They are striving to overcome whatever indifference, isolation and rivalry has marked their relations to each other and thus has distorted Christian witness even to that unity with which God has already blessed them.

3. This document is an attempt to state the implications of the obligation:

- to bear common Christian witness, even while the Churches are divided;
- to avoid in their mutual relations and in their evangelizing activities whatever is not in keeping with the spirit of the Gospel;
- to provide one another, as far as possible, with mutual support for a more effective witness of the Gospel through preaching and selfless service to the neighbor.

4. This document is offered to the Churches. Its reflections and suggestions may serve as a basis of discussion among Christians in varied circumstances, in order to arrive at a line of conduct where they live and witness.

MEANING OF THE TERMS: CHRISTIAN WITNESS, COMMON WITNESS, RELIGIOUS FREEDOM, PROSELYTISM

5. *Christian Witness.*[3] Witness is taken here to mean the continuous act by which a Christian or a Christian Community proclaims God's acts in history and seeks to reveal Christ as the true light which shines for every man. This includes the whole life: worship, responsible service, proclamation of the Good News—all is done under the guidance of the Holy Spirit in order that men may be saved and be gathered into Christ's one and only Body (Col. 1:8; Eph 1:22–23), and attain life everlasting—to know the true God and Him whom he has sent, Jesus Christ (John 17:3).

6. *Common Witness.* Here is meant the witness the Churches, even while separated, bear together, especially by joint efforts, by manifesting before men whatever divine gifts of truth and life they already share in common.

7. *Religious Freedom.*[4] Religious freedom is not used here in the wider biblical sense (e.g. Rom 8:21). It is pointing to the right of the person and of communities to social and civil freedom in religious matters. Each person or community has the right to be free from any coercion on the side of individuals, social groups, or human power of any kind; so that no individual or community may be forced to act against conscience or be prevented from expressing belief in teaching, worship or social action.

8. *Proselytism.*[5] Here is meant improper attitudes and behaviour in the practice of Christian witness. Proselytism embraces whatever violates

---

3. Modern languages use several biblically derived terms which denote particular aspects of the announcements of the Gospel in word and deed: Witness, Apostolate, Mission, Confession, Evangelism, Kerygma, Message, etc. We have preferred to adopt "Witness," because it expresses more comprehensively the realities we are treating here.

4. See WCC, "Christian Witness, Proselytism, and Religious Liberty" (1961); Vatican II, *Dignitatis Humanae* (1965); UN, *Universal Declaration on Human Rights* (1948), esp. article 18. Since the right to religious freedom operates in society, these documents also mention rules which modify the use of it. [Editor's note: See section 1.4 in this volume.]

5. In certain linguistic, cultural, and confessional contexts, the term "proselytism," used without qualification, has acquired this pejorative sense. In those other languages and contexts in which the term still retains its more original meaning of "zeal in

the right of the human person, Christian or non-Christian, to be free from external coercion in religious matters, or whatever, in the proclamation of the Gospel, does not conform to the ways God draws free men to himself in response to his calls to serve in spirit and in truth.

I. COMMON WITNESS

9. There is a growing recognition among the Churches that they must overcome their isolation from each other and seek ways to cooperate in witness to the world. In face, however, of difficulties and obstacles, a clear basis and source of power and hope is needed if the Churches are to embark on this common witness.[6]

10. This basis and source is given in Christ. He is sent into the world by the Father for the salvation of mankind. There is no other Name in which men may find salvation and life (Acts 4:12). Christian Churches confess Christ as God and only Saviour according to the Scriptures, and most adhere to the ancient Creeds which testify to this central truth of faith.

11. Moreover, the Churches believe that they live only by the divine gifts of truth and life bestowed by Christ. Most Churches acknowledge that gifts of divine grace are a reality in other Churches which also provide access to salvation in Christ. Thus all Christian communions, in spite of their divisions, can have a positive role to play in God's plan of salvation.

12. The Churches have the privilege and the obligation of giving witness to the truth and new life which is theirs in Christ. Indeed both privilege and obligation are entrusted to the whole community of Christians to whom God gives a vital role in his plan for the salvation of the world.

13. Therefore Christians cannot remain divided in their witness. Any situations where contact and cooperation between Churches are refused must be regarded as abnormal.

14. The gifts which the Churches have received and share in Christ have demanded and made urgent a common witness to the world. The needs of men and the challenges of a broken and unbelieving world have also compelled the Churches to cooperate with God in deploying his gifts

---

spreading the faith," it will be necessary always to use "proselytism in the pejorative sense" or some phrase which denotes defective attitudes and conduct.

6. See Vatican II, *Ad Gentes* 6, 15 [Editor's note: See section 2.1 in this volume], and the proposals for "Joint Action for Mission," formulated by the 1961 New Delhi Assembly of the WCC and affirmed by the Report of Section II of the 1968 Uppsala Assembly [Editor's note: See WCC, *Uppsala Report 1968*].

for the reconciliation of all men and all things in Christ. This common witness takes place in many areas of social concern, such as

- the development of the whole man and of all men;
- the defence of human rights and the promotion of religious freedom;
- the struggle for the eradication of economic, social and racial injustice;
- the promotion of international understanding, the limitation of armaments and the restoration and maintenance of peace;
- the campaign against illiteracy, hunger, alcoholism, prostitution, the traffic in drugs;
- medical and health and other social services;
- relief and aid to victims of natural disasters (volcanic eruptions, earthquakes, hurricanes, floods, etc.).

15. Cooperation has also extended to include the production, publication and distribution of joint translations of the Scriptures. Moreover, an exploration is being made of the possibility of common texts to be used for an initial catechesis on the central message of the Christian faith. In this connection, cooperation in the field of education and in the use of communications media is already going on in some places.

16. The cooperation of the Churches in these varied fields is increasingly being accompanied by common acts of worship for each other and for the world. Of particular significance is the "Week of Prayer for Christian Unity" which is now celebrated in many places around the world. This practice of common prayer and of acts of worship has greatly helped to create and develop a climate of mutual knowledge, understanding, respect and trust. The World Council of Churches and the Roman Catholic Church have contributed to this improved climate by their studies and guides to common prayer. This fellowship in prayer, nevertheless, sharpens the pain of the Churches' division at the point of Eucharistic fellowship which should be the most manifest witness to the one sacrifice of Christ for the whole world.

17. The central task of the Churches is simply to proclaim the saving deeds of God. This then should be the burden of their common witness; and what unites them is enough to enable them in large measure to speak as one. Indeed all forms of common witness are signs of the Churches' commitment to proclaim the Gospel to all men; they all find in the one Gospel their motivation, their purpose and their content.

18. Whether in witness or service, the Churches are together confronted by the fundamental issues of the nature and destinies of men and

nations; and while they face these questions they encounter men of other religions, or men who are indifferent or unbelievers who hold to a variety of ideologies.

19. But at this vital point of mutual engagement, the Churches become aware not only of their shared understanding of the Gospel but also of their differences. They all believe that Jesus Christ has founded one Church, and one alone; to this Church the Gospel has been given; to this Church every man has been called to belong. Yet today many Christian Communions present themselves to men as the true heritage of Jesus Christ, and this division among the Churches greatly reduces the possibilities of common witness.

20. In the context of religious freedom and the ecumenical dialogue, respect is due to the right of Churches to act according to convictions, which they believe should be held in fidelity to Jesus Christ:

- While it is indeed aware of its pilgrim condition, a Church can be convinced that in it subsists the one Church founded by Christ, that also in it one can have access to all the means of salvation which the Lord offers, that its witness has always remained substantially faithful to the Gospel.
- A Church can regard itself as bound in conscience to proclaim its witness to its own belief, which is distinct from that of the other Churches.
- While the major affirmations of faith, such as those which are formulated in Scripture and professed in the ancient Creeds, are common to almost all the Christian confessions, different interpretations can sometimes call for reservations on this common character.
- The teaching of certain Churches can place limits on cooperation in social concerns, for example, different positions on family ethics (divorce, abortion, responsible parenthood).

Nevertheless, it is not enough to know the limits which the division of Christians places on common witness. The more the need of common witness is grasped, the more apparent does it become that there is a need to find complete agreement on faith—one of the essential purposes of the ecumenical movement.

21. Differences about the content of witness, because of varied ecclesiologies, are by no means the only obstacle to cooperation between the Churches. The rivalries and enmities of the past, the continued resentments due to the memory of ancient or recent wrongs, the conflicts generated by political, cultural and other factors, all these have prevented the Churches

from seeking to bear a common witness to the world. Only the willingness to extend mutual forgiveness of past offences and wrongs and to receive correction from each other will enable the Churches to fulfil their obligation to show forth a common witness to each other and to the world.

22. There is, however, an understandable hesitation of a Church to co-operate in witness where this may trouble and confuse its members. Among other reasons, it may be due also to lack of contact and mutual understanding between the clergy and the laity of Churches. In all such cases, a patient and determined effort should be made to create conditions which favor cooperation.

23. A further obstacle to joint action in witness derives from receiving and interpreting the Gospel in forms so exclusive as to lead to a refusal of all discussion and an unwillingness to recognise that the Spirit can operate in groups other than one's own. This attitude is generally labelled "sectarianism" and such exclusive and excluding groups are often called "sects." When faced with this situation, Churches should first of all recognise the challenge which these groups present to them and examine themselves as to their inadequacy in meeting the profound spiritual needs of their members and of those around them. They must also guard against the very spirit of sectarianism which they so rightly deplore in others. Rather should they strive to hear God's call to renewal and to greater faithfulness to his message of salvation.

24. Moreover, the Churches should pay particular attention to groups which seem open to receive those aspects of the Christian message which those communities have hitherto neglected. The Churches must thus always stand ready for dialogue and to seize every opportunity to extend a fraternal hand and to grasp the hand held out to them.

II. PROSELYTISM AND RELATIONS BETWEEN CHURCHES

25. Christian witness, to those who have not yet received or responded to the announcement of the Gospel or to those who are already Christians, should have certain qualities, in order to avoid being corrupted in its exercise and thus becoming proselytizing. Furthermore, the ecumenical movement itself had made Christians more sensitive to the conditions proper to witness borne among themselves. This means that witness should be completely

- conformed to the spirit of the Gospel, especially by respecting the other's right to religious freedom, and,

- concerned to do nothing which could compromise the progress of ecumenical dialogue and action.

1. Required Qualities for Christian Witness

A

26. In order that witness be conformed to the spirit of the Gospel:

- The deep and true source of witness should be the commandment: "You must love the Lord your God with all your soul and with all your mind. . . . You must love your neighbor as yourself" (Matt 22:37, 39; cf. Lev 19:18; Deut 6:5).
- Witness should be inspired by the true end of the Church: the glory of God through the salvation of men. Witness does not seek the prestige of one's own community and of those who belong to, represent or lead it.
- Witness should be nourished by the conviction that it is the Holy Spirit who, by his grace and light, brings about the response of faith to witness.
- Witness respects the free will and dignity of those to whom it is given, whether they wish to accept or to refuse the faith.
- Witness respects the right of every man and community to be free from any coercion which impedes them from witness to their own convictions, including religious convictions.

B

27. Witness should avoid behavior such as:

a) Every type of physical coercion, moral constraint or psychological pressure which would tend to deprive man of his personal judgement, of his freedom of choice, of full autonomy in the exercise of his responsibility. A certain abuse of mass communications can have this effect.

b) Every open or disguised offer of temporal or material benefits in return for change in religious adherence.

c) Every exploitation of the need or weakness or of lack of education of those to whom witness is offered, in view of inducing their adherence to a Church.

d) Everything raising suspicion about the good faith of others—bad faith can never be presumed; it should always be proved.

e) The use of a motive which has no relation to the faith itself but is presented as an appeal to change religious adherence: for example, the appeal to political motives to win over those who are eager to secure for themselves the protection or favors of civil authority, or those who are opposed to the established regime. Churches which form a large majority in a state should not use legal methods, social, economic or political pressure, in the attempt to prevent members of minority communities from the exercise of their right to religious freedom.

f) Every unjust or uncharitable reference to the beliefs or practices of other religious communities in the hope of winning adherents. This includes malevolent criticism which offends the sensibilities of members of other communities. In general one should compare the good qualities and ideals or the weaknesses and practices of one community with those of the others, not one's ideals with the other's practice.

2. Christian Witness and Relations between the Churches

28. The Lord has willed that his disciples be one in order that the world believe. Thus it is not enough for Christians to conform to the above. They should also be concerned in fostering whatever can restore or strengthen between them the bonds of true brotherhood. Proposed suggestions:

a) In each Church one is conscious that conversion of heart and the renewal of his own community are essential contributions to the ecumenical movement.

b) Missionary action should be carried out in an ecumenical spirit which takes into consideration the priority of the announcement of the Gospel to non-Christians. The missionary effort of one Church in an area or milieu where another Church is already at work depends on an honest answer to the question: what is the quality of the Christian message proclaimed by the Church already at work and in what spirit is it being proclaimed and lived? Here frank discussion between the Churches concerned would be highly desirable, in order to have a clear understanding of each other's missionary and ecumenical convictions, and with the hope that it would help to determine the possibilities of cooperation, of common witness, of fraternal assistance, or of complete withdrawal.[7] In the same manner and spirit the relations between minority and majority Churches should be considered.

c) Particularly all competitive spirit should be avoided by which a Christian community might seek a position of power and privilege, and concern itself less with proclaiming the Gospel to those who have not yet received it, than with profiting by chances to recruit new members among the other Christian communities.

d) To avoid causes of tension between Churches because of the free exercise of the right of every man to choose his ecclesial allegiance and, if necessary, to change it in obedience to conscience, it is vital:

  1. that this free choice should be exercised in full knowledge of what is involved and, if possible, after counsel with the pastors of the two Churches concerned. Particular care is necessary in the case of children and young people; in such cases, the greatest weight and respect should be given to the views and rights of the parents and tutors;

  2. that the Church which admits a new member should be conscious of the ecumenical repercussions, and not draw vain glory from it;

  3. that the Church which has lost a member should not become bitter, or hostile, nor ostracise the person concerned; that it examine its conscience as to how it has done its duty of bringing the Gospel to that person. Has it made an effort to understand how his Christian convictions ought to affect his life, or rather was it content that he should remain a nominal and official member of that community?

  4. that any change of allegiance motivated mainly by the desire to secure some material advantage should be refused.

e) Some points of tension between the Churches are difficult to overcome because what is done by one Church in view of its theological and ecclesiological convictions is considered by the other as implicit

---

7. In speaking of Joint Action for Mission, the World Council of Churches distinguishes presently three degrees of missionary collaboration: surveying the possibilities of missionary action; joint planning; and joint action. The meaning of common witness is wider than that of joint action for mission.

proselytism. In this case, it is necessary that the two sides try to clarify what is really in question and to arrive at mutual understanding of different practices, and if possible, to agree to a common policy. This can be realized only if the carrying out of these theological and ecclesiological convictions clearly excludes every type of witness which would be tainted by proselytism, as described above. Some examples of such tensions:

- The fact that a Church which reserves baptism to adults ("believer's baptism") persuades the faithful of another Church, who have already been baptized as infants, to receive baptism again is often regarded as proselytizing. A discussion on the nature of baptism and its relation to faith and to the Church could lead to new attitudes.

- The discipline of certain Churches concerning the marriage of their members with Christians of other communities is often considered as proselytic. In fact, these rules depend on theological positions. Conversations on the nature of marriage and the family could bring about progress and resolve in a joint way the pastoral question raised by such marriages.

- The Orthodox consider that the existence of the Eastern Catholic Churches is the fruit of proselytism. Catholics level the same criticism against the way in which certain of these Churches have been reunited to the Orthodox Church. Whatever has been the past, the Catholic Church and the Orthodox Church are determined to reject not only proselytism but also the intention even to draw the faithful of one Church to another. An example of this pledge is the common declaration of Pope Paul VI and Patriarch Athenagoras I, on October 28. 1967. The resolution of these questions, evidently important for the ecumenical movement, should be sought in frank discussion between the Churches concerned.

CONCLUSION

29. These reflections and suggestions on common witness and proselytism will, it is hoped, offer the Churches an opportunity of moving more quickly along the way which leads to the restoration of complete communion among them. As they travel that path to unity the Churches realise that Christian witness can never be perfect. They can never cease to strive for a deeper realization and clearer expression of the Good News of the unfathomable

riches of Christ (cf. Eph 3:8), and for a more faithful living in accord with His one message. By fidelity to this striving the Churches will grow together in witness to Christ, "the Faithful and True Witness" (Rev 3:14) in expectation of that day when all things will be perfectly reestablished in him (cf. Eph 1:10; Col 1:20).

2.3

Stuttgart Consultation

WCC/CWME 1987

Editor's Introduction

THIS DOCUMENT WAS PRODUCED at a consultation held at the initiative of the WCC's Commission on World Mission and Evangelism in Stuttgart, Germany, in March 1987. The timing is significant as it was between the publication of the "Ecumenical Affirmation" of the WCC in 1982 and before the Second Lausanne Congress in Manila in 1989. The document seeks, in part, to address the tensions that existed (and still exist) between those who emphasise evangelism as the proclamation of the Gospel and those who give social action and engagement a higher priority. However, there are some paragraphs which highlight the relationship of Evangelism and the Unity of the Church (reproduced below). The excerpt begins with the introductory paragraphs to give context to the statement. The document itself goes on to consider The Nature of Evangelism, Local Christian Communities and Evangelism, Evangelism and the Renewal of the Church, Evangelism and the Unity of the Church (which touches on proselytism), and Evangelism in the Context of Other Faiths.

As an historical aside, both John Stott and David Bosch were present at the consultation.

IN MARCH 1987 THE WCC Commission on World Mission and Evangelism invited representatives of WCC European member churches and agencies for mission and evangelism to a consultation in Stuttgart to consider the place of evangelism in programs of the WCC and its member churches. Attending the meeting were evangelicals belonging to WCC member churches and others not related to the WCC. The consultation statement, using the

WCC's Ecumenical Affirmation as one point of departure, covered a broad range of issues and served as a bridge between conciliar Christians and evangelicals in the period before San Antonio and Lausanne II. The statement is noteworthy for its emphasis on "wholistic" or "integral" evangelism.[1]

STUTTGART CONSULTATION OF EVANGELISM[2]

We have gathered here at Stuttgart from different parts of the world to consider the place of evangelism in the program of the World Council of Churches and of our respective churches and organizations. Of the many who are evangelicals here, some belong to churches that are members of the WCC, while others belong to churches that are not. Some of us are particularly involved in the work of promoting evangelism in our own denomination, local church or area. We have come with varying degrees of ecumenical experience.

Coming from very different theological and ecclesial backgrounds, we have become deeply conscious of our fellowship in the gospel and of our common desire to carry out mission in Christ's way so that God's will may be done. We acknowledge humbly that mission is God's mission and that the evangel is God's good news for humankind. We are unworthy servants, earthenware vessels, who have been entrusted with a priceless treasure (2 Cor 4:7). This treasure we seek to share with all, grateful that this sharing brings a blessing to us as well as to those with whom we share (1 Cor 9:23).

We have heard different emphases on how the gospel is to be shared. Some the sharing of the gospel through resisting oppression and exploitation of the poor and identifying with the marginalized. Others, while not denying the necessity for such an attitude on the part of the churches, have, nevertheless, emphasized the necessity for an explicit invitation to faith in Jesus Christ. While recognizing these different emphases, we have come to a common mind on certain matters, which are set out below. We offer this statement to the CWME in the hope that it will stimulate reflection on the place of evangelism in the conciliar movement, especially in the planning of the 1989 Conference on World Mission and Evangelism.

---

1. This short introduction comes from Scherer and Bevans, *Basic Statements*, 65.

2. Reprinted from WCC, *Mission from Three Perspectives*, 20–31, with kind permission of the WCC

Evangelism and the Unity of the Church

19. "God was in Christ reconciling the world to himself" (2 Cor 5:19). We are called to be ambassadors of and for our reconciling God, ambassadors who bear individually and corporately, the signs of reconciliation—at one with each other as Christ is at one with the Father.

The nature of evangelism will rise out of our understanding of the good news that is being proclaimed and will colour the nature of the good news that is received.

Salvation brings spiritual and total wholeness to the individual at one with God in Jesus Christ. Such wholeness gives people a new identity, not by affirming them in their self-centeredness but by calling them to give themselves to others in Christ's way. The New Testament communities of faith were rebuked when they divided to suit the taste, preference or personal loyalties of individuals (1 Cor 1:10–13).

20. Our Lord Jesus Christ (in John 17) prayed for the unity of his followers. Forms of evangelism that cater primarily to denominational aggrandizement fail to affirm the indivisibility of the one body of Christ. Authentic evangelism calls people into a community with all Christian people, a community that—in spite of denominational and other barriers—lives under the sign of at-one-ment under the cross.

21. We have discerned two related circumstances that jeopardize the unity and the evangelistic effectiveness of the church.

a) In some places, churches that have been present for a long time consider that the unity of Christ's people is not helped by the activities of groups undertaking direct evangelism towards persons who have a traditional relationship to those churches.

b) In the opinion of others, some of these churches appear defensive about "their" nominal members but are unable or perhaps are not even interested in active evangelism towards them. They believe there is an imperative to evangelize in such circumstances.

We need to address these issues with care and creative sensitivity.

22. Any evangelism that does not build up good relationships with other Christians in the community must inevitably come under question. Local churches therefore should be encouraged to pray and work together in a cooperative and loving spirit as a sign of witness and of the attractiveness of the face of Jesus Christ: "See how they love one another."

23. We affirm that Christian unity, important as it is, must never be a unity for its own sake. It is a unity so that all may believe, and in harmony with a mission in Christ's way on behalf of, and in identification with, the poor, the lost and the least in God's creation.

2.4

Orthodox Advisory Group to WCC-CWME

- "Go Forth in Peace: Orthodox Perspectives on Mission" (1986)
- "Final Report of CWME Consultation of Eastern Orthodox and Oriental Orthodox Churches Orthodox" (1988)[1]

Orthodox/CWME

Editor's Introduction

ORTHODOX CHURCHES ENGAGE WITH the World Council of Churches in numerous ways. Of interest here is the Orthodox participation in CWME and especially in the World Mission Conferences that CWME hosts roughly every ten years.

Many Western students are surprised to discover the growth of missiological reflection within the Orthodox Churches. As Petros Vassiliadis notes, "Orthodoxy and mission are two terms that at first glance seem quite incompatible, at least to the Western historians of mission."[2] He argues that "the missional dimension of the Orthodox Church was rediscovered just more than a generation ago thanks to . . . [the] primate of the Albanian Orthodox Church, Archbishop Anastasios (Yannoulatos)."[3] Stamoolis makes the same point: "That the Orthodox Church has any interest in mission work, let alone

---

1. Reproduced with kind permission of the WCC.
2. Vassiliadis, "Orthodox Assessment of the New Mission Statement," 174.
3. Vassiliadis, "Orthodox Assessment of the New Mission Statement," 174-78.

a developed missiology, may come as a new idea to many."[4] *However, much of the material is in the form of scholarly articles and books; there are few formal (and therefore, authoritative) documents available.*[5] *For example, "Go Forth in Peace,"*[6] *is a selection of essays arising from the Orthodox Advisory Group to the WCC. It covers theological and practical aspects of mission as conceived within Orthodoxy and includes an acknowledgement of the existence of "Nominal Christians" within Orthodoxy:*

> First of all, the church's evangelistic witness is for the Christian who is not a Christian. There are many who have been baptized, and yet have put off Christ, either deliberately or through indifference. . . . The re-Christianization of Christians is an important task of the church's evangelistic witness.[7]

The following extract comes from the 1988 consultation of the Orthodox Advisory Group, convened by CWME in preparation for the 1989 San Antonio World Mission Conference. The Report is divided into five sections, each with sub-headings:

I. Witnessing in the Oikoumene Today

    The Apostolic Witness

    Witness in a Secular World

    Witness within a Pluralistic Society and among Believers of Other Faiths

II. Mission and Unity

    Ecclesiological Perspectives

    Common Witness

    Proselytism

III. Social Implications of Sacramental Life

    The Sacramental Dimension of Life

    The Eucharist and Renewal of Life

    Prayer and Repentance

    Witness and the Sacramental Life

IV. The Missionary Imperative and Responsibility in the Local Church

---

4. Stamoolis, *Eastern Orthodox Mission Theology Today*, xi.
5. For Orthodox perspectives, see sections 2.4, 18 in this volume.
6. Bria, *Go Forth in Peace*.
7. Bria, *Go Forth in Peace*, quoted in Scherer and Bevans, *Basic Statements*, 224.

The Mission of the Local Church

Catholicity of the Local Church

Encouraging Various Ministries

Other Mission Challenges

V. *Recommendations to Orthodox Churches*

Two points highlighted under "Other Mission Challenges" are relevant: (1) the rise of various extremist Christian sects and, (2) the dominating attitude of wealthy and powerful churches towards minority local churches

PROSELYTISM

PROSELYTISM, ALONG WITH THE actual disunity among the churches, creates major obstacles for our common witness. Some Christian churches and evangelical bodies are actively engaged in proselytizing Christians already belonging to Orthodox churches. All proselytism by any church should be condemned, and antagonism and unhealthy competition in mission work should be avoided, as constituting a distorted form of mission.

Unfortunately, well financed resources and the power of the media in western Europe and America, often play a key role in maintaining the unchristian missionary zeal of those involved in proselytizing efforts. The Orthodox churches have to continue efforts to persuade those churches and agencies involved in proselytism not to engage in dubious missionary activities detrimental to God's will for unity, and to seek the path of true Christian charity and unity.

At the same time, our Orthodox churches have to pay closer attention to the pastoral, educational and spiritual needs of our people and foster in every possible way a continual spiritual renewal in our parishes and monastic communities. It is especially important to develop ways of strengthening family life and caring for the special needs of youth that they might realize the communal love and concern of the church for their well-being and salvation.

One impetus for the modem ecumenical vision was originally inspired by the committed search for a common witness to the good news of salvation. It still remains the primary objective of our ecumenical involvement—to offer common witness in love to the power of Christ, crucified and risen, so that those who are caught up in this world of division, conflict and death may believe and be transfigured.

2.5

Mission in Christ's Way

Your Will Be Done[1]

CWME World Conference on Mission and Evangelism
San Antonio 1989

Editor's Introduction

THE FOURTH WCC-CWME WORLD Missions Conference took place in San Antonio, Texas, in 1989. The San Antonio Report is divided into four sections: I. "Turning to the Living God"; II. "Participating in Suffering and Struggle"; III. "The Earth is the Lord's"; and IV. "Towards Renewed Communities in Mission." The following extract is taken from the second part of Section I which is sub-divided into five parts:

I. Mission in The Name of The Living God

II. The Living God Calls Us to Unity in Mission

III. Witness in A Secular Society

IV. Witness Among People of Other Living Faiths

V. Communicating the Gospel Today

The Report references the 1987 Stuttgart Consultation and the 1988 CWME-Orthodox Report.[2]

1. Reproduced with kind permission of the WCC.
2. Reproduced in part in sections 2.3, 4 of this volume.

14. ONE OF THE most sensitive areas in our discussions on unity in mission concerned the issue of proselytism. The aim of our evangelism should be the building up of the body of Christ, service in the world, and the glory of God. Instead, evangelism sometimes turns into programmes for denominational aggrandizement. We believe that any evangelism that does not promote good relationships with other Christians in the community must inevitably be called into question (Stuttgart). Our witness may deteriorate into counterwitness, thereby in effect denying the authenticity of the faith experience of other Christians. All unhealthy competition in mission work should be avoided as constituting a distorted form of mission (Orthodox). At the same time we realize that faith communities may become ingrown and stagnant, lose their vision, and become unable or perhaps not even interested in getting involved in evangelism and pastoral renewal in their environment (Stuttgart). In such situations other Christians, rather than ignoring the presence and integrity of the traditional faith communities, may perhaps be privileged to play a catalytic role in renewal for mission. They will, however, only be able to do so if they identify with the local faith community and treat it with sensitivity, respect and integrity.

2.6

Proselytism, Sects, and Pastoral Challenges

Middle East Council of Churches

Unit on Faith and Unity 1989

Editor's Introduction

THIS DOCUMENT WAS WRITTEN for the "Unit on Faith and Unity of the Middle East Council of Churches." This is the third draft, dated July 1989; there is no final version.[1] I have included an edited version as it represents a distinctive voice within the debates around the issue of mission and proselytism. However, some of the document focuses upon pseudo-Christian sects such as Jehovah Witness and I have excluded that aspect of the document.

A note on editing: I have left the document largely unaltered. There are a few examples, therefore, where the grammar is slightly awkward to a native English speaker. I am indebted to Cecil M Robeck Jr. for providing me with a copy of the document, and to the Middle East Council of Churches for permission to reproduce the document.

---

1. "This document proclaims the general principles and the Council is in the process of updating this document in more depth, theological and ecclesiastical, taking into account new data in other words the current ones.... The Council realizes the importance of this issue, especially in its relationship with new modern evangelical and charismatic movement" (MECC, personal correspondence). Reproduced with kind permission of the MECC.

INTRODUCTION

1. PROSELYTISM IS A problem historically rooted. Its manifestations are diverse and it may be presently faced on new grounds.

2. Developments in inter-church relations may allow for an affirmation of a common position against proselytism, still practices occasionally, and which constitutes a "thorny" obstacle on the way towards "Communion of love."

3. Churches that encounter each other in the ecumenical movement face, together, the proselytism practices, in a conscious and organized manner, by sects, parachurch fundamentalist groups and western neo-missionary movements.

4. We are confronted with two problems of different character. The first requires a declaration of principles consolidated by practical guidelines. The second calls for a common pastoral strategy.

5. A number of theological and pastoral issues raised as the churches face the dual problem of proselytism are identical or inter-related (Ecclesiological basis, missiological considerations, approaches to religious freedom)....

DEFINITIONS

6. The most common definition of proselytism emphasizes its means and results. It considers it to be a practice that involves attempts aimed at attracting Christians to a particular church or religious group leading to their alienation from the Church of origin.

7. The joint working group of the WCC and the Roman Catholic Church, in a document on common witness and proselytism, issued in 1970,[2] defined proselytism as a set of inappropriate attitudes and practices in Christian witness. It embraces every violation of the rights of the human person to be free from coercion in religious matters. It refers to whatever, in mission and evangelism, is not in conformity with the ways God chose to draw free human beings to himself.

8. The distinction between proselytism, mission, and evangelism is imperative. Proselytism could be described as a deviation in the practice of mission and evangelism.

9. Proselytism favors individual and group egoism. Instead of emphasizing confidence in God and his economy, it manifests an exaggerated self-confidence and overtrust on one's present methods and programmes.

---

2. See section 2.2 in this volume.

10. Proselytism is often accompanied by ignorance of the other, and in the dissimulation of the truth about them. A distorted image of their faith and religious practices is painted.

11. Refraining, voluntarily, from proselytic practices does not violate religious freedom nor discards it. Moreover, it does not impose any restrictions on the right of every Church, and its duty, to witness in a way that reflects its distinctive character.

PART 1: TOWARDS AN ECUMENICAL APPROACH TO PROSELYTISM

A Historical Approach

12. What we, today, call proselytism was in the heart of the western missionary strategy after failures of attempts to "restore unity" during the fifteenth century.

13. Missionaries adopted a multiplicity of policies. Some were concerned about establishing close relations with church leaders emphasizing unity in faith and its expression through canonical links. Others attempted to change Eastern Christianity from "within" through religious education, schooling and service, paving the way for uniting with Rome. A third category strived to attract small groups and influential individuals through different forms of assistance, alienating them ecclesially and culturally.

The third tendency gained, gradually, more momentum at the expense of the others and led to fragments of Eastern Christianity to unite with the Catholic Church.

14. Missionaries sent out by the revivalist movements within the Anglo-Saxon Churches of the Reformation were, in principle and primarily, preoccupied with evangelizing non-Christians. However, their efforts were actually addressed, gradually, towards Eastern Christians (and members of "united" communities) in a perspective of "renewal." The work of proclamation brought about, consequently, the foundation of new Churches whose members were detached from their communities of origin.

15. The evangelistic practices involving proselytism were legitimized by an ecclesiology expressed in a particular model of Christian unity.

16. Evangelistic practices involving proselytism were nurtured by an affirmation of cultural, political and economic superiority.

17. Those practices succeeded in making use of education and service. They benefited, also, from social divisions, conflicting political and economic interests. They were able to take advantage from the temptation of

"identification with the West" as some Christians hoped it may favor their emancipation from the Ottoman yoke.

18. On the other hand, the proselytic practices reached a measure of success in view of the weakness that the Eastern Churches suffered from.

19. Proselytic practices stressed "personal conversion" and the individual responsibility in choosing one's religious affiliation.

Recent Developments

20. Organized activities of evangelism, including conscious or semi-conscious proselytic practices, has been legitimized, in the twentieth century, on the basis of the necessity to fill "a vacuum." Missionaries claimed to respond to spiritual and cultural needs that could not be dealt with properly, in view of the Eastern Churches hesitancy to be mission-orientated and due to their limited resources.

21. For many reasons, ecclesial, social and political, organized missionary activities lost some of their momentum and were manifest in a few geographical areas only. There have been, during the last decades, a limited number of collective change in Church affiliation.

22. Since the Sixties of this [twentieth] century, organized and self-conscious proselytism had a significantly less important effect in "converting" individuals.

23. However, conscious proselytism did not disappear. Its success was conditioned by its ability to follow indirect paths, adopt new methods and present its justification in an ambiguous manner.

24. The numbers of those who change their Church affiliation may not be, anymore, significant. Yet those who are alienated from their Churches and attracted to other communities or religious groups are not a tiny minority.

25. At present, various Christian schools (their religious education curricula in particular), youth movements, social and cultural organizations, constitute privileged loci for semi-conscious or perhaps unconscious proselytism.

26. In spite of the multiple changes, there are still cases where disagreements of conflicts between the faithful and their clergy constitute occasions for renewed attempts to proselytize.

27. Mixed marriages are often characterized by a certain imbalance at the level of church commitment and religious practice. They maybe, therefore, conducive to a *de facto* proselytism.

28. There are cases, often complex, where semi-conscious or unconscious attempts at changing loyalties are favored by a communitarian understanding whose ecclesial dimension is considered secondary. This is also true of "impatient" ecumenism which may be inclined towards relativism and syncretism. Such ecumenism suggests a diffuse Christian identity and ignores historical consciousness.

29. All the above described cases do not deny that a progress was realized at the level of inter-church relations. Some problems were solved as churches developed deeper knowledge of each other and "purified" their perceptions. Many church leaders expressed genuine openness and an authentic ecumenical commitment, facilitating, thus, consultation and cooperation based on mutual respect. The mere willingness to launch a process of reflection towards a position paper on proselytism indicates a change in mood and mind that cannot be unnoticed.

Towards a Realistic Approach

30. The motives of proselytism are multiple. Its impact on the churches self-understanding and their attitudes towards each other varies from a situation to another. We face, often, the temptation of exaggerating its effect or that of minimizing its role.

31. Subjective consciousness and objective reality are related though not identical. Drawing a distinction is legitimate. However, irrespective of the factual reality, subjective reactions (or, rather, over-reactions) should not be ignored.

32. In order to heal the wounds that were caused by proselytism, the feelings should be taken seriously. These feelings are, often, reflections of a past experience and fears projected into the future. In both cases, they are, in a sense, an integral part of the objective reality.

33. Historical memories condition the various perceptions of proselytism. An ecumenical effort towards a solution of this problem entails a common objective reading of history.

Guidelines for an Ecumenical Approach

34. The first step towards reaching a solution to the thorny problems of proselytism, implies a common declaration. This declaration should be an uncontested reference, it is called to stimulate ecumenical learning and constitute the basis of some more practical and contextual guidelines.

35. The document entitled "Towards a Pastoral Agreement" if adopted by the heads of Churches or in the MECC Executive Committee, could be the nucleus of such a declaration.

36. The declaration of principles should be followed by the setting up of ecumenical commissions, at the national level, whose task is to establish "rules of behaviour" and make sure that concerted efforts are undertaken between church leaders to deal with problems as they arise.

37. A number of issues require further ecumenical reflection, such as:

- Religious freedom and the freedom of conscience.
- Returning to the "mother-church."
- Mixed marriages and religious education.
- Evangelization of nominal Christians.

PART 2: THE CHURCHES AND SECTS: TOWARDS A PASTORAL STRATEGY

38. In opposition to the Churches that have developed a critical attitude towards proselytism, sects, para-church fundamentalist groups and neo-missionary movements practice it, in a conscious and organized manner.

Proselytism is inherent to their mission strategies, they rather consider it identical with evangelism.

39. Sects and groups are numerous, in our region, and throughout the world. They may be classified in five categories:

i. Sects who originated as dissent groups in churches and split subsequently from them. Many of are of the millenarist or messianist type (such as Jehovah Witness and the Mormons).

ii. Western neo-missionary movements, independent from the churches and with a strong fundamentalist inclination and, in many instances, a millenarist tendency.

iii. Sects characterized by syncretism and the claim to universalism that goes beyond different religious expressions and offers a synthesis (such as the Unification Church of Moon).... Some of them advocate a form of Gnosticism.

iv. Groups whose self-understanding is that of renewal movements within the Churches (such as the Charismatics)....

v. Groups attracted by modes of spirituality influenced by Asian religions. They are fascinated by the East as "exported from the West" (such as Transcendental Mediation and Krishna). . . .

(In this paper, we shall leave aside categories 4 and 5.)

40. Proselytic practices of all these groups show similarities in spite of the diversity of "doctrines." (In this paper, we are not primarily concerned with the ideas of the sects and groups but rather with their attitudes and methods).[3] . . .

64. Issues of church renewal and efficient pastoral work are broader than the scope of this paper. We shall, therefore, limit ourselves to five issues that may address, specifically, the challenges of the sects.

a) The emphasis on the membership in the local community. Where the various facets of church experience are lived: sacramental life, interpersonal fraternal relations, common witness. . . . There are many implications with respect to the size of the parish, its dynamism and the ability of its programmes to bring together the personal and the communitarian, the "spiritual" and the "material."

b) The priority, in religious education, to the knowledge of the scriptures in their wholeness and in a way that it involves critical awareness of different types of their misuse. More attention should be given to problems of religion and science, knowledge and revelation. Gnosticism and its various expressions are also worth attention.

c) The place of pastoral psychology and sociology of religion in ministerial formation.

d) The pastoral care addressed towards each and every person in his/her uniqueness and the importance of responding, in an integrated manner, to his/her religious and human needs.

e) The balance between participation and the need for leadership (including spiritual fatherhood).

---

3. [Editor's note: Paragraphs 42–63 consider "Sects." They consider "Some of Their Characteristic Features" (42–47); "What do they offer?" (48–52); Ways of Proselytism (53–60); and "Towards a Pastoral Approach to the Challenge of Sects" (61–64). Paragraph 64 has wider application and is therefore reproduced here.]

2.7

The Balamand Declaration
Uniatism, Method of Union of the Past, and the Present Search for Full Communion[1]

RCC/Orthodox 1993

Editor's Introduction

THE BALAMAND DECLARATION IS *an important addition to this volume although it may be new to many Western students. It is a joint Roman Catholic Church and Orthodox Church document. It arises from the work of the Joint International Commission for the Theological Dialogue Between the Roman Catholic Church and the Orthodox Church which was established in 1980. The Seventh Plenary Session was held in the Balamand School of Theology in Lebanon in June 1993.*

The document addresses the issue of proselytism as experienced between the Orthodox and Roman Catholic Churches in relation to Eastern Catholic Churches, or as they are sometimes called, Uniate Churches. These are Churches that identify as Catholic but not as Roman (Latin) Catholic. Thus, they use non-Latin rites and can be confused with Orthodox Churches in the territories in which they exist. They are in full communion with the Pope and recognise the Catholic sacraments. There has been an uneasy co-existence between the Uniate Churches and the Orthodox Churches which has sometimes involved oppression and violence (see the document below). Many Orthodox

1. Reproduced with kind permission of PCPCU.

have perceived the existence of such Eastern Catholic Churches as a form of proselytism by the Catholic Church against the Orthodox. Whilst receiving a mixed reception, the Balamand Declaration remains a vital step in the process of healing the hurts of centuries of mistrust.

We publish here two items: (1) The Informative Communiqué from the meeting of the seventh plenary session of the joint international commission for theological dialogue between the Catholic Church and the Orthodox Church (Balamand, Lebanon, June 17–24, 1993); 2 (2) the document of the joint dialogue commission on the theme: "Uniatism, method of union of the past, and the present search for full communion."

As with all the results of the joint dialogue commissions, this common document belongs to the responsibility of the Commission itself, until the competent organs of the Catholic Church and of the Orthodox Churches express their judgement in regard to it.

COMMUNIQUÉ

THE SEVENTH PLENARY SESSION of the Joint International Commission for the Theological Dialogue between the Catholic Church and the Orthodox Church took place from June 17 to 24, 1993, within the magnificent framework of Balamand, close to the monastery dating from the twelfth century and in the buildings of the School of Orthodox Theology "St John Damascene" and of the new Orthodox University which is in full development. His Beatitude Ignatius IV Hazim by his personal presence was a living sign of the generous and cordial hospitality shown to all the participants by the Greek Orthodox Patriarchate of Antioch.

The Eucharist was celebrated by the Catholic delegation on Saturday afternoon and by the Orthodox delegation on Sunday morning, each ceremony taking place in the historic church of the monastery with the assistance of a great number of faithful. On Monday, June 21, all the Patriarchs of the territory of Antioch, both Orthodox and Catholic, were guests of His Beatitude Ignatius IV for lunch. An official delegation representing the commission made a courtesy visit to Their Excellencies, the President of the Republic, Mr. Elias Hraoui, and the President of the Parliament, Mr. Nabeh Berri on Tuesday, June 22. The entire Commission then toured the historical center of Beirut and the members were guests at lunch hosted by the Orthodox Archbishop of the capital.

2. JIC, "Seventh Plenary Session."

Representatives of nine autocephalous and autonomous Orthodox Churches were present for this plenary session of the Joint International Commission for dialogue. From the Catholic side, twenty-four members of the Commission took part in the meeting.

The theme of the seventh plenary session was entirely centered on the theological and practical questions presented by the existence and pastoral activity of the Oriental Catholic Churches. The profound changes which have taken place in Central and Eastern Europe, involving the rebirth of religious liberty and the resumption of open pastoral activity by the Oriental Catholic Churches, have made these questions the touchstone of the quality of the relations between the Catholic and the Orthodox Churches.

At Balamand, the Commission had before it a working paper, developed by the coordinating committee of the Commission during its meeting at Ariccia (Rome) in June 1991 which bears the title: "Uniatism, method of union of the past, and the present search for full communion." This text was studied and reworked in common, in a frank and brotherly spirit, accompanied by a deep concern for the continuation of the work of fostering the restoration of full communion between the Orthodox and Catholic Churches.

The text finally adopted at Balamand is composed of two parts: (1) Ecclesiological Principles and (2) Practical Rules. In the spirit of the ecclesiology of communion and because of the fact that the Catholic and Orthodox Churches recognize each other as Sister Churches, it was observed that, in the effort to re-establish unity, what is involved is achieving together the will of Christ for those who are His disciples and the design of God for His Church, by means of a common search for full agreement in faith. It is not a question of seeking the conversion of persons from one Church to the other. This latter type of missionary activity, which has been called "uniatism," cannot be accepted either as a method to follow or as a model for the unity which is being sought by our Churches.

Conscious of the fact that the history of divisions has deeply wounded the memories of the Churches, Catholics and Orthodox are determined to look to the future, with mutual recognition of the necessity for transparent consultation and cooperation at all levels of Church life.

The Joint International Commission for the Theological Dialogue will now submit the document adopted at Balamand to the authorities of the Catholic and Orthodox Churches for approval and application.

TEXT: UNIATISM, METHOD OF UNION OF THE PAST, AND THE PRESENT SEARCH FOR FULL COMMUNION[3]

Introduction

1. At the request of the Orthodox Churches, the normal progression of the theological dialogue with the Catholic Church has been set aside so that immediate attention might be given to the question which is called "uniatism."

2. With regard to the method which has been called "uniatism," it was stated at Freising (June 1990) that "we reject it as method for the search for unity because it is opposed to the common tradition of our Churches."

3. Concerning the Oriental Catholic Churches, it is clear that they, as part of the Catholic Communion, have the right to exist and to act in answer to the spiritual needs of their faithful.

4. The document prepared at Ariccia by the joint coordinating committee (June 1991) and finished at Balamand (June 1993) states what is our method in the present search for full communion, thus giving the reason for excluding "uniatism" as a method.

5. This document is composed of two parts:

(1) Ecclesiological principles and

(2) Practical rules.

Ecclesiological Principles

6. The division between the Churches of the East and of the West has never quelled the desire for unity wished by Christ. Rather this situation, which is contrary to the nature of the Church, has often been for many the occasion to become more deeply conscious of the need to achieve this unity, so as to be faithful to the Lord's commandment.

7. In the course of the centuries various attempts were made to re-establish unity. They sought to achieve this end through different ways, at times conciliar, according to the political, historical, theological and spiritual situation of each period. Unfortunately, none of these efforts succeeded in re-establishing full communion between the Church of the West and the Church of the East, and at times even made oppositions more acute.

8. In the course of the last four centuries, in various parts of the East, initiatives were taken within certain Churches and impelled by outside

---

3. The text was originally drafted in French and translated into English during the meeting.

elements, to restore communion between the Church of the East and the Church of the West. These initiatives led to the union of certain communities with the See of Rome and brought with them, as a consequence, the breaking of communion with their Mother Churches of the East. This took place not without the interference of extraecclesial interests. In this way Oriental Catholic Churches came into being. And so a situation was created which has become a source of conflicts and of suffering in the first instance for the Orthodox but also for Catholics.

9. Whatever may have been the intention and the authenticity of the desire to be faithful to the commandment of Christ: "that all may be one" expressed in these partial unions with the See of Rome, it must be recognized that the reestablishment of unity between the Church of the East and the Church of the West was not achieved and that the division remains, embittered by these attempts.

10. The situation thus created resulted in fact in tensions and oppositions.

Progressively, in the decades which followed these unions, missionary activity tended to include among its priorities the effort to convert other Christians, individually or in groups, so as "to bring them back" to one's own Church. In order to legitimize this tendency, a source of proselytism, the Catholic Church developed the theological vision according to which she presented herself as the only one to whom salvation was entrusted. As a reaction, the Orthodox Church, in turn, came to accept the same vision according to which only in her could salvation be found. To assure the salvation of "the separated brethren" it even happened that Christians were rebaptized and that certain requirements of the religious freedom of persons and of their act of faith were forgotten. This perspective was one to which that period showed little sensitivity.

11. On the other hand certain civil authorities made attempts to bring back Oriental Catholics to the Church of their Fathers. To achieve this end they did not hesitate, when the occasion was given, to use unacceptable means.

12. Because of the way in which Catholics and Orthodox once again consider each other in their relationship to the mystery of the Church and discover each other once again as Sister Churches, this form of "missionary apostolate" described above, and which has been called "uniatism," can no longer be accepted either as a method to be followed nor as a model of the unity our Churches are seeking.

13. In fact, especially since the panorthodox Conferences and the Second Vatican Council, the re-discovery and the giving again of proper value to the Church as communion, both on the part of Orthodox and of

Catholics, has radically altered perspectives and thus attitudes. On each side it is recognized that what Christ has entrusted to his Church—profession of apostolic faith, participation in the same sacraments, above all the one priesthood celebrating the one sacrifice of Christ, the apostolic succession of bishops—cannot be considered the exclusive property of one of our Churches.

14. It is in this perspective that the Catholic Churches and the Orthodox Churches recognize each other as Sister Churches, responsible together for maintaining the Church of God in fidelity to the divine purpose, most especially in what concerns unity. According to the words of Pope John Paul II, the ecumenical endeavor of the Sister Churches of East and West, grounded in dialogue and prayer, is the search for perfect and total communion which is neither absorption nor fusion but a meeting in truth and love (cf. *Slavorum Apostoli* 27).

15. While the inviolable freedom of persons and their obligation to follow the requirements of their conscience remain secure, in the search for re-establishing unity there is no question of conversion of people from one Church to the other in order to ensure their salvation. There is a question of achieving together the will of Christ for his own and the design of God for his Church by means of a common quest by the Churches for a full accord on the content of the faith and its implications. This effort is being carried on in the current theological dialogue. The present document is a necessary stage in this dialogue.

16. The Oriental Catholic Churches who have desired to re-establish full communion with the See of Rome and have remained faithful to it, have the rights and obligations which are connected with this communion. The principles determining their attitude towards Orthodox Churches are those which have been stated by the Second Vatican Council and have been put into practice by the Popes who have clarified the practical consequences flowing from these principles in various documents published since then. These Churches, then, should be inserted, on both local and universal levels, into the dialogue of love, in mutual respect and reciprocal trust found once again, and enter into the theological dialogue, with all its practical implications.

17. In this atmosphere, the considerations already presented and the practical guidelines which follow, insofar as they will be effectively received and faithfully observed, are such as to lead to a just and definitive solution to the difficulties which these Oriental Catholic Churches present to the Orthodox Church.

18. Towards this end, Pope Paul VI affirmed in his address at the Phanar in July 1967: "It is on the heads of the Churches, of their hierarchy,

that the obligation rests to guide the Churches along the way that leads to finding full communion again. They ought to do this by recognizing and respecting each other as pastors of that part of the flock of Christ entrusted to them, by taking care for the cohesion and growth of the people of God, and avoiding everything that could scatter it or cause confusion in its ranks" (*Tomos Agapis* 172). In this spirit Pope John Paul II and Ecumenical Patriarch Dimitrios I together stated clearly: "We reject every form of proselytism, every attitude which would be or could be perceived to be a lack of respect" (December 7, 1987).

Practical Rules

19. Mutual respect between the Churches which find themselves in difficult situations will increase appreciably in the measure that they will observe the following practical rules.

20. These rules will not resolve the problems which are worrying us unless each of the parties concerned has a will to pardon, based on the Gospel and, within the context of a constant effort for renewal, accompanied by the unceasing desire to seek the full communion which existed for more than a thousand years between our Churches. It is here that the dialogue of love must be present with a continually renewed intensity and perseverance which alone can overcome reciprocal lack of understanding and which is the necessary climate for deepening the theological dialogue that will permit arriving at full communion.

21. The first step to take is to put an end to everything that can foment division, contempt and hatred between the Churches. For this the authorities of the Catholic Church will assist the Oriental Catholic Churches and their communities so that they themselves may prepare full communion between Catholic and Orthodox Churches. The authorities of the Orthodox Church will act in a similar manner towards their faithful. In this way it will be possible to take care of the extremely complex situation that has been created in Eastern Europe, at the same time in charity and in justice, both as regards Catholics and Orthodox.

22. Pastoral activity in the Catholic Church, Latin as well as Oriental, no longer aims at having the faithful of one Church pass over to the other; that is to say, it no longer aims at proselytizing among the Orthodox. It aims at answering the spiritual needs of its own faithful and it has no desire for expansion at the expense of the Orthodox Church. Within these perspectives, so that there will be no longer place for mistrust and suspicion, it is necessary that there be reciprocal exchanges of information about various

pastoral projects and that thus cooperation between bishops and all those with responsibilities in our Churches, can be set in motion and develop.

23. The history of the relations between the Orthodox Church and the Oriental Catholic Churches has been marked by persecutions and sufferings. Whatever may have been these sufferings and their causes, they do not justify any triumphalism; no one can glorify in them or draw an argument from them to accuse or disparage the other Church. God alone knows his own witnesses. Whatever may have been the past, it must be left to the mercy of God, and all the energies of the Churches should be directed towards obtaining that the present and the future conform better to the will of Christ for his own.

24. It will also be necessary—and this on the part of both Churches—that the bishops and all those with pastoral responsibilities in them scrupulously respect the religious liberty of the faithful. These, in turn, must be able to express freely their opinion by being consulted and by organizing themselves to this end. In fact, religious liberty requires that, particularly in situations of conflict, the faithful are able to express their opinion and to decide without pressure from outside if they wish to be in communion either with the Orthodox Church or with the Catholic Church. Religious freedom would be violated when, under the cover of financial assistance, the faithful of one Church would be attracted to the other, by promises, for example, of education and material benefits that may be lacking in their own Church. In this context, it will be necessary that social assistance, as well as every form of philanthropic activity be organized with common agreement so as to avoid creating new suspicions.

25. Furthermore, the necessary respect for Christian freedom—one of the most precious gifts received from Christ—should not become an occasion for undertaking a pastoral project which may also involve the faithful of other Churches, without previous consultation with the pastors of these Churches. Not only should every form of pressure, of any kind whatsoever, be excluded, but respect for consciences, motivated by an authentic exigency of faith, is one of the principles guiding the pastoral concern of those responsible in the two Churches and should be the object of their common reflection (cf. Gal 5:13).

26. That is why it is necessary to seek and to engage in an open dialogue, which in the first place should be between those who have responsibilities for the Churches. Those in charge of the communities concerned should create joint local commissions or make effective those which already exist, for finding solutions to concrete problems and seeing that these solutions are applied in truth and love, in justice and peace. If agreement cannot

be reached on the local level, the question should be brought to mixed commissions established by higher authorities.

27. Suspicion would disappear more easily if the two parties were to condemn violence wherever communities of one Church use it against communities of a Sister Church. As requested by His Holiness Pope John Paul II in his letter of May 31, 1991, it is necessary that all violence and every kind of pressure be absolutely avoided in order that freedom of conscience be respected. It is the task of those in charge of communities to assist their faithful to deepen their loyalty towards their own Church and towards its traditions and to teach them to avoid not only violence, be that physical or verbal, but also all that could lead to contempt for other Christians and to a counter-witness, completely ignoring the work of salvation which is reconciliation in Christ.

28. Faith in sacramental reality implies a respect for the liturgical celebrations of the other Church. The use of violence to occupy a place of worship contradicts this conviction. On the contrary, this conviction sometimes requires that the celebration of other Churches should be made easier by putting at their disposal, by common agreement, one's own church for alternate celebration at different times in the same building. Still more, the evangelical ethos requires that statements or manifestations which are likely to perpetuate a state of conflict and hinder the dialogue be avoided. Does not St. Paul exhort us to welcome one another as Christ has welcomed us, for the glory of God (Rom 15:7)?

29. Bishops and priests have the duty before God to respect the authority which the Holy Spirit has given to the bishops and priests of the other Church and for that reason to avoid interfering in the spiritual life of the faithful of that Church. When cooperation becomes necessary for the good of the faithful, it is then required that those responsible to an agreement among themselves, establish for this mutual assistance clear principles which are known to all, and act subsequently with frankness, clarity, and with respect for the sacramental discipline of the other Church.

In this context, to avoid all misunderstanding and to develop confidence between the two Churches, it is necessary that Catholic and Orthodox bishops of the same territory consult with each other before establishing Catholic pastoral projects which imply the creation of new structures in regions which traditionally form part of the jurisdiction of the Orthodox Church, in view to avoid parallel pastoral activities which would risk rapidly degenerating into rivalry or even conflicts.

30. To pave the way for future relations between the two Churches, passing beyond the outdated ecclesiology of return to the Catholic Church connected with the problem which is the object of this document, special attention will be given to the preparation of future priests and of all those who, in any way, are involved in an apostolic activity carried on in a place where the other Church traditionally has its roots. Their education should be objectively positive with respect of the other Church. First of all, everyone should be informed of the apostolic succession of the other Church and the authenticity of its sacramental life. One should also offer all a correct and comprehensive knowledge of history aiming at a historiography of the two Churches which is in agreement and even may be common. In this way, the dissipation of prejudices will be helped, and the use of history in a polemical manner will be avoided. This presentation will lead to an awareness that faults leading to separation belong to both sides, leaving deep wounds on each side.

31. The admonition of the Apostle Paul to the Corinthians (1 Cor 6:1–7) will be recalled. It recommends that Christians resolve their differences through fraternal dialogue, thus avoiding recourse to the intervention of the civil authorities for a practical solution to the problems which arise between Churches or local communities. This applies particularly to the possession or return of ecclesiastical property. These solutions should not be based only on past situations or rely solely on general juridical principles, but they must also take into account the complexity of present realities and local circumstances.

32. It is in this spirit that it will be possible to meet in common the task of re-evangelization of our secularized world. Efforts will also be made to give objective news to the mass-media especially to the religious press in order to avoid tendentious and misleading information.

33. It is necessary that the Churches come together in order to express gratitude and respect towards all, known and unknown—bishops, priests or faithful, Orthodox, Catholic whether Oriental or Latin—who suffered, confessed their faith, witnessed their fidelity to the Church, and, in general, towards all Christians, without discrimination, who underwent persecutions. Their sufferings call us to unity and, on our part, to give common witness in response to the prayer of Christ "that all may be one, so that the world may believe" (John 17:21).

34. The International Joint Commission for Theological Dialogue between the Catholic Church and the Orthodox Church, at its plenary meeting in Balamand, strongly recommends that these practical rules be put into practice by our Churches, including the Oriental Catholic Churches who are called to take part in this dialogue which should be carried on in the

serene atmosphere necessary for its progress, towards the re-establishment of full communion.

35. By excluding for the future all proselytism and all desire for expansion by Catholics at the expense of the Orthodox Church, the commission hopes that it has overcome the obstacles which impelled certain autocephalous Churches to suspend their participation in the theological dialogue and that the Orthodox Church will be able to find itself altogether again for continuing the theological work already so happily begun.

Balamand (Lebanon), June 23, 1993

2.8

The Challenge of Proselytism and the Calling to Common Witness[1]

A Study Document of the Joint Working Group

WCC/RCC 1995

Editor's Introduction

THIS DOCUMENT WAS PRODUCED *in 1995 by the Joint Working Group of the World Council of Churches and the Roman Catholic Church. It is a "study" document and therefore lacks the authority of a "statement" but nonetheless is an informative and important contribution to a contemporary understanding of the issue of proselytism. It was written "in response to concerns expressed by some of our churches in regard to the missionary outreach of other churches that would seem to bear some of the characteristics of proselytism. It is within the concern for full Christian unity and common Christian witness that the question of proselytism is looked at in this document. [This] document may help Christian communities to reflect on their own motivation for mission and also on their methods of evangelizing. Dialogue in a truly ecumenical spirit with those considered to be proselytizing is highlighted."[2]*

---

1. Reproduced with kind permission of PCPCU and the WCC.

2. [Editor's note: quote from the Foreword to the document by His Eminence Metropolitan Elias of Beirut and Most Rev. Alan C. Clark, co-moderators of the Joint Working Group, September 25, 1995.]

I. INTRODUCTION

1. THIS DOCUMENT IS the result of discussions in the Joint Working Group (JWG) and is presented with the conviction that it is timely, and with the hope that it may serve as an impulse for further reflection and action in the churches. The conversations in the JWG were marked both by the grateful recognition of the increase of common witness of Christians from different traditions, and serious concerns about tensions and conflicts created by proselytism in nearly all parts of the world. It is the new reality of common witness and a growth in *koinonia* which forms the backdrop for a critical consideration of proselytism which has been described as conscious efforts with the intention to win members of another church.[3]

2. Even though the JWG has addressed the questions of common witness and proselytism on two previous occasions, recent dramatic events have led it to study these issues once again. Over the past few years we have become more aware of the concern being expressed in new situations and contexts in which people tend to be vulnerable in one way or another, and where proselytizing activity is alleged to be taking place. Some situations invite urgent ecumenical attention, such as:

- within the climate of newly found religious freedom, e.g., in Central and Eastern Europe, where there is a threat felt by some churches that their members are under pressure from other churches to change their allegiance;
- instances in the "developing world" (often easily identified with nations in the southern hemisphere, though also found elsewhere), in which proselytizing efforts take advantage of people's misfortunes—e.g., in situations of poverty in villages, or in the mass migration to the cities where new arrivals have a sense of being lost in anonymity or marginalized and are frequently outside the pastoral structures of their own church—to induce them to change their church affiliation;
- where people of a particular ethnic group, traditionally members of one church, are said to be encouraged by unfair means to become members of other churches;
- the activity of some new missionary movements, groups or individuals, both within our churches and outside them, especially those originating in the newly industrialized nations, which enter countries often uninvited by any church and begin missionary activity among the local people in competition with the local churches;

3. See also the more detailed description of proselytism in para. 18-19.

- in various places the arrival of evangelizing groups making extensive use of the mass media and causing confusion and division among local churches;
- in many parts of the world, the churches are experiencing proselytizing activities of sects and new religious movements.

3. The purpose of this document is to encourage all Christians to pursue their calling to render a common witness to God's saving and reconciling purpose in today's world and to help them to avoid all competition in mission that contradicts their common calling. With this aim the document seeks to facilitate a pastoral response to the continuing challenge of proselytism which not only endangers existing ecumenical relations but is also an additional barrier to our growing together in reciprocal love and trust as brothers and sisters in Christ.

4. Today we thank God for the achievements of ecumenical theological dialogues during recent decades and for a new climate of understanding and friendship in which ecumenical relations are being developed. We are also grateful for all the recent encouraging signs of better mutual understanding and joint perspectives in the area of common witness and proselytism.[4] These are recorded in bilateral and multilateral dialogues among churches and can be seen in significant initiatives of common witness at different levels of church life. These agreements and joint actions provide a basis and encouragement to intensify our efforts to bear together a credible witness to the gospel in the contemporary world.

5. In this study process we wish to affirm what continues to be valid in the two previous WCC-RCC Joint Working Group documents, *Common Witness and Proselytism*[5] and *Common Witness*.[6] We also want to take into account relevant material on evangelism and proselytism from some of the aforementioned dialogues. In addition, this study process will be linked with another possible study on proselytism in the World Council of Churches by Unit II.[7]

---

4. Among many other examples which could be adduced here are "Evangelical-Roman Catholic Dialogue on Mission"; "Summons to Witness to Christ in Today's World"; John Paul II, "Letter to Bishops of Europe"; Pontifical Commission for Russia, *General Principles and Practical Norms*; "Uniatism: Method of Union of the Past"; "US Orthodox/Roman Catholic Consultation"; "Towards Koinonia in Faith, Life, and Witness," 263ff.

5. JWG, "Common Witness and Proselytism" [Editor's note: see section 2.3 in this volume].

6. JWG, *Common Witness*.

7. See also the Report of Section IV from the Fifth World Conference on Faith and Order, "Called to Common Witness for a Renewed World," para. 14, in WCC, *On the*

6. We acknowledge with appreciation similar studies being undertaken by ecumenical bodies such as the Conference of European Churches[8] and the Middle East Council of Churches.[9] Our desire is to invite reflection and action on the part of churches of different traditions in a task to which all are called on our pilgrimage to a fuller expression and experience of visible Christian unity.

II. MISSION AND UNITY: THE CONTEXT OF COMMON WITNESS

7. An essential element of the church is to participate in the mission of God in Jesus Christ to the world by proclaiming through word and action God's revelation and salvation to all people (1 John 1:1–5). Indeed, God's mission towards a "reconciled humanity and a renewed creation" (cf. Eph 1:9–10) is the essential content and impulse for the missionary witness of the church.

8. Mission in this sense of being sent with a message that is addressed to the spiritual and also material needs of people is thus an inescapable mandate for the church. This imperative is affirmed today by many churches and is expressed through their regular activities as well as special efforts (New Evangelization, Decades of Evangelism, Mission 2000). Sent to a world in need of unity and greater interdependence amidst the competition and fragmentation of the human community, the church is called to be sign and instrument of God's reconciling love.[10]

9. Ecumenical relationships, however, have from the beginning of the modern ecumenical movement been shaped by the insight that the search for the visible unity of Christ's church must include the commitment to and the practice of a common missionary witness. In the prayer of Jesus "that they all may be one so that the world may believe" (John 17:21), we are reminded that the unity of Christians and the mission of the church are intrinsically related. Divisions among Christians are a counter-witness to Christ and contradict their witness to reconciliation in Christ.

10. In responding to the appeal for the unity of Christians in effective missionary witness, we need to be aware of the reality of diversity rooted in theological traditions and in various geographical, historical and cultural

---

Way to Fuller Koinonia, 256–57.

8. See "At Thy Word"; CEC, *God Unites*, 182–83.

9. MECC, *Proselytism, Sects, and Pastoral Challenges* [Editor's note: section 2.7 in this volume]; *Signs of Hope in the Middle East*.

10. This perspective is expressed, for example, in Vatican II, *Lumen Gentium* 1; WCC, *Church and World*.

contexts. We recognize, therefore, that the unity we seek is a unity that embraces a legitimate diversity of spiritual, disciplinary, liturgical and theological expressions that enrich common witness. It will include the discovery and appreciation of the many diverse gifts of Christ which we share already now as Christians in "real but imperfect communion," gifts given for the upbuilding of the church (cf. Rom 12:4–8). Even when churches are not in full communion with each other they are called to be truthful to each other and show respect for each other. Such an attitude does not subvert their self-understanding and their conviction to have received the truth but rather facilitates the common search for unity and common witness to God's love for the world.

11. In the growing ecumenical koinonia there must also be a way of witnessing to the gospel to each other in faithfulness to one's own tradition and convictions. Such mutual witness could enrich and challenge us to renew our thinking and life, and could do so without being polemical towards those who do not share the same tradition. "To speak the truth in love" (Eph 4:15) is a challenge and an experience long accepted within the ecumenical movement.

12. The recognition of an already existing, though imperfect, communion among churches is a significant result of ecumenical efforts and a new element in twentieth-century church history. This existing communion should be an encouragement for further efforts to overcome the barriers that still prevent churches from reaching full communion. It should provide a basis for the renewal, common witness and service of the churches for the sake of God's saving and reconciling activity for all humanity and all creation. It should also provide a basis for avoiding all rivalry and antagonistic competition in mission because "the use of coercive or manipulative methods in evangelism distorts koinonia."

13. When Christians by means of efforts towards common witness struggle to overcome such lack of reciprocal love, of mutual understanding and of trust they will be open to the call for repentance and for the renewal of their efforts. This is the way "to come to the unity of the faith and of the knowledge of the Son of God, to maturity, to the measure of the full stature of Christ" (Eph 4:13).

14. These efforts include self-critical reflection on our relationships with other churches, openness to appreciate authentically evangelical expressions of life in them, and to be mutually enriched. They will also include engaging in a more authentic dialogue where we can speak meaningfully and honestly to one another, discussing difficulties as they arise and trying to build up relationships (cf. Eph 4:15).

III. SOME BASIC PRINCIPLES OF RELIGIOUS FREEDOM

15. We acknowledge the right of every person "alone or in community with others and in public or in private" to live in accordance with the principles of religious freedom. Religious freedom affirms the right of all persons to pursue the truth and to witness to that truth according to their conscience. It includes the freedom to acknowledge Jesus Christ as Lord and Saviour and the freedom of Christians to witness to their faith in him by word and deed.

Religious freedom involves the right to freely adopt or change one's religion and to "manifest it in teaching, practice, worship and observance" without any coercion which would impair such freedom.

We reject all violations of religious freedom and all forms of religious intolerance as well as every attempt to impose belief and practices on others or to manipulate or coerce others in the name of religion.

16. Freedom of religion touches on "one of the fundamental elements of the conception of life of the person." The promotion of religious freedom contributes also to the harmonious relations between religious communities and is therefore an essential contribution to social harmony and peace. For these reasons, international instruments and the constitutions and laws of almost all nations recognize the right to religious freedom. Proselytism can violate or manipulate the right of the individual and can exacerbate tense and delicate relations between communities and thus destabilize societies.

17. The responsibility of fostering religious freedom and the harmonious relations between religious communities is a primary concern of the churches. Where principles of religious freedom are not being respected and lived in church relations, we need, through dialogue in mutual respect, to encourage deeper consideration and appreciation of these principles and of their practical applications for the churches.

IV. NATURE AND CHARACTERISTICS OF PROSELYTISM

18. In the history of the church, the term "proselytism" has been used as a positive term and even as an equivalent concept for missionary activity.[11] More recently, especially in the context of the modern ecumenical

---

11. "A historical overview shows that the understanding of 'proselytism' has changed considerably. In the Bible it was devoid of negative connotations. A 'proselyte' was someone who, by belief in Yahweh and acceptance of the law, became a member of the Jewish community. Christianity took over this meaning to describe a person who converted from paganism. Mission work and proselytism were considered equivalent

movement, it has taken on a negative connotation when applied to activities of Christians to win adherents from other Christian communities. These activities may be more obvious or more subtle. They may be for unworthy motives or by unjust means that violate the conscience of the human person; or even if proceeding with good intentions, their approach ignores the Christian reality of other churches or their particular approaches to pastoral practice.

19. Proselytism as described in this document stands in opposition to all ecumenical effort. It includes certain activities which often aim at having people change their church affiliation and which we believe must be avoided, such as the following:[12]

- making unjust or uncharitable references to other churches' beliefs and practices and even ridiculing them;
- comparing two Christian communities by emphasizing the achievements and ideals of one, and the weaknesses and practical problems of the other;
- employing any kind of physical violence, moral compulsion and psychological pressure, e.g., the use of certain advertising techniques in mass media that might bring undue pressure on readers/viewers;[13]
- using political, social and economic power as a means of winning new members for one's own church;
- extending explicit or implicit offers of education, health care or material inducements or using financial resources with the intent of making converts;[14]
- manipulative attitudes and practices that exploit people's needs, weaknesses or lack of education especially in situations of distress, and fail to respect their freedom and human dignity.[15]

20. While our focus in this document is on relationships between Christians, it is important to seek the mutual application of these principles also in interfaith relations. Both Christians and communities of other faiths complain about unworthy and unacceptable methods of seeking converts from their respective communities. The increased cooperation and dialogue

---

concepts until recent times" ("Summons to Witness to Christ in Today's World," para. 32).

12. See JWG, "Common Witness and Proselytism."
13. See "Summons to Witness to Christ in Today's World," para. 32.
14. See "Uniatism: Method of Union," para. 24.
15. See "Evangelical-Roman Catholic Dialogue on Mission," §7.3.

among people of different faiths could result in witness offered to one another that would respect human freedom and dignity and be free of the negative activities described above.

V. SOURCES OF TENSION IN CHURCH RELATIONSHIPS

21. We need to look at some of the sources of tension in church relationships which could lead to proselytism, in order to ground some of this concern. One is the holding of distorted views of another church's teaching or doctrine and even attacking or caricaturing them, e.g. denouncing prayer for the dead as a denial of the need for personal acceptance of Christ as Lord and Saviour; discrediting the veneration of icons as signs of crude idolatry; interpreting the use of art in church buildings as a transgression of the first commandment.

22. Different understandings of missiology and different concepts of evangelization also underlie some inter-church tensions, e.g. seeing God's gift of salvation as coming exclusively through one's own church; seeing the task of mission as exclusively concerned with social matters or exclusively with spiritual matters, rather than in a wholistic way. They can lead to competition or even conflict in missionary practice among the churches rather than a common approach to mission.

23. Different theological and pastoral understandings of the meaning of certain concepts can also contribute to tension in relationships. For example, some aim at the re-evangelization of baptized but non-practicing members of other churches. But there are different interpretations of who is "unchurched," or a "true" Christian believer. Efforts to understand the perspectives of other Christian communities on these matters are therefore necessary.

24. The varieties of understanding of membership existing among churches can also be an unnecessary source of tension. There are theological issues involved. The way of becoming a member and even the way of terminating membership in particular churches can be understood very differently. The duties and responsibilities of members also differ from church to church. This diversity of understanding influences the way we see changes in church affiliation.

25. Unfortunately, there are occasions when the personal and cultural confusion of people, their social-political resentments, the tensions within a church, or their hurtful experiences in their own church can be played upon to persuade them to be converted.

26. Sometimes, evangelizers can be tempted to take advantage of the spiritual and material needs of people or their lack of instruction in the faith in order to make them change their church affiliation because they may interpret this as a lack of pastoral care and attention to these people on the part of churches to which they belong. But in fact, pastoral care, even if it could be more adequate, may be available to the person in his or her own church. Here again there may be different perceptions as to what is adequate and what is inadequate in the field of pastoral care. However the churches must always look for ways to improve the pastoral care they give to their people, especially the quality of instruction in the faith.

27. Tensions also arise on occasion because of the unjust interference on the part of the state in church matters in order to influence people to change church membership.

28. In other situations where a church identifies with the government or works in collusion with it to the extent that it fails to exercise its prophetic role, tensions can arise within the Christian community from what may be seen as preferential treatment by the government for that particular church.

29. Tensions can result in evangelizing activity when there is a lack of sufficient regard for people's culture and religious traditions. There can also be dangers if we lose sight of the fact that the gospel must take root in the soil of different cultures, while it cannot be limited to any culture.

30. Finally, there can be a lack of respect for the beliefs and practices of minority groups in contexts dominated by a majority church, and an inability to see them as full and equal partners in society that causes tensions in relationships. In some cases, a dominant Christian tradition has allowed restrictive laws to be framed by the state which disfavour Christians of another tradition.

VI. STEPS FORWARD

31. Despite all efforts to combat it, the problem of proselytism is still with us, causing painful tensions in church relationships and undermining the credibility of the church's witness to God's universal love. Ultimately, proselytism is a sign of the real scandal which is division. By placing the issue of proselytism in the context of church unity and of common witness we suggest a perspective which makes it possible to approach the problem within an adequate theological framework.

32. As responsible ecumenical relationships in many different contexts are a complex reality requiring study and theological dialogue, prayer and practical collaboration, we would like to recommend the following to the

churches, keeping in mind that the movement for Christian unity can also contribute to breaking down barriers between people in the wider society as well:

- to encourage churches to pray for one another and for Christian unity in response to the prayer of our Lord, that his disciples "may all be one ... so that the world may believe" (John 17:21);
- to prepare more adequate Christian formation programmes within our churches so that people are better equipped to share their own faith, as well as ecumenical programmes that will foster respect for the integrity of other Christian churches and openness to receive from them;
- to develop a sensitivity to existing ecclesial realities in a given area so that when providing the required pastoral care for one's own church members, it can be done in an atmosphere of communication and appropriate consultation;[16]
- to condemn publication of unverified alleged events or incidents concerning church activities that only fan feelings of fear and prejudice, and of one-sided or prejudicial reports on religious developments which can undercut efforts towards cooperation;[17]
- to try to understand history from the perspective of other churches in order to arrive at a shared common understanding of it and, where necessary, at reconciliation, mutual forgiveness and healing of memories;
- to study together the nature of diakonia in order that the characteristics of Christian service be made clear and transparent; that is, that it may be truly inspired by the love of Christ and that it may not be a reason for tension, nor a means of proselytism;
- to help people to a greater awareness of the phenomenon of sects and new religious movements, through collaborative efforts, and also to consider the question of how to respond pastorally but firmly to coercive religious practices by persons and groups that are not in keeping with the principles of religious liberty;
- to include in any future study of proselytism the significant participation of Christians, both within and outside World Council of Churches and Roman Catholic circles of influence, especially those accused of

---

16. See "Uniatism: Method of Union," para. 22.
17. See "US Orthodox/Roman Catholic Consultation," para. 2.

these practices and those who have changed church affiliation through the efforts of another church.[18]

33. These efforts will be effective and successful to the extent that relationships of reciprocal trust are built between the churches.

VII. CONCLUSION

34. Knowing that our common faith in Jesus, Lord and Saviour, unites us and that baptism is an effective sign of unity, we are called to live our Christian vocation in unity and to give visible witness to it.

35. Therefore, it is not enough to denounce proselytism. We need to continue to prepare ourselves for genuine common Christian witness through common prayer, common retreats, Bible courses, Bible sharing, study and action groups, religious education jointly or in collaboration, joint or coordinated pastoral and missionary activity,[19] a common service (diakonia) in humanitarian matters and theological dialogue. The immensely rich Christian spiritual patrimony of contemplative prayer can be a resource for all. We acknowledge that our current divisions limit the extent to which we can engage in common witness. We recall and make our own the principle cited in the third world conference on Faith and Order at Lund, Sweden, 1952:

> We earnestly request our churches to consider whether they are doing all they ought to do to manifest the oneness of the people of God. Should not our churches ask themselves whether they are showing sufficient eagerness to enter into conversation with other churches and whether they should not act together in all matters except those in which deep differences of conviction compel them to act separately . . . ? Obedience to God demands also that the churches seek unity in their mission to the world.[20]

36. There is also an urgent need to continue to work collaboratively in order to transcend the lines that society draws between those at the center and those on the peripheries, between those who have an abundance of resources and those marginalized because of race, economics, gender or for other reasons. These societal divisions often provide the context for

---

18. WCC, *On the Way to Fuller Koinonia*, 256–57
19. JWG, *Common Witness*, para. 44.
20. Tomkins, *Third World Conference on Faith and Order*, 16.

proselytism and therefore challenge our divided churches to closer collaboration that will be a common Christian witness.²¹

37. In all of these reflections we take our inspiration from the gospel itself:

> This is my commandment: love one another, as I have loved you. No one can have greater love than to lay down his life for his friends. . . . You did not choose me, no, I chose you; and I commissioned you to go out and to bear fruit, fruit that will last; so that the Father will give you anything you ask him in my name. My command to you is to love one another (John 15:12-13, 16-17)

NOTE ON THIS STUDY DOCUMENT

As proselytism is a reality that obliges churches to seek a solution, and a question that continues to surface at different meetings, including the WCC central committee and the assembly in Canberra, the Joint Working Group, at its meeting in Wennigsen, Germany, in March 1992, decided to work on a new study document on proselytism, as this would be a broader forum to gather some of the findings from various meetings, including the bilateral dialogues, and to make a synthesis of solutions proposed.

At subsequent JWG executive meetings, decisions were made to base the new study document on the 1970 document "Common Witness and Proselytism" and the 1982 document "Common Witness." Mr. Georges Lemopoulos and Sr. Monica Cooney were asked to prepare an outline for the work. Consultations were held with various people both within the WCC and outside. A draft outline, prepared with the help of Fr. Karl Müller, svd, and Prof. Dr. Reinhard Frieling, was then submitted to the JWG executive meetings, and a first draft was presented to the JWG plenary meeting in Crete, June 1994.

Dr. Günther Gassmann and Monsignor John Radano were then appointed as drafters. They presented an amended draft to the JWG executive in Geneva in October 1994, after which both WCC Programme Unit II and Programme Unit III (CCIA) were consulted (the latter on the question of religious freedom).

A final draft was discussed at the JWG plenary in Bose, Italy, May 1995, and finalized at the executive, Geneva, September 1995.

---

21. The theological basis for this common witness and further suggestions may be found in JWG, *Common Witness*, para. 44.

This document points out the problem of proselytism, noting the different realities in a variety of contexts as it is not a problem of any two churches in a particular area. It is prepared in the conviction that while we continue to proselytize and to accuse one another of proselytism, instead of speaking the truth in love, we cannot respond to the call to common witness, nor can we live the command to love one another as God has first loved us.

2.9

Evangelization, Proselytism, and Common Witness

The Report from the Fourth Phase of the International Dialogue 1990–1997 between the Roman Catholic Church and Some Classical Pentecostal Churches and Leaders[1]

RCC/Pentecostal 1997

Editor's Introduction

THIS IS A REPORT from the Roman Catholic Church and Pentecostal leaders, dated 1997. The previous three phases focused on (1) the Baptism in the Holy Spirit, Christian Initiation, and the Charisms, Scripture and Tradition and the Human Person and the Gifts (1972–1976), (2) Faith and Religious Experience, Speaking in Tongues, and the Role of Mary (1977–1982), and (3) koinonia (Christian Communion and Fellowship) (1985–1989). (From para. 5 of the current document). It is refreshingly honest with both Catholic and Pentecostal voices echoing the pain experienced, a delightful growing depth of relationship, and repentance where necessary.[2]

---

1. Reproduced with kind permission of PCPCU.
2. PCPCU, "Evangelization, Proselytism, and Common Witness."

INTRODUCTION

(1) THIS IS A report from the participants of the fourth phase of the international Dialogue (1990–1997) between the Pontifical Council for Promoting Christian Unity and some classical Pentecostal denominations and leaders. The Dialogue began in 1972....

(4) We, the participants, have sought to represent faithfully the positions held by our churches. However, we have made no decisions for the churches since we have no authority to make such decisions. The churches are free to accept or reject the report either in whole or in part. Yet as responsible persons, representing our traditions either officially or in some other way, we have come together over a period of years to study the issues of evangelization, proselytism, and common witness. In accordance with our understanding of the Gospel we are making proposals to our churches. We, the participants hereby submit our findings to our respective churches for review, evaluation, correction and reception.

I. Mission and Evangelization

II. The Biblical and Systematic Foundation of Evangelization

III. Evangelization and Culture

IV. Evangelization and Social Justice

V. Proselytism

VI. Common Witness . . .

V. PROSELYTISM[3]

1. Moving Towards a Common Position on Proselytism

(68) Since 1972 members of this Dialogue have committed themselves to address the issue of proselytism. That this discussion has at last begun is a sign of the growing trust and maturation of Pentecostal Catholic relations. Both teams in this International Roman Catholic-Pentecostal Dialogue entered into a conversation on this topic with a number of misgivings. It is difficult enough to address this subject as an abstract object of study.

---

3. The papers done for this section were by John C. Haughey, SJ, of Loyola University, Chicago ("Evangelization and Social Justice: An Inquiry into Their Relationship"), and by Mud O. Dirkson, PhD, and Karen Carroll Mundy, PhD, (Church of God) of Lee University, Cleveland, TN ("Evangelization and Social Justice: A Pentecostal Perspective").

But Catholic-Pentecostal relationships in many parts of the world have been troubled at times with accusations of insensitivity to the presence of long-standing Christian communities, charges of proselytism, and counter charges of persecution. Some people, in both traditions, have made it clear that they do not want Catholics and Pentecostals to speak to one another. Others have made it clear that they did not even want the topic of proselytism itself addressed. Both the Catholic and the Pentecostal teams debated within themselves, and then together, the wisdom of undertaking such a discussion in the light of possible repercussions on our mutual and growing relationship. Indeed, even the Dialogue itself could suffer, we feared. In spite of these significant concerns, we decided that the urgency of the situation and the need to proclaim the Gospel in a credible manner demanded a beginning to this discussion.

(69) The members of the Dialogue observed that proselytism exists, in large part, because Pentecostals and Catholics do not have a common understanding of the Church. To give one illustration, they do not agree on the relationship between the church, on one hand, and baptism as an expression of living faith, on the other.

Nonetheless in our previous discussions we have expressed the ways in which we perceive the bonds between us that already exist. Catholics, for example, hold that everyone who believes in the name of the Lord Jesus and is properly baptized[4] is joined in a certain true manner to the body of Christ which is the Church. For Pentecostals, "the foundation of unity is a common faith and experience of Jesus Christ as Lord and Savior through the Holy Spirit. This implies that to the extent that Pentecostals recognize that Roman Catholics have this common faith in and experience of Jesus as Lord, they share a real though imperfect koinonia with them."[5] This is true even though each has different understandings of the Church.

(70) Still members of the Dialogue think that Pentecostals and Catholics already agree on critical points of faith. Recognition of this fact makes it possible for each of our communities to act in ways that do not impede the growth of the other. Lack of mutual recognition, however, has led at times to dismissive charges and countercharges (e.g. "sects"; "unbelievers," "syncretists," etc.) and actions and counteractions (e.g., unilateral decisions for the good of one community, often at the expense of the other community) by members of both communities. These charges and actions have detracted from the ability of Catholics and Pentecostals to witness credibly before the world to the reconciling power of God through Jesus Christ.

---

4. Cf. "Perspectives on Koinonia," §54.
5. "Perspectives on Koinonia," §55.

(71) A primary example of such a conflict may be found in the tensions which exist between Christians who are not in fellowship with one another. It is not our purpose in this document to give priority to the interests of one particular Church over those of another. While in the example given in the following paragraphs, the Catholic Church is described as the long-established Church and the Pentecostals as the newcomers, such as may be the case in any given European country, there are instances such as in the case of Northeast Zimbabwe in which Pentecostals may be described as the long-established Church and the Catholics as newcomers. In the use of our example, our concern is merely to illustrate, in concrete terms, the tensions which may arise with respect to mission in a given region between two such churches.

(72) Catholics, for instance, may have preached the Gospel and established churches in a region centuries ago. Through the centuries these churches have played an important role in the lives of the people of that region. The role which the church has played has extended far beyond the walls of the congregation, permeating every aspect of the culture of the people from art, to music, to social institutions, to festivals and other public celebrations. The lives of the people flow easily between church and the wider culture because the church has impacted the culture in a major way.

(73) However, there is another side to this. Often the earlier Christianization of a given culture by Catholicism takes for granted that it remains permeated by faith. As with an individual, so also with a culture, critique by the Word and on-going transformation are necessary.

(74) The time and investment in the church by devout Catholics have been significant in many cultures. Sometimes their attempt to live the life of faith has come at a great price—persecution, even martyrdom. Actively embracing the challenges of living and transforming the society to which the Gospel has been brought is no small feat. The faithful have struggled to maintain the Gospel, even at times when the society has not wanted to hear it. The local church has rejoiced when the Gospel has taken root, and sorrowed when it has failed to do so. In other words, evangelization is an on-going need for any culture.

(75) Conflict erupts when another community of Christians enters into the life of an already religiously-impacted community and begins to evangelize without due consideration of the price that has been paid for witness to the Gospel by believers who have preceded them. Difficulties arise when there is no acknowledgment of the significant role which the church plays in all aspects of the lives of those who are citizens of this region. This conflict comes about because the two Christian communities are separated and have not recognized the legitimacy of one another as members of the

one Body of Christ. They have been separated from one another. They have not spoken with one another. Certain assumptions have been made by each about the other. Judgements have taken place without proper consultation between them.

(76) Even if the motives of newcomers are irreproachable with respect to the welfare of the people in this region, including a genuine concern to see that the citizens of the region have really heard the Gospel, their method of entry into the region often contributes to misunderstanding and conflict, and perhaps even to a violent response. Courtesy would seem to call for some communication with the leaders of the older church by the new evangelizers. Without this, the older church and culture are easily violated. The people and church leaders in some of these areas have often been offended by what they see as disrespect or disregard of pastoral activities that have been exercised for a long time. It is easy to see why serious tensions might arise.

(77) The conflicts which have occurred between us demonstrate clearly the problem which disunity creates even for well-intentioned Christians. Disunity isolates us from one another. It leads to suspicion between us. It contributes to a lack of mutual understanding, even to an unwillingness for us to try to understand each other. And all of these things have resulted in a general state of hostility between us in which we even question the Christian authenticity of each other. Our different readings of the Gospel reached in our isolated states have led to doctrinal differences which have only further contributed to the question of whether or not the other truly proclaims the Gospel.

(78) If each perceives the other through the lens of this disunity, the result is all too often that one sees the other as an adversary to its own mission and may, therefore, feel the need to place impediments in the way of the other. There may be public denunciations, even persecution, of one another. Both sides have suffered, Pentecostals in particular since they have usually been the minority. But the main tragedy, and on this both the Catholic and Pentecostal teams agree, is that the conflict resulting from the disunity of Christians always "scandalizes the world, and damages that most holy cause, the preaching of the Gospel to every creature."[6] What needs to be faced honestly, and examined with great care, are the reasons behind these conflicts. What we both desire is the pure preaching of the Gospel. Most of our conflicts would diminish if we agreed that this is what evangelization is all about.

---

6. Vatican II, *Unitatis Redintegratio* 1.

(79) Instead of conflict, can we not converse with one another, pray with one another, try to cooperate with one another instead of clashing with one another? In effect, we need to look for ways in which Christians can seek the unity to which Christ calls his disciples (cf. John 17:21) starting with basic respect for one another, learning to love one another.

2. Replacing Dissatisfaction with Hope

(80) By the fourth century church and state were deeply involved in the life of each other. Since then both have occasionally resorted to coercion to assure political-religious homogeneity in society. This has been expressed in the repression of heresy (inquisition) and of other religions (the expulsion of Jews and Muslims from various European countries). The same concern shaped the principle cuius regia, eius religia ("all citizens must accept the religion of their ruler") which was enforced in Europe, especially during the sixteenth and seventeenth centuries. The process by which churches and states moved, first, to religious toleration and then to religious freedom only began in the late eighteenth century and did not become more or less universal in the West until the mid-twentieth century.

(81) In this historical context, Catholics are well aware that attempts at Christianization have often been attached to political and economic expansion (e.g., Latin America) and that sometimes pressure and violence have been used. They also acknowledge that prior to Vatican II, Catholic doctrine has been reluctant to support full religious freedom in civil law.

(82) Today Catholics and Pentecostals condemn coercive and violent methods. Nevertheless, all too often, aggressiveness still characterizes our interaction. Words have become the new weapons. Catholics are affronted when some Pentecostals assume that they are not even Christians, when they speak disrespectfully of the Catholic Church and its leaders or when Pentecostals lead Catholic members into newly established Pentecostal fellowships. Pentecostals are affronted when some Catholics in some parts of the world view them as "rapacious wolves," when they are ridiculed as "panderetas o aleluyas" (tambourines or alleluias), or when they are indiscriminately classified as "sects."

(83) Further proof of the fact that neither Catholics nor Pentecostals are satisfied with the state of division which exists between them can be seen in their own discussions of proselytism. An initial working definition of proselytism is that it is a disrespectful, insensitive and uncharitable effort to transfer the allegiance of a Christian from one ecclesial body to another.

Actions have already been taken by several traditions which reveal that they believe that "proselytism" is something to be condemned.[7]

(84) Pentecostals did not participate directly in the development of those documents, but Pentecostals have also demonstrated their concern over proselytism, on a more limited scale. They have enacted various bylaws, adopted statements on ministerial ethics, and developed other guidelines which provide leadership to their ministers on issues such as how close together congregations can be planted, what permissions need to be obtained from other pastors in the area in which a new work is being planted, and what type of relationship a minister must maintain when working within the parish of another minister of the same denomination, or within a district that is not his or her own. These bylaws, codes of ethics, and other guidelines have been developed to resist any temptation which one minister might have to proselytize (cf. 2 Cor 10:16). These guidelines work because there is mutual recognition between those who are subject to them.

(85) The early writings of Pentecostals reveal a number of rich and fertile visions of unity among Christians, even if at times they were triumphalistic. Among them was the vision of Charles F. Parham who viewed himself as called by the Holy Spirit to serve as an "apostle of unity." Another was repeatedly published by the African-American pastor William J. Seymour of the famous Azusa Street Mission, in the Apostolic Faith, that the movement stood for "Christian unity everywhere." The ministers of the Assemblies of God, in their organizational meeting of April 1914 went so far as to state that they opposed the establishment of "unscriptural lines of fellowship or disfellowship" since such lines stood counter to Jesus' desire for unity as expressed in John 17:21. A number of other early Pentecostal leaders shared these sentiments also, and read this impulse toward unity as one which was birthed by the Holy Spirit.

(86) While some Pentecostal bodies, especially some indigenous groups in Latin America and Africa, have retained their original visions for unity, most Pentecostals around the world have chosen to pursue more limited visions of unity. This has happened due to a number of factors. Fundamentalists outside Pentecostalism publicly criticized existing Pentecostal

---

7. On the Catholic side, the theme has been addressed in several international bilateral dialogues in which the Roman Catholic Church has been involved, namely, with Evangelicals ("Evangelical-Roman Catholic Dialogue on Mission"); with Baptists ("Summons to Witness to Christ in Today's World"); and with the Orthodox ("Uniatism: Method of Union"). On the multilateral level, the Joint Working Group between the Roman Catholic Church and the World Council of Churches has recently published a study document (JWG, *Challenge of Proselytism*) [section 2.9 in this volume]. In so doing, Catholics, like many Protestant and Orthodox groups, have expressed the desire to condemn all proselytism.

cooperation with many other Christians as inconsistent with biblical teaching. The adoption by some Pentecostals of certain eschatological interpretations popular among Fundamentalists and Evangelicals led to growing suspicion of the modern movements toward unity among Protestants. Peer pressure which suggested that Pentecostals would be granted acceptance as full members of the Evangelical community if they would cut existing ties with certain other Christians, further compromised the original visions of unity.[8] Many Pentecostals also withdrew their support of larger movements toward unity when they believed that their own priorities were not being taken seriously. Vestiges of these original visions of unity are still to be found among the published statements which outline the raison d'etre of many Pentecostal organizations including the Pentecostal World Conference.

(87) The Pentecostal members of this Dialogue lament the impact of the factors which have led to the loss of the original visions of unity. They would like to challenge Pentecostals to look once again at their roots that they might rediscover the richness of their earliest call to facilitate unity between all Christians, by internalizing anew the role the Holy Spirit has presumably played in the birth of these deep yearnings.

(88) All members of this Dialogue also wish to encourage Pentecostals to share their visions of greater Christian unity with other Christians. In turn, we urge the latter to bring their own visions of unity to the discussion. In this way, we believe that together we can "discover the unfathomable riches of the truth" thereby deepening our own understanding of what we believe the Holy Spirit has caused to emerge within us. We are all called to be stewards of this precious gift of unity which we already enjoy and to which we yet aspire in the bond of peace (cf. Eph 4:3).

(89) In the light of these realities which have contributed to our own coming together for dialogue, the members of both teams felt keenly the need to acknowledge that neither Catholics nor Pentecostals have fulfilled sufficiently the demands of the Gospel to love one another. While the past cannot be undone and is not even wholly retrievable, we must make every effort to know and express it as accurately as possible.

3. Defining the Challenge

(90) The term "proselytism" is not found in the Bible, but the term "proselyte" is. It is originally derived from the Old Testament vocabulary relating to those strangers and sojourners who moved into Israel, believed in Yahweh, and accepted the entire Torah (e.g., Exod 12:48–49). This term carried

8. Robeck Jr., "Assemblies of God and Ecumenical Cooperation," 107–50.

a positive meaning, i.e., to become a convert to Judaism. In the New Testament, proselytes were present in Jerusalem on the day of Pentecost (cf. Acts 2:11), and at least one of them was chosen to serve the widows (cf. Acts 6:5). But in recent times, "proselytism," as used within Christian circles, has come to carry a negative meaning associated with an illicit form of "evangelism."

(91) An issue between Catholics and Pentecostals that relates to the problem of proselytism concerns the way a living faith is perceived in the life of an individual Christian or in a community. Through dialogue we have learned that Pentecostals and Catholics may have different ideas about who is "unchurched," different understandings of how living in a deeply Christian culture can root the Christian faith in someone's life. They may have different ideas of how to assess whether, or in what way, pastoral needs are being met in a Christian community or in a person's life. They may have different ways of interpreting whether or not a person can be considered an evangelized Christian.

(92) The Dialogue has taught us that because of these differences there is a continual need to learn from one another so as to deepen mutual knowledge and understanding of each others' doctrinal traditions, pastoral practices and convictions. We need to learn to respect the integrity and rights of the other so as to avoid judgements that create unnecessary conflict in regard to evangelization and obstacles to the spreading of the Gospel, in addition to those already caused by our divisions.

(93) Attempts to define proselytism reveal a broad range of activities and actions that are not easily interpreted. These tend to be identified and evaluated differently by the parties involved. In spite of these difficulties, we have concluded that both for Catholics and for Pentecostals, proselytism is an unethical activity that comes in many forms. Some of these would be:

- all ways of promoting our own community of faith that are intellectually dishonest, such as contrasting an ideal presentation of our own community with the weaknesses of another Christian community;
- all intellectual laziness and culpable ignorance that neglect readily accessible knowledge of the other's tradition;
- every wilful misrepresentation of the beliefs and practices of other Christian communities;
- every form of force, coercion, compulsion, mockery or intimidation of a personal, psychological, physical, moral, social, economic, religious or political nature;

- every form of cajolery or manipulation, including the exaggeration of biblical promises, because these distortions do not respect the dignity of persons and their freedom to make their own choices;
- every abuse of mass media in a way that is disrespectful of another faith and manipulative of the audience;
- all unwarranted judgements or acts which raise suspicions about the sincerity of others;
- all competitive evangelization focused against other Christian bodies (cf. Rom 15:20).

(94) All Christians have the right to bear witness to the Gospel before all people, including other Christians. Such witness may legitimately involve the persuasive proclamation of the Gospel in such a way as to bring people to faith in Jesus Christ or to commit themselves more deeply to Him within the context of their own church. The legitimate proclamation of the Gospel will bear the marks of Christian love (cf. 1 Cor 13). It will never seek its own selfish ends by using the opportunity to speak against or in any way denigrate another Christian community, or to suggest or encourage a change in someone's Christian affiliation. Both the Pentecostal and Catholic members of this Dialogue view as proselytism such selfish actions as an illegitimate use of persuasive power. Proselytism must be sharply distinguished from the legitimate act of persuasively presenting the Gospel. Proselytism must be avoided.

(95) At the same time we acknowledge that if a Christian, after hearing a legitimate presentation of the Gospel, freely chooses to join a different Christian community, it should not automatically be concluded that such a transfer is the result of proselytism.

(96) For the most part, people hear the preaching of the Gospel within their own particular church where their own spiritual needs are also met. It may also happen, on a given occasion, that members of different Christian communities help to organize an evangelistic campaign, in which they also participate. The primary aim of such an evangelistic campaign should always be the proclamation of the Gospel. We believe that the Reverend Billy Graham has provided an important model in this regard. Respecting the ecclesial affiliation of the participants, he organizes such campaigns only after he has sought the support and agreement of the churches in the area, including Catholics and Pentecostals. When those who are already part of a Christian community respond to his call to commit themselves more deeply to Christ, the pastoral resources from their own church are immediately made available to help them in their renewed commitment.

Thus, proselytism is avoided. The churches involved receive the respect and regard they deserve, illustrating the results of communication and cooperation, demonstrating a measure of real, visible unity.

(97) Confusion has resulted when the terms "proselytism" and "evangelism" have been used as though they were synonyms. This confusion has impacted the civil realm. Some countries, for instance, have passed so-called "anti-proselytism" laws which prohibit or greatly restrict any kind of Christian evangelism or missionary activity. We deplore this.

4. Promoting Religious Freedom

(98) Mention of these anti-proselytism laws introduces us to the complex matter of religious freedom. There is general agreement that religious liberty is a civil right. For Christians there is also the religious freedom they are to accord to one another as brothers and sisters in Christ, and to all human beings since they are made in the image and likeness of God.

(99) Religious freedom is promoted by both secular society, for example, in statements from the United Nations[9] and by the church.[10] Pentecostals and Catholics are in full agreement in the support of religious freedom, whether it is seen as a civil right or as one of the principles that should guide their relationships with each other.

(100) Religious freedom as a civil right is very complex in the way it is pursued and resisted in the endlessly varied political situations that have church related to state and state to church. Catholics and Pentecostals need to stand as one in respecting and promoting this civil right for all peoples and for one another.

(101) Historically, Pentecostals have not enacted broadly representative resolutions on the subject of religious freedom largely because of their minority status in the societies where they have functioned. They have recently, however, joined with other Christians when issues of religious freedom have been at stake. They have also led efforts to end persecution or to promote legislation towards religious freedom, especially in countries where in the past the rights of their Pentecostal sisters and brothers have been violated (e.g. Italy, and a number of Latin American countries). It is clear, therefore, that they believe that the state has a legitimate role in guaranteeing religious freedom.

(102) Because of these convictions, members of the Dialogue reject:

9. See UN, *Universal Declaration on Human Rights*; *Declaration on the Elimination of all Forms of Intolerance* 1.1.

10. See, e.g., Vatican II, *Dignitatis Humanae*.

- all violations of religious freedom and all forms of religious intolerance as well as every attempt to impose belief and practices on others or to manipulate or coerce others in the name of religion;
- inequality in civil treatment of religious bodies, although, we affirm, as Vatican II affirmed, that in exercising their rights individuals and social groups "are bound by the moral law to have regard to the rights of others, to their own duties toward others and for the common good of all."[11]

(103) Catholics believe that the state is obliged to give effective protection to the religious liberty of all citizens by just laws and other suitable means, and to ensure favorable conditions for fostering religious life.[12]

(104) Religious freedom has also been the subject of significant ecumenical dialogue.[13] A statement that is even more comprehensive in scope is that of the Joint Working Group between the Catholic Church and the World Council of Churches. With them we agree that "religious freedom affirms the right of all persons to pursue the truth and witness to the truth according to their conscience. It includes the freedom to acknowledge Jesus Christ as Lord and Savior and the freedom of Christians to witness to their faith in him by word and deed."[14] Religious freedom includes the freedom to embrace a religion or to change one's religion without any coercion which would impair such freedom.[15]

5. Resolving Conflicts in the Quest for Unity

(105) Conflicts among Christian groups are not unusual. Difficulties experienced by Protestant missionary movements of the nineteenth and twentieth centuries highlighted the need to resolve tensions among denominations. It became obvious that divisions were obstacles to the preaching of the Gospel. These concerns led to the first World Missionary Conference at Edinburgh, Scotland, in 1910, at which an international body of Protestants and Anglicans assembled to discuss ways to cooperate rather than compete in mission. This conference led to other movements for Christian cooperation. As we approach the end of the century virtually all major Christian families, Anglican, Catholic, Orthodox, Pentecostal, and Protestant, are now involved

---

11. Vatican II, *Dignitatis Humanae* 7.
12. Cf. Vatican II, *Dignitatis Humanae* 6.
13. E.g., "Summons to Witness."
14. JWG, "Challenge of Proselytism," 15.
15. JWG, "Challenge of Proselytism," 15.

in efforts to find ways to work together, to overcome misunderstandings, and to resolve doctrinal differences, so that these will no longer be obstacles to the proclaiming of the Gospel of Jesus Christ.

(106) These concerns have implications for Pentecostals and Catholics where conflict arises from mission activities. Two points need to be kept in mind. On the one hand, we affirm that the principles of religious freedom are basic for evangelization. On the other hand, divided Christians have real responsibilities for one another because of the bonds of koinonia they already share.[16] In facing conflicts, the right to religious freedom must be seen in relationship to the responsibility to respond to Christ's call for the unity of his disciples. Christ calls Christians to live their freedom. At the same time, He calls Christians to unity "so that the world may believe" (John 17:21).

(107) The call of the Lord of the Church cannot be ignored. It is reinforced by the Apostle Paul who exhorted the Ephesians to make "every effort to maintain the unity of the Spirit in the bond of peace" (Eph 4:3) for "there is one body, and one spirit . . . one Lord, one faith, one baptism, one God and Father of all" (Eph 4:4–5). Christians, who have been reconciled to God and entrusted with the ministry of reconciliation (cf. 2 Cor 5:18), need to be reconciled with each other in order to carry out their ministry effectively. Ongoing division jeopardizes the impact of the Gospel.

(108) We realize that some of our readers will think that our conclusions are idealistic. We do not agree. We recognize that not everyone has had the same experience and the same opportunity that we have had to work together, to pray together, and to learn from one another. We have come to recognize, in a fresh way, that with God all things are possible to those who believe (cf. Mark 9:23). The Scriptures teach us that Christ calls us and the apostle invites us to unity (cf. John 17:21; Eph 4:3). The patterns of our relationships in the past have not reflected this call. We engaged in this dialogue because of what we understand is the will of Christ which our past relationships have not reflected. Our efforts are intended as a contribution to re-thinking the lack of conformity between Pentecostal/Catholic relationships and the call of Christ. We commend our findings to our readers recognizing that some will find them to be a real challenge.

(109) We look forward to the day when leaders within our two communities will be able to pray together, develop mutual trust, and deal with tensions which arise. Through our theological dialogue, now twenty-five years old, we have gained a deeper understanding of the meaning of faith in Christ and a mutual respect for one another. We covet for our leaders these

---

16. Cf. "Perspectives on Koinonia," §54–55.

same gifts and believe such relationships might yield greater sensitivity on issues of mutual concern. The relationship might even yield a code of ecclesial etiquette to help prevent difficulties from arising.

All of this seems possible and desirable. Are we not, as believers, being prepared for a future in which we will be judges not only of the world but also of the angels? (cf. 1 Cor 6:2–3). Would it not be a sign of contradiction if we had to hand over our present disputes to the judgement of the world? But this is what is happening when we arrive at impasses. "Can it be," Paul asks, "that there is no one among you wise enough to decide between one believer and another?" (1 Cor 6:5).

6. Affirming Principles for Mutual Understanding

(110) The discussion on the nature of proselytism leads very quickly into practical matters. Even if Pentecostals and Catholics explicitly or implicitly denounce proselytism, many people may need practical guidance on how to live up to this commitment. The members of the Dialogue have agreed upon the following principles which seek to express the spirit of Christian love as it is portrayed in Scripture (cf. 1 Cor 13). They submit these principles for consideration by their respective churches.

(111) The deep and true source of any Christian witness is the commandment "You shall love the Lord your God with all your heart, and with all your soul, and with all your mind and you shall love your neighbor as yourself" (Matt 22:37, 39; cf. Lev 19:18; Deut 6:5). Christian witness brings glory to God. It is nourished by the conviction that it is the Holy Spirit whose grace and light brings about the response of faith. It respects the free will and dignity of those to whom it is given, whether or not they wish to accept.

(112) Pentecostals and Catholics affirm the presence and power of the Gospel in Christian communities outside of their own traditions. Pentecostals believe that all Christians of whatever denomination, can have a living personal relationship with Jesus as Lord and Savior. Catholics believe that only in their own visible communion "the fullness of the means of salvation can be attained." But they also believe that "some, even very many, of the significant elements and endowments which together go to build up and give life to the Church itself, can exist outside the visible boundaries of the Catholic Church."[17] It is the responsibility of all Christians to proclaim the Gospel to all who have not repented, believed, and submitted their lives to the Lordship of Christ. It is imperative for every Christian to speak "the

---

17. Vatican II, *Unitatis Redintegratio* 3.

truth in love" (Eph 4:15) about all Christian communities. We affirm the obligation to portray the beliefs and practices of other Christian communities accurately, honestly and charitably, and wherever possible, in cooperative efforts with them. We pray and work "for building up the body of Christ, until all of us come to the unity of the faith and of the knowledge of the Son of God, to maturity, to the measure of the full stature of Christ" (Eph 4:12–13).

(113) Individual Christians have the right and responsibility to proclaim the Gospel boldly (Acts 4:13, 29; Eph 6:19) and persuasively (cf. Acts 17:3; Rom 1:14). All people have the right to hear the Gospel preached in their own "language" in a culturally sensitive fashion. The Good News of Jesus Christ addresses the whole person, including his or her behavioural, cognitive, and experiential dimensions. We also affirm responsible use of modern technology as a legitimate means to communicate the Gospel.

(114) In the light of these issues, we offer the following proposals to our communities:

- to incorporate these principles in our own daily lives and ministries;
- to pursue contacts with Christian leaders for consideration of these issues;
- to conduct our preaching, teaching, and pastoral ministry in the light of these principles;
- to invite scholarly and professional societies at all levels to discuss this document;
- to incorporate these insights into the various programs for educators, ministerial students and other church workers;
- to encourage the development of relationships of mutual understanding and respect which will enable us to work together on these issues.

(115) We encourage prayer for and with each other. Above all, we pray that Pentecostals and Catholics will be open to the Holy Spirit who will convince the hearts of all Christians of the urgency, and the biblical imperative of these concerns.

(116) Without a doubt, proselytism is a sensitive issue among Pentecostals and Catholics, but we believe that through open and honest dialogue and docility to the Spirit, we can respond to the challenge before us. This may not always be easy, but the love of Christ compels us to deal with "a humility and gentleness, with patience, bearing with one another in love, making every effort to maintain the unity of the Spirit in the bond of peace"

(Eph 4:3). It is only then that we will give credible witness to Christ in a world which urgently needs to hear the Good News. . . .

Appendix 2: A List of Official Documents of the Roman Catholic Church Used in This Report

Second Vatican Council

- *Lumen gentium* [Dogmatic Constitution on the Church]
- *Gaudium et spes* [Pastoral Constitution on the Church in the Modern World]
- *Unitatis Redintegratio* [Decree on Ecumenism]
- *Apostolicam actuositatem* [Decree on the Apostolate of Lay People]
- *Ad Gentes* [Decree on the Church's Missionary Activity]
- *Dignitatis humanae* [Declaration on Religious Liberty]

Pope Paul VI, *Evangelii nuntiandi* [Evangelization in the Modern World]

Synod of Bishops, *De iustitia in mundo* [Justice in the World]

2.10

Towards Common Witness
A Call to Adopt Responsible Relationships in Mission and to Renounce Proselytism[1]

WCC 1997

Editor's Introduction

THIS DOCUMENT IS ANOTHER World Council of Churches contribution from 1997.[2]

PREFACE

WITHIN THE ECUMENICAL MOVEMENT and the World Council of Churches the concern for common witness and the unity of the churches has always been a priority,[3] and proselytism has been recognized as a scandal and

---

1. Reproduced with kind permission of the WCC.
2. WCC, "Towards Common Witness."
3. In fact, concern about proselytism as an ecumenical issue antedates the establishment of the WCC. The 1920 *Encyclical of the Ecumenical Patriarchate*, which proposed the foundation of a "koinonia" of churches, asked for the cessation of proselytizing activities. In the preliminary Faith and Order and Life and Work meetings, which took place in the same year, the issue of proselytism was again raised. Since the very establishment of the WCC, the issue of proselytism has been identified as one of the hindrances to Christian unity. As early as 1954, the Central Committee in Evanston decided that in view of difficulties which were affecting relationships between WCC

counterwitness. Ecumenical statements have repeatedly expressed the need for the clearer practice of responsible relationships in mission, a sharper commitment to witness in unity and renunciation of all forms of proselytism. Yet during these almost fifty years of ecumenical fellowship in the WCC, proselytism has continued to be a painful reality in the life of the churches.

The issue of proselytism is again being raised as a major factor dividing the churches and a threat to the ecumenical movement itself. In the face of such a complex situation, the Central Committee in Moscow, 1989, requested the former Commission on World Mission and Evangelism to "take up this issue [of proselytism] for further study and action, examining also the existing statements for up-dating if necessary." A similar request was made by the Fifth World Conference on Faith and Order (Santiago de Compostela, 1993), which asked for a "new and broader study of mission, evangelism and proselytism."

The present document, which has been elaborated by Programme Unit II, is in response to these requests. In order to reflect accurately on current realities and find appropriate ways forward, the Unit embarked on a broad consultative study process. Mission agencies, churches, missiologists and theologians, local congregations and monastic orders in different parts of the world participated by correspondence. Furthermore a series of consultations was organized: "Towards Responsible Relationships in Mission" (Chambésy, 1993); an Orthodox consultation on "Mission and Proselytism" (Sergiev Possad, Russia, 1995); "Called to Common Witness" (Manila, 1995); and "Common Witness" (Bossey, 1996). Special efforts were made to bring together in dialogue the "proselytizers" and "proselytized" and to involve not only WCC member churches but members of the evangelical, Pentecostal and charismatic constituencies. Documents and statements on this issue from churches and other organizations have been carefully studied

---

member churches, a commission should be appointed to study further the issue of proselytism and religious liberty. After a number of years of laborious study, a statement on *Christian Witness, Proselytism, and Religious Liberty in the Setting of the World Council of Churches*, drafted by the commission and revised twice by the Central Committee (1956 and 1960), was received by the WCC Third Assembly (New Delhi, 1961).

Issues of proselytism and common witness have also been on the agenda of the Joint Working Group between the Roman Catholic Church and the World Council of Churches, which has elaborated three important study documents: *Common Witness and Proselytism* (1970); *Common Witness* (1982); and *The Challenge of Proselytism and the Calling to Common Witness* (1996).

Furthermore, many documents and declarations on the issue of common witness and proselytism have been produced recently by local and international bilateral dialogues between churches. Studies have also been done by the Conference of European Churches and the Middle East Council of Churches.

and analyzed and their insights incorporated in the present statement. Permanent contact has been maintained with the Joint Working Group in a spirit of mutual cooperation and sharing. Its study document, "The Challenge of Proselytism and the Calling to Common Witness" (1995), was one of the basic texts used in the elaboration of this statement. The Unit II study, however, was undertaken with much broader participation, and emphasizes the missiological and pastoral implications of proselytism in the life of local churches on the way towards common witness and Christian unity. An earlier draft of this statement was used as a resource paper at the Conference on World Mission and Evangelism in Salvador, Brazil (1996).

This statement is presented in the conviction that it is both timely and important for churches in all parts of the world. Its genesis also reflects the spirit of the WCC's "Common Understanding and Vision" document, in that it has provided space for wider participation in ecumenical discussions.

INTRODUCTION

Dramatic develoments in different parts of the world in recent years have compelled the ecumenical family to re-examine issues related to common witness and proselytism in greater depth. For the WCC the situation is made even more urgent by the fact that complaints of proselytistic activities are being made against some of its own member churches as well as churches and groups outside its fellowship.

Among present-day realities damaging the relationships between churches in different parts of the world and thus requiring the urgent attention of the ecumenical family are:

- competitive missionary activities, especially in Central and Eastern Europe, Africa, Asia and Latin America, carried out independently by foreign missionary groups, churches and individuals, often directed at people already belonging and committed to one of the churches in those countries, and often leading to the establishment of parallel ecclesial structures;
- the re-emergence of tensions between the Orthodox and the Roman Catholic Church concerning the Eastern Rite Catholic churches;[4]

---

4. The Eastern Rite Catholic churches originated in those groups of former Orthodox who entered into full communion with the Roman Catholic Church around the bishop of Rome while retaining various Eastern liturgical and canonical traditions inherited from their mother churches.

- a sharp increase in the number of new mission agencies based in the South working independently in other parts of the world, often without contact with the churches in those countries;
- growing frustration among churches, especially in the South, whose members are being lured to other churches by offers of humanitarian aid;
- the humanitarian work done among immigrants, poor, lonely and uprooted people in big cities intended to influence them to change their denominational allegiance;
- the growth of religious fundamentalism and intolerance;
- the growing impact of sects and new religious movements in many parts of the world;
- the discrediting of established minority Christian churches in multifaith communities.

The aims of this statement are: (1) to make churches and Christians aware of the bitter reality of proselytism today; (2) to call those involved in proselytism to recognize its disastrous effects on church unity, relationships among Christians and the credibility of the gospel and, therefore, to renounce it; and (3) to encourage the churches and mission agencies to avoid all forms of competition in mission and to commit themselves anew to witness in unity.

I. CHRISTIAN WITNESS AND RELIGIOUS FREEDOM

1. The Mission Imperative

Christian mission is primarily and ultimately God's mission—the *missio Dei*. It is centered in the loving and eternal purpose of the triune God for humankind and all of creation, revealed in Jesus Christ. Central to God's mission is the life-giving presence of the Holy Spirit, who continues the mission of Christ through the church and remains the source of its missionary dynamism. The WCC Canberra assembly (1991) described a vision of mission in unity: "A reconciled humanity and renewed creation (cf. Eph 1:9–10) is the goal of the mission of the church. The vision of God uniting all things in Christ is the driving force of its life and sharing."[5]

As the body of Christ, constituted, sustained and energized by the life-giving presence of the Holy Spirit, the church is missionary by nature. It

---

5. WCC, *Signs of the Spirit*, 100.

proclaims that in Jesus Christ the incarnate Word, who died and rose from the dead, salvation is offered to all as God's gift of love, mercy and liberation.

Participating in God's mission is an imperative for all Christians and all churches, not only for particular individuals or specialized groups. It is an inner compulsion, rooted in the profound demands of Christ's love, to invite others to share in the fullness of life Jesus came to bring (cf. John 10:10).

Mission in Christ's way is *holistic*, for the whole person and the totality of life are inseparable in God's plan of salvation accomplished in Jesus Christ. It is *local*—"the primary responsibility for mission, where there is a local church, is with that church in its own place."[6] It is also *universal*, that is, to all peoples, beyond all frontiers of race, caste, gender, culture, nation to "the ends of the earth" in every sense (cf. Acts 1:8; Mark 16:15; Luke 24:47).

2. Common Witness: Mission in Unity

Numerous WCC documents have recalled the intrinsic relation between the credibility of the mission of the church in the world and the unity among Christians—underscored in the prayer of Jesus "that they all may be one . . . so that the world may believe" (John 17:21) and historically realized among the apostles in Jerusalem already on the day of Pentecost. Common witness is "the witness that the churches, even while separated, bear together, especially through joint efforts, by manifesting whatever divine gifts of truth and life they already share and experience in common."[7] It may be thought of as "a eucharistic vision of life which gives thanks for what God has done, is doing, and will do for the salvation of the world through acts of joyous self-offering."[8]

Despite the many barriers which keep the churches apart, the WCC member churches have been able to recognize a certain degree of ecclesial communion among themselves, imperfect though that may yet be. Confessing "the Lord Jesus Christ as God and Saviour according to the scriptures," they seek through the WCC to "fulfil together their common calling to the glory of one God, Father, Son and Holy Spirit."[9] On this basis, other grounds for common witness to the whole world can be affirmed together. Mutual recognition of baptism (as expressed in the WCC's "Baptism, Eucharist and Ministry" text) is the foundation for Christian unity and common witness.

6. Duraisingh, *Called to One Hope*.
7. Stransky, "Common Witness," 197.
8. WCC, *On the Way to Fuller Koinonia*, 254.
9. "Basis," in WCC, "Constitution and Rules of the World Council of Churches."

Authentic common witness presupposes respect and understanding for other traditions and confessions. What should be emphasized is that which is common and can be done together, rather than the barriers which separate. Even when apparently irreconcilable differences remain on certain issues, the truth should be spoken in love (Eph 4:15), for the building up of the church (Eph 4:12), rather than for giving prominence to one's position over against that of others. There is more that unites the churches than separates them. These unifying elements should be looked for in building up witness in unity.

3. Mission in the Context of Religious Freedom

God's truth and love are given freely and call for a free response. Free will is one of the major gifts with which God has entrusted humans. God does not force anyone to accept God's revelation and does not save anyone by force. On the basis of this notion, the International Missionary Council and the World Council of Churches (in process of formation) developed a definition of religious freedom as a fundamental human right. This definition was adopted by the WCC First Assembly in Amsterdam (1948), and at the suggestion of the WCC's Commission of the Churches on International Affairs it was subsequently incorporated in the Universal Declaration of Human Rights: "Everyone has the right to freedom of thought, conscience and religion. This right includes the freedom to change his/her religion or belief, and freedom, either alone or in community with others, in public or in private, to manifest his/her religion or belief, in teaching, practice, worship and observance." The same principle is to be applied in mission work.

The WCC Fifth Assembly (1975) reaffirmed the centrality of religious liberty, stating that "the right to religious freedom has been and continues to be a major concern of member churches and the WCC. However this right should never be seen as belonging exclusively to the church.... This right is inseparable from other fundamental human rights. No religious community should plead for its own religious liberty without active respect and reverence for the faith and basic rights of others. Religious liberty should never be used to claim privileges. For the church this right is essential so that it can fulfil its responsibilities which arise out of the Christian faith. Central to these responsibilities is the obligation to serve the whole community."[10] One's own freedom must always respect, affirm and promote the freedom of

---

10. See WCC, *Breaking Barriers*, 106, and the report of the Orthodox Consultation in Vassiliadis, "Mission and Proselytism."

others; it must not contravene the golden rule: "In everything do to others as you would have them do to you" (Matt 7:12).

II. PROSELYTISM—A COUNTERWITNESS

While the word "proselyte" was originally used to designate a person who became a member of the Jewish community by believing in Yahweh and respecting the Law of Moses, and subsequently, in early Christian times, for a person of another faith who converted to Christianity, proselytism in later centuries took on a negative connotation due to changes in the content, motivation, spirit and methods of "evangelism."

"Proselytism" is now used to mean the encouragement of Christians who belong to a church to change their denominational allegiance, through ways and means that "contradict the spirit of Christian love, violate the freedom of the human person and diminish trust in the Christian witness of the church."[11]

Proselytism is "the corruption of witness."[12] On the surface, proselytism may appear as genuine and enthusiastic missionary activity; and some people involved in it are genuinely committed Christians who believe that they are doing mission in Christ's way. It is the aim, spirit and methodology of this activity which make it proselytism.

Some of the characteristics which clearly distinguish proselytism from authentic Christian witness are:

- Unfair criticism or caricaturing of the doctrines, beliefs and practices of another church without attempting to understand or enter into dialogue on those issues. Some who venerate icons are accused of worshipping idols; others are ridiculed for alleged idolatry towards Mary and the saints or denounced for praying for the dead.

- Presenting one's church or confession as "the *true* church" and its teachings as "the *right* faith" and the only way to salvation, rejecting baptism in other churches as invalid and persuading people to be rebaptized.

- Portraying one's own church as having high moral and spiritual status over against the perceived weaknesses and problems of other churches.

---

11. See report of the Sergiev Possad consultation in Vassiliadis, "Mission and Proselytism."

12. See "Revised Report on Christian Witness, Proselytism, and Religious Liberty," in WCC, *Minutes and Reports*, 214.

- Taking advantage of and using unfaithfully the problems which may arise in another church for winning new members for one's own church.
- Offering humanitarian aid or educational opportunities as an inducement to join another church.
- Using political, economic, cultural and ethnic pressure or historical arguments to win others to one's own church.
- Taking advantage of lack of education or Christian instruction which makes people vulnerable to changing their church allegiance.
- Using physical violence or moral and psychological pressure to induce people to change their church affiliation. This includes the use of media techniques profiling a particular church in a way that excludes, disparages or stigmatizes its adherents, harassment through repeated house calls, material and spiritual threats, and insistence on the "superior" way to salvation offered by a particular church.
- Exploiting people's loneliness, illness, distress or even disillusionment with their own church in order to "convert" them.

Common witness is constructive: it enriches, challenges, strengthens and builds up solid Christian relationships and fellowship. Through word and deed, it makes the gospel relevant to the contemporary world. Proselytism is a perversion of authentic Christian witness and thus a counterwitness. It does not build up but destroys. It brings about tensions, scandal and division, and is thus a destabilizing factor for the witness of the church of Christ in the world. It is always a wounding of koinonia, creating not fellowship but antagonistic parties.

Nevertheless, it must be acknowledged that some people may move from one church to another out of true and genuine conviction, without any proselytistic pressure or manipulation, as a free decision in response to their experience of the life and witness of another church.

The churches must continually assess their own internal life to see whether some of the reasons people change church allegiance may lie with the churches themselves.

III. GUIDELINES FOR RESPONSIBLE RELATIONSHIPS IN MISSION

1. Issues for Further Study and Reflection

- Growth towards responsible relationships in mission which promote genuine Christian common witness and avoid proselytism will require further dialogue, reflection and study in a number of important ecclesiological, theological and other areas:
- historical and social factors, including (1) diversity of experience among different churches, (2) unawareness or different understandings of the history of one's own church and other churches, leading to wounded memories, and (3) dissimilar perspectives and perceptions among majority and minority churches in contexts where a single church has come to be identified with a given nation, people or culture;
- different and even contradictory understandings of the content of Christian faith—regarding worship, sacraments and the teaching authority of the church—and of the limits of legitimate diversity in these areas;
- different understandings of the nature of an individual's church membership and Christian commitment, particularly reflected in the use of expressions conveying value judgments (such as "nominal," "committed," "true" or "born-again Christian," "unchurched," "evangelization" and "re-evangelization"), which are often a source of tension among the churches, leading to accusations of proselytism;
- different understandings of the aim of mission, leading to differences in ethos and style of mission, particularly around those concepts of "church growth" and "church expansion" which seem to give priority to the number of "converts" and thus seem to encourage mission among those who are already members of a Christian church;
- different understandings of the universality of mission, particularly around the validity of the early Christian principle of "canonical territory," according to which the local church already present in any place is primarily responsible for the Christian life of the people there and no other Christian individual, group or church may act or establish ecclesial structures without consulting and cooperating with the local church.

2. The Way Forward: Practical Proposals

Despite the problems still to be overcome, ecumenical reflection and experience in the last few decades have demonstrated that reconciliation and mutual understanding are possible and that witness in unity can become a reality on an even greater scale.

As new contexts call for new initiatives in proclaiming the gospel in unity, churches in partnership in mission commit themselves to:

- deepened understanding of what it means to be church in today's world, and acceptance and celebration of their inter-relatedness in the one body of Christ (cf. 1 Cor 12:12);
- deepened conviction that it is God's mission in which the churches share as God's co-workers, not their own;
- efforts to come to a greater common understanding and vision of their missionary role in contemporary society;
- reaching out together in Christ's way to new frontiers of mission—listening, accompanying, walking with, resourcing, receiving from one another;
- renewed determination to manifest together "the one hope of [their] calling" (Eph 4:4) in order to share more fully in the divine plan of salvation for the reconciliation and gathering up of all peoples and all things in Christ (cf. Eph 1:9–10).

Because the way to evangelizing in ecumenical fellowship and partnership is still long, churches in partnership in mission must:

- repent of past failures and reflect more self-critically on their ways of relating to one another and their methods of evangelizing, in order to overcome anything in their theological or doctrinal expressions or missionary policies and strategies which shows lack of love, understanding and trust of other churches;
- renounce all forms of denominational competition and rivalry and the temptation to proselytize members of other Christian traditions as contrary to Jesus' prayer for the unity of his disciples (John 17:21);
- avoid establishing parallel ecclesial structures, but rather stimulate, help and cooperate with the existing local churches in their evangelistic work in society at large as well as in relation to their own people, especially so-called nominal members;

- condemn any manipulation of humanitarian assistance to individual Christians or churches to induce people into changing their denominational allegiance or to further the missionary goals of one church at the expense of another;
- learn to "speak the truth in love" to one another when they consider others to be proselytizing or engaging in dishonest practices in evangelism.

This Christian fellowship and partnership will not be possible unless Christians and churches:

- listen to one another in genuine dialogue aimed at overcoming ignorance, prejudices or misunderstandings, understanding their differences in the perspective of Christian unity and avoiding unjust accusations, polemics, disparagement and rejection;
- ensure greater sharing of information and accountability in mission at all levels, including prior discussion before launching programmes for evangelism;
- encourage, strengthen and complement one another in missionary activity in an ecumenical spirit, including prior consultation with the church in an area to see what are the possibilities of missionary collaboration and witness in unity;
- demonstrate willingness to learn from others—for example, from their dynamism, enthusiasm and joy in mission, their sense of community, their rejoicing in the Spirit, their spirituality;
- make greater efforts for inner renewal in their own traditions and cultural contexts.

CONCLUSION

With the Salvador World Mission conference, "We decry the practice of those who carry out their endeavors in mission and evangelism in ways which destroy the unity of the body of Christ, human dignity, and the very lives and cultures of those being evangelized; we call on them to confess their participation in and to renounce proselytism."

Called to one hope, we commit ourselves to our common call to mission and to work towards mission in unity. We actively seek a new era of "mission in Christ's way" at the dawn.

> *As you, Father, are in me and I am in you, may they also be in us, so that the world may believe that you have sent me. The glory that you have given me I have given them, so that they may be one, as we are one, I in them and you in me, that they may become completely one, so that the world may know that you have sent me and have loved them even as you have loved me.* (John 17:20–23)

RECOMMENDATIONS

In addition to commending the document "Towards Common Witness" to the churches for their reflection and action, Central Committee approved the following recommendations to facilitate the implementation of the document:

1. That the churches and related agencies:

   a) make greater efforts to educate their own faithful in local congregations, Sunday schools, training centers and seminaries to respect and love members of other churches as sisters and brothers in Christ;

   b) actively promote knowledge of the heritages and contributions of other churches that, despite differences, confess the same Jesus Christ as God and Saviour, worship the same triune God and are engaged in the same witness in the world;

   c) promote efforts towards reconciliation by addressing historical wounds and bitter memories;

   d) initiate (with the assistance of the WCC when necessary) encounter and dialogue at the local, national and regional levels with those engaging in mission work that is perceived as proselytism, in order to help them understand their motivations, make them aware of the negative impact of their activities, and promote responsible relationships in mission;

   e) seek opportunities for working together with other churches on pastoral and social issues that affect local communities and countries as a whole, and be open to authentic cooperation with others in addressing the needs of the people being served;

   f) together renounce proselytism as a denial of authentic witness and an obstruction to the unity of the church, and urge support for common witness, unity and understanding among the churches proclaiming the gospel;

g) continue to pray together for Christian unity, allowing God's Spirit to lead the churches into fuller truth and faithfulness.

2. That the World Council of Churches:

a) strengthen its emphasis on ecumenical formation using all resources of its education sector, in view of the growing trend towards confessionalism and confessional rivalries;

b) undertake a study on ecclesiology and mission, since many of the points of tension and division in relation to common witness stem from conflicting understandings in these areas.

Although it is recognized that the main responsibility for implementing the "Towards Common Witness" document lies with the churches, the WCC should play a facilitating role in stimulating the dialogue within and among the churches.

2.11

Statement on Religious Liberty, Evangelism, and Proselytism[1]

Seventh-Day Adventist Statement 2000

Editor's Introduction

THIS CONCISE STATEMENT IS an important addition to this volume. It reveals that the issue is wider than the "mainstream" Churches and denominations and affects other Christian bodies as well.[2]

SEVENTH-DAY ADVENTISTS BELIEVE THAT freedom of religion is a basic human right. As Christians, they are persuaded that the dissemination of religion is not only a right, but a joyful responsibility based on a divine mandate to witness.

God has called Christians to evangelism—the proclamation of the good news of salvation in Christ (Matt 28:19–20). This is central to Christian life and witness. Thus Christianity is missionary by its very nature.

In affirming global mission and evangelization, Adventists are motivated by willing obedience to Christ's commission and by a sincere desire that every human being be saved and inherit eternal life. They are also motivated by a sense of urgency in expectation of the imminence of Christ's

---

1. This statement was voted by the General Conference of Seventh-Day Adventists Administrative Committee (ADCOM), for release at the time of the General Conference Session in Toronto, Canada, June 29–July 9, 2000. Reproduced with kind permission of the Seventh-Day Adventist Church.

2. Seventh-Day Adventist Church. "Religious Liberty, Evangelism, and Proselytism."

return. In endeavoring to fulfill the gospel commission, Seventh-Day Adventists are thus witnessing, preaching, and serving today in more than 200 countries.

In the context of the dissemination of religion, the issue of "proselytism" has arisen because the term "proselytism" is defined in a number of ways and increasingly is being given a pejorative connotation, associated with unethical means of persuasion, including force. Seventh-Day Adventists unequivocally condemn the use of such methods. They believe that faith and religion are best disseminated when convictions are manifested and taught with humility and respect, and the witness of one's life is in harmony with the message announced, evoking a free and joyous acceptance by those being evangelized.

Evangelistic and missionary activity needs to respect the dignity of all human beings. Individuals need to be truthful and transparent when dealing with other religious groups. Terminology should be used which avoids offending other religious communities. Statements which are false or ridicule other religions should not be made.

Conversion is an experience of the Spirit, and should therefore in no way be connected to offering and receiving material inducements. While the right to engage in humanitarian activities must be fully recognized, such action must never be linked to evangelism in a way that exploits vulnerable people by offering financial and material incentives to entice them to change religion.

Seventh-Day Adventists are committed to serving their fellow men by preaching the everlasting gospel to every nation, and kindred, and tongue, and people (Rev 14:6).

2.12

Communicating the Message
Common Witness/Evangelism/Proselytism[1]

WCC 2001

Editor's Introduction

THIS IS AN ARTICLE from the CWME journal, "International Review of Mission," 2001. As such it represents a World Council of Churches perspective. Jacques Matthey, in his editorial, notes:

> This issue of IRM is fully dedicated to an important consultation which took place from July 8–15, 2000 . . . in Germany. For the first time for many years two [Commissions] . . . Faith and Order and Mission and Evangelism, prepared and organized a meeting together. . . . In the past, the two constituencies and the World Council of Churches (WCC) commissions representing them had not found many opportunities to act in common. . . . The consultation can be described as a crossroad of two study processes. One, directed by Faith and Order, concerns ecclesiology. The other, undertaken by Mission and Evangelism, centers on the new missiological challenges that exist in the current context of globalization. . . . The approach to witness is based on an official WCC document on mission and evangelism, the so-called "Ecumenical Affirmation," approved by the central committee in 1982.[2]

1. Reproduced with kind permission of the WCC.
2. Matthey, "Editorial."

I. COMMON WITNESS

WE HAVE BEFORE US, and are pleased to affirm, two recent texts: "Towards Common Witness" and "The Challenge of Proselytism and the Calling to Common Witness."[3]

We see common witness not primarily as a way of avoiding unnecessary, counter-productive conflicts, but as a task inspired by a vision of the ultimate goal and purpose of the church and Christian mission: salvation. This goal is unity in love, joy and peace—in all the gifts of the Holy Spirit—unity among people, unity of the entirety of humanity collectively, unity of the entire creation, with God: Father, Son and Holy Spirit. If we keep the vision of this ultimate goal before us, so much of what has had to be said or written about missionary deviations and problems would no longer concern us. As we continue our ecumenical journey it is essential that we keep its ultimate destination in mind and heart.

The inspiration and vitality for our missionary pilgrimage is our experience of the joy with which the gospel begins and ends: the joy of Christ coming to us at his birth, his baptism, his evangelical preaching, his cross, death, burial and resurrection, his ascension, and our participation here and now in the beauty, love, joy and peace of his eternal reign. It is this paschal/eschatological experience, made possible by the power and gift of the Holy Spirit that motivates and energizes this journey. The church is both the visible sign of this reality and our entrance into it, always pointing beyond herself to the coming Lord and his kingdom. It is therefore our sadness that some do not know, or have never known this joy, that impels us to evangelize. To evangelize means to pray, to preach, to teach, to baptize, to found churches, to ordain, celebrate, proclaim, and to dedicate ourselves to living and working for the fulfilment of God's saving plan among people everywhere. For it is his will that all people come to the knowledge of the truth.

In reality, our shared experiences indicate that a common witness to the joy of the good news is unfortunately rare. All too often the focus on the common eschatological goal is lost. Christians instead fix on or even idolise the means rather than the goal. These means include conversion, church construction, religious education, liturgical celebration; all these are the activities one expects from a local congregation. However, it must be clear that these legitimate activities are only the means and not the ends of mission.

---

3. WCC, "Towards Common Witness," 16. A document commended to the churches by the central committee of the World Council of Churches. JWG, "Challenge of Proselytism." This document was adopted in 1995 and served as a basis for the 1997 WCC text mentioned above.

The church must continually examine and reflect upon the context in which she lives, and ask what prevents the people in this context from experiencing the abundant life Christ offers. In any given local situation, what is it that makes it difficult or even impossible for people to enter into the love and joy of the Holy Spirit? Indeed, if the doctrinal divisions or internal conflicts between Christians constitute such obstacles, the churches themselves can become barriers to the fulfilment of God's mission.

Common witness can be viewed from three perspectives, depending on the stage of development in a local situation.

1. At the initial stage of a particular mission, common witness could mean cooperation among Christians, so that at least potential converts are not faced with the scandalizing spectacle of Christians slandering each other or fighting among themselves.

2. As the mission progresses and various local denominational congregations arise, common witness may mean mutual solidarity, sharing resources, and participating in common expressions of devotions—even when respective faith traditions remain distinct. Such collaboration is possible and genuine insofar as each community remains sincerely committed to its own approach to and understanding of the gospel, as common witness necessitates that each listen to and respect the other's faith experience, the "stories" of the other Christian traditions in that place.

3. At a later stage, each community will eventually ask itself to discern God's will for their community. Here common witness can reveal the presence of Christ which all Christians within that particular context are summoned to manifest. This can entail shared or interrelated ministries of education, counselling, social and charitable outreach, as well as mutual intercession. Common witness, then, need not mean a single unified conception or programme; rather, it describes any mutually supportive approach to common challenges, concerns and problems.

In practice, however, we know this type of common witness seldom arises. All too often, churches define their mission in terms of membership and income, assessing their success in terms of numerical increase, infrastructure and financial reports. As missions become autonomous and self-sustaining their founders and supporters judge their work to have been successful, even if the missio Dei may in fact have been poorly served. Rival churches are apt to spend so much time and energy competing with or criticizing each other that they seldom reflect upon what God would rather have them do. Such narrow understandings of mission inevitably fail to promote progress towards the love and joy, which are the signs of the kingdom of God.

Recommendations

Common witness is often frustrated by a lack of coordination between WCC member churches and Christians who do not participate in the World Council, nor abide by its recommendations concerning mission and proselytism. A new challenge therefore arises from the need to draw these groups into dialogue with the WCC.

More than once in plenary and group sessions, participants in this consultation expressed an interest in developing a positive expression of Orthodox mission: not a statement about evangelism vs. proselytism, but rather of mission to society and to the world, in love and service. The commissions and teams on Faith and Order (F&O) and Mission and Evangelism (CWME) may wish at some point to sponsor a consultation on a positive elucidation of Orthodox mission.

II. EVANGELISM

We discussed evangelism as traditional missionary outreach, i.e., as the initial stage of congregational building. In practice, it is at this level that cooperation and harmony are often the least likely to occur. Since most societies on the planet have already heard the gospel message in some form, the introduction of a new faith tradition into a particular geographic region often leads directly to conflict rather than cooperation, to interconfessional rivalry rather than healthy competition. This latter, in an atmosphere of mutual respect, can in fact have a strongly positive effect on church life. In the experience of several participants, the presence of a friendly alternative requires each community to retain or restore a certain evangelical vigour that might otherwise have been lost.

Recommendation

Despite the theological and practical reflections and recommendations of numerous conferences and consultations that have been convened, we continue to experience the pain and trauma of divisive missionary tactics, and conflicting theologies and practices. Especially following the recommendations made at the Santiago de Compostela F&O world conference, we suggest further work by F&O/CWME to implement a process of sharing stories of reconciliation, with the goal of a "healing of memories." The suffering of particular Christian groups inevitably enters into their collective consciousness and has often become constitutive of their identity. Unless and until these stories are told and acknowledged, wounds cannot fully heal. Christians need to heal each other in mutual acceptance and reconciliation.

III: PROSELYTISM

When members of one Christian community fail or refuse to listen to the memory of another, the danger of proselytism increases. One can speak of this refusal to listen, or to share, as one of the characteristics of a proselytizing spirit.

Proselytism derives from a mythology created around the host culture in effect the ignorance of its ecclesiology, tradition, history and religious life. Proselytism can often be motivated by the desire of profit, rather than by love. In such cases mission is transformed into a pursuit that will produce a satisfactory return on one's investment. It follows that one measure of proselytism has to do with the exploitation of vulnerability—economic, social, psychological—of the host community.

Another way to detect proselytism might be to consider the spiritual condition of a particular group before and after their exposure to the work of a given mission. Naturally, both converts and proselytes will be in some sense dissatisfied with or alienated from their original spiritual home. But if, by exposure to the work of a particular mission, they move to a greater potential for love, joy, forgiveness—the gifts of the Spirit—this is evidence of a genuine Christian transformation, of authentic conversion. If, on the other hand, their change in religious allegiance was prompted by a desire for or the promise of economic or social advantages, or if it results in a transformation which reduces people's potential for experiencing the gifts of the Spirit, this is evidence of proselytism.

Churches can help to defend their own flocks from the negative impact of proselytism by better educating and meeting the spiritual needs of their members, and addressing any alienation, dissatisfaction or ignorance they might be experiencing. In this way, believers in the community are equipped to become missionaries themselves, filled with joy, love and peace.

Recommendation

Members of the WCC have on several occasions analyzed, defined and condemned proselytism, and the texts cited above are excellent examples. Yet the issues remain, as does the practice of proselytism—at times involving also WCC member churches. Surely the proliferation of some lay missionary organizations not subject to the guidance and control of ecclesiastical authorities makes it difficult or even impossible satisfactorily to address this continuing problem. Yet F&O/CWME might explore ways in which the World Council could enter into a sharing of memories of the stories that motivate and inspire evangelism and mission, in particular with those groups which have not previously been receptive to WCC affirmations on ecclesiology, missiology, evangelism and proselytism.

2.13

Church, Evangelization, and the Bonds of *Koinonia*

A Report of the International Consultation between the Catholic Church and the World Evangelical Alliance (1993–2002)[1]

Editor's Introduction

THE EXCERPTS REPRODUCED HERE are from a World Evangelical Alliance Report from 2003.[2] The selected paragraphs come from "Part II. Catholics, Evangelicals, and Evangelization in Light of Koinonia." The Appendix to the document gives some helpful background:

> Increasing contacts between Evangelicals and Catholics during the 1970s and 1980s provide a background for the international consultations between the World Evangelical Fellowship and the Catholic Church that have taken place since 1993.
>
> Among these contacts, an international dialogue on mission between some Evangelicals and Roman Catholics took place between 1978 and 1984. On the Catholic side it was sponsored by the Vatican's Secretariat (after 1988, Pontifical Council) for

---

1. Reproduced with kind permission of the Department for Theological Concerns of World Evangelical Alliance.
2. For the full report, see ICCCWEA, "Church, Evangelization."

> *Promoting Christian Unity*. Evangelical participants included some prominent leaders such as John Stott, but the participants came on their own authority, without officially representing any evangelical body. This dialogue led to an important report, published in 1985, the first in which Evangelicals and Catholics discussed together such themes as salvation, evangelization, religious liberty, and proselytism.

(61) CONCERNING "PROSELYTISM," IT should be pointed out that the understanding of the word has changed considerably in recent years in some circles. In the Bible the word proselyte was devoid of negative connotations. The term referred to someone apart from Israel who, by belief in Yahweh and acceptance of the law, became a member of the Jewish community. It carried the positive meaning of being a convert to Judaism (Exod 12:48–49). Christianity took over this positive and unobjectionable meaning to describe a person who converted from paganism. Until the twentieth century, mission work and proselytism were largely synonymous and without objectionable connotations (B 32, 33). It is only in the twentieth century that the term has come to be applied to winning members from each (B 33), as an illicit form of evangelism (P 90). At least, in some Evangelical circles proselytism is not a pejorative term; in Catholic and most ecumenical circles it is. The attempt to "win members from each other" (B 33) by unworthy means is negative and pejorative proselytism. Members of our communions have been guilty of proselytism in this negative sense. It should be avoided.

(62) We affirm, therefore, "the following things should be avoided: offers to temporal or material advantages . . . improper use of situations of distress . . . using political, social and economic pressure as a means of obtaining conversion . . . casting unjust and uncharitable suspicion on other denominations; comparing the strengths and ideals of one community with the weakness and practices of another community" (B 36). This issue of seeking to win members from other churches has ecclesiologically and missiologically significant consequences, which require further exploration.

(63) Unethical methods of evangelization must be sharply distinguished from the legitimate act of persuasively presenting the Gospel. If a Christian, after hearing a responsible presentation of the Gospel, freely chooses to join a different Christian community, it should not automatically be concluded that such a transfer is the result of proselytism (P 93, 94).

(64) Catholic-Evangelical relations have been troubled by the practice of seeking to evangelize people who are already members of a church, which causes misunderstanding and resentment, especially when Evangelicals seek

to "convert" baptized Catholics away from the Roman Catholic Church. This is more than a verbal conflict about different uses of terms like conversion, Christian, and church. Evangelicals speak of "nominal Christianity," referring to those who are Christians in name, but only marginally Christian in reality, even if they have been baptized. Nominal Christians are contrasted with converted believers, who can testify to a living union with Christ, whose confession is biblical and whose faith is active in love. This is a sharp distinction common among Evangelicals, who see nominal Christians as needing to be won to a personal relation with the Lord and Savior. Evangelicals seek to evangelize nominal members of their own churches, as well as of others; they see this activity as an authentic concern for the Gospel, and not as a reprehensible kind of "sheep-stealing" (E.iii). Catholics also speak of "evangelizing" such people, although they refer to them as "lapsed" or "inactive" rather than as "nominal," and still regard them as "Christian" since they are baptized believers. They are understandably offended whenever Evangelicals appear to regard all Roman Catholics as nominal Christians, or whenever they base their evangelism on a distorted view of Catholic teaching and practice.

(65) We agree that a distinction must be made between one's estimate of the doctrines and practices of a church and the judgment that bears on an individual's spiritual condition, e.g., his or her relationship to Christ and to the Church.

(66) As to an individual's spiritual or religious condition, whether a person is nominal, lapsed, inactive, or fallen away, a negative judgment is suspect of being intrusive unless the person to be evangelized is the source of that information. The spiritual condition of a person is always a mystery. Listening should be first, together with a benevolent presumption of charity, and in all cases we may share our perception and experience of the Good News only in a totally respectful attitude towards those we seek to evangelize. This attitude should also be the case apart from evangelization in all attempts at persuading brothers and sisters in what we believe to be true.

(67) Evangelicals and Catholics are challenged to repent of the practice of misrepresenting each other, either because of laziness in study, or unwillingness to listen, prejudice, or unethical judgments (E.i). We repent of the culpable ignorance that neglects readily accessible knowledge of the other's tradition (P 93). We are keenly aware of the command: "Thou shall not bear false witness against thy neighbor" (Exod 20:16).

(68) We repent of those forms of evangelization prompted by competition and personal prestige, and of efforts to make unjust or uncharitable reference to the beliefs or practices of other religious communities in order to win adherents (E.i, p.91, J.19). We repent of the use of similar means

for retaining adherents. We deplore competitive forms of evangelism that habitually pit ourselves against other Christians (P 93).³ All forms of evangelization should witness to the glory of God.

(69) We repent of unworthy forms of evangelization which aim at pressuring people to change their church affiliation in ways that dishonor the Gospel, and by methods which compromise rather than enhance the freedom of the believer and the truth of the Gospel (B 31).

(70) Thus agreeing, we commit ourselves to seeking a "newness of attitudes" in our understanding of each other's intentions.⁴

DIALOGUE DOCUMENTS

B: *Summons to Witness to Christ in Today's World: A Report on the Baptist-Roman Catholic International Conversations* 1984–1988, Pontifical Council for Promoting Christian Unity, *Information Service [IS]* 72 (1990/I) 5–14.

E: *The Evangelical-Roman Catholic Dialogue on Mission* 1977–1984, *A Report*, Basil Meeking and John Stott, eds. (Grand Rapids, 1986); see also *IS* 60 (1986/I-II) 71–97.

J: Joint Working Group Between the Catholic Church and the World Council of Churches, "The Challenge of Proselytism and the Calling to Common Witness", *The Seventh Report*, Appendix C (Geneva, 1998) 43–52; see also *IS* 91 (1996/I–II) 77–83.

P: *Evangelization, Proselytism and Common Witness, The Report from the Fourth Phase of the International Dialogue (1990-1997) Between the Roman Catholic Church and Some Classical Pentecostal Churches and Leaders, IS* 97 (1998/I–II) 38–56; see also *Pneuma* 21:1 (1999) 11–51.

---

3. Cf. *Dignitatis Humanae* 4, 12; John Paul II, "Tertio Millennio Adveniente" 35
4. Cf. Vatican II, *Unitatis Redintegratio* 7; Eph 4:23.

2.14

Proselytism Policy Statement[1]
A Paper from the Micah Network Disaster Management Working Group, South Asia

Micah Network 2007

CONTEXT

THE ARREST OF SHELTER NOW workers in Afghanistan for "proselytizing" in August 2001 led to intense media interest in the way Christian aid and development organizations work in a country without religious freedom. The ensuing coverage was generally critical of Christian organizations and saw them as guilty, at worst, of using people's vulnerability in order to entice them to change their religion or, at best, of hiding their true intentions from the authorities. This paper seeks to give guidance with reference to this issue for Micah Network members.

DEFINING PROSELYTISM

THE DICTIONARY DEFINITION OF "proselytism" refers only to conversion from one opinion, creed or party to another. However, members of various religious traditions and of the international development community and media have come to understand "proselytism" as involving

---

1. Reproduced with kind permission of the Micah Network. For the original, see Micah Network, "Proselytism Policy Statement."

unjustified manipulation or use of coercive techniques or force to achieve conversion. This policy statement addresses this expanded understanding of "proselytism."

While recognizing that Christians have been guilty of proselytizing in this expanded sense we believe that the practice is inconsistent with New Testament teaching on conversion. Jesus decisively rejected the use of all types of coercion in establishing his kingdom when he was tempted at the beginning of his public ministry. After his resurrection Jesus sent his disciples, filled with the Holy Spirit, into the world with nothing but the message of the gospel, works of love and miraculous signs. The New Testament clearly rejects the use of human force, of any sort, as a means to conversion.

EVANGELISM, CONVERSION, AND PROSELYTISM

We, as Micah Network members exist to show and tell the good news of God's love in Jesus Christ and we long to see people's lives transformed as a result of an encounter with Jesus. This statement expounds how our view of evangelism and conversion differs from a manipulative and coercive proselytism.

STATEMENT

1. While longing to see people coming to a personal faith in Jesus Christ we reject manipulative or coercive proselytism as a way of propagating the Christian faith

2. It is absolutely abhorrent to us to exploit people's vulnerability in order to put pressure on them to convert to our religion. Conversions gained in this way are often superficial and bring no credit to the converts or the Christian faith in general.

3. There is a crucial difference between using aid in order to put pressure on needy people to convert and dispensing aid while hoping and praying that those who receive it come to believe in Jesus Christ.

4. We unequivocally affirm the Code of Conduct for the International Red Cross and Red Crescent Movement and NGO's in Disaster Relief,[2]

---

2. The relevant part of this Code is section 3: "*Aid will not be used to further a particular political or religious standpoint.* Humanitarian aid will be given according to the need of individuals, families and communities. Notwithstanding the right of Non Governmental Humanitarian Agencies to espouse particular political or religious opinions,

which says that aid will not be used to further a particular political or religious standpoint. Compliance of NGOs from all religious and political traditions, which sign up to this code, should be stringently tested.

5. We are not involved in giving relief to the needy so that we can evangelise but because it is our Christian calling to give relief to the needy. Where there is freedom to evangelise our calling to help the needy is not be affected.

6. We do not believe that it is possible to dissociate what we are as Christians from what we do. We are prepared to accept the restriction placed upon us by certain governments that hinder us from taking the initiative in sharing our faith with those we serve. However, we believe that governments have no authority to stop us truthfully explaining our faith when we are asked to do so. If someone asks why we are serving them then we claim the right to say that it is out of obedience to Jesus Christ and in response to his love. Religious traditions other than Christianity value truthfulness and honesty and, therefore, we can expect these virtues to be respected even in Christians. The challenge for us as Christians is to make sure that our motivation in serving the poor is indeed obedience to and love for Jesus.

7. We believe that it is unreasonable of governments to expect us not to behave as Christians when serving the poor in their country. Praying and reading the Bible privately and with other Christians are activities that are fundamental to our lives as Christians. Therefore, we should be allowed to have Bibles and a reasonable amount of other Christian literature. We should also be free to associate with other Christian workers, as is appropriate for the purpose of fellowship and worship.

8. Where there is a Christian community, however small, we believe that it is reasonable that aid workers from outside that community should be allowed to associate with them. However, we recognize the crucial importance of being sensitive to the position of a local church and of doing everything possible to avoid doing anything that will make their position more difficult than it is.

9. In seeking official entry to serve the needy in countries that restrict Christian activity we will be very open about our Christian identity

---

we affirm that assistance will not be dependent on the adherence of the recipients to those opinions. We will not tie the promise, delivery or distribution of assistance to embracing or acceptance of a particular political or religious creed." [Editor's note: see IFRC et al., "Code of Conduct."]

and motivation. It is our intention to be open in our actions and motivations, able to defend any accusation of manipulative or coercive proselytism by our transparency.

10. While seeking transparency in our official relationship with any government we appreciate that it is often difficult for local organizations to operate in the same way.

11. We reject the use of coercion of any sort in the process of conversion or in keeping people as adherents of a particular faith. As Christians we affirm the principles of freedom of religion and tolerance of differences of belief, which arise from our understanding of the biblical view of humanity and the nature of Christian mission as shown to us by Christ and his apostles. We can appreciate the unease of zealous religious people of various traditions when they see freedom of religion become freedom of irreligion in many Western countries but we still believe that to be religious because one wants to be is superior to being religious because one has to be.

12. We endorse Article 18 of the International Covenant on Civil and Political Rights which states, "Everyone shall have the right to freedom of thought, conscience and religion. This right shall include freedom to have or to adopt a religion or belief of his choice, and freedom, either individually or in community with others and in public or private, to manifest his religion or belief in worship, observance, practice and teaching."

CONCLUSION

Believing that God the Father has called us to serve the poor in the name of Jesus and in the power of the Holy Spirit, we are prepared to go anywhere to fulfil our calling. We do not hide the fact that we go as servants of Jesus Christ. However, we recognise that we all inevitably carry with us the burden of those aspects of our own culture that are profoundly godless. Our prayer is that as we serve we will be able to see and reject what is bad in our culture and that those we serve will be able to distinguish between the cultural godlessness of our own culture and the Christian values that inform and shape our lives and practice.

2.15

Lausanne Movement Documents[1]

- Lausanne Covenant (1974)
- Lausanne Occasional Papers 10 and 19 (1980)
- Manila Manifesto (1989)
- The Cape Town Commitment (2011)
- South Asia Regional Consultation (2012)

Editor's Introduction

THE LAUSANNE MOVEMENT BEGAN in 1974 with the first International Congress on World Evangelization, under the leadership of Billy Graham and John Stott. "Graham perceived the need for a global congress to re-frame Christian mission in a world of political, economic, intellectual, and religious upheaval. The church, he believed, had to grasp the ideas and values behind rapid changes in society."[2] The Congress was held in Lausanne, Switzerland (where the World Evangelical Fellowship, now the World Evangelical Alliance, had its head office), in July 1974. "A year later, the Lausanne Committee for World Evangelization (LCWE, now known as the Lausanne Movement) was formed. Its aim then, as now, is to facilitate global collaboration in making Christ known to all people."[3]

One characteristic of the LCWE/LM is the production of many documents that have helped define and shape evangelical missions in the ensuing decades. The most notable is The Lausanne Covenant, arising directly from

---

1. Reproduced with kind permission of Lausanne Movement.
2. Lausanne Movement, "Legacy of the Lausanne Movement."
3. Lausanne Movement, "Legacy of the Lausanne Movement."

the first Congress. Both subsequent Congresses have produced important statements: *The Manila Manifesto* (1989) and *The Cape Town Commitment* (2011). However, in the intervening years there have been many Lausanne Occasional Papers (LOPs), arising from smaller conferences and consultations.[4] I reproduce here selections from various documents. Proselytism, per se, is not a strong theme within Lausanne documents, but religious liberty, mission and evangelism feature strongly.

The first document is an extract from the 1974 Lausanne Covenant, firstly on Spiritual Conflict (in which the authors acknowledge that, "that we ourselves are not immune to worldliness of thoughts and action . . . desirous to ensure a response to the gospel, we have compromised our message, [and] manipulated our hearers through pressure techniques") and then on Freedom and Persecution.

This is followed by a paragraph from "Christian Witness to Nominal Christians among Roman Catholics" (LOP 10) and by a lengthy quote from "Christian Witness to Nominal Christians among the Orthodox" (LOP 19). These illustrate the approach to intra-Christian relationships adopted by an influential segment of the evangelical constituency. However, "The Manila Manifesto," the next document, offers a welcome and more nuanced perspective.

The Cape Town Commitment develops this view further, and the final quote, from the "South Asia Regional Consultation: Report and Commitment" (2013), shows a further development in approach.

THE LAUSANNE COVENANT[5] (1974)

12. Spiritual Conflict

WE BELIEVE THAT WE are engaged in constant spiritual warfare with the principalities and powers of evil, who are seeking to overthrow the Church and frustrate its task of world evangelization. We know our need to equip ourselves with God's armour and to fight this battle with the spiritual weapons of truth and prayer. For we detect the activity of our enemy, not only in false ideologies outside the Church, but also inside it in false gospels which twist Scripture and put people in the place of God. We need both watchfulness and discernment to safeguard the biblical gospel. We acknowledge that we ourselves are not immune to worldliness of thoughts and action, that is, to a surrender to secularism. For example, although careful studies

---

4. At time of writing, there are sixty-six Lausanne Occasional Papers. See Lausanne Movement, "Content Library."

5. See also Stott, *Lausanne Covenant*.

of church growth, both numerical and spiritual, are right and valuable, we have sometimes neglected them. At other times, desirous to ensure a response to the gospel, we have compromised our message, manipulated our hearers through pressure techniques, and become unduly preoccupied with statistics or even dishonest in our use of them. All this is worldly. The Church must be in the world; the world must not be in the Church (Eph 6:11–18; 2 Cor 2:17; 4:2–4; 10:3–5; John 17:15; 1 John 2:18–26; 4:1–3; Gal 1:6–9).

13. Freedom and Persecution

It is the God-appointed duty of every government to secure conditions of peace, justice and liberty in which the Church may obey God, serve the Lord Jesus Christ, and preach the gospel without interference. We therefore pray for the leaders of nations and call upon them to guarantee freedom of thought and conscience, and freedom to practice and propagate religion in accordance with the will of God and as set forth in The Universal Declaration of Human Rights. We also express our deep concern for all who have been unjustly imprisoned, and especially for those who are suffering for their testimony to the Lord Jesus. We promise to pray and work for their freedom. At the same time we refuse to be intimidated by their fate. God helping us, we too will seek to stand against injustice and to remain faithful to the gospel, whatever the cost. We do not forget the warnings of Jesus that persecution is inevitable (1 Tim 1:1–4; Acts 4:19; 5:29; Col 3:24; Heb 13:1–3; Luke 4:18; Gal 5:11; 6:12; Matt 5:10–12; John 15:18–21).

LAUSANNE OCCASIONAL PAPERS 10 AND 19 (1980)[6]

Christian Witness to Nominal Christians among Roman Catholics[7]

Introduction

Among approximately one billion people in the world who are classified as "Christians" it is recognized that many still need to be evangelized. They are "nominal Christians" who have not committed themselves to Jesus Christ and do not acknowledge his claims on their lives. These nominal Christians

---

6. See also Lausanne Movement, "Statement to the Churches on Nominality."

7. Lausanne Movement, *Christian Witness to Nominal Christians among Roman Catholics*.

are found extensively among Protestants, Orthodox, and Roman Catholics. This document will focus on the third category. Other study groups are concentrating on evangelizing nominal Christians among Protestants and Orthodox.

Christian Witness to Nominal Christians among the Orthodox[8]

1. Introduction

The history of the Orthodox churches goes back to the early centuries. Throughout many centuries of persecution, these churches bravely proclaimed the gospel and were very much alive.

This history reflects the reality of the often-quoted axiom, "The blood of the martyrs is the seed of the church." Today, however, many of its members are Christians only in name. *A nominal Christian Orthodox is any person who is born into an Orthodox family and is baptized by his church. He may or may not attend his church and may participate in the sacraments, but he does not have a personal experience of salvation and a relationship with our Lord Jesus Christ.*[9] The objectives of this paper, therefore, are to outline the historical development of the theology of the Orthodox Church, to survey the contemporary situation in matters of faith and practice, and to suggest appropriate approaches....

A. Terminology

B. Membership

C. Expansion

D. Government

E. Stages in the History of Christendom

2. Historical Development of Orthodox Theology

A. The Church of the General Councils (325–787)

(i) The Council of Nicaea (325)

(ii) The Council of Constantinople (381)

(iii) The Council of Ephesus (431)

---

8. Lausanne Movement, *Christian Witness to Nominal Christians among the Orthodox*. [Editor's note: I have edited the text down but left the headings and sub-headings to give the reader a sense of the context and structure of the entire paper.]

9. [Editor's note: emphasis added.]

    (iv) The Council of Chalcedon (451)

    (v) The Council of Constantinople (553)

    (vi) The Council of Constantinople (680–681)

    (vii) The Council of Nicaea (787)

B. The Church during the Byzantine Empire

C. The Great Schism (1054)

D. The Orthodox Church under Islam

E. The Orthodox Church and the Reformation

F. Theology and Worship]

3. Contemporary Situation

A. Eastern Europe[10]

Political and Cultural: Culturally, if not politically, the lands of Eastern Europe present such a varied "mosaic" of diversified elements that no generalizations are possible. There are countries which prior to 1939 were characterized by high industrial development (East Germany) and Western democracy (Czechoslovakia), while others contained some of Europe's most backward communities (Albania, Bulgaria). Stalin attempted to impose by force the same form of totalitarianism on all, but the results varied in each case.

Approaching the Orthodox in these countries need not, however, involve us in a detailed political examination of each main relevant country (USSR, Poland, Romania, Yugoslavia, Bulgaria, and Albania). It is much more important to know the religious/cultural background of each country; and, for practical purposes, the shortcut to this is the study produced by the British Council of Churches, written by Trevor Beeson in 1974 and entitled "Discretion and Valour: Religious Conditions in Russia and Eastern Europe." To understand the cultural background of Orthodoxy, however, more extended study is necessary, and not only study, but a willingness to empathise, such as very few Evangelical Christians have ever been willing to do.

---

10. I have included Eastern Europe because many allegations of proselytism by evangelicals against the Orthodox communities arise within the former Soviet countries.

To generalise, there are probably about one hundred twenty Protestant missions active in Eastern Europe today. Of course, many of these are very small, and, among them, there is hardly anyone well enough versed in Orthodox theology to make a meaningful approach possible. . . .

[B. Western Europe

C. Greece, Cyprus, Istanbul

D. India

E. Middle East

F. Egypt

G. Ethiopia

H. United States and Canada

I. Australia and New Zealand

J. Other countries] . . .

4. *Strategy of Witnessing to Nominal Christians among the Orthodox*

In dealing with the issue of a Christian witness among nominal Christians from any tradition, one must have a deep sense of the lostness of religious people. Just because a person is named among Christian peoples and has a form of godliness does not mean that he has the life-changing power of the gospel. The most subtly lost people are those who rely on the thought that they are Christians, without really knowing what that means. Orthodox people are hard to reach with the gospel message, because most of them believe they do not need to be reached. Working with the rough nominal Orthodox will require positive, definite means and a carefully planned strategy.

A. Hindrances from Without

(i) Political Hindrances:

(a) *In communist countries* the political hindrance is paramount. . . .

(b) *The Nationalistic Problem* appears in some countries because church and state are united and inter-related. This makes it difficult for the people to separate themselves from their church without being accused of denouncing their national and cultural heritage. The confusion of religious and patriotic zeal also detracts from the average person's understanding of the gospel.

(c) *In countries where governments are influenced by other religions* (Muslim, Hindu, Buddhist, etc.) the authorities often put pressure on Christians, in order to hinder the progress of Christianity.

(ii) *Material Hindrances* ...

B. Hindrances from Within Orthodoxy

(i) *Cultural Hindrances* ...

(ii) *Pride, Ignorance, Prejudice, and Fanaticism* ...

(iii) *Credibility of the Priests* ...

(iv) *Cardinal Doctrinal Differences* ...

Christian Influence Considered Foreign:
Through the years, the Lord used missionaries from other countries to bring the gospel to Orthodox countries. Thousands of people have been saved, and hundreds of churches have been established, Foreign missionaries are still needed today, according to local circumstances and cultures. (They cannot reside in most countries of Eastern Europe, and there is a limited scope of what they can do.) However Orthodox people have a pride which inhibits their welcoming foreigners, who are considered, by many, to be agents of foreign propaganda. We realise that missions have helped very much in spreading the gospel through institutions, literature, schools, hospitals, orphanages, and in other ways. Missionaries who come from abroad should not ignore the culture of the people, but rather need to adjust themselves to the local situation. We see the need for a closer co-operation between churches and missions.

C. Hindrances from Within the Evangelical Community

(i) *Fragmented witness* ...

(ii) *Lack of zeal and readiness* ...

(iii) *Spiritual immaturity* ...

(iv) *Lack of knowledge and respect for Orthodoxy:*

Among Evangelicals, even in Orthodox countries, there is widespread ignorance of the tradition and faith of the Orthodox church. Often wisdom is not used in evangelism. Many Evangelicals ignore that which is positive in Orthodox theology and practice, assuming that everything in Orthodoxy is wrong.

Protestants in Western Europe and North America are almost totally unaware of the recent history of the persecuted church in Eastern Europe. They do not help the persecuted church as much as they would desire because of government restrictions. A major educational and support programme needs to be undertaken by the Christians who subscribe to the Lausanne Covenant.

(v) Lack of co-ordination of mission efforts . . .

D. Overcoming the Hindrances

(i) By showing love and respect to nominal Orthodox. . . .

(ii) By showing respect to the Orthodox tradition as the oldest Christian church with her rich history which is beneficial to Christians of all traditions.

(iii) By exploiting things we share in common with Orthodoxy. . . .

(iv) By presenting the gospel to the Orthodox. . . .

MANILA MANIFESTO[11] (1989)

Editor's Introduction

THE MANILA MANIFESTO AROSE *out of the Second Lausanne Congress held in Manila in 1989. It begins with Twenty-One Affirmations, followed by three main sections: A. The Whole Gospel; B. The Whole Church; and C. The Whole World, with a short Conclusion. There are twelve numbered sections (1–4 in A; 5–9 in B and 10–12 in C).*

I reproduce below B.9 and C.11–12. These show a more nuanced approach to ecumenical relationships than is evidenced from the preceding LOPs (§9–10), and develop the thinking of Lausanne on religious freedom (§12).

B. The Whole Church

THE WHOLE GOSPEL HAS to be proclaimed by the whole church. All the people of God are called to share in the evangelistic task. Yet without the Holy Spirit of God all their endeavors will be fruitless.

9. Cooperating in Evangelism

Evangelism and unity are closely related in the New Testament. Jesus prayed that his people's oneness might reflect his own oneness with the Father, in order that the world might believe in him, and Paul exhorted the Philippians to "contend as one person for the faith of the gospel." In contrast to this biblical vision, we are ashamed of the suspicions and rivalries, the dogmatism over non-essentials, the power struggles and empire-building which spoil our evangelistic witness. We affirm that co-operation in evangelism is indispensable, first because it is the will of God, but also because the gospel of reconciliation is discredited by our disunity, and because, if the task of world evangelization is ever to be accomplished, we must engage in it together.

"Cooperation" means finding unity in diversity. It involves people of different temperaments, gifts, calling and cultures, national churches and mission agencies, all ages and both sexes working together.

We are determined to put behind us once and for all, as a hangover from the colonial past, the simplistic distinction between First World sending and Two-Third World receiving countries. For the great new fact of our era is the internationalization of missions. Not only are a large majority of all evangelical Christians now non-Western, but the number of Two-Thirds World missionaries will soon exceed those from the West. We believe that

---

11. Lausanne Movement, *Manila Manifesto*.

mission teams, which are diverse in composition but united in heart and mind, constitute a dramatic witness to the grace of God.

Our reference to "the whole church" is not a presumptuous claim that the universal church and the evangelical community are synonymous. For we recognize that there are many churches which are not part of the evangelical movement. Evangelical attitudes to the Roman Catholic and Orthodox Churches differ widely. Some evangelicals are praying, talking, studying Scripture, and working with these churches. Others are strongly opposed to any form of dialogue or cooperation with them. All evangelicals are aware that serious theological differences between us remain. Where appropriate, and so long as biblical truth is not compromised, cooperation may be possible in such areas as Bible translation, the study of contemporary theological and ethical issues, social work, and political action. We wish to make it clear, however, that common evangelism demands a common commitment to the biblical gospel.

Some of us are members of churches which belong to the World Council of Churches and believe that a positive yet critical participation in its work is our Christian duty. Others among us have no link with the World Council. All of us urge the World Council of Churches to adopt a consistent biblical understanding of evangelism.

We confess our own share of responsibility for the brokenness of the body of Christ, which is a major stumbling block to world evangelization. We determine to go on seeking that unity in truth for which Christ prayed. We are persuaded that the right way forward towards closer cooperation is frank and patient dialogue on the basis of the Bible, with all who share our concerns. To this we gladly commit ourselves (John 17:11, 20–23; Phil 1:3–5, 15, 17, 27; 2:3, 4; Rom 14:1–15:2; Eph 2:14–16; 4:1–7; Acts 20:4).

C. The Whole World

The whole gospel has been entrusted to the whole church, in order that it may be made known to the whole world. It is necessary, therefore, for us to understand the world into which we are sent (Mark 16:15).

11. The Challenge of AD 2000 and Beyond

The world population today is approaching six billion people. One third of them nominally confess Christ. Of the remaining four billion half have heard of him and the other half have not. In the light of these figures, we evaluate our evangelistic task by considering four categories of people.

First, there is the potential missionary work force, the committed. In this century this category of Christian believers has grown from about forty million in 1900 to about five hundred million today, and at this moment is growing over twice as fast as any other major religious group.

Secondly, there are the uncommitted. They make a Christian profession (they have been baptized, attend church occasionally, and even call themselves Christians), but the notion of a personal commitment to Christ is foreign to them. They are found in all churches throughout the world. They urgently need to be re-evangelized.[12]

Thirdly, there are the unevangelized. These are people who have a minimal knowledge of the gospel, but have had no valid opportunity to respond to it. They are probably within reach of Christian people if only these will go to the next street, road, village, or town to find them.

Fourthly, there are the unreached. These are the two billion who may never have heard of Jesus as Savior, and are not within reach of Christians of their own people. There are, in fact, some two thousand peoples or nationalities in which there is not yet a vital, indigenous church movement. We find it helpful to think of them as belonging to smaller "people groups" which perceive themselves as having an affinity with each other (e.g., a common culture, language, home, or occupation). The most effective messengers to reach them will be those believers who already belong to their culture and know their language. Otherwise, cross-cultural messengers of the gospel will need to go, leaving behind their own culture and sacrificially identifying with the people they long to reach for Christ. . . .

12. Difficult Situations

Jesus plainly told his followers to expect opposition. "If they persecuted me," he said, "they will persecute you also." He even told them to rejoice over persecution, and reminded them that the condition of fruitfulness was death.

These predictions, that Christian suffering is inevitable and productive, have come true in every age, including our own. There have been many thousands of martyrs. Today the situation is much the same. We earnestly hope that glasnost and perestroika will lead to complete religious freedom in the Soviet Union and other Eastern bloc nations, and that Islamic and Hindu countries will become more open to the gospel. We deplore the recent brutal suppression of China's democratic movement, and we pray that it will not bring further suffering to the Christians. On the whole, however, it seems that ancient religions are becoming less tolerant, expatriates less welcome, and the world less friendly to the gospel.

In this situation we wish to make three statements to governments which are reconsidering their attitude to Christian believers.

---

12. [Editor's note: emphasis added.]

First, Christians are loyal citizens, who seek the welfare of their nation. They pray for its leaders, and pay their taxes. Of course, those who have confessed Jesus as Lord cannot also call other authorities Lord, and if commanded to do so, or to do anything which God forbids, must disobey. But they are conscientious citizens. They also contribute to their country's well-being by the stability of their marriages and their homes, their honesty in business, their hard work, and their voluntary activity in the service of the handicapped and needy. Just governments have nothing to fear from Christians.

Secondly, Christians renounce unworthy methods of evangelism. Though the nature of our faith requires us to share the gospel with others, our practice is to make an open and honest statement of it, which leaves the hearers entirely free to make up their own minds about it. We wish to be sensitive to those of other faiths, and we reject any approach that seeks to force conversion on them.

Thirdly, Christians earnestly desire freedom of religion for all people, not just freedom for Christianity. In predominantly Christian countries, Christians are at the forefront of those who demand freedom for religious minorities. In predominantly non-Christian countries, therefore, Christians are asking for themselves no more than they demand for others in similar circumstances. The freedom to "profess, practice, and propagate" religion, as defined in the Universal Declaration of Human Rights, could and should surely be a reciprocally granted right.

We greatly regret any unworthy witness of which followers of Jesus may have been guilty. We determine to give no unnecessary offense in anything, lest the name of Christ be dishonored. However, the offense of the cross we cannot avoid. For the sake of Christ crucified we pray that we may be ready, by his grace, to suffer and even to die. Martyrdom is a form of witness which Christ has promised especially to honor (John 12:24; 15:20; Matt 5:12; Jer 29:7; 1 Tim 2:1–2; Rom 13:6–7; Acts 4:19; 5:29; 1 Cor 1:18, 23; 2:2; 2 Cor 4:1, 2; 6:3; Phil 1:29; Rev 2:13; 6:9–11; 20:4).

Cape Town Commitment: A Confession of Faith and a Call to Action[13] (2011)

Editor's Introduction

THE THIRD LAUSANNE CONGRESS was held in Cape Town, South Africa, in 2010 as part of the various events to acknowledge the influence of Edinburgh 1910. It was preceded by many smaller preparatory events. These included the Lausanne Theology Working Group which reflected upon the theme of The Whole Church Taking the Whole Gospel to the Whole World.[14]

The Cape Town Commitment (CTC) begins with the Foreword and Preamble, and is followed by two major parts: I. For the Lord We Love: The Cape Town Confession of Faith, and II. For the World We Serve: The Cape Town Call to Action.

The language used is that of love: "The mission of God flows from the love of God. The mission of God's people flows from our love for God and for all that God loves. World evangelization is the outflow of God's love to us and through us" ([1] "We love because God first loved us"), and this love is directed to (2) the living God, (3) the Father, (4) the Son, (5) the Holy Spirit, (6) God's Word, (7) God's World, (8) the gospel of God, (9) the people of God, and (10) the mission of God. Part II is the Call to Action, exemplified by A. Bearing witness to the truth of Christ in a pluralistic, globalized world; B. Building the peace of Christ in our divided and broken world; C. Living the love of Christ among people of other faiths; D. Discerning the will of Christ for world evangelization; E. Calling the Church of Christ back to humility, integrity and simplicity; and F. Partnering in the body of Christ for unity in mission. As is usual, it closes with a Conclusion.

I reproduce passages below that are relevant to proselytism.

I. For the Lord We Love: The Cape Town Confession of Faith

9. WE LOVE THE people of God

The people of God are those from all ages and all nations whom God in Christ has loved, chosen, called, saved and sanctified as a people for his own possession, to share in the glory of Christ as citizens of the new creation. As those, then, whom God has loved from eternity to eternity and throughout all our turbulent and rebellious history, we are commanded to love one another. For "since God so loved us, we also ought to love one another," and thereby "be

---

13. Lausanne Movement, *Cape Town Commitment*.
14. See Lausanne Movement, *Whole Gospel*; *Whole Church*; *Whole World*.

imitators of God . . . and live a life of love, just as Christ loved us and gave himself up for us." Love for one another in the family of God is not merely a desirable option but an inescapable command. Such love is the first evidence of obedience to the gospel, the necessary expression of our submission to Christ's Lordship, and a potent engine of world mission [2 Thess 2:13-14; 1 John 4:11; Eph 5:2; 1 Thess 1:3; 4:9-10; John 13:35].[15]

(A) *Love calls for unity.* Jesus' command that his disciples should love one another is linked to his prayer that they should be one. Both the command and the prayer are missional—"that the world may know you are my disciples," and that "the world may know that you [the Father] sent me" [John 13:34-35; 17:21]. A most powerfully convincing mark of the truth of the gospel is when Christian believers are united in love across the barriers of the world's inveterate divisions—barriers of race, colour, gender, social class, economic privilege or political alignment. However, few things so destroy our testimony as when Christians mirror and amplify the very same divisions among themselves. We urgently seek a new global partnership within the body of Christ across all continents, rooted in profound mutual love, mutual submission, and dramatic economic sharing without paternalism or unhealthy dependency. And we seek this not only as a demonstration of our unity in the gospel, but also for the sake of the name of Christ and the mission of God in all the world.

(B) *Love calls for honesty.* Love speaks truth with grace. No one loved God's people more than the prophets of Israel and Jesus himself. Yet no one confronted them more honestly with the truth of their failure, idolatry and rebellion against their covenant Lord. And in doing so, they called God's people to repent, so that they could be forgiven and restored to the service of God's mission. The same voice of prophetic love must be heard today, for the same reason. Our love for the Church of God aches with grief over the ugliness among us that so disfigures the face of our dear Lord Jesus Christ and hides his beauty from the world—the world that so desperately needs to be drawn to him.

(C) *Love calls for solidarity.* Loving one another includes especially caring for those who are persecuted and in prison for their faith and witness. If one part of the body suffers, all parts suffer with it. We are all, like John, "companions in the suffering and kingdom and patient endurance that are ours in Jesus" [Heb 13:1-3; 1 Cor 12:26; Rev 1:9]. We commit ourselves to share in the suffering of members of the body of Christ throughout the world, through information, prayer, advocacy, and other means of support.

---

15. [Editor's note: in the original, biblical quotes were placed in footnotes, but I have placed them within the text in brackets.]

We see such sharing, however, not merely as an exercise of pity, but longing also to learn what the suffering Church can teach and give to those parts of Christ's body that are not suffering in the same way. We are warned that the Church that feels itself at ease in its wealth and self-sufficiency may, like Laodicea, be the Church that Jesus sees as the most blind to its own poverty, and from which he himself feels a stranger outside the door.[16]

Jesus calls all his disciples together to be one family among the nations, a reconciled fellowship in which all sinful barriers are broken down through his reconciling grace. This Church is a community of grace, obedience and love in the communion of the Holy Spirit, in which the glorious attributes of God and gracious characteristics of Christ are reflected and God's multi-coloured wisdom is displayed. As the most vivid present expression of the kingdom of God, the Church is the community of the reconciled who no longer live for themselves, but for the Saviour who loved them and gave himself for them. . . .

II. Living the Love of Christ among People of Other Faiths

1. "Love your neighbor as yourself" includes persons of other faiths

In view of the affirmations made in *The Cape Town Confession of Faith* section 7d, we respond to our high calling as disciples of Jesus Christ to see people of other faiths as our neighbors in the biblical sense. They are human beings created in God's image, whom God loves and for whose sins Christ died. We strive not only to see them as neighbors, but to obey Christ's teaching by being neighbors to them. We are called to be gentle, but not naïve; to be discerning and not gullible; to be alert to whatever threats we may face, but not ruled by fear.

We are called to share good news in evangelism, but not to engage in unworthy proselytizing. *Evangelism*, which includes persuasive rational argument following the example of the Apostle Paul, is "to make an honest and open statement of the gospel which leaves the hearers entirely free to make up their own minds about it. We wish to be sensitive to those of other faiths, and we reject any approach that seeks to force conversion on them."[17] *Proselytizing*, by contrast, is the attempt to compel others to become "one of us," to "accept our religion," or indeed to "join our denomination."

   A. We commit ourselves to be scrupulously ethical in all our evangelism. Our witness is to be marked by "gentleness and respect, keeping a clear

---

16. Lausanne Movement, *Lausanne Covenant* 4–5.
17. Lausanne Movement, *Manila Manifesto* 12.

conscience" [1 Pet 3:15–16; cf. Acts 19:37]. We therefore reject any form of witness that is coercive unethical, deceptive, or disrespectful.

B. In the name of the God of love, we repent of our failure to seek friendships with people of Muslim, Hindu, Buddhist and other religious backgrounds. In the spirit of Jesus, we will take initiatives to show love, goodwill and hospitality to them.

C. In the name of the God of truth, we (i) refuse to promote lies and caricatures about other faiths, and (ii) denounce and resist the racist prejudice, hatred and fear incited in popular media and political rhetoric.

D. In the name of the God of peace, we reject the path of violence and revenge in all our dealings with people of other faiths, even when violently attacked.

E. We affirm the proper place for dialogue with people of other faiths, just as Paul engaged in debate with Jews and Gentiles in the synagogue and public arenas. As a legitimate part of our Christian mission, such dialogue combines confidence in the uniqueness of Christ and in the truth of the gospel with respectful listening to others. . . .

4. Love respects diversity of discipleship

So called "insider movements" are to be found within several religions. These are groups of people who are now following Jesus as their God and Saviour. They meet together in small groups for fellowship, teaching, worship and prayer centered around Jesus and the Bible while continuing to live socially and culturally within their birth communities, including some elements of its religious observance. This is a complex phenomenon and there is much disagreement over how to respond to it. Some commend such movements. Others warn of the danger of syncretism. Syncretism, however, is a danger found among Christians everywhere as we express our faith within our own cultures. We should avoid the tendency, when we see God at work in unexpected or unfamiliar ways, either (i) hastily to classify it and promote it as a new mission strategy, or (ii) hastily to condemn it without sensitive contextual listening.

A. In the spirit of Barnabas who, on arrival in Antioch, "saw the evidence of the grace of God" and "was glad and encouraged them all to remain true to the Lord" [Acts 11:20–24], we would appeal to all those who are concerned with this issue to:

(1) Take as their primary guiding principle the apostolic decision and practice: "We should not make it difficult for the Gentiles who are turning to God" [Acts 15:19].

(2) Exercise humility, patience and graciousness in recognizing the diversity of viewpoints, and conduct conversations without stridency and mutual condemnation [Rom 14:1–3]. . . .

6. Love works for religious freedom for all people

Upholding human rights by defending religious freedom is not incompatible with following the way of the cross when confronted with persecution. There is no contradiction between being willing personally to suffer the abuse or loss of our own rights for the sake of Christ, and being committed to advocate and speak up for those who are voiceless under the violation of their human rights. We must also distinguish between advocating the rights of people of other faiths and endorsing the truth of their beliefs. We can defend the freedom of others to believe and practice their religion without accepting that religion as true.

Let us strive for the goal of religious freedom for all people. This requires advocacy before governments on behalf of Christians *and* people of other faiths who are persecuted. Let us conscientiously obey biblical teaching to be good citizens, to seek the welfare of the nation where we live, to honor and pray for those in authority, to pay taxes, to do good, and to seek to live peaceful and quiet lives. The Christian is called to submit to the state, unless the state commands what God forbids, or prohibits what God commands. If the state thus forces us to choose between loyalty to itself and our higher loyalty to God, we must say No to the state because we have said Yes to Jesus Christ as Lord [Jer 29:7; 1 Pet 2:13–17; 1 Tim 2:1–2; Rom 13:1–7; Exod 1:15–21; Dan 6; Acts 3:19–20; 5:29]. In the midst of all our legitimate efforts for religious freedom for all people, the deepest longing of our hearts remains that all people should come to know the Lord Jesus Christ, freely put their faith in him and be saved, and enter the kingdom of God. . . .

III. Partnering in The Body of Christ for Unity in Mission

Paul teaches us that Christian unity is the creation of God, based on our reconciliation with God and with one another. This double reconciliation has been accomplished through the cross. When we live in unity and work in partnership we demonstrate the supernatural, counter-cultural power of the cross. But when we demonstrate our disunity through failure to partner together, we demean our mission and message, and deny the power of the cross.

1. Unity in the Church

A divided Church has no message for a divided world. Our failure to live in reconciled unity is a major obstacle to authenticity and effectiveness in mission.

We lament the dividedness and divisiveness of our churches and organizations. We deeply and urgently long for Christians to cultivate a spirit of grace and to be obedient to Paul's command to "make every effort to maintain the unity of the Spirit in the bond of peace." While we recognize that our deepest unity is spiritual, we long for greater recognition of the missional power of visible, practical, earthly unity. So we urge Christian sisters and brothers worldwide, for the sake of our common witness and mission, to resist the temptation to split the body of Christ, and to seek the paths of reconciliation and restored unity wherever possible.

2. Partnership in global mission

Partnership in mission is not only about efficiency. It is the strategic and practical outworking of our shared submission to Jesus Christ as Lord. Too often we have engaged in mission in ways that prioritize and preserve our own identities (ethnic, denominational, theological, etc.), and have failed to submit our passions and preferences to our one Lord and Master. The supremacy and centrality of Christ in our mission must be more than a confession of faith; it must also govern our strategy, practice and unity.

We rejoice in the growth and strength of emerging mission movements in the majority world and the ending of the old pattern of "from the West to the Rest." But we do not accept the idea that the baton of mission responsibility has passed from one part of the world Church to another. There is no sense in rejecting the past triumphalism of the West, only to relocate the same ungodly spirit in Asia, Africa, or Latin America. No one ethnic group, nation, or continent can claim the exclusive privilege of being the ones to complete the Great Commission. Only God is sovereign.

We stand together as church and mission leaders in all parts of the world, called to recognize and accept one another, with equality of opportunities to contribute together to world mission. Let us, in submission to Christ, lay aside suspicion, competition and pride and be willing to learn from those whom God is using, even when they are not from our continent, nor of our particular theology, nor of our organization, nor of our circle of friends.

Partnership is about more than money, and unwise injection of money frequently corrupts and divides the Church. Let us finally prove that the Church does not operate on the principle that those who have the most money have all the decision-making power. Let us no longer impose our own preferred names, slogans, programmes, systems and methods on other parts of the Church. Let us instead work for true mutuality of North and

South, East and West, for interdependence in giving and receiving, for the respect and dignity that characterizes genuine friends and true partners in mission.

South Asia Regional Consultation: Report and Commitment (2013)

Editor's Introduction

THIS DOCUMENT ORIGINATED IN *November 2012 at a regional consultation held in Sri Lanka. It "brought together thirty two evangelical leaders from five South Asian nations namely, Sri Lanka, Nepal, Bhutan, Pakistan and India to joyfully witness to the truth and transforming power of the Gospel of Jesus Christ among our diverse peoples, and to prayerfully deliberate on how the Cape Town Commitment (CTC) affirms and clarifies the faith and action of the South Asian church in the specific context of our many challenges. Nine relevant themes derived from the CTC "Call to Action" provided a framework to discern the challenges facing the South Asian church, and our priorities for missional engagement."*[18] *The nine themes are developed, followed by a series of "Commitments" relevant to each. The short extract below is from Theme A, "Confessing Christ in a Pluralistic Context."*

1. WE ARE CALLED to share the good news in evangelism, but not unworthy proselytism. We must reject the indiscriminate use of "warfare" vocabulary, numerical growth as an end in itself and an attitude of socio-cultural superiority. Rather, our witness must be characterized by grace, respect and sensitivity. This we do in the spirit of humility and servanthood, perhaps even entailing suffering and death.

---

18. Lausanne Movement, *South Asia Consultation*, 1.

2.16

Christian Witness in a Multi-Religious World

Recommendations for Conduct[1]

WCC/RCC/WEA 2011

Editor's Introduction

THIS IS A DOCUMENT *jointly produced by the World Council of Churches, Pontifical Council for Interreligious Dialogue and the World Evangelical Alliance, dating from 2011. Whilst this document does not directly address the issue of proselytism, nonetheless, it was acknowledged in the drafting and publishing that many of the Recommendations within this document also have relevance within the debates about proselytism. It is included within this Reader for this reason.*

PREAMBLE

MISSION BELONGS TO THE very being of the church. Proclaiming the word of God and witnessing to the world is essential for every Christian. At the same time, it is necessary to do so according to gospel principles, with full respect and love for all human beings.

---

1. Reproduced with kind permission of the Department for Theological Concerns of World Evangelical Alliance.

Aware of the tensions between people and communities of different religious convictions and the varied interpretations of Christian witness, the Pontifical Council for Interreligious Dialogue (PCID), the World Council of Churches (WCC) and, at the invitation of the WCC, the World Evangelical Alliance (WEA), met during a period of five years to reflect and produce this document to serve as a set of recommendations for conduct on Christian witness around the world. This document does not intend to be a theological statement on mission but to address practical issues associated with Christian witness in a multi-religious world.

The purpose of this document is to encourage churches, church councils and mission agencies to reflect on their current practices and to use the recommendations in this document to prepare, where appropriate, their own guidelines for their witness and mission among those of different religions and among those who do not profess any particular religion. It is hoped that Christians across the world will study this document in the light of their own practices in witnessing to their faith in Christ, both by word and deed.

A BASIS FOR CHRISTIAN WITNESS

1. For Christians it is a privilege and joy to give an accounting for the hope that is within them and to do so with gentleness and respect (cf. 1 Pet 3:15).

2. Jesus Christ is the supreme witness (cf. John 18:37). Christian witness is always a sharing in his witness, which takes the form of proclamation of the kingdom, service to neighbor and the total gift of self even if that act of giving leads to the cross. Just as the Father sent the Son in the power of the Holy Spirit, so believers are sent in mission to witness in word and action to the love of the triune God.

3. The example and teaching of Jesus Christ and of the early church must be the guides for Christian mission. For two millennia Christians have sought to follow Christ's way by sharing the good news of God's kingdom (cf. Luke 4:16–20).

4. Christian witness in a pluralistic world includes engaging in dialogue with people of different religions and cultures (cf. Acts 17:22–28).

5. In some contexts, living and proclaiming the gospel is difficult, hindered or even prohibited, yet Christians are commissioned by Christ to continue faithfully in solidarity with one another in their witness to

him (cf. Matt 28:19–20; Mark 16:14–18; Luke 24:44–48; John 20:21; Acts 1:8).

6. If Christians engage in inappropriate methods of exercising mission by resorting to deception and coercive means, they betray the gospel and may cause suffering to others. Such departures call for repentance and remind us of our need for God's continuing grace (cf. Rom 3:23).

7. Christians affirm that while it is their responsibility to witness to Christ, conversion is ultimately the work of the Holy Spirit (cf. John 16:7–9; Acts 10:44–47). They recognize that the Spirit blows where the Spirit wills in ways over which no human being has control (cf. John 3:8).

PRINCIPLES

Christians are called to adhere to the following principles as they seek to fulfil Christ's commission in an appropriate manner, particularly within interreligious contexts.

1. Acting in God's love. Christians believe that God is the source of all love and, accordingly, in their witness they are called to live lives of love and to love their neighbor as themselves (cf. Matt 22:34–40; John 14:15).

2. Imitating Jesus Christ. In all aspects of life, and especially in their witness, Christians are called to follow the example and teachings of Jesus Christ, sharing his love, giving glory and honor to God the Father in the power of the Holy Spirit (cf. John 20:21–23).

3. Christian virtues. Christians are called to conduct themselves with integrity, charity, compassion and humility, and to overcome all arrogance, condescension and disparagement (cf. Gal 5:22).

4. Acts of service and justice. Christians are called to act justly and to love tenderly (cf. Mic 6:8). They are further called to serve others and in so doing to recognize Christ in the least of their sisters and brothers (cf. Matt 25:45). Acts of service, such as providing education, health care, relief services and acts of justice and advocacy are an integral part of witnessing to the gospel. The exploitation of situations of poverty and need has no place in Christian outreach. Christians should denounce and refrain from offering all forms of allurements, including financial incentives and rewards, in their acts of service.

5. Discernment in ministries of healing. As an integral part of their witness to the gospel, Christians exercise ministries of healing. They are called to exercise discernment as they carry out these ministries, fully respecting human dignity and ensuring that the vulnerability of people and their need for healing are not exploited.

6. Rejection of violence. Christians are called to reject all forms of violence, even psychological or social, including the abuse of power in their witness. They also reject violence, unjust discrimination or repression by any religious or secular authority, including the violation or destruction of places of worship, sacred symbols or texts.

7. Freedom of religion and belief. Religious freedom including the right to publicly profess, practice, propagate and change one's religion flows from the very dignity of the human person which is grounded in the creation of all humans beings in the image and likeness of God (cf. Gen 1:26). Thus, all human beings have equal rights and responsibilities. Where any religion is instrumentalized for political ends, or where religious persecution occurs, Christians are called to engage in a prophetic witness denouncing such actions.

8. Mutual respect and solidarity. Christians are called to commit themselves to work with all people in mutual respect, promoting together justice, peace and the common good. Interreligious cooperation is an essential dimension of such commitment.

9. Respect for all people. Christians recognize that the gospel both challenges and enriches cultures. Even when the gospel challenges certain aspects of cultures, Christians are called to respect all people. Christians are also called to discern elements in their own cultures that are challenged by the gospel.

10. Renouncing false witness. Christians are to speak sincerely and respectfully; they are to listen in order to learn about and understand others' beliefs and practices, and are encouraged to acknowledge and appreciate what is true and good in them. Any comment or critical approach should be made in a spirit of mutual respect, making sure not to bear false witness concerning other religions.

11. Ensuring personal discernment. Christians are to acknowledge that changing one's religion is a decisive step that must be accompanied by sufficient time for adequate reflection and preparation, through a process ensuring full personal freedom.

12. Building interreligious relationships. Christians should continue to build relationships of respect and trust with people of different religions so as to facilitate deeper mutual understanding, reconciliation and cooperation for the common good.

RECOMMENDATIONS

The Third Consultation organized by the World Council of Churches and the PCID of the Holy See in collaboration with World Evangelical Alliance with participation from the largest Christian families of faith (Catholic, Orthodox, Protestant, Evangelical and Pentecostal), having acted in a spirit of ecumenical cooperation to prepare this document for consideration by churches, national and regional confessional bodies and mission organizations, and especially those working in interreligious contexts, recommends that these bodies:

- *Study* the issues set out in this document and where appropriate formulate guidelines for conduct regarding Christian witness applicable to their particular contexts. Where possible this should be done ecumenically, and in consultation with representatives of other religions.
- *Build* relationships of respect and trust with people of all religions, in particular at institutional levels between churches and other religious communities, engaging in on-going interreligious dialogue as part of their Christian commitment. In certain contexts, where years of tension and conflict have created deep suspicions and breaches of trust between and among communities, interreligious dialogue can provide new opportunities for resolving conflicts, restoring justice, healing of memories, reconciliation and peace-building.
- *Encourage* Christians to strengthen their own religious identity and faith while deepening their knowledge and understanding of different religions, and to do so also taking into account the perspectives of the adherents of those religions. Christians should avoid misrepresenting the beliefs and practices of people of different religions.
- *Cooperate* with other religious communities engaging in interreligious advocacy towards justice and the common good and, wherever possible, standing together in solidarity with people who are in situations of conflict.
- *Call* on their governments to ensure that freedom of religion is properly and comprehensively respected, recognizing that in many countries

religious institutions and persons are inhibited from exercising their mission.

- *Pray* for their neighbors and their well-being, recognizing that prayer is integral to who we are and what we do, as well as to Christ's mission.

APPENDIX: BACKGROUND TO THE DOCUMENT

1. In today's world there is increasing collaboration among Christians and between Christians and followers of different religions. The Pontifical Council for Interreligious Dialogue (PCID) of the Holy See and the World Council of Churches' Programme on Interreligious Dialogue and Co-operation (WCC-IRDC) have a history of such collaboration. Examples of themes on which the PCID/WCC-IRDC have collaborated in the past are: Interreligious Marriage (1994–1997), Interreligious Prayer (1997–1998) and African Religiosity (2000–2004). This document is a result of their work together.

2. There are increasing interreligious tensions in the world today, including violence and the loss of human life. Politics, economics and other factors play a role in these tensions. Christians too are sometimes involved in these conflicts, whether voluntarily or involuntarily, either as those who are persecuted or as those participating in violence. In response to this the PCID and WCC-IRDC decided to address the issues involved in a joint process towards producing shared recommendations for conduct on Christian witness. The WCC-IRDC invited the World Evangelical Alliance (WEA) to participate in this process, and they have gladly done so.

3. Initially two consultations were held: the first, in Lariano, Italy, in May 2006, was entitled "Assessing the Reality" where representatives of different religions shared their views and experiences on the question of conversion. A statement from the consultation reads in part: "We affirm that, while everyone has a right to invite others to an understanding of their faith, it should not be exercised by violating others' rights and religious sensibilities. Freedom of religion enjoins upon all of us the equally non-negotiable responsibility to respect faiths other than our own, and never to denigrate, vilify or misrepresent them for the purpose of affirming superiority of our faith."

4. The second, an inter-Christian consultation, was held in Toulouse, France, in August 2007, to reflect on these same issues. Questions on

Family and Community, Respect for Others, Economy, Marketing and Competition, and Violence and Politics were thoroughly discussed. The pastoral and missionary issues around these topics became the background for theological reflection and for the principles developed in this document. Each issue is important in its own right and deserves more attention that can be given in these recommendations.

5. The participants of the third (inter-Christian) consultation met in Bangkok, Thailand, January 25–28, 2011, and finalized this document.

2.17

Together Towards Life[1]

WCC/CWME 2013

Editor's Introduction

"TOGETHER TOWARDS LIFE" (TTL) *is the product of several years' work by CWME. It was formally approved by the Central Committee of the WCC in September 2012, and presented to the tenth WCC Assembly in Busan, Korea, in 2013.*

The document is built around four themes: Spirit of Mission: Breath of Life; Spirit of Liberation: Mission from the Margins; Spirit of Community: Church on the Move; and, Spirit of Pentecost: Good News for All. It begins with an introductory section, Together Towards Life: Introducing the Theme, and ends with a section entitled, Feast of Life: Concluding Affirmations.

It complements and builds upon the 1982 WCC statement, "Mission and Evangelism: An Ecumenical Affirmation."

Below are extracts from TTL relevant to the themes of proselytism and religious liberty.

SPIRIT OF COMMUNITY: CHURCH ON THE MOVE

God's Mission and the Church's Unity

62. THE HIGHLY COMPETITIVE environment of the free market economy has unfortunately influenced some churches and para-church movements to seek to be "winners" over others. This can even lead to the adoption of

---

1. Reproduced with kind permission of the WCC.

aggressive tactics to persuade Christians who already belong to a church to change their denominational allegiance. Seeking numerical growth at all costs is incompatible with the respect for others required of Christian disciples. Jesus became our Christ not through power or money but through his self-emptying (*kenosis*) and death on the cross. This humble understanding of mission does not merely shape our methods but is the very nature and essence of our faith in Christ. The church is a servant in God's mission and not the master. The missionary church glorifies God in self-emptying love.

63. The Christian communities in their diversity are called to identify and practice ways of common witness in a spirit of partnership and co-operation, including through mutually respectful and responsible forms of evangelism. Common witness is what the "churches, even while separated, bear together, especially through joint efforts, by manifesting whatever divine gifts of truth and life they already share and experience in common."[2]

. . .

SPIRIT OF PENTECOST: GOOD NEWS FOR ALL

The Call to Evangelize

82. Today's world is marked by excessive assertion of religious identities and persuasions that seem to break and brutalize in the name of God rather than heal and nurture communities. In such a context, it is important to recognize that proselytism is not a legitimate way of practicing evangelism.[3] The Holy Spirit chooses to work in partnership with people's preaching and demonstration of the good news (see Rom 10:14–15; 2 Cor 4:2–6), but it is only God's Spirit who creates new life and brings about rebirth (John 3:5–8; 1 Thess 1:4–6). We acknowledge that evangelism at times has been distorted and lost its credibility because some Christians have forced "conversions" by violent means or the abuse of power. In some contexts, however, accusations of forced conversions are motivated by the desire of dominant groups to keep the marginalized living with oppressed identities and in dehumanizing conditions.

83. Evangelism is sharing one's faith and conviction with other people and inviting them to discipleship, whether or not they adhere to other religious traditions. Such sharing is to take place with both confidence and humility and as an expression of our professed love for our world. If we claim to love God and to love our fellow human beings but fail to share the

---

2. Best and Gassmann, *On the Way to Fuller Koinonia*, 254.
3. WCC, "Towards Common Witness."

good news with them urgently and consistently, we deceive ourselves as to the integrity of our love for either God or people. There is no greater gift we can offer to our fellow human beings than to share and or introduce them to the love, grace, and mercy of God in Christ. ...

Evangelism in Christ's Way

86. Evangelism is sharing the good news both in word and action. Evangelizing through verbal proclamation or preaching of the gospel (*kerygma*) is profoundly biblical. However, if our words are not consistent with our actions, our evangelism is inauthentic. The combination of verbal declaration and visible action bears witness to God's revelation in Jesus Christ and of his purposes. Evangelism is closely related to unity: the love for one another is a demonstration of the gospel we proclaim (John 13:34-35) while disunity is an embarrassment to the gospel (1 Cor 1).

87. There are historical and contemporary examples of faithful, humble service by Christians, working in their own local contexts, with whom the Spirit has partnered to bring about fullness of life. Also, many Christians who lived and worked as missionaries far away from their own cultural contexts did so with humility, mutuality, and respect; God's Spirit also stirred in those communities to bring about transformation.

88. Regrettably, sometimes evangelism has been practiced in ways which betray rather than incarnate the gospel. Whenever this occurs, repentance is in order. Mission in Christ's way involves affirming the dignity and rights of others. We are called to serve others as Christ did (cf. Mark 10:45; Matt 25:45), without exploitation or any form of allurement.[4] In such individualized contexts, it may be possible to confuse evangelism with buying and selling a "product," where *we* decide what aspects Christian life we want to take on. Instead, the Spirit rejects the idea that Jesus' good news for all can be consumed under capitalist terms, and the Spirit calls us to conversion and transformation at a personal level, which leads us to the proclamation of the fullness of life for all.

89. Authentic evangelism is grounded in humility and respect for all and flourishes in the context of dialogue. It promotes the message of the gospel, of healing and reconciliation, in word and deed. "There is no evangelism without solidarity; there is no Christian solidarity that does not involve sharing the message of God's coming reign."[5] Evangelism, therefore,

---

4. WCC et al., "Christian Witness in a Multi-Religious World."

5. WCC, *San Antonio Report*, 26; *Mission and Evangelism*, §34; Duraisingh, *Called to One Hope*, 38.

inspires the building of inter-personal and community relationships. Such authentic relationships are often best nourished in local faith communities and based in local cultural contexts. Christian witness is as much by our presence as by our words. In situations where the public testimony to one's faith is not possible without risking one's life, simply living the gospel may be a powerful alternative.

90. Aware of tensions between people and communities of different religious convictions and varied interpretations of Christian witness, authentic evangelism must always be guided by life-affirming values, as stated in the joint statement on "Christian Witness in a Multi-Religious World: Recommendations for Conduct."[6] ...

Evangelism, Interfaith Dialogue, and Christian Presence

96. Particularly important is dialogue between people of different faiths, not only in multi-religious contexts but equally where there is a large majority of a particular faith. It is necessary to protect rights of minority groups and religious freedom and to enable all to contribute to the common good. Religious freedom should be upheld because it flows from the dignity of the human person, grounded in the creation of all human beings in the image and likeness of God (Gen 1:26). Followers of all religions and beliefs have equal rights and responsibilities. ...

FEAST OF LIFE: CONCLUDING AFFIRMATIONS

110. *We affirm that dialogue and cooperation for life are integral to mission and evangelism.* Authentic evangelism is done with respect for freedom of religion and belief, for all human beings as images of God. Proselytism by violent means, economic incentive, or abuse of power is contrary to the message of the gospel. In doing evangelism it is important to build relations of respect and trust between people of different faiths. We value each and every human culture and recognize that the gospel is not possessed by any group but is for every people. We understand that our task is not to bring God along but to witness to the God who is already there (Acts 17:23–28). Joining in with the Spirit, we are enabled to cross cultural and religious barriers to work together towards life.

---

6. See section 2.16 in this volume.

2.18

Orthodox Perspectives

- Official Documents of the Holy and Great Council of the Orthodox Church
- Russian Orthodox Church, "Basic Principles of Attitude to the Non-Orthodox."

Orthodox

Editor's Introduction

BELOW ARE EXTRACTS FROM *three different Orthodox statements. The first two are "Official Documents of the Holy and Great Council of the Orthodox Church," which "commenced on the Sunday of Pentecost, June 19, 2016, with the Pan-Orthodox concelebration of all the Primates of the participating Orthodox Churches."[1] As such, these are the most authoritative current statements within the Orthodox Church. The Council consisted of delegates from the Ecumenical Patriarchate, the Patriarchate of Alexandria, the Patriarchate of Jerusalem, the Church of Serbia, the Church of Romania, the Church of Cyprus, the Church of Greece, the Church of Poland, the Church of Albania, and the Church of the Czech lands and Slovakia. The third extract is from the Russian Orthodox Church, from a document dealing with the "Basic Principles of Attitude to the Non-Orthodox."[2]*

Proselytism is a significant issue for most Orthodox Churches, and there are many references to it within texts from Orthodox theologians and leaders;

1. Office of the Panorthodox Secretariat, *News Bulletin*, Number 1, 21 June 2016.
2. Russian Orthodox Church, Department for External Church Relations, "Basic Principles of Attitude to the Non-Orthodox."

however, such texts are best viewed as "personal theological opinions."[3] As such they carry significantly reduced authority compared to the three documents reproduced in part below.

OFFICIAL DOCUMENTS OF THE HOLY AND GREAT COUNCIL OF THE ORTHODOX CHURCH

Relations of the Orthodox Church with the Rest of the Christian World[4]

Editor's Introduction

THIS DOCUMENT FROM THE Holy and Great Council of 2016 explains the ecumenical vision of the Orthodox Church in twenty-four paragraphs. The relevant paragraph is 23.

THE ORTHODOX CHURCH HAS a common awareness of the necessity for conducting inter-Christian theological dialogue. It therefore believes that this dialogue should always be accompanied by witness to the world through acts expressing mutual understanding and love, which express the "ineffable joy" of the Gospel (1 Pet 1:8), eschewing every act of proselytism, uniatism, or other provocative act of inter-confessional competition. In this spirit, the Orthodox Church deems it important for all Christians, inspired by common fundamental principles of the Gospel, to attempt to offer with eagerness and solidarity a response to the thorny problems of the contemporary world, based on the prototype of the new man in Christ.

The Mission of the Orthodox Church in Today's World[5]

Editor's Introduction

THE SUB-TITLE OF THIS document is "The contribution of the Orthodox Church in realizing peace, justice, freedom, fraternity and love between peoples, and in the removal of racial and other discriminations." After a few introductory paragraphs the document is divided into six sections: A. The Dignity of the Human Person; B. Freedom and Responsibility; C. Peace and Justice; D. Peace and the Aversion of War; E. The Attitude of the Church Toward

---

3. Orthodox priest in conversation with the editor.
4. https://www.holycouncil.org/-/rest-of-christian-world.
5. https://www.holycouncil.org/-/mission-orthodox-church-todays-world.

Discrimination; and F. The Mission of the Orthodox Church As a Witness of Love through Service. Each section is further divided into numbered paragraphs. The reference to proselytism is found in the Introductory paragraphs, reproduced below.

For God so loved the world that he gave his Only Son, that whoever believes in him should not perish but have eternal life (John 3:16). The Church of Christ exists *in the world*, but is *not of the world* (cf. John 17:11, 14–15). The Church as the Body of the incarnate Logos of God (John Chrysostom, *Homily before Exile*, 2 PG 52, 429) constitutes the living "presence" as the sign and image of the Kingdom of the Triune God in history, proclaims the good news of a *new creation* (2 Cor 5:17), of *new heavens and a new earth in which righteousness dwells* (2 Pet 3:13); news of a world in which *God will wipe away every tear from people's eyes; there shall be no more death, nor sorrow, nor crying. There shall be no more pain* (Rev 21:4–5).

Such hope is experienced and foretasted by the Church, especially each time the Divine Eucharist is celebrated, bringing *together* (1 Cor 11:20) the *scattered children of God* (John 11:52) without regard to race, sex, age, social, or any other condition into a single body where *there is neither Jew nor Greek, there is neither slave nor free, there is neither male nor female* (Gal 3:28; cf. Col 3:11).

This foretaste of the *new creation*—of a world transfigured—is also experienced by the Church in the countenance of her saints who, through their spiritual struggles and virtues, have already revealed the image of the Kingdom of God in this life, thereby proving and affirming that the expectation of a world of peace, justice, and love is not a utopia, but the *substance of things hoped for* (Heb 11:1), attainable through the grace of God and man's spiritual struggle.

Finding constant inspiration in this expectation and foretaste of the Kingdom of God, the Church cannot remain indifferent to the problems of humanity in each period. On the contrary, she shares in our anguish and existential problems, taking upon herself—as the Lord did—our suffering and wounds, which are caused by evil in the world and, like the Good Samaritan, pouring oil and wine upon our wounds through words of *patience and comfort* (Rom 15:4; Heb 13:22), and through love in practice. The word addressed to the world is not primarily meant to judge and condemn the world (cf. John 3:17; 12:47), but rather to offer to the world the guidance of the Gospel of the Kingdom of God—namely, the hope and assurance that evil, no matter its form, does not have the last word in history and must not be allowed to dictate its course.

The conveyance of the Gospel's message according to the last commandant of Christ, *Go therefore and make disciples of all nations, baptizing them in the name of the Father and of the Son and of the Holy Spirit, teaching them to observe all that I have commanded you* (Matt 28:19) is the diachronic mission of the Church. This mission must be carried out not aggressively or by different forms of proselytism, but in love, humility and respect towards the identity of each person and the cultural particularity of each people. All the Orthodox Church have an obligation to contribute to this missionary endeavor.

Drawing from these principles and the accumulated experience and teaching of her patristic, liturgical, and ascetical tradition, the Orthodox Church shares the concern and anxiety of contemporary humanity with regard to fundamental existential questions that preoccupy the world today. She thus desires to help resolve these issues, allowing the *peace of God, which surpasses all understanding* (Phil 4:7), reconciliation, and love to prevail in the world.

THE RUSSIAN ORTHODOX CHURCH

Editor's Introduction

THE EXTRACT BELOW IS *from "Basic Principles of Attitude to the Non-Orthodox," from the Department for External Church Relations of the ROC. This document is again divided into paragraphs: (1) The unity of the Church and the sin of human divisions; (2) The quest for the restoration of the unity; (3) Orthodox witness before the non-Orthodox world; (4) Dialogue with the non-Orthodox; (5) Multilateral dialogue and participation in the work of inter-Christian organizations; (6) Relations of the Russian Orthodox Church with the non-Orthodox on her canonical territory; (7) Internal tasks in relation to dialogue with non-Orthodox confessions; and (8) Conclusion.*

6.1. THE RELATIONS OF the Russian Orthodox Church with non-Orthodox Christian communities in the CIS and Baltic states should be carried out in the same spirit of fraternal co-operation in which the Orthodox Church works with other traditional confessions in order to co-ordinate social work, promote social harmony and put an end to proselytism on the canonical territory of the Russian Orthodox Church.

6.2. The Russian Orthodox Church maintains that the mission of the traditional confessions is possible only if it is carried out without proselytism and not at the expense of "stealing" the faithful, especially with the aid of material benefits. The Christian communities in the CIS and Baltic countries are called to unite their efforts for reconciliation and the moral revival of society and to raise their voice in the defence of human life and human dignity.

6.3. The Orthodox Church draws a clear distinction between the non-Orthodox confessions which declare their faith in the Holy Trinity and the divine-human nature of Jesus Christ, on the one hand, and the sects which reject fundamental Christian doctrines on the other. While recognizing the right of non-Orthodox Christians to witness to their faith and conduct religious education among the population groups that traditionally belong to them, the Orthodox Church is against any destructive missionary activity on the part of sects.[6]

Editor's Commentary

"Proselytism" is not defined within these statements, although several characteristics stand out from the Orthodox perspective: proselytism is provocative and competitive in nature; it comes in various forms, and can be aggressive; it is associated with "'stealing' the faithful" and may involve material inducements. It is contrasted with: mutual understanding and love, joy in the Gospel, Gospel principles, humility and respect of persons and cultural identity, and social engagement and harmony. Proselytism may also be closely associated with "canonical" territories. Additionally, two of these statements concern the relationship of the Orthodox Church with non-Orthodox "confessions" based on the acceptance of the Holy Trinity and the dual, divine-human nature of Jesus Christ. In the broader context of these documents (not reproduced here) the context for this relationship is through ecumenical organizations (such as the World Council of Churches), or bi- or multi-lateral dialogues with other Churches or global bodies.

One such example of this dialogue occurred in February 2016 when Patriarch Kirill met with Pope Francis in Havana, Cuba. One outcome of the meeting was the "Joint Declaration of Pope Francis and Patriarch Kirill of Moscow and All Russia."[7] Paragraph 24 (of 30) highlights proselytism, again set within the context of mutual respect, peace and love.

Orthodox and Catholics are united not only by the shared Tradition of the Church of the first millennium, but also by the mission to preach the

---

6. https://mospat.ru/en/documents/attitude-to-the-non-orthodox/vi.
7. https://mospat.ru/en/2016/02/13/news128178.

Gospel of Christ in the world today. This mission entails mutual respect for members of the Christian communities and excludes any form of proselytism. We are not competitors but brothers, and this concept must guide all our mutual actions as well as those directed to the outside world. We urge Catholics and Orthodox in all countries to learn to live together in peace and love, and to be "in harmony with one another" (Rom 15:5). Consequently, it cannot be accepted that disloyal means be used to incite believers to pass from one Church to another, denying them their religious freedom and their traditions. We are called upon to put into practice the precept of the apostle Paul: "Thus I aspire to proclaim the gospel not where Christ has already been named, so that I do not build on another's foundation" (Rom 15:20).

2.19

Common Declaration of His Holiness Francis and His Holiness Tawadros II[1]

RCC/Coptic Orthodox 2017

Editor's Introduction

ON MAY 10, 1973, Pope Paul VI and the Pope of Alexandria Shenouda III issued a joint Declaration. The meeting and declaration were historic for a number of reasons, not least the "centuries of difficult history" that have existed between the two Churches. One aspect of this history was the mutual accusations of proselytism which the two Popes addressed in their Declaration:

> In the name of this charity [rooted in total fidelity to the one Lord Jesus Christ and in mutual respect for each one's traditions], we reject all forms of proselytism, in the sense of acts by which persons seek to disturb each other's communities by recruiting new members from each other through methods, or because of attitudes of mind, which are opposed to the exigencies of Christian love or to what should characterize the relationships between Churches. Let it cease, where it may exist. Catholics and Orthodox should strive to deepen charity and cultivate mutual consultation, reflection and cooperation in the social and intellectual fields and should humble themselves before God, supplicating Him who, as He has begun this work in us, will bring it to fruition.[2]

---

1. Francis and Tawadros II, "Common Declaration." Reproduced with kind permission of PCPCU.
2. Paul VI and Amba Shenouda III, "Common Declaration."

The Declaration of Pope Francis and Pope Tawadros II, reproduced below, shows how the two Churches have continued to build "the bonds of fraternity and friendship," and, in particular, they mention religious freedom in §8 and repeat baptism in §11.

1. WE, FRANCIS, BISHOP of Rome and Pope of the Catholic Church, and Tawadros II, Pope of Alexandria and Patriarch of the See of Saint Mark, give thanks to God in the Holy Spirit for granting us the joyful opportunity to meet once more, to exchange a fraternal embrace and to join again in common prayer. We glorify the Almighty for the bonds of fraternity and friendship existing between the See of Saint Peter and the See of Saint Mark. The privilege of being together here in Egypt is a sign that the solidity of our relationship is increasing year by year, and that we are growing in closeness, faith and love of Christ our Lord. We give thanks to God for this beloved Egypt, the "homeland that lives inside us," as His Holiness Pope Shenouda III used to say, the "people blessed by God" (cf. Isa 19:25) with its ancient Pharaonic civilization, the Greek and Roman heritage, the Coptic tradition and the Islamic presence. Egypt is the place where the Holy Family found refuge, a land of martyrs and saints.

2. Our deep bond of friendship and fraternity has its origin in the full communion that existed between our Churches in the first centuries and was expressed in many different ways through the early Ecumenical Councils, dating back to the Council of Nicaea in 325 and the contribution of the courageous Church Father Saint Athanasius, who earned the title "Protector of the Faith." Our communion was expressed through prayer and similar liturgical practices, the veneration of the same martyrs and saints, and in the development and spread of monasticism, following the example of the great Saint Anthony, known as the Father of all monks.

This common experience of communion before the time of separation has a special significance in our efforts to restore full communion today. Most of the relations which existed in the early centuries between the Catholic Church and the Coptic Orthodox Church have continued to the present day in spite of divisions, and have recently been revitalized. They challenge us to intensify our common efforts to persevere in the search for visible unity in diversity, under the guidance of the Holy Spirit.

3. We recall with gratitude the historic meeting forty-four years ago between our predecessors, Pope Paul VI and Pope Shenouda III, in an embrace of peace and fraternity, after many centuries when our mutual bonds of love were not able to find expression due to the distance that had arisen between us. The Common Declaration they signed on May 10, 1973, represented a milestone on the path of ecumenism, and served as a starting point

for the Commission for Theological Dialogue between our two Churches, which has borne much fruit and opened the way to a broader dialogue between the Catholic Church and the whole family of Oriental Orthodox Churches. In that Declaration, our Churches acknowledged that, in line with the apostolic tradition, they profess "one faith in the One Triune God" and "the divinity of the Only-begotten Son of God . . . perfect God with respect to his divinity, perfect man with respect to his humanity." It was also acknowledged that "the divine life is given to us and is nourished in us through the seven sacraments" and that "we venerate the Virgin Mary, Mother of the True Light," the "*Theotokos*."

4. With deep gratitude we recall our own fraternal meeting in Rome on May 10, 2013, and the establishment of May 10 as the day when each year we deepen the friendship and brotherhood between our Churches. This renewed spirit of closeness has enabled us to discern once more that the bond uniting us was received from our one Lord on the day of our Baptism. For it is through Baptism that we become members of the one Body of Christ that is the Church (cf. 1 Cor 12:13). This common heritage is the basis of our pilgrimage together towards full communion, as we grow in love and reconciliation.

5. We are aware that we still have far to go on this pilgrimage, yet we recall how much has already been accomplished. In particular, we call to mind the meeting between Pope Shenouda III and Saint John Paul II, who came as a pilgrim to Egypt during the Great Jubilee of the year 2000. We are determined to follow in their footsteps, moved by the love of Christ the good Shepherd, in the profound conviction that by walking together, we grow in unity. May we draw our strength from God, the perfect source of communion and love.

6. This love finds its deepest expression in common prayer. When Christians pray together, they come to realize that what unites them is much greater than what divides them. Our longing for unity receives its inspiration from the prayer of Christ "that all may be one" (John 17:21). Let us deepen our shared roots in the one apostolic faith by praying together and by seeking common translations of the Lord's Prayer and a common date for the celebration of Easter.

7. As we journey towards the blessed day when we will at last gather at the same Eucharistic table, we can cooperate in many areas and demonstrate in a tangible way the great richness which already unites us. We can bear witness together to fundamental values such as the sanctity and dignity of human life, the sacredness of marriage and the family, and respect for all of creation, entrusted to us by God. In the face of many contemporary challenges such as secularization and the globalization of indifference, we are

called to offer a shared response based on the values of the Gospel and the treasures of our respective traditions. In this regard, we are encouraged to engage in a deeper study of the Oriental and Latin Fathers, and to promote a fruitful exchange in pastoral life, especially in catechesis, and in mutual spiritual enrichment between monastic and religious communities.

8. Our shared Christian witness is a grace-filled sign of reconciliation and hope for Egyptian society and its institutions, a seed planted to bear fruit in justice and peace. Since we believe that all human beings are created in the image of God, we strive for serenity and concord through a peaceful co-existence of Christians and Muslims, thus bearing witness to God's desire for the unity and harmony of the entire human family and the equal dignity of each human being. We share a concern for the welfare and the future of Egypt. All members of society have the right and duty to participate fully in the life of the nation, enjoying full and equal citizenship and collaborating to build up their country. Religious freedom, including freedom of conscience, rooted in the dignity of the person, is the cornerstone of all other freedoms. It is a sacred and inalienable right.

9. Let us intensify our unceasing prayer for all Christians in Egypt and throughout the whole world, and especially in the Middle East. The tragic experiences and the blood shed by our faithful who were persecuted and killed for the sole reason of being Christian, remind us all the more that the ecumenism of martyrdom unites us and encourages us along the way to peace and reconciliation. For, as Saint Paul writes: "If one member suffers, all suffer together" (1 Cor 12:26).

10. The mystery of Jesus who died and rose out of love lies at the heart of our journey towards full unity. Once again, the martyrs are our guides. In the early Church the blood of the martyrs was the seed of new Christians. So too in our own day, may the blood of so many martyrs be the seed of unity among all Christ's disciples, a sign and instrument of communion and peace for the world.

11. In obedience to the work of the Holy Spirit, who sanctifies the Church, keeps her throughout the ages, and leads her to full unity—that unity for which Jesus Christ prayed:

Today we, Pope Francis and Pope Tawadros II, in order to please the heart of the Lord Jesus, as well as that of our sons and daughters in the faith, mutually declare that we, with one mind and heart, will seek sincerely not to repeat the baptism that has been administered in either of our Churches for any person who wishes to join the other. This we confess in obedience to the Holy Scriptures and the faith of the three Ecumenical Councils assembled in Nicaea, Constantinople and Ephesus.

We ask God our Father to guide us, in the times and by the means that the Holy Spirit will choose, to full unity in the mystical Body of Christ.

12. Let us, then, be guided by the teachings and the example of the Apostle Paul, who writes: "[Make] every effort to keep the unity of the Spirit in the bond of peace. There is one body and one Spirit, just as you too were called to the one hope of your calling, one Lord, one faith, one baptism, one God and Father of all, who is over all and through all and in all" (Eph 4:3–6).

Cairo, April 28, 2017

Part 3

ARTICLES BY INDIVIDUAL COMMENTATORS

Editor's Introduction

THE FINAL SECTION BRINGS together seven articles from knowledgeable commentators, each of whom brings a distinct perspective to bear. I have chosen these articles to ensure that different voices are heard, alongside a geographical focus on Eastern Europe and the Middle East. There are legal and theological voices, combined with discussion on the ethics of evangelism and proselytism.

It is inevitable that some voices are not heard here. I plead limited space and time but suggest that the bibliography will give enthusiastic readers some suggestions for further research and study.

3.1

Fishing in the Neighbor's Pond
Mission and Proselytism in Eastern Europe[1]

Miroslav Volf

International Bulletin of Missionary Research 20.1 (1996) 26–31

A GOOD WAY TO describe the situation in Eastern Europe today is to say that yesterday's dreams have turned into today's nightmares.[2] This holds true not only in politics and economy but also in church life. One need not be an expert in Eastern European Christianity to know that at the very center of the religious turmoil are the issues of mission and proselytism. What precisely is the problem? One way to put it is to say that what Protestants (mainly of the evangelical kind) consider to be legitimate mission Catholics

1. Reprinted with permission of the *International Bulletin of Mission Research*, which is owned by the Overseas Ministries Study Center and published by Sage Publications.

2. This essay was prepared for a conference at the Overseas Ministries Study Center, New Haven, CT. Some portions were originally presented at the Consultation on Theological Education and Leadership Development in Post-Communist Europe, October 18, 1994, in Oradea, Romania. The proceedings of that conference will be published under the title "Eastern European Faces of Jesus." When I speak below about Eastern Europe, I am primarily referring to the eastern portion of the region marked by the former iron curtain, that is, exclusive of Central Europe.

and Orthodox (whom I will refer to as established churches) consider to be illegitimate and culturally damaging proselytism.

For all churches in Eastern Europe the peaceful revolution of 1989 seemed a dawn of a new era. They had been discriminated against and even persecuted under Communist totalitarianism; now under democracy they were hoping for unhindered flourishing. Instead, new conflicts emerged, this time not with the government, but with each other. Churches were now politically free to pursue their respective goals, but they became trapped in the battle over their own colliding goals.

Catholics and Orthodox were hoping that some of the significant social influence they had before the Communists came into power would be regained. After all, for centuries they served as guardians of various Eastern European cultures, preserving the identity of their peoples. Hence to be Croatian was to be a Catholic Christian, to be Serbian was to be an Orthodox Christian, and so forth. Yet the years of Communist domination had partly de-Christianized Eastern European cultures. Moreover, the new democratic order has brought a wide variety of other cultural shapers (both Christian and non-Christian) into play and indeed guarantees them the right of existence. The same historical change that freed established churches to exert themselves again as a major cultural force has provided space for a wide variety of other forces that compete with the established churches. Conflict was preprogrammed. It was only a question of how it would be carried out: within the bounds set by the new democratic order, or using the skills honed in the totalitarian past; through civil dialogue, or through brute force; with regard and love for one another, or with indifference and even hate.

Evangelical Protestants, always a small minority in Eastern European countries, also had great hopes for democracy. Above all, they wanted freedom to worship God and proclaim the Good News to non-Christians. The trouble was that their definition of who were non-Christians included most members of the established churches. What compounded the trouble, however, was the zeal of various Christian groups from abroad who saw the lifting of the iron curtain as the unique opportunity to proclaim Jesus Christ within what they used to call an "evil empire." In a 1993 study, the Center for Civil Society in Seattle determined that approximately 760 different Western religious groups, churches, and parachurch organizations were at work in former Communist nations of Europe. There were 200 to 350 different groups in the Commonwealth of Independent States, for instance, and 120 to 200 in Romania alone.

The following statement by Patriarch Alexy II of Moscow and All Russia at the Conference of European Churches in 1992 expresses well the sentiment of the established churches:

> We thought with certitude that after we received freedom, the solidarity of our Christian brothers in the West would help us to organize and restore our witness to Christ in our country, and our catechetical and missionary work in order to enlighten those educated in atheism and still ignoring Christ. And this would be in the spirit of the manifestation of the "joint witness" to Christ excluding and condemning any proselytism . . .
>
> And the long-endured [anti-religious system] and desired changes for the best came. The atheist totalitarian system of prohibiting the free witness to Christ broke down. And what happened?
>
> When the territories of central and eastern Europe were opened for the public missionary endeavor and evangelism, the peoples rooted in millennial Orthodox traditions became objects of proselytism for numerous zealots calling themselves missionaries and preachers who came from outside to the new markets. We had a different idea about the joint Christian witness and the brotherly solidarity in strengthening our preaching of Christ and promoting cooperation in the ecumenical community in conditions of freedom. . . . Of course our people will also survive this invasion, as it survived even worse times of persecution and attacks from the atheist propaganda. We withstood at that time, we shall withstand also now, since God was with us at that time and will be with us now.[3]

From the perspective of the established churches, foreign missionaries, equipped with the latest fishing gear, are eagerly fishing for poor souls in the Orthodox pond, left partly unattended during decades of Communist rule. It is understandable that the primates of the Orthodox churches would issue a message stating that "the consideration of these [Orthodox] countries as 'terra missionis' is unacceptable, since in these countries the Gospel has already been preached for many centuries"[4] and insisting that genuine mission is properly "carried out in non-Christian countries and among non-Christian people."

From the perspective of Protestants, however, the negative reaction of the Orthodox and Catholics to what evangelical missionaries present as the Gospel just confirms the conviction that they need to be evangelized. When

3. Lodwick, *Remembering the Future*, 73.
4. "Message of the Primates."

the statements by patriarchs are given political legitimacy by legislation that prohibits or strongly curtails work of evangelical groups, then these groups feel that their fears are confirmed—the "black Mafia" may turn out to be more hostile to genuine Christianity than the "red Mafia" ever was; the established churches are interested in democracy only when it serves to consolidate their power.

Before identifying some significant differences between Protestant and established churches in Eastern Europe that contribute to the conflict over mission and proselytism, I want to underline that the problem of proselytism in Eastern Europe is not confined to the encounter between evangelicals and the established churches. On one hand, there are non-Christian religious groups (like the Moonies) seeking a foothold in the space that has been opened after the fall of the iron curtain. Here proselytism is an interfaith issue involving encroachment by non-Christian sects with established churches sometimes unable or unwilling to distinguish between evangelical organizations and the non-Christian sects.

On the other hand, a good deal of proselytizing occurs within the Protestant churches themselves. Pastors of Baptist and Pentecostal churches often complain about independent charismatic churches coming into their cities, enlisting their best (or the most troublesome) coworkers, and stealing their sheep, especially the young ones. In the process the old sheepfold is maligned as unspiritual and culturally backward (because the shepherds in charge do not believe in quite the same amount of miracles as the newcomers and will not tolerate some contemporary styles of worship and dress). Here, for the most part, the problem of proselytism is an issue of personal power, cultural taste, generational difference, and financial independence; differences in theology are secondary.[5]

DIFFERING PERSPECTIVES

The most disturbing problems surrounding the issue of proselytism in Eastern Europe involve fundamental differences in perspective. First, there are

---

5. In the midst of an explanation as to why he participated in a successful coup mounted against a number of older presbyters in a local Pentecostal church in former Yugoslavia, a young spiritual "revolutionary" offered to me as evidence that these people needed to be deposed of the fact that one of them did not know how to pronounce "Coca Cola"—the elder man pronounced it the way the words would be read if they were Serbian words rather than the way Americans pronounce them. Never mind that the presbyter was a true saint of God who had served the church selflessly for years. He was unfit as a spiritual leader of the modern educated generation, my young friend seemed to suggest.

differing perspectives on the relation between church and culture. Established churches consider themselves as guardians of the existing cultures and peoples, who need to be freed both from Communist and negative Western influences. They want to preserve the Orthodox or Catholic character of their cultures. In sharp contrast, Protestants in Eastern Europe tend to see themselves as addressing individuals, often with the purpose of freeing them from the weight of traditional culture. They see the Gospel for the most part in contrast to existing culture.

Second, there are *differing perspectives on the relation between church and state.* Established churches in Eastern Europe have, for the most part, not yet consciously accepted all the implications of democracy as a political system such as cultural pluralism and a free market of goods and ideas. They are not prepared to see themselves as simply one among many players in the social game.

Evangelical Protestants, I believe, are split on the issue. Those more rooted in Eastern European traditions tend to welcome democracy because it means freedom, but at the same time they desire to have it without pluralism and competition; their understanding of the basic pattern of church/state relations is the same as that of the established churches, even if they find themselves on opposite sides of particular issues. Those evangelicals more influenced by Western ideas tend, in contrast, to accept plurality as a good that needs to be protected, and competition of ideas as a value to be cherished. Their understanding of the basic pattern of relations between state and church tends to be different from that of the established churches.

Third, there are *differing perspectives on what it means to be a Christian*. Established churches are like mothers who embrace all children born to them—that is, all those who were baptized. There are various degrees of belonging to the church. There is a place for saints, and there is a place for sinners; are all welcome. Protestants, however, are like stern fathers and accept only those who behave—who actively believe in Jesus Christ as their Savior and Lord and act in accordance with their belief. Hence for Protestants, all those who do not "behave"—believe and act—are legitimate objects of evangelization. Moreover, they ought to be encouraged to leave the places where they are not challenged to behave and join the communities of behavers—the true believers.

Fourth, there are *differing perspectives on the church.* For established churches, on the one hand, the church is one, and it is visible. If there is in fact more than one church, or bodies that call themselves church, this is a serious problem that must be overcome by ecumenical efforts (or, in some more conservative circles, by all others joining the one true church that has existed through the centuries). Switching from one church to the other is not allowed on theological grounds. For Protestants, on the other hand, the church that is one is invisible. There are many visible churches. Some are bad and ought to be left; others are good and can be joined if they suit one's personality, interests, and needs. Switching from one church to the other, provided the new one is "Bible believing," is not unlike switching from Pepsi to Coke (or, as many Eastern European Protestants might say, from Budweiser to Heineken).

These major differences of perspective are not simply theological in nature; they have an important sociological dimension. The internal culture and institutions of the established churches in Eastern Europe are to a large extent still more fitted to premodern than to modern societies, which is exactly opposite for the evangelical churches.[6] Since the Eastern European societies are caught in transition from premodern to modern societies, social conflicts involved in such transition are also felt in the life of the church. Some conversions, though authentically spiritual, are also triggered by important social factors—they are protests against the old social status quo in favor of more flexible and pluralistic democratic social structures.

Instead of addressing these major differences between established and Protestant churches in greater detail, I want to indicate three related tasks facing Protestant churches in Eastern Europe. I believe that if we as evangelical Protestants pursue the mission of proclaiming Christ along with these tasks, there is hope that the conflict between established churches and Protestants over mission and proselytism will be significantly reduced.

CONTEXTUAL THEOLOGY

Protestant churches in Eastern Europe need to develop a theology that, in addition to being rooted in the Scriptures, is sensitive to the needs, struggles, and aspirations of the churches and the peoples in diverse Eastern European countries. This will be a *contextual* theology.

When we talk about contextual theology, I find it helpful to make a simple but important distinction between "contextual products" and "contextual advertising." For example, an international firm such as Coca-Cola or McDonalds comes to Eastern Europe with a ready-designed product that it wants to sell. In order to sell it, however, it has to persuade locals to buy it. So it may use local people and local symbols to lure people into buying a nonlocal product. This is contextual advertising. In contrast, a contextual

---

6. I am using here "premodern" and "modern" as descriptive rather than evaluative terms, well aware that modernity is a rather mixed blessing and premodernity is by no means a curse.

product is one that a firm in Romania or Russia designs and makes for use in Romania or Russia.

What we need, I propose, is not a Coca-Cola or McDonald's kind of contextualization, not contextual advertising, but contextual—local—products. Our theological schools should not be simply import agencies and local advertising firms for foreign theological companies. I am not suggesting that we should not import, translate, and publish important works produced elsewhere. But this is not all we should do, and this is not the main thing we should do. We must learn from our brothers and sisters in other parts of the world, from those who have a centuries-long and rich tradition of Protestant theological reflection (as in the West) and from those who live in contexts similar to ours (those in the so-called Two-Thirds World). For a while it will be good to have some of them on site as expert consultants. We cannot isolate ourselves from others, because there is only one Lord, and the church of Jesus Christ around the world is one. But in communion with all the saints, we should create and disseminate our own products. If we do not, we will rightly be criticized by our compatriots as foreigners or, in some countries, as Westernizers. Our churches and theological institutions should be places where local products are developed, products that can be shared with the rest of the world.

In a very important sense, though, we followers of Jesus Christ are not supposed to be inventing anything. The Gospel is one and the same for the whole world. It is the story of our Lord Jesus Christ, who came into the world to proclaim and enact the Good News, to die and rise for the salvation of the world. When we talk about contextual products, we need to keep in mind that the Gospel is first of all something given to us rather than created by us. Yet, our own context requires that we preach the one Gospel in our own language and think with our own heads how the Gospel intersects with the specific cultures in which God has placed us. The voices that respond to the voice of the one Good Shepherd are shaped by the cultures from which they come.

I was at one of the many conferences organized in the wake of the downfall of Communism whose purpose was to explore the mission in Eastern Europe. I profoundly appreciate the enthusiasm and efforts of such gatherings, though occasionally the zeal is misplaced. A first-rate video presentation was shown at one of the conferences I attended. A line from it stuck with me. With pictures of Red Square with its beautiful church on the screen, the narrator insisted with much passion that we "need to bring Jesus" to Russia. That was probably an innocent comment, but is set me thinking about how Western Christians talk about the mission and how they sometimes carry it out. I understand, I thought to myself, the need to preach the Gospel in Russia. But what kind of a poor little Jesus would that be whom we would have to bring to Russia (or to any other part of the globe for that matter)? Shall we put him in a box like some dumb idol, write on it "Fragile, handle with care," and transport him over, hoping for his safe arrival? I could not help wondering who is serving whom when people carry their gods into foreign lands. Even in the furthest regions of the world, Jesus Christ is already there before we ever set foot on them, though he may not be recognized or worshiped. In Eastern Europe Jesus Christ has been not only present but also worshiped by millions of people for centuries. Maybe he was worshiped in a wrong way, maybe only half-heartedly, maybe even only with lips. Yet he was there, and he was worshiped. Jesus does not need to be brought to Eastern Europe. What we need to do is to wash the face of Jesus, that beautiful face that has been dirtied not only by Communist propaganda but also by so many compromises our churches—both the established and evangelical—have made through the centuries.

If one aspect of our mission is to wash the face of Jesus, an important aspect of our evangelical theologizing must be to rediscover the authentic Eastern European faces of Jesus. Does Jesus have Eastern European faces, a Moldavian or a Macedonian face, you may ask? Yes, he does. He is "the true light, which enlightens everyone"; he is the unconquerable light that "shines in the darkness, and the darkness cannot overcome it." When he comes into any culture, he does not come to a strange land but "to what is his own." This holds true even if that culture holds him a stranger, even if only a few receive him and "believe in his name" (John 1:5, 9, 11, 12). The eternal light of God shines in the darkness of our world refracted through the prisms of our multiple cultures. To change the image, our task is not to import Jesus, like some exotic article from a foreign land. We must proclaim Jesus and, in obedience to his message of salvation, (re)discover the Croatian, Slovakian, Hungarian, or Serbian face of Jesus.

HEARING AND SPEAKING THE TRUTH

The need to (re)discover the Eastern European faces of Jesus brings me to the second task for evangelical Christians. It concerns the religious context in Eastern Europe. The culture of most Eastern European countries has been shaped profoundly and indelibly by Orthodox Christianity and Catholicism. Since I am dealing here mainly with Eastern Europe (as distinct from Central Europe), I will concentrate my comments on the relation between Protestants and Orthodox. Similar observations apply in other settings, however, for the relation between Protestants and Catholics.

There are many reasons for the tensions between the Orthodox Church and various Protestant churches in Eastern Europe. Some are theological, others sociological, one of them being the uncertainty of the Orthodox Church in dealing with the processes of democratization. How can we as Protestants deal with the tensions?

In the heat of the battle, especially when one is part of a weak minority, it is difficult to do anything other than fight back. But we are the followers of the Messiah who, when abused, did not abuse; when he suffered, he did not threaten (1 Pet 2:23). We should have both the courage and the strength not to cross swords with our presumed enemy but to extend our hand. It is sometimes tempting to repay theological abuse with theological abuse. Orthodox believers call Protestants intruders and innovators; they will not recognize Protestants as a church, insisting that they are a dangerous sect. What do we do? We accuse Orthodox priests of being power-hungry, denounce them as promoters of false human traditions, and insist that they are part of an apostate church.

I think Protestants need to do all they can to resist being drawn into such an exchange of theological abuses. We should rather suffer violence than inflict it; we should return insult with blessing (1 Pet 3:9). From the perspective of pop psychology or quasi-revolutionary rhetoric, such a refusal to fight would be at best described as unhealthy and at worst thought of as worthy only of "despicable rubble," as Karl Marx put it.[7] In fact, it speaks of sovereign strength and sets a profound and genuinely Christian revolution in motion. In all our relationships we need to be trained in this revolutionary refusal to let our behavior be defined by our enemies but to follow in the footsteps of the crucified Messiah.

Most Protestants in Eastern Europe would agree with this exhortation. They know better than to go after the Orthodox with the sword in their hand. But I am not so sure that they are willing to extend to them a brotherly or sisterly hand. The impression one gets from various publications and speeches is that evangelical theology stands in almost complete opposition to Orthodox theology and that evangelical churches stand in total opposition to Orthodox churches. To pick up the terminology from 1 Peter that I used earlier, Protestants do not abuse them as the Orthodox seem to abuse Protestants, but neither do they bless them. What would happen, however, if we repaid the seeming abuse with blessings, as 1 Peter teaches us? What would happen if we started praying for a spiritual renewal within the Orthodox church, a renewal that would not be without precedent in Orthodox history? What would happen if we praised them for preserving the right

---

7. See Marx and Engels, *Werke*, 4:200.

doctrine about Christ and the Trinity, and for fighting strenuously today against the forces that find these doctrines wrong and oppressive? What would happen if we admired them for preserving the memory of some profoundly Christian men and women whom we would do well to emulate?

Orthodox theology indeed differs from Protestant theology on many issues. The question is, What should we do with these differences? One thing we certainly should not do is pretend that they do not exist or that they are unimportant. Whoever disregards differences in the name of some superficial love will trip over those differences in surprising places. Yet the way to deal with differences is not to state what we believe and tell the Orthodox Church that we are absolutely right and they are absolutely wrong. Even if God's Word is absolute, our knowledge of God's Word is not. We are not gods but limited human beings, and sinful ones at that.

How, then, should we proceed? First we need to *listen*. We need to listen to what the Orthodox Church says about itself. If we disagree with Orthodox theology, we should disagree with what they actually believe, and not with what we imagine they believe, or even with what we have read in one or two of their books. Moreover, as we want to portray to them the best possibilities of our theology, we should listen to the best presentations of their theology (while not disregarding how sometimes good theology gets corrupted when translated at the popular level). In addition to listening to what they say about themselves, we should listen carefully to what they say about us, to their criticism of our theology and practice. Often those with whom we are in conflict distort our image, but sometimes in such distorted images we can discover a truth about ourselves that we and our friends are too blind to see or too cowardly to say.

Second, we must *testify*. This second step is as important as the first. We must testify to the Orthodox Church about what we believe to be the truth of God's Word as intelligently as we can, as gently as we can, and above all as faithfully to the Gospel of Jesus Christ as we can. Jesus said: "My teaching is not mine but his who sent me" (John 7:16). How much more is this true of us, his disciples! Our teaching is not ours but belongs to the one who sent us. We are not at liberty to change what we believe to be true in order to reach some cheap consensus; we have a mandate "to testify to the *truth*" (John 18:37), not to find the least common denominator. Truth does not necessarily lie halfway between two opposing opinions. And it does not necessarily lie in either of the opinions, or (as some master dialecticians would want us to believe) in both of them. Truth lies where it lies, and our task is to point to it, wherever it lies, with us or with others. For it is the truth that will set us free.

If we put together the need to listen and the need to testify, and apply them not only to the Orthodox Church but to culture at large, the results will be astounding. If we are persistent, there will emerge among us indigenous theologies that let the Romanian or Russian face of Jesus Christ shine upon Romanian or Russian lands. The question is, Do we have enough humility, discernment, and courage to speak the truth and to hear the truth when spoken to us? It is the possession of the theological virtues of humility, discernment, and courage, more than the right perspectives on any single theological issue, that we need in Eastern Europe today. Our churches must be training grounds for humble, discerning, and courageous people who will fearlessly put their minds in the service of God's kingdom for the good of God's people and of culture at large.

BREAKING DOWN THE DIVIDING WALL

With respect to culture at large, many Protestants in Eastern Europe highlight the need for moral education and social involvement as the key issues that need addressing. They are right to do so. In Marxist societies both moral reflection and moral behavior have seriously atrophied. Moral reflection, we were told, was the bourgeois thing to do; the socialist thing to do was to change the structures. Moral behavior, though officially encouraged (what society can afford not to encourage it?), was seriously undermined by lack of philosophical grounding and by irrational laws and corrupt officials. As Christians, we need to recover the moral vision and build communities that will embody moral practices. To live virtuous lives, we need both union with Christ and communion with our brothers and sisters. The church, as a community of those who follow Christ, provides what sociologists call "plausibility structures," which make transmission of moral values and moral practices effective.

There is no theme touching social involvement I do not find addressed by many Protestants but is absolutely crucial in Eastern Europe, as it is in the rest of the world today. It is the theme of *social conflict and reconciliation*. Official Marxist ideology told us that we lived in the best of all worlds, from which the causes of social conflict have been removed. Under the lid of official ideology and secret service surveillance, however, conflicts were brewing.

There is one particular area where conflicts have exploded in Eastern Europe. The feelings of ethnic belonging (often associated with religious belonging) that were repressed for decades have reasserted themselves with a vengeance, not only in former Yugoslavia but also in many other parts of Eastern Europe. I believe that the problem of proselytism is closely related to this matter. As James H. Billington observed recently about the Russian context, authoritarian nationalists "want to build on the privileged position that orthodoxy obtained in the late Soviet period to become a force for social discipline and for the periodic purging of corrupting foreign influences."[8] The pressures in the direction of instrumentalization of the established churches are present in many countries of Eastern Europe. To the extent that local governments give in to such pressures, any presence of non-Orthodox (or non-Catholic) forms of Christianity would be unwelcome, any public proclamation of the Gospel by them construed as proselytism, any of their attempts to influence public affairs understood as unwelcome foreign intrusion.

As is well known, ethnocentrism of nation-states is one of the most dangerous political phenomena. It breeds totalitarianism in which the priests of the nationalistic idolatry are ready to place everything on the altar of national interests. In relation to other states, writes Nicholas Wolterstorff,[9] nationalist totalitarianism "acts solely in its own self-interest, breaking treaties when it sees fit, waging wars when it finds the advantage, thumbing its nose at international conventions and organizations. National self-assertion is its only goal. All that restrains it is a balance of terror." Within its own state, nationalist totalitarianism knows only of the rights of a particular nation, not of the rights of individuals—not of the rights of individuals that belong to the dominant ethnic group, and even less of the rights of those who belong to ethnic minorities. Ethnic minorities, who live mixed with the dominant population in all nation-states, are left with "only two choices: either to emigrate, under varying degrees of duress, or to accept the status of second-class citizens, with varying degrees of deprivation of rights and repression. *There is never any other choice.*"

What we need is an effective response to the problems of ethnicity and ethnic conflicts that are tearing Eastern European societies apart and leaving a trail of blood and ashes. This is not a place to develop a theology of ethnicity.[10] I should say here only that in addition to theological explorations of this topic, we need common church commitments, something like the Barmen Declaration, produced by the Confessing Church under the leadership of Karl Barth in the struggle against the Nazi regime.[11] How

---

8. Billington, "Orthodoxy."

9. Wolterstorff, *Until Justice and Peace Embrace*, 109, 114.

10. See Volf, "Exclusion and Embrace"; "When the Unclean Spirit Leaves"; "Vision of Embrace."

11. One such example of a common confession seeking to overcome racial division is the South African "Belhar Confession" (1986). [Editor's note: see DRMC, "Belhar

would a confessional statement, addressed to the problem of ethnic conflict, read? I suggest something like the following:

> "You were slaughtered and by your blood you ransomed for God saints from every tribe and language and people and nation" (Rev 5:9). "There is no longer Jew or Greek, there is no longer slave or free, there is no longer male and female; for all of you are one in Christ Jesus" (Gal 3:28).
>
> All the churches of Jesus Christ, scattered in diverse cultures, have been redeemed for God by the blood of the Lamb to form one multicultural community of faith. The "blood" that binds them as brothers and sisters is more precious than the "blood," language, customs, political allegiances, or economic interests that may separate them.
>
> We reject the false doctrine that a church should place allegiance to the culture it inhabits and the nation to which it belongs above the commitment to Jesus Christ and the brothers and sisters from other cultures and nations, servants of the one Jesus Christ, their common Lord, and members of God's new community.

Imagine the impact on Eastern European societies if all our churches, established and Protestant, were to adopt and act in accordance with such a confession.

PATTERNS OF CONFORMATION

We Protestants need to discover the Eastern European faces of Jesus, I have argued; we need to listen to what our brothers and sisters in established churches have to say to us and testify to them to the truth of the Gospel; we need to break down the wall of hostility between cultures and nations. If we attend to these theological tasks, our mission in Eastern Europe will be enriched, and we will find ourselves more at peace with our neighbors who belong to Orthodox and Catholic traditions. In conclusion, let me point out one major danger that lurks in a project of discovering the Eastern European faces of Jesus.

When I was a boy, I used to read the Old Testament and be amazed at how easily the Israelites would abandon Yahweh and follow after strange gods. "How could they do such a thing, after God has led them through the Red Sea, settled them in the land where milk and honey flowed, and took such good care of them?" I used to ask myself. Little did I know how

Confession"; Barth, "Theological Declaration of Barmen."]

dangerous my question was. Simply to ask means to be blind about ourselves. For the question is not "how *they* could do such a thing" but "how *we* repeatedly do the same."

When I was a young student of theology, I was shocked to find many theologians giving up basic Christian doctrines. I used to ask myself, "How could these 'liberal' theologians accommodate so shamelessly to the spirit of the age when the plain truth of the Gospel has been revealed to us in God's Word?" Little did I know that the question of the student about "liberal" theologians was as dangerous a question as the boy's about the faithless Israelites. I thought accommodation was the problem of liberals not of conservatives. I did not realize that whereas I saw their accommodation clearly, I was either blind or very lenient toward my own.

No doubt "liberals"—and in Eastern Europe, Protestants would say, Catholics and Orthodox—have accommodated too often. I am sorry for their accommodations, but what I fear more are our own accommodations as conservative evangelicals. Let me take an example from a different part of the world—the question of race in such a good evangelical denomination as the Assembly of God in the United States, as analyzed recently by Cecil M. Robeck Jr. in a paper entitled "Historical Roots of Racial Unity and Division in American Pentecostalism." In 1945 the denomination made an official resolution "that we encourage the establishment of Assembly of God churches for the colored race." The wording would make one believe that the denomination was seeking to overcome racial divisions that plagued US society and recover the biblical vision in which there was neither Jew nor Greek, neither slave nor free. But this was not the case. In the same official document we read: "Conforming to American Law and society our work amongst the Colored People will remain distinct and separate, and the Colored Branch when formed shall be under the supervision of the Home Missions Department."[12] The whites kept separate from the blacks but made sure that they were in charge.

Contrast this discrimination with the birth of the Pentecostal movement in Azusa Street, Los Angeles. The leader of the nascent movement was William J. Seymour, an African-American preacher from the southern United States who moved to California. For him, the Gospel overcame the boundaries between people, between black and white, rich and poor, Mexican and Chinese—which is how the Pentecostal movement lived, at least in its first years. "People of all nations came and got their cup full," we read in a book from 1915. Though even then "some of our white brethren" had

---

12. Assembly of God quoted in Robeck Jr., "Historical Roots of Racial Unity and Division."

"prejudice and discrimination," the movement insisted that "we must love all men as Christ commands," a Christ who "takes in all people in his Salvation" and who "is neither black nor white man, nor Chinaman nor Hindu, nor Japanese, but God."[13]

As the Pentecostal movement grew, however, it started moving away from its original gospel vision of racial unity toward conformity to US social practices of racial segregation. What is equally disturbing as the insistence on separation and division is the kind of justification given for it in the official documents of the church: "*Conforming to American Law and society* our work amongst the Colored People will remain distinct and separate," the minutes read. The original holy conformation to the gospel vision has been replaced by the godless conformation to "American Law and society," and this was done in good conscience by good Christians who believed in the Bible as the infallible Word of God, affirmed all evangelical doctrines, and desired to live holy lives. They accommodated, and they even explicitly stated that they accommodated, yet they seemed to have been unaware of doing so. They were trapped inside their own culture but believed they were free followers of Jesus Christ alone. Being trapped inside our own cultures and our prejudices with the Bible in our hands is what I fear for Protestants in Eastern Europe.

Conflict over mission and proselytism in Eastern Europe is unlikely to go away any time soon. We need to work to overcome these conflicts because they are a counterwitness to the world. If the church is itself profoundly divided, it cannot be a sign of God's reconciliation in a world torn apart by social and ethnic hostilities. Our goal must therefore be to end the strife of churches over mission and proselytism and proclaim together the message of Jesus Christ as the one Lord of the one world.

We must ensure that our continuing disputes over mission and proselytism are not over our prejudices but over the truth of the Gospel, and that all encounters are carried out in the spirit of humility appropriate to the followers of the crucified Messiah.

---

13. Seymour, *Doctrines and Discipline*, 12, 13.

3.2

Mission and Proselytism
A Middle East Perspective[1]

David A. Kerr

International Bulletin of Missionary Research 20.1 (1996) 12–16, 18–22

The approximately ten to twelve million Christians of West Asia/North Africa (i.e., of the so-called Middle East) represent a kaleidoscope of Christian churches and cultural traditions.[2] The great majority are Orthodox, members of the Oriental and Eastern Orthodox churches, which account for more than 75 percent of the total Christian population of the region. Catholic churches of both Eastern and Western (Latin) rites account for about another 20 percent. The evangelical or Protestant churches form a minority of between 3 and 4 percent.[3] These figures, based on David Barrett's

---

1. Reprinted with permission of the *International Bulletin of Mission Research*, which is owned by the Overseas Ministries Study Center and published by Sage Publications.

2. The author acknowledges their indebtedness and expresses gratitude to Carolyn Sperl, coordinator of Reference and Interlibrary Loan Services, Hartford Seminary, for her assistance in researching the disparate literature relevant to this study. The colonialist associations and geographic ambiguities of the term "Middle East" and its variant "Near East" call for the less prejudicial (albeit less elegant) terminology "West Asia/North Africa," which will be used throughout.

3. Recent introductory studies of these churches include Roberson, *Eastern Churches*,

calculations, relate to the churches that are today members of the Middle East Council of Churches (MECC), probably the world's most inclusive regional ecumenical council. Successor to the predominantly Protestant Near East Council of Churches, it embraces four families of churches (Oriental Orthodox, Eastern Orthodox, Catholic, and Protestant), with the Assyrian Church of the East (so-called Nestorian) possibly joining in the future as a fifth family.[4]

This ecumenical achievement is a positive sign of reconciliation between the indigenous churches, which for centuries have lived in disunity and mutual mistrust. It expresses their growing willingness to resolve historical problems of division by a concerted witness to the Gospel's power of renewal and reconciliation in a politically torn region.

Among the ecclesial issues on the MECC agenda is the problem of proselytism. This was the subject of a special report, *Proselytism, Sects, and Pastoral Challenges: A Study Document*, which the Commission on Faith and Unity prepared for the MECC's Fifth General Assembly in 1989.[5] As the most ecumenical document on the issue in the West Asian/North African perspective, it provides an appropriate starting point for this essay.

PROSELYTISM: THE MECC DEFINITION

The MECC study document defines proselytism as "a practice that involves attempts aimed at attracting Christians from a particular Church or religious group, leading to their alienation from their Church of origin." It is treated as an issue of ecumenical malpractice that contravenes biblical

---

which deals with the Oriental and Eastern Orthodox and the Catholic churches of West Asia/North Africa and elsewhere (but excludes the Protestants); and Horner, *Guide to Christian Churches in the Middle East*, which includes information on the Protestant churches as well as the Oriental and Eastern Orthodox and the Catholics. A briefer summary appears in Teague, *Turning a New Leaf*. For a sociopolitical overview of these Christian communities, see Betts, *Christians in the Arab East*. For the contemporary statement of an Arab Christian, see Raheb, *I Am a Palestinian Christian*. Standard scholarly reference works include Atiyah, *History of Eastern Christianity*; Arberry, *Judaism and Christianity*.

4. For the MECC's account of the churches of its region, see MECC, "Who Are the Christians of the Middle East?"

5. The preamble of the document reads: "After a discussion process started in December 1986, the Commission on Faith and Unity studied in its last meeting (July 1989), before the Vth General Assembly, a third draft. It has agreed that it should be considered 'A Study Document' submitted to the Executive Committee of the MECC and to the Churches and made available to institutions, groups or individuals concerned." See 2.7 of this volume.

understandings of how God relates to humankind, how Christians relate to one another, and respect for the human right to be free from coercion in religious matters. The problem is analyzed as having psychological roots in "individual and group egoism," political manifestations in "feelings of cultural, political and economic superiority," and institutional dimensions in "an overtrust in one's present methods and programmes." It is perpetuated by ignorance of Christian traditions other than those of one's own cultural or political background, and it may include the willful "dissimulation of the truth about them." Proselytism is therefore seen as the opposite of authentic evangelism, which emphasizes "confidence in God and His economy" as the basis of mission.[6]

The MECC document addresses two dimensions of the issue. In historical terms it is related to the "western missionary strategy" of the medieval Catholic missions and their Protestant successors.[7] The contemporary dimension is identified mainly with "sects"—by which the MECC means millenarian or messianic groups, independent "neo-missionary" groups of fundamentalist persuasions, groups that represent syncretistic forms of religious universalism, charismatic renewal movements within established churches, and new religious movements that claim to draw upon Asian forms of religious spirituality.[8] While proselytism in West Asia/North Africa occurs unconsciously as well as consciously, its underlying presupposition is that a missionary "vacuum" exists throughout the region, where indigenous churches are considered to be lacking missionary motivation and resources.[9]

With this understanding of proselytism, the present essay will examine manifestations of the problem in the complex history of the Eastern churches' experience of the Western church and its missions. It will then review contemporary initiatives in intra-Christian dialogue, one of the benefits of which has been the emergence of a clearer understanding of how the Orthodox churches understand Christian witness. Attention will be given to the MECC's suggested remedies, and in conclusion we shall examine some of the contextual issues that shape the identity of Eastern churches.

---

6. MECC, *Proselytism, Sects, and Pastoral Challenges*, para. 6–11. For an elaboration of these definitions, see Sabra, "Proselytism, Evangelism, and Ecumenism."

7. MECC, *Proselytism, Sects, and Pastoral Challenges*, para. 13–14.

8. MECC, *Proselytism, Sects, and Pastoral Challenges*, para. 39.

9. MECC, *Proselytism, Sects, and Pastoral Challenges*, para. 20–29.

HISTORICAL DIMENSIONS

Eastern Patriarchates

For the indigenous West Asian/North African Christian communities, it is a matter of historic pride and contemporary self-understanding that Christianity has been continuously present throughout the region since apostolic times. The cities of Jerusalem, Antioch, Alexandria, and Etchmiadzin are quite as important for Christians as are Mecca, Medina, and Jerusalem for Muslims, and Jerusalem for Jews. They are the places where the apostles proclaimed the Gospel and founded the first churches that carried forward the Christian mission.

In ecclesiastical language, they constitute the "patriarchates" of the East. They have always seen themselves as existing in an equal apostolic relationship with the Western patriarchates of Rome and Constantinople. From the fourth century, Rome was accorded a spiritual primacy as *primus inter pares*, though without the universal authority that Catholics later invested in the papacy. Constantinople (originally known by its Greek pre-Christian name of Byzantium) held political primacy within the Byzantine Empire, to which most of the Eastern churches belonged. But in ecclesial terms the Easterners have always insisted on the coequal autonomy of each patriarchate as the institutional reality of the biblical conception of the universal church; as the human body is made up of many members, so the apostolic churches are the members of the body of Christ.

The patriarchates have always been the centers of Eastern Christian liturgy, theology, witness, and church administration, expressed in their ancient ethnic languages (Syriac and Aramaic in Antioch and Jerusalem; Coptic in Alexandria). This continued to be true long after the seventh century, when the rise of Islam, its military conquests, and the extension of its political power under the Islam caliphate reduced the Eastern patriarchates socially to the role of Christian minorities in increasingly Muslim societies.

To the northeastern frontier of the Byzantine Empire lay the kingdom of Armenia. Here the church traces its foundation to the apostles Thaddeus and Bartholemew. The Armenian monarchy recognized Christianity as the national religion from the beginning of the fourth century, even before the conversion of the Byzantine emperor Constantine.[10] Armenian Christians have ever since looked to Etchmiadzin as the seat of what they call their

---

10. King Tiridate's conversion to Christianity at the hands of St. Gregory the Illuminator (301) predates the baptism of Emperor Constantine (337).

"catholicosate," which, in terms of Armenian canon law, has higher authority than a patriarchate.[11]

Despite the diversity of cultural, linguistic, and social characteristics that they represented, the five patriarchates and the Armenian catholicosate preserved the common faith of the Nicean Creed (325) until the early fifth century. This is remembered as the period of "the undivided church." Over the following centuries this ecumenical fellowship proved vulnerable to centrifugal forces. The ecumenical Council of Ephesus (431) excommunicated the eastern members of the patriarchate of Antioch. To escape the persecution of those whom the Byzantine rulers declared heretics, these Assyrian Christians took refuge in Persia.[12] Twenty years later the Council of Chalcedon (451) witnessed doctrinal cleavage between the Copts (Egyptians) of Alexandria, the remaining Syrians of Antioch, and the Armenians of Etchmiadzin on the one hand, and the churches of Constantinople and Rome on the other.[13]

Oriental Orthodox

Since Chalcedon, the Copts, Syrians, and Armenians, together with the church of Kerala (India) and the church of Ethiopia, have formed the family of Oriental Orthodox churches. They are "autocephalous," or self-governing, but united in creed and liturgy. Each is inseparably identified with the people and culture in which it exists and in this sense can be described sociologically as ethnic churches. Contextually, this characteristic has been a source of strength throughout their histories and helps explain their remarkable tenacity to the Christian faith, despite their being under Islamic rule. Their numerical decline through the medieval centuries did not diminish the quality of their spiritual life, which is evident in a wealth

---

11. In Armenian canon law the catholicosate has global authority over Armenians, in contrast to the patriarchate, which has only regional jurisdiction. The church comprises two patriarchates (Jerusalem and Constantinople), which are dependent upon the catholicosate of Etchmiadzin. In the fifteenth century a second catholicosate was created for the Armenian diaspora in Cilicia, Syria (modern-day Lebanon).

12. The name "Assyrian" reflects their claim to descend from the ancient people of Nineveh. Alternatively, they call themselves "Chaldean." In either case they reject their designation by other churches as Nestorian, after the fifth-century theologian Nestorius, whom the Council of Ephesus condemned for allegedly teaching Dyophysitism, the view that the person of Jesus Christ included two separate natures.

13. The doctrinal issue turned once again on the problem of defining the person of Jesus Christ. Was he of a single divine nature, as the Orientals were alleged to have asserted (Monophysitism), or of two natures that were united without confusion, change, division, or separation, as the Western Christians insisted (Chalcedonianism)?

of theological writing and liturgical expression.[14] Today they continue to account for the majority of West Asian and North African Christians.

Eastern Orthodox

After the Chalcedonian separation, smaller communities of Christians in Antioch and Alexandria remained in communion with Constantinople and technically with Rome. Often referred to as Melkites (from Arabic *malik*, meaning "king," in reference to the Byzantine emperor), their orthodoxy is of the Chalcedonian kind. In MECC ecumenical parlance they constitute the Eastern Orthodox family. Historically their presence has been strongest in the cosmopolitan coastal regions of West Asia and North Africa. Though historical links with the Greek church continue, especially in the patriarchate of Jerusalem, the Eastern Orthodox patriarchate of Antioch identifies itself as the church of the Arabs.[15] It has contributed in diverse ways to the development in the nineteenth and twentieth centuries of Arab nationalism and is committed to social coexistence with Islam. Relations between the Eastern and Oriental Orthodox, though strained in the past, have grown more intimate through a series of pan-Orthodox conferences that began in Addis Ababa in 1965.

Eastern Catholics

This historical survey has so far exposed factors that resulted in the disunity of the Eastern churches. The refusal of one church to recognize the ecclesial validity of another is the soil in which proselytism is seeded. It was with the extension of Western Catholicism into West Asia, in consequence of Rome's denial of the ecclesial integrity of the Eastern patriarchates under what it deemed as their heretical doctrines, that the growth of proselytism began.

To avoid generalization, it is important to emphasize at the outset of this discussion that the oldest and largest indigenous community of West Asian Catholics are the Maronites. Exactly as we have seen to be the case with the Oriental and Eastern Orthodox sense of ethnic identity, the Maronites have strong ethnic ties to Lebanon, where land and faith have combined

---

14. The recovery of the theological output of these churches within Muslim societies and culture is the goal of important contemporary research, much of which has been pioneered by Samir Khalil. For a recent example of this in English, see Khalil and Nielsen, *Christian Arabic Apologists*.

15. The Arabization of the episcopate and election of the first Arab patriarch at the end of the nineteenth century stands as one of the early milestones of Arab nationalism.

in the Maronite sense of being a national church. Their union with Rome was gradually consolidated from the era of the Latin Crusades (between the eleventh and thirteenth centuries), and though their ecclesiastical customs were subject to extensive Latinization, they never lost their original Syriac identity, which today they often proudly reaffirm.

In contrast to the Maronites, who claim to have been Catholic from their origins between the fifth and seventh centuries, other Catholic communities have sprung up as the result of the later missionary activity of the Western Catholic church. Following the mutual anathemas exchanged between Rome and Constantinople in 1054 and the subsequent failure of the Council of Ferrara-Florence (1437–1439) to heal the rift between Latin Catholicism and Eastern Orthodoxy, the Catholic Church developed a strategy for reunion with the East by the conversion of the Oriental and Eastern Orthodox churches to Catholicism. Western Catholic missions, initially led by the Franciscans and later by the Jesuits, exerted a powerful Latinizing influence upon the Maronites and won converts from the other churches. Thus, corresponding to each Oriental and Eastern Orthodox church, a Catholic equivalent arose: Chaldean (Assyrian) Catholic (1553), Syrian Catholic (1663), Melkite (Greek) Catholic (1724), Armenian Catholic (1742), and Coptic Catholic (1895). By recognizing these convert churches as the canonical heirs of the ancient Eastern patriarchates, Rome claimed to be reuniting the church.[16] Together with the Latin Catholic Patriarchate of Jerusalem,[17] these Catholic patriarchates are defined by the Second Vatican Council as part of "the divinely revealed and undivided heritage of the universal Church."[18]

The Vatican designates these churches as Eastern-rite Catholics, in distinction from the Roman (or Latin) Catholic rite of the West. This label emphasizes the Catholic view that they enrich the universal Catholic Church by preserving distinctive elements of their original canonical traditions. Their alternative designation as "Uniate" churches (i.e., united with Rome), while having long historical currency, emphasizes rather the fact of

---

16. In fairness to the Roman position, it must be acknowledged that Rome viewed the Eastern-rite churches within the Catholic communion as symbols of the full communion with the Eastern and Oriental Orthodox churches that is yet to be achieved. They were provisional models of reunion, or as the Second Vatican Council stated: "All these directives of law are laid down in view of the present situation, until such time as the Catholic Church and the separated Eastern Churches come together into complete unity" (Vatican II, *Orientalium Ecclesiarum* [Abbott, *Documents of Vatican II*, 385]).

17. Created by the Latin Crusaders after their conquest of Jerusalem in 1099, this patriarchate did not survive the end of the Latin Kingdom of Jerusalem but was reconstituted by the Vatican in 1847.

18. Abbott, *Documents of Vatican II*, 373.

their conversion, which incurs the Eastern and Oriental Orthodox charge of proselytism. The very existence of these churches is therefore problematic; what the Catholics have regarded as a symbol of reunion, the Orthodox have treated as "a major obstacle to the progress of the dialogue" with the Catholic Church.[19] The fact that significant progress has recently been made in this dialogue is an ecumenical achievement to which we shall return later in this article.

Evangelical Churches

In the nineteenth century, Eastern churches, led by the Maronites, joined cause in laying the charge of proselytism this time against the evangelical missions that had arrived in West Asia. In 1823 the first missionaries of the American Board of Commissioners for Foreign Mission (ABCFM) began evangelistic work in Beirut and Mount Lebanon. The Maronite patriarch greeted them with an encyclical that condemned their version of the Bible and forbade Maronites to associate with the English *bibliyyun* ("biblicists"). In May of that year, Pope Leo XII backed the patriarch by issuing a further condemnation of "a certain Bible society" which had printed and distributed a corrupt version of the Scriptures.[20]

The aim of the missionaries was the revival of "nominal Christians," who, by becoming "Christian in heart," were expected to advance the evangelization of Muslims and Jews. The initial ABCFM policy was stated by Rufus Anderson as follows:

> Not to subvert them [the indigenous churches]; not to pull them down and build anew. It is to reform them; to revive among them ... the knowledge and spirit of the Gospel.... It is not part of our object to introduce Congregationalism or Presbyterianism among them.... We are content that their present ecclesiastical organization should remain, provided the knowledge and spirit of the Gospel can be revived under it.[21]

This statement did not prevent the emergence of separate evangelical churches. Some of the missionaries found it impossible to credit the indigenous

---

19. For example, see Zissis, "Uniatism."

20. For analyses of the history of nineteenth-century evangelical missionary theory and practice in West Asia by indigenous scholars, see Badr, "Mission to 'Nominal Christians'"; Semaan, *Aliens at Home*.

21. Badr, "Mission to 'Nominal Christians,'" 164–65. Anderson's study of this issue is found in his *History of the Missions*.

churches with any spiritual vitality.[22] Orthodox and Catholic Christians who associated with the evangelical missionaries were ostracized by their church hierarchies, the case of the Maronite As'ad Shidyaq becoming the cause celebre when he was imprisoned by the Maronite patriarch and died in jail (ca. 1823).[23] When in 1826 two Armenians, Gregory Wortabet and Dionysius Carabet, asked to be received into an evangelical fellowship, the missionaries decided to form themselves into a church.

The first evangelical church was established in Beirut. "Being desirous of enjoying Christian ordinances," its founding members determined (in the words of their charter) "to adopt with some variations, the Articles of Faith and the Form of Covenant, used by the First Church in Hartford, Connecticut, to be publicly read on the admission of members."[24] Increase in the number of converts during the mid-nineteenth century, and the need for an appropriate form of institutional organization within the Ottoman millet system of religious communities encouraged the missionaries to develop a fourfold policy: the conversion of indigenous "nominal" Christians, the organization of convert evangelical churches, the training of an indigenous ministry, and the publication of Christian literature.[25] Anderson acquiesced in the missionaries' practice as a result of his 1844 visit through the region, and his original policy of nonproselytism evolved to "the restoration of pre-Constantinian and primitive (Pauline) Christianity ... [by] the formation not only of exemplary individuals in their [i.e., the Eastern churches'] midst but of exemplary communities as well."[26] But he recognized the consequence of this policy change when he later wrote: "This admission of converts into a church, without regard to their previous ecclesiastical relation, was a practical ignoring of the old church organizations in that region. It was so understood, and the spirit of opposition and persecution was roused to the utmost."[27]

---

22. For example, see Jessup, *Greek Church and Protestant Missions*.

23. A contemporary American missionary, Isaac Bird, was the first to write on this incident in his *Martyr of Lebanon*. Rufus Anderson later wrote a chapter, "The Martyr of Lebanon, Assaad Shidyak" (see Anderson, *History of the Missions*, 1:52).

24. Badr, "Mission to 'Nominal Christians,'" 100–2; cf. Semaan, *Aliens at Home*, 82–85. The missionary significance of the First Church in Hartford lay in its minister from 1818 to 1867, Joel Hawes, who played a leading role in the Second Great Awakening. Hawes was a friend and supporter of Rufus Anderson as well as his traveling companion on an extended visit to West Asia in 1844. On Joel Hawes, see Walker, *History of the First Church in Hartford*.

25. Badr, "Mission to 'Nominal Christians,'" 254.

26. Badr, "Mission to 'Nominal Christians,'" 264.

27. Anderson, *History of the Missions*, 1:47.

The ABCFM policy in this regard is but a concise example of the practice of the nineteenth-century Anglican, Lutheran, and Reformed missions in Turkey, Palestine, and Egypt. An Anglican bishopric was established in Jerusalem in 1841 largely through the efforts of Britain's Church Missionary Society. German missionaries created the Evangelical Lutheran Church of Jordan around 1860. In addition to the work of the ABCFM in Lebanon, which gave rise to the present National Evangelical Synod of Syria and Lebanon, its activity in Turkey spawned an Armenian evangelical congregation in 1846, which has grown to become the Union of Armenian Evangelical Churches in the Near East. American Presbyterians in Cairo founded the Coptic Evangelical Church in 1853, which is today the largest and most influential Protestant denomination in the region.[28]

In his discussion of the evangelical churches of West Asia, Norman Homer notes that "the vast majority of their membership came originally from Orthodox and Eastern-rite Catholic churches. This has left a residue of mutual suspicion and ill will that can be overcome only by more creative ecumenical relationships than yet exist, especially between Protestant and Orthodox churches."[29]

INTRA-CHRISTIAN DIALOGUE

Our overview of centuries of church history in the West Asian/North African region will have served its purpose if it illustrates the ubiquity of intra-Christian proselytism as an issue with which the contemporary churches must deal. It sets discomforting questions against the cherished Western maxim that the modern ecumenical movement evolved from the history of missions. The Western trajectory of mission has been experienced as profoundly antiecumenical by the Eastern churches, compounding the disunity that already existed and arguably weakening the situation of Christian minorities within Muslim societies.

Against this background the ecumenical achievements of the MECC are the more remarkable. Mutual recognition among the different member families of churches has offset the absolutist demands that continue to be heard in other regions affected by similar historical problems (e.g., the demand by some Orthodox that Uniatism be abolished by the absorption of the Uniates into the Latin rite of Roman Catholicism).[30]

---

28. See Horner, *Guide to Christian Churches in the Middle East*, 65–79, for a full list of Anglican and Protestant churches in West Asia/North Africa.
29. Horner, *Guide to Christian Churches in the Middle East*, 72.
30. Zissis, "Uniatism," 22. Defining uniatism as no more than "a method of

The process of healing these historical wounds can be illustrated by two significant examples, both of which have had a positive impact on the life of the MECC, though the initiatives originated elsewhere. The first involves the Catholic and Eastern Orthodox churches, which, since 1990, have been trying to resolve the issue of the Eastern-rite Catholic (Uniate) churches. Their joint "Statement on the Subject of Uniatism," published as the Freising Declaration of 1990, became the basis of a continuing dialogue in which it has been agreed that while the Eastern-rite Catholic churches have come into existence as part of the historic search for unity, Uniatism no longer provides a model or method for Catholic-Orthodox rapprochement. In the contemporary ecumenical understanding of the church as a communion of those who receive the "gifts and graces" of the Holy Spirit,[31] neither Catholics nor Orthodox claim exclusive possession of the Holy Spirit's authenticating marks. They embrace one another as pilgrims in a Spirit-guided journey toward perfect communion. In this pilgrimage the Eastern-rite Catholics/Uniates serve not as intermediaries between sister churches but as fellow pilgrims who seek to make their own specific contribution to the growth of Christian koinonia.[32] Although a certain ambiguity remains about the specific ecumenical role of the Eastern-rite Catholics, agreement that Uniatism is no longer a model for ecclesial reunion represents a significant defusing of tensions created by proselytism.

A second example of intra-Christian dialogue is the growth since the late 1980s of bilateral conversations between Western evangelical missions and the indigenous churches of West Asia/North Africa. An annual conference of Evangelicals for Middle East Understanding (EMEU), founded in 1987, provides a framework for dialogue between indigenous Christians and Western evangelicals who are exploring cooperative rather than competitive understandings of mission. Speaking to evangelicals, EMEU director Donald Wagner calls for "a new day for mission . . . [in which] we must strive to become authentic partners with the churches of the Middle East. We will discover that God is already at work in Jerusalem, the West Bank, Beirut, Cairo, Baghdad, and throughout this region. We will not only learn from our sisters and brothers in the faith in these lands, but will find the true

---

proselytizing the East," Zissis argues that it is a "fraudulent union" that should be abolished, asking that the Uniates be "incorporated in the Latin rite of Roman Catholicism."

31. Vatican II, *Lumen Gentium* (Abbott, *Documents of Vatican II*, 34).

32. Summary of salient points in the Joint Commission's 1991 working document (see JIC, "Uniatism"). For an interpretation of this document by an Eastern-rite Catholic priest, see Loya, "Uniatism in Current Ecumenical Dialogue," 83–86.

meaning of being the church in new ways that will honor the Lord and the gospel he gave us."[33]

An example of this sort of dialogue has been published in *Turning Over a New Leaf: Protestant Missions and the Orthodox Churches of the Middle East*. This book introduces Western evangelicals to the life of the indigenous churches of West Asia in a concise, informed, and sensitive manner that seeks to replace negative stereotypes by "a kinder, gentler understanding."[34] It explores aspects of Orthodox theology that evangelicals find difficult (e.g., works/faith relationship, the Eucharist, Mariology and the communion of saints, apostolic succession) and develops a frank discussion of differences between their respective understandings of salvation and spiritual renewal. It is especially helpful in showing how Orthodox spiritual renewal draws inspiration from the Orthodox liturgy of worship.

These examples show evidence of a process of reconciliation at least between churches (Catholic-Orthodox) and mission groups (Western evangelicals) whose understanding of mission centers upon the church and the local Christian community. It must be admitted, however, that these positive developments have little impact on those groups that, as noted above, the MECC terms "sects." From the EMEU perspective, Donald Wagner has expressed concern about what he sees as "the western orientation and cultural insensitivity" of the evangelical AD 2000 movement. He also subjects the theology and policies of the International Christian Embassy-Jerusalem to critical scrutiny, concluding that it "allows the gospel and lordship of Jesus Christ to become subservient to the modern political ideology of Zionism . . . reducing the Christian church to a mere 'parenthesis' and rejecting the local Christian community."[35]

ORTHODOX UNDERSTANDINGS OF MISSION

Perhaps the most sensitive issue for continuing dialogue between Western and Eastern churches is the nature of mission itself. On grounds that the ethnic identity of Eastern churches is assumed to deprive them of a real sense of mission, evangelicals sometimes continue the nineteenth-century practice of justifying a proselytizing evangelism of Eastern Christians so

33. Wagner, *Anxious for Armageddon*, 181–82; see also 57–58, 186–87. For a report on the 1991 Cyprus meeting, see Lawton, "Other Peace Conference."

34. David Teague's phrase, which he uses as the title of the chapter in which he speaks of what he learned through personal encounter with Coptic Orthodoxy in Egypt. See Teague, *Turning Over a New Leaf*, 63–84.

35. Wagner, *Anxious for Armageddon*, 181, 96–113.

that they might become effective channels of indigenous evangelism. Orthodox response to being treated as *terra missionis* often caricatures Western missions as a continuation of the medieval Crusades and has resulted in denunciation of the word "mission." With its Latin connotations of "sending forth," they associate mission negatively with their historic experience of the imperial ambitions of the Holy Roman Empire and its successor European states.

Orthodox churches generally prefer the Greek term *martyria* (witness). The following paragraphs attempt to summarize the content that modern Orthodox have given this term in their recent missiological writings and consultations.

Witness as Liturgy

The heart of the Orthodox understanding of witness is the liturgy. "The Liturgy," writes Metropolitan Anastasios of Albania (formerly professor at the University of Athens),

> is a continuous transformation of life according to the prototype Jesus Christ, through the power of the Spirit. If it is true that in the Liturgy we not only hear a message but we participate in the great event of liberation from sin and of *koinonia* (communion) with Christ through the real presence of the Holy Spirit, then this event of our personal incorporation into the Body of Christ, this transfiguration of our little being into a member of Christ, must be evident and be proclaimed in actual life. The Liturgy has to be continued in personal, everyday situations. . . . Without this continuation the Liturgy remains incomplete.[36]

Liturgy After the Liturgy

The idea of continuity between the liturgy and witness in life is expressed in the phrase "liturgy after the Liturgy." Ion Bria, the Romanian Orthodox theologian who served as Orthodox adviser in the World Council of Churches' Commission on World Mission and Evangelism, explains it thus: "The mission of the Church rests upon the radiating and transforming

---

36. This often-cited quotation appears, for example, in Bria, *Martyria/Mission*, 66–67. See also Bria, *Go Forth in Peace*, 38.

power of the Liturgy. It is the stimulus in sending out the people of God to the world to confess the Gospel and to be involved in man's liberation."[37]

Liturgy as witness/mission means the church being in the midst of the human community it serves in order to transform it into the Christ-like image and likeness of God (*theosis*). This necessitates the radical conversion of societies and individuals whose lives are characterized by sin, separation from God, and submission to the evils of idolatry (social and political as much as religious). Accordingly, a group of Orthodox theologians who met in Bucharest in 1974 to discuss the topic "Confessing Christ Today" analyzed witness under its "vertical" (divine-human) and "horizontal" (social-individual) dimensions. They emphasized that "the first method of evangelistic witness is the sharing of love by those who have acknowledged the love of God for them." They argued that this primary expression of witness, this self-giving quality of Christian lives that invite emulation, is a more effective way of transforming human communities than "the bold announcement of Christ as Saviour to a world which has already heard the words and still remains unresponsive."[38]

The Context of Witness

The ethnic and national identity of Orthodox churches means that the primary context of their witness is their own people and nations. For much of the twentieth century, Orthodox churches living under the restrictions of Communist regimes had no opportunity to witness beyond their own societies. But contemporary Orthodox theologians insist that their understanding of witness is not contingent on a particular sociopolitical circumstance. It flows from the Orthodox ecclesiology, which identifies the church with the people (*laos*) as "the people's church."[39] This understanding gives missiological priority to the indigenization of faith in a particular culture so that the latter is transformed by gospel values. The Orthodox consultation "Confessing Christ Today" identified four dimensions of such indigenous evangelization: (1) the evangelization of those who are Christian in name but ignore their baptism either deliberately or through indifference; (2) the penetration of superficially Christian cultures with the transforming power of the Holy Spirit reaching into "every nook and cranny" of national life; (3) the evangelization of "the structures of this world," especially in the social, economic, and political spheres, where the church should give voice to

37. Bria, *Martyria/Mission*, 68.
38. Bria, *Martyria/Mission*, 226.
39. Bria, *Martyria/Mission*, 10.

the poor and oppressed; and (4) the evangelization of secularized men and women for whom transcendence, forgiveness, and the sacramental have no meaning.[40]

Evangelism

The notion of the people's church must at the same time be understood within the historic order of the ministries within the Orthodox Church. The primary evangelists are the bishops, their presbyters and deacons, and the monastic orders. The monastic community has the specific evangelistic role of living as "a sign, a paradigm, an anticipation and foretaste of the Kingdom," sanctifying time and seeking the renewal of the inner life through unceasing prayer.[41] Modern Orthodoxy is rediscovering the power of the laity, especially through the development of various Orthodox youth movements. Given the persecution that many Orthodox churches have experienced from hostile political authorities, it is important to recognize the evangelistic value of the faithful who suddenly find themselves called to physical martyrdom. Evangelism, therefore, while the calling of the whole church, is effectively exercised by particular representatives who witness "from within the faith and truth of the body of the Church."[42]

Cross-Cultural Witness

The Orthodox churches' firm emphasis on culturally indigenized witness may seem to beg the question, often asked by Western missionaries, of the place of cross-cultural witnessing in Orthodox priorities. However, Orthodox history proudly records the evangelization of the Slavs by the ninth-century Greek brothers Saints Cyril and Methodius. This century has seen innovative forms of intra-Orthodox missionary cooperation in Africa, Alaska, and the Far East, regions of what is sometimes called the Orthodox diaspora. Cross-cultural evangelism has not figured significantly in the witness of Orthodox churches living under restrictive political (e.g., the former Soviet Union and Eastern Europe) or socioreligious (e.g., Islam) conditions, which we have already acknowledged. Recent political change in Russia and Eastern Europe opens new opportunities, though the recurrence in Eastern

---

40. Bria, *Martyria/Mission*, 228

41. On the role of monastic witness in Orthodoxy, see Bria, *Martyria/Mission*, 243–48.

42. Bria, *Martyria/Mission*, 230.

Europe of previously suppressed animosities between Eastern-rite Catholics and Orthodox, on the one hand, and evangelicals and Orthodox, on the other, has revived Orthodox suspicions of mission as involving one church transgressing the ethnic context of another. Where cross-cultural evangelization is possible, Orthodox agree that its subjects must be non-Christians, not Christians from other Orthodox, Catholic, or evangelical churches.[43]

Christian Witness within Islam

Since the seventh century, Islam has provided the social, cultural, and political framework of Orthodox presence in West Asia and North Africa. It exceeds the scope of this article to review this long history of Orthodox-Muslim relations.[44] The contribution of Father Joseph el-Zahlaoui, an Antiochian Orthodox living in Lebanon, to the compendium *Your Will Be Done: Orthodoxy in Mission* offers a good example of a contemporary Orthodox whose concern is with witness in the context of Islam.[45]

Rejecting the view that the Orthodox communities have been introverted by the social experience of Islam, el-Zahlaoui reminds us of important ways in which Orthodox Christians have contributed to the cultural, ideological, and scientific renaissance of Arab societies in different periods of their history. His general point is that "Christianity became an essential spiritual force in the cultural, social and political life of Arab Muslims."

The contemporary resurgence of conservative religious trends throughout the region confronts all minorities with difficult problems. Many Christians feel threatened, even to the point of fearing for their survival. As in previous times of crisis, many Christians opt to emigrate out of the region, usually to the West, with the result that the remaining Christian presence is seriously weakened. Hard as this situation makes it for many Christians to give confident witness, el-Zahlaoui insists on the responsibility of the church to relate the Gospel to this crisis. "The witness of the Gospel challenges us to transform the prevailing destructive suspicion between the minorities and majorities into constructive confidence."

In practical terms, this means that the church must identify with the cause of all victims of injustice in "a fidelity to Christ who calls us to assume on behalf of everybody all true human solidarity." In the Lebanese context

---

43. Case studies of cross-cultural witness appear in Lemopoulos, *Your Will Be Done*.

44. For a sociohistorical analysis, see Haddad, *Syrian Christians in Muslim Society*. For a more theological perspective, see Vaporis, *Orthodox Christians and Muslims*.

45. "Witnessing in the Islamic Context," in Lemopoulos, *Your Will Be Done*, 95–104, from which the following quotations are taken.

el-Zahlaoui emphasizes the church's medicosocial and educational services, through which it witnesses the presence of God within human suffering and manifests the reconciliatory power of the Incarnation.[46]

The most serious impediment to effective Christian witness is the disunity of Christian churches. "Where the Church should be a manifestation of God's love to all human beings and a united community in God's peace, it often appears as a gathering of sects, mutually exclusive of one another." Such disunity invites the criticism of Muslims whose scripture, the Qur'an, argues that disunity is a sign of God's punishment upon Christians who have neglected their divine covenant (5:15).[47] The challenge of Christian witness within Muslim societies, el-Zahlaoui concludes, demands concerted "spiritual and theological reflection on the meaning of our faith and of our beliefs in the Islamic context in which we live."[48]

A PASTORAL APPROACH TO ISSUES OF PROSELYTISM

The MECC document with which this essay began calls for "a pastoral agreement" among churches for the resolution of historical and contemporary problems of proselytism.[49] The key to this approach is "a dialogue of love"[50] in which Christians of different traditions learn to listen to one another in their search for mutual correction and enrichment. The examples we have given point to the growth of such dialogue between churches and with missionary agencies that operate with an ecclesial commitment, however varied this may be. The MECC study document lists several issues that call for discussion under the category of "unconscious" proselytism, such as religious freedom and the freedom of conscience, the issue of "returning

---

46. For further information, see Khouri, "Mission of the Orthodox Youth in Lebanon," 181–83.

47. "For those, too, who call themselves Christians, We did take a Covenant, but they forgot a good part of the Message that We sent them. So We estranged them, with enmity and hatred between one and another, to the Day of Judgment. And soon will God show them what they have done" (Qur'an 5:15).

48. The leading contemporary Orthodox theologian to have addressed the issue of the Christian relationship to Islam is Metropolitan Georges Khodr of Lebanon. See Khodr, "Christianity in a Pluralistic World." For a discussion of the contextualization of Christian theology—including Orthodox contributions—in Palestinian Muslim society, see Mazawi, "Palestinian Local Theology."

49. MECC, *Proselytism, Sects, and Pastoral Challenges*, para. 34–37.

50. The phrase is used by the former MECC general secretary Gabriel Habib in his letter to Evangelicals, "Renewal, Unity, and Witness in the Middle East." See also Michael Roemmele's reply in the same issue (260–62).

to the mother church," mixed marriages and religious education, and the evangelization of nominal Christians.

Is dialogue possible with what the MECC terms "sects," for which, in its judgment, "proselytism is a constitutive element of their identity"? If the MECC has less confidence in dialogue in this respect, there being "not enough basis for a constructive dialogue," it nevertheless recommends "a pastoral strategy" that specifically rejects the option of trying to suppress the freedom of sects to operate. No haven is offered to the argument that civil law should be invoked against the sects. On the contrary, the study document insists that the freedom of the sects to operate must be upheld, as also the right of the individual to choose his or her religious affiliation.[51]

A pastoral approach to the sects should include challenge in two senses of the word: challenge to the sects by monitoring their activities and raising "awareness of the religious and human threats of this phenomenon"; and the challenge of the sects, in that the churches should be energized for renewal, expressed in "a more efficient pastoral work that 'recaptures what has been lost' and immunizes (the) faithful against the temptations of 'religious consumerism.'" Without elaborating further, the document emphasizes the need for continuing renewal of religious education, ministerial formation, pastoral care, and "the balance between participation and the need for leadership" (which this author reads as meaning the new relationship between clergy and laity).

ISSUES FOR INTRA-CHRISTIAN DIALOGUE

The MECC's call for dialogue between Eastern and Western churches implicitly requires us to consider the sociopolitical context in which proselytism continues to evoke contentious argument. At least three dimensions of Christian identity need to be kept in mind.

---

51. MECC, *Proselytism, Sects, and Pastoral Challenges*, para. 61–64. On this point, George Sabra argues that an appeal to secular authorities, or to the courts other than in cases where proselytizing groups breach national laws, infringes the religious rights of individuals, denies the spirit of the Gospel, and betrays the witness of the earliest Christians, who courageously stood for freedom of faith against the political, legal, military, and social pressures of the Roman Empire. See Sabra, "Proselytism, Evangelization, and Ecumenism," 26–28.

Christian Religious Identity in West Asia/North Africa

The Lebanese theologian George Sabra reminds us that religion continues to function as a primary factor of social identity throughout the West Asian/North African region. He draws a helpful distinction between the "denominational" (or sociological) identity of a Christian community and the "ecclesial" (or faith) commitment of its members. These two dimensions may be continuous with each other. But modern forces of secularization have tended to erode the ecclesial vitality of many Christians who nonetheless continue to be socially defined by their denomination. In this context, Sabra argues, the purpose of evangelization is to enhance the ecclesial identity of individuals and communities. He then poses the question, If the faith renewal of an individual or group leads to a change of ecclesial affiliation, is this evangelization or proselytism?[52]

Two variables tend to influence the way this question is answered. Where continuity between church and ethnicity is strong (e.g., in the Oriental Orthodox churches and the Maronite church), change of ecclesial affiliation from the mother church is unconscionable and treated as a betrayal of community. In cases where ecclesiology has reduced or eliminated the sense of ethnicity (e.g., in Protestant churches), the quality of personal faith commitment/salvation is the primary value of evangelism.

Here the second variable becomes evident. Where faith is understood in individualistic terms as a personal relationship with God, freedom of religious conviction and the right to change religious affiliation tend to be given priority. This is typically the case with Protestant Christianity, which has been so much influenced by principles of the Western Enlightenment. A quite different worldview pertains among those churches that are historically rooted in the cultural and intellectual traditions of West Asia/North Africa, where community provides the social and spiritual context within which individual faith is nurtured. This is at the heart of the monastic tradition of Christianity and is inherent in the shape and content of the liturgy. In different ways it is no less evident in the Islamic religious consciousness, which has influenced the social character of indigenous Christianity. Evangelism in this context is understood in terms of the renewal of an individual's ecclesial identity within his or her denominational identity, not in separation from it. Orthodox witness makes this very clear and amounts to a conceptual (and thus practical) resistance to the many Western notions of mission.

---

52. Sabra, "Proselytism, Evangelization, and Ecumenism," 29–31.

Christian Cultural Identity in West Asia/North Africa

The intricate relationship between language and culture is richly evidenced in the indigenous Christian communities in West Asia/North Africa. Our review of the churches has emphasized the diversity of linguistic cultures (Aramaic, Armenian, Coptic, and Syriac) that distinguished the ancient Eastern patriarchates from each other and from the West (Greek and Latin). With the rise and expansion of Islam from the seventh century, however, Arabic has become the lingua franca of most of the peoples of the region. The wealth of Christian theological writing from the mid-eighth century in Arabic as well as in their ethnic languages is a literary monument of their bilingual traditions. Sydney Griffith, a leading scholar of this genre of Christian literature, observes that Christians "actually adopted a way of presenting the traditional teachings of the church in an Arabic idiom conditioned by the Islamic frame of reference in the midst of which they lived."[53] Rarely have Western missions been sensitive to this achievement. Indeed, if recognized at all, it has usually been regarded with suspicion as an incipient paganism that must be expunged. The conversion of indigenous Christians to Western forms of Christianity has had the effect of deracinating them from their cultural-linguistic traditions, marking them out as "aliens at home"[54] and burdening them with the criticism of being cultural proselytes.

Christian Political Identity in West Asia/North Africa

Under the Ottoman Empire the Christian communities of West Asia/North Africa were recognized for legal and political purposes as millets—autonomous minorities within Muslim society, represented by their clerical hierarchies. For four hundred years (early sixteenth to early twentieth centuries) this was the juridical framework of George Sabra's sociological category of "denominational" identity. While the millet system has been formally abolished in the constitutions of the modern Arab states, it continues to exert informal influence in terms of political psychology and practice. This is strikingly evident in Lebanon, where a "confessional" system of public life guarantees (in theory) that each religious community in the state is represented proportionately to its size in relation to the other religious communities. While political leadership is exercised on constitutionally secular lines, confessionalism allows the religious hierarchies of both Christian and

---

53. Griffith, "Faith and Reason in Christian Kalām," 5.
54. See Semaan, *Aliens at Home*.

Muslim communities to continue to exert considerable influence behind the scenes, and openly if political life breaks down in civil or military disorder.

Against this background the antagonism of indigenous churches to proselytism has certain political resonance. This may be construed as a case of clerical hierarchies protecting their political influence from further erosion. But since this is how the political culture continues to operate, it can also be argued that a politically influential clergy is a positive asset for Christian minorities in societies that are themselves undergoing various forms of Islamic religious and social renewal. Burdened by a feeling of vulnerability, many Arab Christians look for the strengthening of their traditional institutions of leadership and feel politically undermined and endangered by proselytism.

CONCLUSION

This article has attempted to elucidate the controversial issue of proselytism in West Asia/North Africa in a dispassionate manner, based on historical evidence and contemporary documentation, analyzed from the point of view of the indigenous Christian communities. In conclusion, the author wishes to commend the statement of George Sabra that "ecumenism is simply incompatible with proselytism."[55] The weight of historical evidence shows that proselytism almost invariably becomes the dynamic of intra-Christian relations where disunity prevails among churches or sectarianism is fostered by exclusivist groups. Ultimately, it is evangelism itself that becomes the casualty of "sheep-stealing" mission.

If the renewal of the church arises from the renewal of Christian witness, the qualitative wealth of Christian traditions in West Asia/North Africa (notwithstanding their quantitative decline) suggests that this region has an important role to play in the twenty-first century, as it did in the first. But this promise will be realized only to the degree that the churches of the future can regain the ecumenical fellowship of the early Christian centuries. Drawing once again from Sabra's sociological analysis, we can well support his hope that in a truly ecumenical situation "the evangelizers could aim at reviving . . . sociological Christians in and for their own (ecclesial) traditions."[56]

---

55. Sabra, "Proselytism, Evangelization, and Ecumenism," 25.
56. Sabra, "Proselytism, Evangelization, and Ecumenism," 33.

3.3

Mission and the Issue of Proselytism[1]

CECIL M. ROBECK JR.

International Bulletin of Missionary Research 20.1 (1996) 2–8

PROSELYTISM IS A BLIGHT on the veracity of the Christian message and on the effectiveness of Christian mission. Almost weekly one can pick up a local newspaper or Christian periodical and find a story in which the members of one group are charged with attempting to lure members of another group into their ranks.[2] The heat and animosity generated by such allegations and activities hold explosive potential in many parts of the world.[3]

Proselytism, as G. R. Evans observes, "is a sign that the sense of sharing a common mind has broken down."[4] This breakdown may be observed at two levels. First, it can be seen in the multitude of Christian communities that do not respect or recognize the genuineness or fullness of ecclesial

---

1. Reprinted with permission of the *International Bulletin of Mission Research*, which is owned by the Overseas Ministries Study Center and published by Sage Publications.

2. See Alta/Baja California Bishops, "Dimensions of a Response to Proselytism"; John Paul II, "Opening Address to Fourth General Conference," 321–32, esp. 326; Mycio, "America Losing Luster in Ukraine"; Margolis, "Wave of Religious Revival Splits Brazil"; Dahlburg, "Russian Law Curbs Foreigner Preaching"; "Lebanon Meeting Statement Rejects Proselytism," 166–69; Haynes, "Brazil's Catholics Launch 'Holy War,'" 74–75; Dellinger, "Evangelicals View Hispanic Evangelization Differently," 10–11.

3. In particular, I think of recent attempts to pass legislation in the Commonwealth of Independent States that would restrict a great deal of evangelization and that would have the potential of aiding more repressive elements in the current parliament.

4. Evans, *Church and the Churches*, 70.

claims made by other communities that call themselves Christian. Second, it can be observed in our inability or unwillingness to work together on a common definition of terms. To date, one group's evangelization is still another group's proselytism.

Besides the disparity between definitions of the problem, even the assumptions that undergird certain definitions are not shared by all. Evans argues, "If I think you are already in Christ in his Church where you are, I shall not want to win you for my Church. Indeed, I shall regard you as already a member of it."[5] But many of us can think of situations in which this basic assumption is not shared, and evangelistic or missional activity continues unabated. As a result, sincere efforts of Christian witness may be seen as proselytism, creating division rather than reconciliation.

What is proselytism? How is it being defined? And who is defining it? It is not my concern to redefine or to do away with the term "proselytism" but to explore its common usages in such a way as to preserve the legitimate place for a noncoercive, sensitive evangelism.

In January 1994 Armenian Orthodox Catholicos Karekin II visited the United States. While he was in Southern California, he shared some of his concerns about the interface between the Orthodox and evangelicals. Since the collapse of Communism in Eastern Europe, he reported, many evangelicals have made trips to that region of the world to engage in what they call evangelism. Some of them met with Catholicos Karekin himself. When they did, they found him dressed in clerical attire, wearing a cross. Although they knew who he was, they nevertheless pressed him on the question of whether or not he knew Jesus.

"They ignore the fact that Eastern Orthodox Christians are just that— Christians," he protested. He went on to point out that "Christianity is not something we have inherited from the West but something that has been with us since the beginning of the Christian era."[6] Such stories are common among Orthodox leaders in Eastern Europe and the former Soviet Union, and they serve notice to evangelicals on the whole that they could use some lessons both in theology and church history—not to mention the kindness and common courtesy of 1 Corinthians 13:4–5.

Evangelicals know remarkably little about Eastern Orthodoxy. But this is not the total story. The Orthodox know far too little about evangelicals. One need only note the action of Archbishop Iakovos, archbishop of the Greek Orthodox Archdiocese of North and South America, who issued an encyclical letter in September 1994 declaring Seventh-Day Adventists, the

---

5. Evans, *Church and the Churches*, 70.
6. Finnegan, "Armenian Pope Delights Faithful."

Assemblies of God, and Pentecostals to be "religious groups which are not of the Christian tradition."[7] Fortunately, the damage has been somewhat ameliorated through the issuance of a corrective that declares that "most congregations of the Assemblies of God, Pentecostals and Seventh-Day Adventists are of the Christian Tradition. Some are not."[8]

Much more positive is the work undertaken in a joint evangelization project called Mission Volga.[9] Beginning in the spring of 1992 some leaders in the Russian Orthodox Church and a number of evangelical parachurch leaders worked out an evangelistic program that resulted in one hundred thousand people responding to invitations; through a series of televized events, Mission Volga was seen by some twenty-five million people.

The ignorance of some evangelicals often leads to what can only be called proselytism. On other occasions, such as occurred with Mission Volga, there may be cooperative efforts that are both evangelistically effective and successful in avoiding the proselytism label. But in still other situations, the charge of proselytism would appear to be unwarranted. Rules that are unilaterally declared regarding geographic or cultural boundaries are clearly debatable. Consider, for example, unchurched Hispanic Catholics who are contacted by evangelizing Protestants. On one hand, any charge that such Protestants do not take Hispanic history and culture seriously or that they do not understand the Roman Catholic theology of baptism must be answered.[10] On the other hand, some Roman Catholic leaders, such as Cardinal Augusto Vargas Alzamora, are prepared to recognize that "the number of baptized Catholics who live a life totally indifferent to their faith is dramatically changing the face of the culture."[11] Whatever might have once been said about a strong Hispanic Catholic culture must now be modified.

Although proselytism possesses a neutral or positive meaning in the Bible,[12] today most connotations are derogatory. But it is equally clear that

7. Archbishop Iakovos to the Pastors and Reverend Priests of the Greek Orthodox Archdiocese of North and South America. See "Archbishop Calls Pentecostals Non-Christian," 42

8. Protocol no. 13 from the Reverend Dr. Milton B. Efthimiou to the Reverend Fathers of the Greek Orthodox Archdiocese of North and South America, May 22, 1995.

9. See Nicastro Jr., "Mission Volga."

10. Alta/Baja California Bishops, "Dimensions of a Response to Proselytism," 667.

11. Bermudez, "Evangelizing All Over Again," 12.

12. In the Old Testament the original proselyte was a Gentile foreigner and came under the protection of God in the midst of Israel (Exod 22:21; Deut 29:10–15). Later, as they assimilated into the whole of Israel's life, proselytes were seen as Gentiles who believed in Israel's God, with or without the mark of circumcision. The term appears in the New Testament only four times (Matt 23:15; Acts 2:10; 6:5; 13:43). Only in Matthew

despite widespread agreement about the negative character of proselytism, definitions differ dramatically, depending upon who employs the term. A few examples will make the point.

THE ORTHODOX AND THE ISSUE OF PROSELYTISM

Although concern over proselytism against the Orthodox is not new, events in Eastern Europe over the past half dozen years have highlighted the problem. The uninvited entry of Protestant missionaries into the Orthodox communities of the Middle East spans more than a century and a half. As Norman A. Horner has noted, the charge of proselytism may have emerged when Protestant missionaries were disappointed in their efforts to evangelize Muslims, so that they turned their attention instead to members of the various Orthodox communities already present in the region.[13] A number of studies on the subject have been undertaken by the Middle East Council of Churches and individual members of the council.[14]

In more recent years, the Orthodox Church throughout Eastern Europe and the former Soviet Union has been deeply troubled by what it perceives to be an invasion of groups bent upon proselytizing those whom it understands to be part of its legitimate flock.[15] Many groups—from historic Protestant denominations to younger churches, independent evangelists, parachurch organizations, and so-called sects, cults, and new religious movements—have rejoiced at the new freedoms available in the whole of Eastern Europe and the former Soviet Union, or Commonwealth of Independent States (CIS).[16] Many have taken advantage of the situation to carry their message into Eastern Europe and the CIS. Sometimes they are sensitive

---

23:15 is there a negative connotation to the term.

13. Horner, "Problem of Intra-Christian Proselytism," 314–15.

14. See Sabra, "Proselytism, Evangelization, and Ecumenism"; Middle East Council of Churches, *Proselytism, Sects, and Pastoral Challenges*. The latter document was submitted to the executive committee of the MECC and distributed to the churches [see section 2.7 in this volume].

15. See, for example, "Message of the Primates," 57–60.

16. George Otis Jr. and his staff at the Sentinel Group in Seattle, WA, gave a report in which the breadth of work undertaken in the whole of Eastern Europe by new groups is displayed. The work of Pentecostals and charismatic groups is viewed as evangelism and mission activity. It is noted, however, that "proselytizing by cults is another problem in the former Soviet republics. Mormon, Hindu, Baha'i, and Buddhist groups are recruiting members, as are various proponents of occult and New Age doctrines" (Otis Jr., "Holy Spirit around the World," 59).

to the cultural and religious histories of the region, but often they are not. Zeal frequently outruns knowledge.

It is equally clear that the Orthodox Church, dominant in this region for a millennium, counts on its cultural link with the past to move ahead after the era of Soviet suppression. Yet the seventy-year presence of Communism, with its intense persecution of the churches, has produced an enormous spiritual vacuum. The national churches, Orthodox and otherwise, find themselves with inadequate resources to fill this vacuum. Protestant and other groups from the West are entering the region with a distinct advantage. They are often able to afford to do things that the Orthodox churches can still only dream of.[17]

As a result of this "invasion," the primates of the Orthodox churches issued a formal statement on March 15, 1992, in which they charged that the traditional Orthodox countries are now being viewed as "missionary territories" by a variety of groups that are setting up missionary networks and proselytizing. Of particular note in this statement is the reference to the then-unresolved Uniate issue in the Ukraine, Romania, East Slovakia, the Middle East, and elsewhere; as well as the rise of Protestant fundamentalist (and evangelical) missionary activity "in Orthodox countries which were under communist regime."[18] The primates maintain that the behavior of Protestant fundamentalists (and evangelicals) is inappropriate, and that the outsiders' view of these countries as terra missionis is unacceptable, "since in these countries the Gospel has already been preached for many centuries."[19] Genuine mission, the primates go on to point out, is properly "carried out in non-Christian countries and among non-Christian people."[20]

The cultural and ecclesial insensitivity of some contemporary groups has been extremely disturbing to Orthodox and other Christians who paid

---

17. On this point, see the irenic, enlightening article by Leonid Kishkovsky, "Orthodoxy at a Crossroads," 15–16.

18. "Message of the Primates," 58. Since the message was issued in 1992, the Uniate problem has been largely resolved. See the work of the Pontifical Commission for Russia (PCR, "Principles and Norms," 301–4) as well as the report of the Joint International Commission for the Theological Dialogue between the Roman Catholic Church and the Orthodox Church (JIC, "Uniatism," 4–7).

19. "Message of the Primates," 58. Leaders from two former Soviet republics, the Ukraine and Armenia (the one political, the other ecclesiastical), have made similar comments in the American press. Mary Mycio quotes Dmytro Karchynsky of the Ukrainian National Assembly as ridiculing the missionaries who preach on Kiev's Independence Square: "They come from a country that didn't exist three hundred years ago to preach in a country that was Christianized one thousand years ago." "Even more galling," reports Mycio, "they use Russian translators" (Mycio, "America Losing Luster in Ukraine," H2).

20. "Message of the Primates," 59.

a severe price for their faithfulness in the midst of Communist oppression. Such insensitivity needs to be challenged.

But it also appears that the Orthodox, who admittedly are ill prepared to rush into a fully democratic, societal pluralism, have overreacted. In late 1994 the theological commission of the Russian Orthodox Church recommended to the governing synod that it withdraw from membership in the World Council of Churches "in protest over continuing 'missionary intrusions' in Russia by other churches."[21] Their claims seem to overlook the impact of the seventy-year reign of atheistic ideals, as though to deny that it had any effect. The region is claimed as "Orthodox," which must be understood as "Christian," merely because in times past the Gospel has been preached there, the culture has been Christianized, and the Orthodox Church is entitled to cultural hegemony. The Orthodox have essentially defined proselytism so broadly that any missionary or evangelistic activity undertaken by non-Orthodox within these countries is labeled illegitimate, and those who are active in such practices are frequently described as thieves.

ROMAN CATHOLICS AND THE ISSUE OF PROSELYTISM

A similar situation exists in Latin America, where it is the Roman Catholic Church that raises the charge of proselytism. The arguments used by Roman Catholics in Latin America, which are deeply rooted in claims to cultural hegemony, are similar to those used by the Orthodox elsewhere. Similarly, alleged proselytizers are accused of theological and cultural insensitivity.

At Vatican II, the Roman Catholic Church condemned proselytism. In its "Decree on the Church's Missionary Activity" (*Ad Gentes*), the council noted, "The Church strictly forbids that anyone should be forced to accept the faith, or be induced or enticed by unworthy devices."[22] No one should be "forced to act against his convictions nor is anyone to be restrained from acting in accordance with his convictions in religious matters."[23]

It is noteworthy that while the council wished to safeguard people from coercion, inducements, and enticements, it did not wish to discourage mission. This is stated clearly in the "Decree on the Apostolate of Lay People" (*Apostolicam actuositatem*). "A member who does not work at the growth of the body to the extent of his possibilities," the bishops noted, "must be considered useless both to the Church and to himself." Members were encouraged to engage in evangelization as well as acts of charity. In

---

21. "Ecu News," 16.
22. Vatican II, *Ad Gentes* 13.
23. Vatican II, *Dignitatis Humanae* 2.

order to safeguard these acts of charity from criticism such as the charge of proselytism, the bishops encouraged members to look for the imago Dei in those to whom they sought to minister. "The liberty and dignity of the person helped must be respected with the greatest sensitivity," they argued. "Purity of intention should not be stained by any self-seeking or desire to dominate. The demands of justice must first of all be satisfied."[24]

In 1993 Cardinal Cassidy, president of the Pontifical Council for Promoting Christian Unity, made a helpful distinction between "sects" and those who may at times exhibit sectarian attitudes.[25] This distinction, he noted, was made as a result of two important dialogues that have included evangelicals and Pentecostals.[26]

In spite of these welcome and obvious changes at the upper levels of the Roman curia, the word on the street is that evangelicals continue to be viewed and treated as though they were proselytizing sectarians, especially in Latin America. A speech that John Paul II gave on October 12, 1992, in Santo Domingo, Dominican Republic, as he began the Episcopal Conference of Latin American Bishops, clearly employed the language of "sects" to describe non-Catholic movements. While it is unclear whether the pope intended to include evangelicals and, in particular, Pentecostals in the category of "rapacious wolves," other Catholic voices certainly did.[27]

---

24. Vatican II, *Apostolicam Actuositatem* 2, 8. On human dignity, see Vatican II, *Gaudium et Spes* 26; *Dignitatis Humanae*.

25. It is indeed gratifying and significant to note Cardinal Cassidy's informed and carefully nuanced distinction between "sects or new religious movements" that do not participate in ecumenical dialogue and those groups that have participated in ecumenical dialogue, even if on a relatively limited scale. He notes, "We must be careful, however, not to confuse the issue by lumping under the term 'sect,' groups that do not deserve that title. I am not speaking here, for instance, about the evangelical movement among Protestants, nor about Pentecostalism as such. The Pontifical Council has had fruitful dialogue and significant contacts with certain evangelical groups and with Pentecostals. Indeed, one can speak of a mutual enrichment as a result of these contacts" (Cassidy, "Prolusio," 122). While the Pontifical Council for Promoting Christian Unity has made it clear that many evangelicals and Pentecostals do not fall under the categories that are the focus of the 1986 document *Sects or New Religious Movements*, much of the language of the document leaves open the possibility that bishops may apply this work to evangelicals and Pentecostals. This seems particularly the case in Latin America. See "Vatican Reports on Sects, Cults," 2-10. Haynes, "Brazil's Catholics Launch 'Holy War,'" highlights the work of Bishop Sinesio Bohn in this regard. Quite understandably, Latin American Protestants resent being referred to as sects, a term they reserve for groups such as the Mormons and Jehovah's Witnesses.

26. On these two dialogues, see Meeking and Stott, *Evangelical-Roman Catholic Dialogue on Mission*; *Pneuma* 12.1 (1990) 77-142.

27. John Paul II, "Opening Address to Fourth General Conference," 326. In an interesting exchange on this issue, of which I have been a part, Edward L. Cleary, OP,

Evangelicals and Pentecostals are viewed as the most substantive part of the "problem of the sects" in Latin America.[28] Pentecostals are especially singled out by the bishops of California and of the Sonoran region of Mexico as being among the "sects or new religious groups . . . most aggressive in their proselytizing."[29] As such, they would be viewed and treated according to the 1986 Vatican report *Sects, Cults, and New Religious Movements.*

This stance is grounded in the assumption of historical and cultural continuity. "Many . . . Hispanic people have lived all their lives in a thoroughly Catholic environment and have been formed as Christians by the tradition, culture, piety and religious practices of the Catholic Church."[30] But this is an unfair judgment on two counts. First, it does not take seriously the presence of evangelicals who are themselves Hispanic and who have been part of the Hispanic culture for a century or more. Second, evangelicals are being told that even though vast multitudes of Hispanic people rarely ever darken the doorway of a church, they should be considered Christian; they remain Roman Catholic and are therefore off-limits to non-Roman Catholic mission. "We feel," write the bishops of Alta and Baja California, that evangelicals display "a lack of understanding and appreciation both of the rich history of the Catholic faith in Hispanic culture and of the theology of baptism."[31]

---

wrote "John Paul Cries 'Wolf,'" 7–8, in which he lamented the pope's language, which tends to feed old stereotypes, especially about Pentecostals. In response, I wrote a letter to the editor that was printed under the title "What the Pope Said." In my letter I affirmed Cleary's point and applauded the pope's recommendations to his bishops on steps to stop the problem of "fleeing sheep." The pope had suggested that the flock was not receiving adequate feeding from the church. I argued that the very issues the pope addressed to the bishops were the issues that Pentecostals and evangelicals had lifted up throughout this century. A rebuttal to my letter came from James Chichetto, CSC, "Dubious Tactics," in which he argued that evangelicals and Pentecostals are indeed "rapacious wolves" bent upon "destructive proselytism." Cleary submitted a subsequent edition, printed under the title "El maltrato de la jerarquia catolica a los pentecostales." An excerpt from my letter to Commonweal was printed at the end.

28. Serbin, "Latin America's Catholics," 405–6; Ramirez, "Crisis in Ecumenism among Hispanic Christians," 663.

29. Alta/Baja California Bishops, "Dimensions of a Response to Proselytism," 666–67.

30. Alta/Baja California Bishops, "Dimensions of a Response to Proselytism," 667. The Orthodox make a parallel argument in Eastern Europe.

31. Alta/Baja California Bishops, "Dimensions of a Response to Proselytism," 667. The relationship between faith and culture or Gospel and culture is clearly an area that Roman Catholics and Pentecostals need to study together, but it would be inaccurate to suggest that Pentecostals simply misunderstand the nature of Christian baptism as practiced by Roman Catholics. In "Perspectives on Koinonia," the report from the third quinquennium of this dialogue, it was apparent that there was much about baptism on

Over against the "sects" the bishops list the "historic churches"—the Orthodox Church, Protestant churches stemming from the Reformation, and the Anglican Church. These are viewed as ecumenical because of their search for Christian unity and their respect for "all religious beliefs."[32] This suggests that very little, if any, evangelization is being undertaken by these churches in Latin America, which may account for their relative lack of growth as compared with evangelicals throughout that region. These churches do not challenge Roman Catholic claims to cultural hegemony and thus do not threaten the place of Roman Catholicism in Latin American life.

Latin America is not the only region of the world where the Roman Catholic Church has been concerned about the issue of proselytism. In preparation for the special synod of African bishops in 1994, a working paper titled "Evangelizing Mission of the Church in Africa" astutely described both the problems and the possibilities for the evangelization of Africa by Roman Catholics, one of the problems being the rapid growth of what are termed "sects and new religious movements." Among these groups are included the many African Independent Churches, which are accused of embracing an "unyielding fundamentalism or aggressive proselytizing." Other groups are also charged with proselytism, defined as "pressuring people to conversion by methods unworthy of the gospel, and offensive propaganda against fellow Christians." Competition between groups is also portrayed as problematic within the African context, especially in relation to such things as "initial proclamation [evangelization], rivalries over schools, the siting of churches and the presenting of candidates for public office."[33]

Two documents produced over the past decade—one officially in relation to the Pontifical Council for Promoting Christian Unity, and the other a more recent and unofficial statement produced in the United States—have addressed the subject of proselytism. In each of these cases, evangelicals have contributed to the discussion in significant ways. The second of the two statements, *Evangelicals and Catholics Together: The Christian Mission in the Third Millennium*, has produced considerable reflection, discussion, and consternation on the part of the constituencies of both traditions. It is obvious from the wording of the title that the drafters capitalized on some

---

which Pentecostals and Roman Catholics have agreement. But there is also much on the topic over which they disagree, and some of those disagreements are based upon the rejection of the theology of the other, not merely upon misunderstanding or an overemphasis on some aspect of baptism, as the bishops have suggested. See "Perspectives on Koinonia," esp. §41, 47–51. See also Robeck Jr. and Sandidge, "Ecclesiology of Koinonia and Baptism."

32. Alta/Baja California Bishops, "Dimensions of a Response to Proselytism," 667.
33. "Evangelizing Mission of the Church in Africa," 653; see §81–89.

of the hard work done by certain bilateral texts and on some of the documents of Vatican II. The document charges both evangelicals and Catholics with attempting "to win 'converts' from one another's folds." It condemns the practice of "sheep stealing" because it undermines Christian mission, reflects poor stewardship, and involves practices that violate the Gospel. The drafters recognize that both faith communities possess the "opportunity and means of growth in Christian discipleship." They call for respect for those who are "active adherents of another Christian community" and for the decisions made by people who have joined one group or the other. They condemn various forms of coercion, the bearing of false witness, the presentation of unjust and unbalanced caricatures and stereotypes, and other unworthy practices. Also condemned is "denominational or institutional aggrandizement," examples of which are not given; this is a charge, like the use of coercion, that shows up repeatedly in recent documents on proselytism.[34]

In some respects, the earlier document, *Evangelical-Roman Catholic Dialogue on Mission* (ERCDOM), is more thoughtfully constructed. Proselytism, according to ERCDOM, is a perversion of genuine evangelism, a form of "unworthy witness." The drafters explore the reasons for proselytism, including definitional problems over categories of church members such as "lapsed," "inactive," and "nominal," and the problems inherent in the ecclesiological distinction between the "visible" and the "invisible" church. Finally, drawing from the 1970 document, *Common Witness and Proselytism*, (produced by a joint theological commission of the Roman Catholic Church and the World Council of Churches), they emphasize three aspects of the document. Proselytism occurs wherever the evangelizer's motive is unworthy, the methods are unworthy, or the message is "unjust or uncharitable" in its portrayal of the other's faith community.[35]

PROSELYTISM AND THE WORLD COUNCIL OF CHURCHES

Proselytism has been on the agenda of the World Council of Churches at least since 1954. Following the Evanston Assembly, the Central Committee of the WCC appointed a commission to study the subject of proselytism

---

34. "Evangelicals and Catholics Together," 21; Meeking and Stott, *Evangelical-Roman Catholic Dialogue on Mission*, 89–91. For criticisms of "Evangelicals and Catholics Together," see Taylor, "Catholic-Evangelical Agreement Criticized by Latino Baptists," A11; "Evangelical Catholic Statement Criticized," 520–21.

35. Meeking and Stott, *Evangelical-Roman Catholic Dialogue on Mission*, 89–91.

and religious liberty. This was undertaken because of "difficulties which had arisen affecting relationships between member churches."[36] The commission produced its report in July 1956. It was revised by the Central Committee (July 28–August 4, 1956) and finally passed at the New Delhi Assembly (1967), published that fall under the title "Christian Witness, Proselytism, and Religious Freedom."[37]

Providing the groundwork for continuing discussions within the council itself *Christian Witness* also held implications for the relationship between council members and churches that were not part of the council. Proselytism, which was termed a "corruption of witness," included such actions as cajolery, bribery, intimidation, placing an organization's success before Christ's honor, comparing one's strengths with the weaknesses of others, bearing false witness against other churches, and the replacing of love for souls with self-aggrandizing motives.[38] It is worth observing that this paper was adopted by the WCC at a time when a number of Orthodox groups joined the council and when the International Missionary Council was incorporated within the structure of the WCC.[39]

The WCC continued to work on the topic throughout the 1960s, in particular, with the Roman Catholic Church immediately following Vatican II. In May 1970 a Joint Theological Commission released *Common Witness and Proselytism: A Study Document* and recommended that it be studied by the Joint Working Group, which had been established in 1965 to facilitate common agenda items between the WCC and the Vatican. The Joint Working Group went on to recommend that the member churches of the WCC also examine the document.[40]

In *Common Witness and Proselytism* the definition of proselytism focuses on "whatever violates the right of the human person, Christian or non-Christian, to be free from external coercion in religious matters, or whatever, in proclamation of the Gospel, does not conform to the ways God draws free men to himself in response to his calls to serve in spirit and in truth." The document describes various actions that should be avoided, actions thus identified as proselytizing activities. Included is the condemnation of coercion, whether physical, moral, or psychological, which would tend to deprive human beings of freedom of choice and full autonomy. Here

36. WCC, "Christian Witness, Proselytism, and Religious Liberty," 48.
37. "Revised Report of the Commission"; WCC, *Evanston to New Delhi*, 239–45.
38. "Revised Report of the Commission," 80, 82.
39. Loffler, "Proselytism," 829; cf. Horner, "Problem of Intra-Christian Proselytism," 305.
40. JWG, "Common Witness and Proselytism," 9.

the document points out that "certain abuse of mass communications can have this effect." Offers of aid, whether "open or disguised," given with the expectation that someone would receive them if he or she converts, are condemned. The offering of inducements, exploitation of weakness, the raising of suspicions about others, improper motivations linked to "social, economic, or political pressure," and the use of "unjust and uncharitable references" about other religious communities are also included in the broader definition of proselytism.[41]

A decade later, Norman Horner authored a helpful historical overview of discussions on proselytism. He concluded that especially in the Middle East, where the Orthodox had lived for centuries as a highly restricted minority, other Christians, including Catholics, Protestants, and what he called "a variety of small, sectarian groups," needed to develop better definitions for evangelism and proselytism, and a better understanding of the culture in which these ancient Orthodox churches exist.[42]

In 1988–1989, Raymond Fung, secretary for evangelism for the WCC, published a series of letters on the topic, which have now been collected in his book *Evangelistically Yours*. He began by noting that proselytism constitutes "sheep-stealing or coercive and improper attempts to convert." Fung went on to ask also about the concrete circumstances that give rise to proselytism. His collection of letters from Ethiopia, the United States, Costa Rica, the Philippines, Pakistan, and the Netherlands is revealing. Fung concluded his study by referring to the 1970 document *Common Witness and Proselytism* and by offering several observations. He suggested that as the issue of common witness is emphasized, there will be a corresponding decrease in proselytism. He called for theological and missiological exchanges on the subject. And he urged his readers to engage in preaching the Gospel without worrying about whether one's own group would grow as a result.[43]

During the 1990s, the World Council of Churches has been engaged in another major study on the issue of proselytism. Certain staff members of the WCC met in the Orthodox Center in Chambesy, Switzerland, on February 24–27, 1993. The results of that meeting were subsequently published under the title *Towards Responsible Relations in Mission*. The group stated that "commitment to evangelism is inseparable from the commitment to the unity of the Body of Christ." Of most significance is the claim that participants in this study group "shared the reality of the pain that unilateral and insensitive mission activity has caused." "Invasion" language is used to

---

41. JWG, "Common Witness and Proselytism," 11; 18–19; see also 17.
42. Horner, "Problem of Intra-Christian Proselytism," 312–13.
43. Fung, *Evangelistically Yours*, 188, 219–23.

describe the "proselytizing activities of sects and new religious movements" and the "unilateral mission work by churches, groups and agencies who are not members of the WCC."[44]

The report attempts to think theologically about the relationship between proselytism and "communion of churches." One result is that if the idea of koinonia is allowed to serve as a basis for understanding the church, "competition in mission activities, proselytism, the creation of parallel church structures and interference in the life of already existing churches would be avoided."[45]

In August 1993 the Fifth World Conference on Faith and Order of the WCC convened in Santiago de Compostela, Spain, with the issue of proselytism again on the agenda. Perhaps more than at any time since 1970, new concerns were factored into the discussion. The idea of a fuller koinonia was central to the meeting. Proselytism was viewed as including the use of coercive and manipulative methods in the act of "evangelism" that lead to the distortion of "the real though imperfect koinonia Christians already share."[46]

The conference delegates proposed that the WCC undertake a new study of "mission, evangelism, and proselytism," for which they offered a four-point rationale. First, Christians who are not part of the WCC are often charged with proselytism, but seldom are they part of the discussion in which such charges emerge. This needs to change. Second, those who have succumbed to the "proselytizing" efforts of others are seldom if ever debriefed by the community they leave. Representative "proselytes" should be included in future discussions; their testimony may have value. Third, churches that are losing their sheep need to have an opportunity to ask why. Fourth, a forum is needed in which the accusers and the accused may face one another in a constructive way such as is outlined in Matthew 18.

Finally, two affirmations emerged from the group. First, it was affirmed that most persons engaging in proselytism "do so out of a genuine concern for the salvation of those whom they address."[47] Second, it was acknowledged that churches that show signs of spiritual vitality in "faith, life, and witness" appear to be relatively immune to losses resulting from proselytism.

Georges Lemopoulos reports that, in follow up to the meeting in Spain, the WCC's Unit II has pursued the subject, and that, in cooperation

---

44. "Towards Responsible Relations in Mission," 235, 236, 238.
45. "Towards Responsible Relations in Mission," 238.
46. Best and Gassmann, *On the Way to Fuller Koinonia*, 256.
47. Best and Gassmann, *On the Way to Fuller Koinonia*, 257.

with Faith and Order and Unit II, the Joint Working Group has completed a study document titled *The Challenge of Proselytism and the Calling of Common Witness*.

THE WCC AND INTERRELIGIOUS PROSELYTISM

In spite of all these conferences and study groups, proselytism persists as a major concern. This is true for two reasons. First is the collapse of Communism in the former Soviet Union and the changing social and religious landscape that has followed. Second is the transformation or broadening of ecumenical commitments by some members of the WCC to include Jews and, for that matter, members of other world religions. In the first instance, we can see the rise of concern as is evidenced by the cries of the Orthodox. In regard to the second, we need to look briefly at the issue of what might be called interreligious proselytism.

A troubling understanding of proselytism is one that is receiving considerable attention within many conciliar and Roman Catholic circles and that is also beginning to receive discussion in evangelical circles.[48] It involves the idea that the evangelization of people of other living faiths may ultimately prove to be an act of proselytism. Certainly within countries such as those in which Islam is the dominant religion, anti-Christian evangelization laws exist. The Islamic majority clearly labels violations of these laws as acts of proselytism. But it is troubling that many Christians seem to be coming to similar conclusions.

Evangelicals, however, are bound to insist that the message of the Gospel is intended to go out both to the Jew and to the Gentile (Rom 1:16–17). Evangelicals hold, therefore, that the message of God's salvation, made available uniquely and ultimately in Jesus Christ, is something to be proclaimed to every person and to every race. The Jewish people, and peoples of other living faiths, are no exception to Jesus' Great Commission (Matt 28:19–20).

The World Council of Churches clearly held to this position in the past. In its 1948 Assembly convened in Amsterdam, the WCC received a report entitled *The Christian Approach to the Jews*, in which this issue was spelled out explicitly: "All of our churches stand under the commission of our common Lord, 'Go ye into all the world and preach the Gospel to every creature.' The fulfillment of this commission requires that we include the Jewish people in our evangelistic task."[49]

---

48. See, for instance, Stackhouse Jr., "Evangelicals Reconsider World Religions," in which the author studies the recent thought of Clark Pinnock and John Sanders.

49. WCC, *Theology of the Churches and the Jewish People*, 5.

Because the Holocaust lay in such close proximity to the founding of the WCC, it is understandable that the WCC and its various constituencies should seek greater understanding of the Jewish people and their faith. Dialogue between a number of different WCC member denominations and the Jews, as well as between Roman Catholics and Jews, has raised a number of very important questions about the covenantal relationship between God and the Jews, between God and the church, and between the church and the Jews before God. But the verdict is still out on whether, on theological grounds, Israel still has a "valid covenant with God" or whether the churches may need to "proscribe all proselytism of Jews."[50]

The latter position, set forth by Allan Brockway, is at best premature, but it is not difficult to detect movement in this direction by some of the member churches of the WCC. Simon Schoon observes that in recent years "the WCC and its member churches [have moved] away from the missionary approach to the Jews towards a dialogical relationship between the churches and the Jewish people." For many, this has been accompanied by a parallel movement away from direct missionary effort. Dialogue, as the Presbyterian Church (USA) noted in its 1987 study *A Theological Understanding of the Relationship Between Christians and Jews*, "is not a cover for proselytism."[51] The idea that proselytism and dialogue—real, genuine, give-and-take dialogue—could go hand in hand violates the meaning of both terms.

From an evangelical perspective, the point of disagreement comes when evangelization and proselytism are equated.[52] In an increasingly pluralistic world, when dialogue is set against a negative idea such as proselytism, and when proselytism is viewed as a synonym for evangelism, the implications are entirely unacceptable to evangelicals.

Eugene Stockwell has recently noted that the issue of pluralism is posing a whole new set of questions for the church. If dialogue qua dialogue replaces evangelism or mission, one must ask, Does the missionary mandate of the church get lost? Do the exclusive claims of Jesus Christ, and therefore the claims of the Gospel, get lost as well? What happens if some churches or even the WCC ultimately decides that a "pluralism of faiths" is actually God's intention rather than the long-held idea that God intends

50. This action is suggested by Allan Brockway in WCC, *Theology of the Churches and the Jewish People*, 186.

51. WCC, *Theology of the Churches and the Jewish People*, 173, 114.

52. The Presbyterian Church does not employ "evangelization" and "proselytization" synonymously. Brockway, who at the time this book was published was program secretary for Jewish-Christian relations at the WCC, appears to be at odds with the Presbyterians in this matter.

"that everyone on earth should be a Christian"?[53] Is the next step to suggest that the evangelization of people of other "living faiths" is in fact proselytism and therefore ought to be banned?

CONCLUSION

Speaking from an evangelical perspective, I conclude with five observations. First, definitions and applications of the term "proselytism" differ, depending upon who defines them and where they are applied. Second, those who use the term have defined it for evangelicals rather than with evangelicals. Third, when the term is defined for another group and then unilaterally applied to that group, the issue becomes one of ecclesial oppression. Fourth, since those who most frequently invoke the charge of proselytism against younger churches were themselves in earlier times engaged in similar activities, the older churches may well run the risk of self-incrimination. Fifth, it would be wrong to judge evangelicals as not having any sympathy for the wrongness or inappropriateness of proselytism, for they have publicly recognized its evils.

I believe that most evangelicals would agree that those who have a demonstrably active living faith in Jesus Christ should not be treated as persons to be evangelized. I also believe that evangelicals would agree that any form of evangelization that is coercive, deceptive, or manipulative in nature is unworthy of the name and should be labeled as proselytism and condemned. The term "proselytism," however, cannot be applied indiscriminately to all evangelistic activity. Space must be left for legitimate evangelistic efforts directed at persons of other religious communities when the affiliation of such persons is merely nominal.

---

53. Stockwell, "Conciliar Missions," 25.

3.4

Mission, Evangelism, and Proselytism in Christianity

Mainline Conceptions as Reflected in Church Documents

JOEL A. NICHOLS

Emory International Law Review 12 (1998) 563–650[1]

Editor's Introduction

THIS IS A VERY *heavily edited version of a long document (over thirty thousand words). It originally appeared in the Emory International Law Review. Joel Nichols was "Candidate for JD, Emory University School of Law, and MDiv, Candler School of Theology (May 1998). BA, Abilene Christian University (1995)" and therefore brings both a legal and a theological perspective to the article.*

The original article offers a brilliant and historical overview of the major mission and evangelism texts from the four main Christian bodies up to 1998 (Nichols uses a categorization of Roman Catholic, Evangelical Protestant, Conciliar Ecumenical, and Orthodox).

In editing his work I have been ruthless and have attempted to highlight only those sections that deal explicitly with proselytism, or with human rights

---

1. This edited version is reproduced with the kind permission of the copyright holder, Joel A. Nichols, and the *Emory International Law Review*.

and religious freedom insofar as they impinge upon proselytism. The reader may find that I have broken the flow of argument and writing in my editing: I freely admit that I have therefore done Nichols a dis-service but the intent is to offer an overview of how such texts touch on (or do not touch on) proselytism. However, in an attempt to make the paper more accessible I start with his "Summary and Conclusions." I then follow this with my edited version of his more detailed work on the major Statements, speeches and papers from the four different traditions.

The benefits of this paper include his reference to a wide variety of primary and secondary sources (hidden within the footnotes), along with his analysis of those sources. This is a long article despite ruthless editing but the "Summary and Conclusions" are worth reading.[2]

SUMMARY AND CONCLUSIONS

THIS ARTICLE HAS SHOWN that the problem of proselytism is not simply a legal issue—it is also a theological issue. The problem of proselytism is not limited to methods of persuasion and conversion; it grows out of the differing theologies of religious groups. In the case of Christianity, the theologies and missiologies differ among the four major segments of Christianity.

The Roman Catholic Church has written much on the subject of mission and evangelism. Catholics view the Church as missionary by its very nature, stemming from the missionary nature of God. The mission of the Church should be carried out through both proclamation and social action, including solidarity with the poor and oppressed. The Eucharist also serves a missionary purpose. Other religions are respected by the Catholic Church, partly because those religions possess "seeds of the Word." People should be called to come to God, but they should always be free to make their own decisions. Proselytism is condemned, but is undefined. The unity of the Church is emphasized, as all baptized persons are called to be together in one flock.

The Catholic documents tend to be rather opaque and lack specificity. While this affords some flexibility in interpretation, the lack of specific definitions of such terms as proselytism, nominal, Christians, missionary lands, and appropriate methods of evangelism leaves much to be desired. The Catholic Church's definition of a Christian is quite broad, encompassing all those who have been baptized, even if they are not currently practicing. This definition engenders criticism from many Protestant groups, who believe that Christianity involves a personal commitment. A further criticism of

2. Nichols, "Mission, Evangelism, and Proselytism in Christianity."

the Catholic Church is that by ceding as much as they do to other religions, they are compromising the uniqueness of the Christian message. Catholics would disagree and contend that salvation still comes through Christ alone, though not through only one method of salvation. However, such an assertion requires a firmer basis and rationale for missions than appears in official documents.

Evangelical Protestants can be characterized by looking at the Lausanne Movement. Evangelicals believe in the primacy of proclamation in evangelism. The rationale for evangelism stems from the Biblical commands of Jesus, and from a conviction that those outside the Church are lost. While persons of other religions should be respected, they need the truth of the distinctive Christian message. Evangelicals believe that Christianity involves a personal decision and a commitment to follow Christ. Unworthy methods of evangelism are denounced, but not spelled out clearly. Persons should be free to hear and respond to the Christian invitation.

Like the Catholic documents, the Evangelical documents lack sufficient specificity. While this allows individual denominations to craft their own specific missionary guidelines, it also leaves open the possibility that evangelical missionaries will not practice appropriate methods of evangelism. Evangelicals do not provide a mechanism for interreligious dialogue, and consider nominal Christians as appropriate candidates for evangelism. By defining who is a Christian in a narrow fashion, evangelicals provoke charges of proselytism. A further criticism is that by focusing on the proclamative aspect of evangelism, evangelicals neglect the social and cultural situation of those being evangelized.

The conciliar ecumenical movement, as seen in WCC documents, promotes unity in the churches as primary. Thus, competitive churches are viewed as unhealthy and detrimental to Christian witness. Unfortunately, no clear delineation is set forth concerning what constitutes competition among churches, for no firm definition of a Christian can be agreed upon. Ecumenicals emphasize all aspects of evangelism, including solidarity with humanity, especially the poor, and working for justice in the world. Respecting human dignity as primary, ecumenicals both encourage local churches to retain their own cultural identities and to foster interreligious dialogue. Proselytism is denounced and religious liberty advanced, but only the latter term is given clear definition.

The WCC documents make more ambitious attempts at defining and delimiting terms associated with evangelism than Catholics or evangelicals, but still fall short of complete definition. There is no definition of nominal Christians, nor a detailing of who is to evangelize them if they are to be evangelized at all. No single definition of proselytism is agreed upon. No set definition of a Christian is given, and what is implied is a quite broad definition. This raises concerns from the evangelicals' perspective, who further claim that overemphasis on the unity and ecumenicity of the church can lead to a lack of attention given to the individual believer. A further criticism is the same as that leveled against the Catholics—that by entertaining the possibility of interreligious dialogue, ecumenicals are compromising the uniqueness and sufficiency of Jesus Christ.

Eastern Orthodox churches ground the concept of mission in the trinitarian nature of God. The Church is primarily a place of communion, and life in God is that of communion. Unity of the Church is crucial, as it evidences community in God. The missionary task of the Church is to mediate and model to the world what life in God is like. Thus, eucharistic celebration and a commitment to unity are more important than proclamation. Orthodoxy closely associates Christianity with culture, retaining cultural and national lines as imaginary boundaries within which only one local church should operate. All those who have been baptized into the Church are considered members of the Orthodox Church. No mention is made of nominal Christians, though the tacit understanding is that only the Orthodox Church has the right to evangelize (or re-evangelize) these persons.

The situation surrounding the new Russian law "On Freedom of Conscience and on Religious Associations" is understood much better if it is contextualized within this theological framework. The law is not merely an invention of bureaucrats to suppress foreigners and support a nationalistic programme. Neither is the purpose of the law merely to regulate non-Christian sects. Rather, there are theological reasons underlying the law's passage which are grounded in the theology of Orthodoxy.

This is not to condone the law as it stands, but rather to help understand it. Some of the feelings of the ROC are legitimate.[3] The Church was oppressed under the Communist regime. Its parishioners were taken away. Its priests were murdered. Its buildings were confiscated. Its funds, spiritual and material, were virtually depleted. Then, after the fall of communism, the ROC found itself having to compete with foreign, non-Orthodox Christians within Russia. As the ROC explains it, the ROC was in a weakened position and has had difficulty alongside these new missionaries.

However, the situation is more complex than that. The stated arguments of the ROC concerning proselytism often do not get to the heart of the issue. The theological understanding of Orthodoxy differs radically from

---

3. For a documentary history of how churches fared under the Soviet state, see Corley, *Religion in the Soviet Union*.

prevailing Western theologies. Russian Orthodoxy considers the entire Russian people to be Christian, to be Russian Orthodox. Russian Orthodoxy considers Christianity something into which a person is baptized at birth; that person is subsequently a permanent church member. Russian Orthodoxy views interreligious competition and parallel Christian structures as fundamentally un-Christian, and contrary to what it means to be the Church and to witness to the world. They call such competition "proselytism."

These positions contrast sharply with the views of many non-Orthodox Christians—especially evangelicals. Evangelicals view Christianity as a personal decision, not a cultural, communal existence. Evangelicals view proclamation as the primary method of evangelism, not witness through the Eucharist nor only social action. Evangelicals view nominal Christians, of any denomination, as ripe for evangelism. Evangelicals view Russia, as they view every nation, as a land in need of evangelism.

It is no wonder that evangelicals are among the groups with whom the ROC has the most disagreement and competition. Truly, "[o]ne group's evangelization is another group's proselytism."[4] In situations such as the one in Russia, we would be wise to remember that human rights law cannot provide all of the answers when theology is so deeply implicated.

While legal dialogue must occur, so too must theological dialogue. While non-Orthodox Christians can learn much from the Orthodox Church's theology and her consistent witness through years of persecution under communism, the Orthodox Church would do well to consider carefully the various theologies and missiologies held by her sister Christian churches and to reconsider the depths of her own theology.[5] Those theologies and missiologies contain resources for discussing and coping with issues of evangelism and proselytism in different and, arguably, more appropriate ways....

---

4. Robeck Jr., "Mission and the Issue of Proselytism," 2, 4. [Editor: see preceeding paper in this volume.] ("The Orthodox have essentially defined proselytism so broadly that any missionary or evangelistic activity undertaken by non-Orthodox within these countries is labeled illegitimate, and those who are active in such practices are frequently described as thieves.")

5. See Newbigin, *Dialogue of Gospel and Culture* (arguing that it is necessary to challenge the ROC to let go of the "old territorial principle that regards the presence on Russian soil of any form of Christianity other than its own as illegitimate," while at the same time contending that missionaries to Russia should learn from the ROC and the long and costly history it endured under communism).

INTRODUCTION

Through the centuries different names have been given to this missionary enterprise: witness (*martyria*), proselytism, mission, evangelism. Spreading the faith has occurred through a variety of methods: proclamation, witness, eucharistic celebration, social activism, martyrdom, and, unfortunately, the use of force. The Crusades, pogroms, forced baptisms, and tortured confessions emerge, as examples from history of Christians forcibly spreading their message. Unhappily, theological justification has been offered for the use of force since the time of St. Augustine. Using Jesus' parable of a great feast (Luke 7:15–24), Augustine interpreted the words "*compelle intrare*" (compel them to come in) as applicable to those who believed something other than orthodox doctrine: the heretics. Augustine's interpretation gave theological justification to all manner of pressure and persecution of the heterodox over the centuries.[6] . . .

The word "proselytism" in recent years has come to convey a sense of improper evangelism.[7] Christian groups condemn proselytism and routinely use the term only in its negative sense.[8] All agree that proselytism is wrong, but none admit engagement in it. In discussing proselytism, one helpful distinction to bear in mind is between "in-reach proselytism," trying to claim the baptized but still immature believers, or "nominal Christians,"

---

6. For an excellent rendering of this history, see Tierney, "Religious Rights," 17, 19–21. Unfortunately, theologians such as Thomas Aquinas continued to use Augustine's interpretation through the years.

7. For an evaluation of the prevailing international human rights norms regarding proselytism, see Lerner, "Proselytism, Change of Religion." The best look at official Christian statements and positions on human rights can be found in Shupack, "Churches and Human Rights." See also Witte Jr., "Law, Religion, and Human Rights."

8. Note that this is a different usage from common legal terminology, which adopts a neutral connotation for the word. In legal circles, "proselytism" is commonly used to designate all kinds of evangelistic activities, with a distinction then drawn between "legitimate proselytism" and "illegitimate proselytism." Christian groups make a similar distinction, but use the terms "evangelism" and "proselytism" to denote these two ideas. Cf. "Proselytism," in *Webster's Ninth New Collegiate Dictionary*, 945: "To induce someone to convert to one's faith [or] to recruit someone to join one's party institution, or cause"; "Proselytism," in Garner, *Dictionary of Modern Legal Use*, 444 (confirming this usage in the legal realm); "Proselytism," in Richardson and Bowden, *Westminster Dictionary of Christian Theology*, 475–76: "Today, proselytism is used in a negative sense to characterize [improper] evangelism. . . . Both the World Council of Churches since the 1960s and the Vatican more recently have accepted the term proselytism to describe any kind of manipulation of another or encroachment upon their personal freedom to choose"); "Proselytism" in O'Collins and Farrugia, *Concise Dictionary of Theology*, 195: "Proselytism almost always now has the negative meaning of forcing or otherwise manipulating people into accepting a particular faith."

while sustaining mature believers, and "out-reach proselytism," attempting to convert believers of different or no faiths, and thereby gain new adherents. Christian groups believe strongly in inreach proselytism because it concerns their own denomination. Most disputes arise over out-reach proselytism, and Christian groups lack a uniform view on this topic.

Discussions about proselytism and religious freedom, at their core, implicate the various theologies and missiologies of the groups involved. Discerning the relevant theologies and missiologies of the various Christian confessions requires careful parsing of their respective theological and missiological statements. Only through such a parsing can one embark on an informed discussion concerning evangelism and proselytism. . . .

I. ROMAN CATHOLICISM

A. Ad Gentes

The foundation for modern Roman Catholic missiology was laid by the Second Vatican Council. The seminal document is the "Decree on the Church's Missionary Activity" (*Ad Gentes*). . . . *Ad Gentes* begins by reaffirming that "the Church on earth is by its very nature missionary."[9] The missionary nature of the Church is derivative of the mission of the Son and the Holy Spirit. Just as the Father sent the Son and the Spirit into the world through His love, so the Church is now sent into the world through God's love. . . .

Ad Gentes explains that non-Christians should "freely turn to the Lord."[10] Though the heart of the non-Christian must be opened by the Holy Spirit before such "free" turning can occur, the freedom of the act is critical. The document denounces all forms of evangelism that involve any form of coercion: "The Church strictly forbids that anyone should be forced to accept the faith, or be induced or enticed by unworthy devices; as it likewise strongly defends the right that no one should be frightened away from the faith by unjust persecutions."[11] Thus, although the word "proselytism" does not appear in *Ad Gentes*, the sentiment against it clearly does. However, this statement comprises the extent of the discussion of illegitimate evangelism. No details concerning inappropriate methods or modes of evangelism are listed, though some guidelines for appropriate evangelism are listed in the latter part of the document. . . .

---

9. Vatican II, *Ad Gentes* 2.
10. Vatican II, *Ad Gentes* 13.
11. Vatican II, *Ad Gentes* 13.

Ad Gentes never considers who is a candidate for evangelism. The document uses the term "non-Christian," but never defines it. The inference can be drawn that all persons who are baptized are Christians, since "all baptized people are called upon to come together in one flock."[12] However, no mention is made of persons who were once baptized and are no longer active members of Christian communities. Such persons seem to be Christians in name only ("nominal Christians"). The document does *not* denote whether such persons should be placed in the category of "Christians" or the category of "non-Christians."

This simple Christian versus non-Christian typology introduces a fundamental tension between Catholic (and often Orthodox) understandings and some Protestant missiologies. It is over nominal Christians that many skirmishes are fought. Non-Catholics often consider such persons proper candidates for Christian evangelism while Catholics consider such persons as still members of the Church, though not fully participating members. Such a difference in viewpoint can lead to major differences in evangelistic approaches and can cause hostile feelings when the Catholic Church feels its members (the nominal Christians) are being "proselytized" by other Christian groups. Recent flare-ups in once predominantly Catholic Latin American and Eastern European countries are examples of this problem.

Just as only two categories of people exist according to *Ad Gentes*, similarly, only two kinds of territories exist. The document designates these two places as "lands which are already Christian" and as "missionary lands."[13] Once again, the distinction is set forth vaguely. This leads to a similar problem with non-Catholics. On one hand, many Protestant groups are uncomfortable labeling *any* land as "already Christian," since Christianity is an individual choice and not a choice made by a country as a whole. Many Orthodox Christians, on the other hand, would recognize Christian countries. But they explain that Catholics apply a different standard to their lands and treat the Orthodox countries as missionary lands when in fact they are already Christian lands. So, although *Ad Gentes* indicates that "missionary lands" are the proper place for evangelism, that designation has not proved useful in the broader ecumenical discussion of proselytism and evangelism.

Finally, *Ad Gentes* addresses cooperation in mission efforts, principally focusing on cooperation among various Catholic churches and dioceses.[14] The document lacks any indication regarding whether cooperation with other professing Christian groups should be undertaken. In organizing

---

12. Vatican II, *Ad Gentes* 6.
13. Vatican II, *Ad Gentes* 41.
14. Vatican II, *Ad Gentes* 35–41.

mission activity, *Ad Gentes* advocates consolidation of mission efforts under one segment ("Sacred Congregation for the Propagation of the Faith") and indicates that "the rights of the Eastern Churches must, however, be safeguarded."[15] This reference to "the Eastern Churches" is somewhat vague: it may be a reference solely to the Orthodox churches, or may include the Uniate churches.[16] If it includes the Uniate churches, this seems an inadequate way to deal with the tension aroused between the Catholic Church and the Orthodox Church. If it does not include Uniate churches, then no mention is made of Uniate churches and the document does not address one of the fundamental concerns of Christian groups outside the Catholic Church concerning proselytism.

Ad Gentes is a landmark document that establishes a baseline from which all discussions of Catholic missions must start. The document is neither a legal code nor a manual of mission ethics, but a statement of fundamental principles. . . .

Ad Gentes is also the benchmark by which all other Catholic statements on evangelism and proselytism must be measured. A host of documents have been produced by other Catholic sources, from the Pope to individual priests and bishops, concerning specific applications of the ideas promulgated by the Second Vatican Council. These subsequent developments will now be considered.

B. Evangelii Nuntiandi

Ten years after the adjournment of the Second Vatican Council, Pope Paul VI promulgated an apostolic exhortation entitled "On Evangelization in the Modern World" (*Evangelii Nuntiandi*).[17] This landmark work was an attempt to systematize and prescribe an appropriate theology and framework for missions. . . .

Evangelii Nuntiandi proclaims boldly that "the task of evangelizing all people constitutes the essential mission of the Church.[18] . . . *Evangelii Nuntiandi* touches briefly on "nominal Christians." In the context of Christian witness, one of the questions an evangelizer must ask is whether the

---

15. Vatican II, *Ad Gentes* 29.

16. Uniate churches practice the liturgy and adornments of the Orthodox churches, but recognize the Pope of the Catholic Church as having received the primary mandate from God. Frequent disagreements exist between Orthodox churches and Catholic churches concerning these Uniate churches.

17. Paul VI, *Evangelii Nuntiandi*.

18. *Declaration of the Synod Fathers* 4, quoted in Paul VI, *Evangelii Nuntiandi* 14.

people with whom he is working "live as nominal Christians but according to principles that are in no way Christian."[19] Though the document later asserts that evangelism is appropriate for such a person,[20] it does not outline what kind of evangelistic effort should ensue nor does it imply what the person's standing is with God and with the Church. More importantly, the document omits any comment concerning whether nominal Christians are appropriate candidates for evangelism by members of other religions, other Christian confessions, or solely by the Catholic Church. . . .

Interestingly, the document next mentions those Christians who are not in full communion with the Church. The Church would be "lacking in her duty if she did not give witness before them of the fullness of the revelation whose deposit she guards."[21] The text goes no further in explaining what this witness should be. This statement seemingly opens the door to evangelism of persons who are, to some degree, already adherents of the Christian faith. If so, then this would be, almost by definition, proselytism. . . .

Evangelii Nuntiandi tackles the topic of proselytism fairly directly at the close of the document. The discussion is couched in terms of the evangelizer possessing an ever increasing love for those whom he is evangelizing. One consequence of this love is respect for the dignity and freedom of the subject of evangelism. The specific religious and spiritual situation of those being evangelized must be kept constantly in mind. "[N]o one has the right to force them excessively";[22] consciences and convictions must be respected. Once again, a solid theological basis has been laid, but the ramifications of the statements are not explained.

Evangelii Nuntiandi further addresses religious liberty in the following section, but shifts the focus from the rights of the evangelized to the right of the evangelizers to proclaim the Gospel message. An interlocutor in the text asserts that "to impose a way, be it that of salvation, cannot but be a violation of religious liberty. Besides . . . why proclaim the Gospel when the whole world is saved by uprightness of heart?"[23] The papal response is grounded in the documents of Vatican II, particularly *Dignitatus Humanae* and *Ad Gentes*. The pope agrees that it would be a grievous error to "impose something" on the consciences of other persons. However, to propose

---

19. Paul VI, *Evangelii Nuntiandi* 21.
20. Paul VI, *Evangelii Nuntiandi* 52, discussing those "people who have been baptized but who live quite outside the Christian life."
21. Paul VI, *Evangelii Nuntiandi* 54.
22. Paul VI, *Evangelii Nuntiandi* 79.
23. Paul VI, *Evangelii Nuntiandi* 80.

"the truth of the Gospel" and to identify the free options which that Gospel presents—"without coercion, or dishonorable or unworthy pressure"[24]—is not an attack on religious liberty, but is rather the fullest respect of that liberty.[25] The pope proceeds to claim that the respectful presentation of Christ is not only the right of Christians, but their duty. The "right" that is involved is the right of persons who have not heard the Gospel message to hear a free presentation of the message of salvation and then to possess the freedom to make an educated decision about that message.[26] . . .

Overall, then, *Evangelii Nuntiandi* builds upon the foundation of *Ad Gentes*. While it clarifies some of the concepts the Council set forth, it does not resolve all ambiguities. Once again, this is an asset for interpretation in a variety of ways, but does not clarify the position of the Catholic Church as much as one would like on issues of proselytism. . . .

C. Redemptoris Missio

The most recent authoritative statement on mission which amplifies *Ad Gentes* is *Redemptoris Missio* (Mission of the Redeemer)[27] . . . an encyclical letter of Pope John Paul II concerning "the permanent validity of the Church's missionary mandate." Encyclicals carry the highest authority within Catholic circles, below only such infallible conciliar statements as *Ad Gentes*.

Redemptoris Missio further sets forth the groundwork for missions. Citing the emphasis on missionary activity in *Ad Gentes*, the encyclical claims that the third millennium is a "great springtime for Christianity."[28] This springtime should not be simply watched as it comes, but ushered in through increased mission activity.

Like *Ad Gentes*, *Redemptoris Missio* uses the term "non-Christians" without definition.[29] The omission is striking. One cannot evangelize "non-Christians" unless that category of persons is clearly demarcated from those who are "Christians." . . . The underlying assumption in *Redemptoris Missio* seems to be that anyone who is baptized is a Christian, regardless of whether their "faith" or "commitment" to the Church is actual or nominal.[30] This

24. Vatican II, *Dignitatis Humanae*, quoted in Paul VI, *Evangelii Nuntiandi* 80.
25. Paul VI, *Evangelii Nuntiandi* 80.
26. Paul VI, *Evangelii Nuntiandi* 80.
27. John Paul II, *Redemptoris Missio*.
28. John Paul II, *Redemptoris Missio* 2, 86.
29. John Paul II, *Redemptoris Missio* 4.
30. See John Paul II, *Redemptoris Missio* 50 ("it is true that some kind of communion,

has serious implications for evangelism, because any evangelism by other groups directed towards even those who are nominal Catholic adherents is considered to be proselytism by the Catholic hierarchy.

The pope implicitly says this in discussing ecumenical activity and the problem of "sects." Ecumenical activity is praised as biblically mandated, but "Christian and paraChristian sects are sowing confusion by their activity." "The expansion of these sects represents a threat for the Catholic Church" and for those with whom the Catholic Church is working.[31] Categorizing those groups not organically connected to the Catholic Church as "sects" lends an aura of authorization to the activities of the Catholic Church and her partners while reflecting poorly on the other groups. Other groups, however, might maintain a different definition of who is Christian. For example, a person may have been baptized into the Catholic Church as an infant, yet not have attended mass or other activities during the course of their lives. The Catholic Church would likely consider this person a Christian; some non-Catholic groups would claim the person has no knowledge or understanding of God, and therefore is not a Christian and is an appropriate candidate for evangelism. The Catholic Church would call the activity "proselytism by sects" while the evangelizing group would dub the activity "evangelism by a legitimate Christian organization."[32]

Redemptoris Missio emphasizes freedom of conscience. The pope quotes the Second Vatican Council:

> The human person has a right to religious freedom. . . . All should have immunity from coercion by individuals, or by groups, or by any human power, that no one should be forced to act against his conscience in religious matters, nor prevented from acting according to his conscience, whether in private or in public, whether alone or in association with others, within due limits.[33]

All persons should be able to make free choices concerning their religious beliefs and affiliations, a freedom that grows out of the freedom given to humans by God. God offers restoration and love to humans, but humans are

---

though imperfect, exists among all those who have received Baptism in Christ").

31. John Paul II, *Redemptoris Missio* 50.

32. See, e.g., discussion in Sigmund, "Religious Human Rights in Latin America," 467, 472. See also Alta/Baja California Bishops, "Dimensions of a Response to Proselytism," 666 (a scathing attack on "sects and new religious groups" and their purported methods of conversion).

33. Vatican II, *Dignitatis Humanae* 2, quoted in John Paul II, *Redemptoris Missio* 8.

free to reject the offer.[34] Since God gives humans such latitude concerning a free response to God's love, human mission activity should also allow for a free response.

The act of proclaiming Christ and bearing witness to him, "when done in a way that respects consciences, does not violate freedom."[35] In this way, the Church advocates freedom of religion and of expression while maintaining its theological basis and right to mission activity. Religious freedom is "the premise and guarantee of all the freedoms that ensure the common good of individuals and peoples."[36] Regardless of whether Catholicism constitutes a majority or minority in a country, *Redemptoris Missio* advocates religious freedom in all countries, for it is "an inalienable right of each and every human person."[37]

Additionally, this freedom involves the right of every person to hear the "Good News" of God through Christ.[38] This is a critical point, since the aim of proclamation is *Christian conversion*, which means making a personal decision to accept "the saving sovereignty of Christ and becom[e] his disciple."[39] The pope defends this call to conversion against accusations that it is "proselytism." He says those outside the Catholic Church claim that "it is enough to help people become more human or more faithful to their own religion, that it is enough to build communities capable of working for justice, freedom, peace, and solidarity."[40] Aptly stated, such claims do not respect the right of the Catholic Church to proclaim the Good News nor the right and freedom of the recipient to respond to that message in the manner he or she chooses. . . .

D. Other Documents

These three major documents on missions, evangelism, and proselytism form the framework for discussion of Roman Catholic missions within the past twenty-five years. These broad documents must be amplified at more local levels. One such amplification is *Go and Make Disciples*, a document produced by the United States Catholic Conference.[41] This document cites

34. John Paul II, *Redemptoris Missio* 7.
35. John Paul II, *Redemptoris Missio* 8.
36. John Paul II, *Redemptoris Missio* 39.
37. John Paul II, *Redemptoris Missio* 39.
38. John Paul II, *Redemptoris Missio* 46.
39. John Paul II, *Redemptoris Missio* 46.
40. John Paul II, *Redemptoris Missio* 46.
41. USCC, *Go And Make Disciples*.

Euangelii Nuntiandi, Redemptoris Missio, and the Bible liberally as it defines and describes the Catholic mission to the United States. Evangelization has a definition adapted directly from *Evangelii Nuntiandi*: "evangelizing means bringing the Good News of Jesus into every human situation and seeking to convert individuals and society by the divine power of the Gospel itself."[42] This conversion is described as "the change of our lives that comes about through the power of the Holy Spirit."[43]

Impetus for evangelization is grounded in the commands of Jesus.[44] Evangelism is for all people:

> Catholics should continually share the Gospel with those who have no church community, with those who have given up active participation in the Catholic Church, as well as welcoming those seeking full communion with the Catholic Church . . . . At the same time, we Catholics cannot proselytize—*that is, manipulate or pressure anyone to join our Church*. Such tactics contradict the Good News we announce and undermine the spirit of invitation that should characterize all true evangelization.[45]

. . . Although documents from *Ad Gentes* and *To the Ends of the Earth*[46] contain much information on missions and evangelism, it is somewhat hard to discern precisely the official beliefs of the Catholic Church. There is no clear discussion of who is a Christian, nor who is an appropriate candidate for evangelism. There is no clear statement concerning where missionary activity is to take place. Much theological argument is offered but it is neither clear nor cogent. While flexibility is advantageous for authoritative documents ensuring that interpretation of those documents can change with time, the lack of some clear statements, definitions, or clarifications of potential contradictions is unhelpful for our current study. This flexibility also leaves non-Catholics a bit unsure as to what to expect from the Roman Catholic Church regarding missionary activity of non-Catholic persons. Neither can non-Catholics anticipate how and when the Catholic Church will respond when it feels inappropriate missionary incursions are occurring on adherents of Catholic beliefs.

---

42. USCC, *Go And Make Disciples* 2 (citing Paul VI, *Evangelii Nuntiandi* 18).
43. USCC, *Go And Make Disciples* 2 (citing Paul VI, *Evangelii Nuntiandi* 18).
44. USCC, *Go And Make Disciples* 4.
45. USCC, *Go And Make Disciples* 8 (emphasis added).
46. NCCB, *To The Ends Of The Earth*. While *Redemptoris Missio* was not yet written at the release of *To the Ends of the Earth*, thoughts from the former were incorporated into NCCB, *Celebrating "To The Ends Of The Earth."*

II. EVANGELICAL PROTESTANTISM

. . .

A. The Lausanne Covenant

The Lausanne Covenant[47] seeks to maintain a respect for human rights and human freedom. The drafters admit that, in the past, they have been guilty of "manipulat[ing] hearers through pressure techniques," and they repent of this.[48] Moreover, the drafters clearly articulate their desire for "peace, justice, and liberty" in all places so the followers of God may worship Him freely and obey Him. The Universal Declaration of Human Rights is specifically endorsed,[49] and the adherents of the Lausanne Covenant pledge their support to the continuing advancement of human rights. The Lausanne Covenant states, "Because [men and women are] made in the image of God, every person, regardless of race, religion, colour, culture, class, sex or age, has an intrinsic dignity because of which he or she should be respected and served, not exploited."[50] It is on this premise of God-given dignity that the drafters stand to advocate religious freedom and toleration. . . .

B. The Manila Manifesto

The twenty-one affirmations which open the Manila Manifesto[51] are brief, one-line sentences, each of which endorses a basic tenet of evangelical Christianity, especially as it pertains to evangelism. This important section of the document opens with a recommitment to the *Lausanne Covenant* as the basis for cooperation in the Lausanne Movement.[52] The affirmations next discuss common Evangelical Protestant themes: the authority of the Bible as the Word of God and the sinfulness of humans.[53] The brevity of all

---

47. Lausanne Movement, "Lausanne Covenant," in Douglas, *Let the Earth Hear His Voice*, 3–10. Of course, not all evangelical groups adhere to the Lausanne Covenant, since it is entirely voluntary. Some evangelical groups would feel that the Lausanne Covenant is not conservative enough, while others would feel it is not open enough.

48. Lausanne Movement, *Lausanne Covenant*, para. 12.

49. Lausanne Movement, *Lausanne Covenant*, para. 13.

50. Lausanne Movement, *Lausanne Covenant*, para. 5.

51. Lausanne Movement, "Manila Manifesto," in Schere and Bevans, *Basic Statements*, 292–305.

52. Lausanne Movement, *Manila Manifesto*, aff. 1.

53. Lausanne Movement, *Manila Manifesto*, aff. 2–4.

of the affirmations is worth noting. While brevity lends itself more readily to agreement among various evangelical groups, this brevity does not clarify the issues as much as one would like for analytical purposes. As in the Catholic documents, the opaqueness is both beneficial and detrimental because it leads to multiple possible interpretations.

Significantly, the seventh affirmation states: "We affirm that other religions and ideologies are not alternative paths to God, and that human spirituality, if unredeemed by Christ, leads not to God but to judgment, for Christ is the only way."[54] The uniqueness of Christ is claimed as the basis for missions by the evangelicals. This is important because implicit in the above statement is a rejection of interreligious dialogue as advantageous for salvation purposes. Claiming Christ as the only way to salvation provides a clear rationale for missions. However, simply claiming Christ as the only way does not eliminate all problems for evangelism. First there is still the question of who should be evangelized? That is, who is already saved and thus does not need to hear the Gospel message? If the message is preached to such persons, is it proselytism? Second, claiming Christ's uniqueness for salvation opens the door to charges of insensitivity and illegitimate proselytism from non-Christian groups. . . .

The Manila Manifesto turns to the Universal Declaration of Human Rights for guidance on religious freedom, advocating the freedom to "profess, practice, and propagate" religion. Evangelicals do not desire freedom only for Christianity, but seek freedom of religion for all people. This means that Christians are seeking no more religious freedom than they desire to give. This freedom of religion has limits, however. All "unworthy methods of evangelism" are denounced. Even though Christians desire to share their faith with others, the practice should be "to make an open and honest statement of it, which leaves the hearers entirely free to make up their own minds about it." Therefore, any evangelistic approach which "seeks to force conversion" on any nonbeliever is rejected.[55] While unworthy methods are denounced, though, there is no clear delineation of precisely what forms of evangelism are approved and what are not. The only hint given is the statement that any method which seeks to "force conversion" is unworthy. . . .

The *Manila Manifesto* is not clear concerning what evangelicals believe about nonevangelical groups which profess a belief in Christ; but it appears that *everyone* who does not fit the evangelical definition of a "Christian" needs to be evangelized and converted.

---

54. Lausanne Movement, *Manila Manifesto*, aff. 7.
55. Lausanne Movement, *Manila Manifesto*, para. C12.

It is precisely on this point that criticism of evangelicals often becomes most severe and most warranted. The critique is that evangelicals define who is a Christian too narrowly. *The Manila Manifesto* states that any cooperation with Roman Catholic and Orthodox Churches should occur in areas where "biblical truth is not compromised," but "common evangelism demands a common commitment, to the biblical gospel."[56] Further, while some evangelical groups are members of the World Council of Churches, there are other groups that are not members. Even so, "all of us urge the World Council of Churches to adopt a consistent biblical understanding of evangelism."[57] This statement by itself makes clear that the evangelicals do not currently agree with the WCC's understanding of evangelism.[58] If these statements concerning the Catholics, Orthodox, and conciliar churches are taken at face value, it is not difficult to imagine how some evangelical churches could oppose those groups quite strongly. If this opposition is grounded in a belief that other groups are not "Christian" according to the evangelical definition, then other groups become appropriate candidates for evangelization. Skirmishes often erupt over this fine line between proselytism and evangelism. The problem of proselytism is most acute in precisely this kind of situation. . . .

However, evangelicals have precious little to say (in their consensus documents) about proper missionary techniques. Since they lack a principle of interreligious dialogue, they are much more susceptible to charges of proselytism. Without clearly stating what activities are licit and illicit for evangelism, evangelicals leave the door open to such charges. This problem is exacerbated if evangelicals adhere to a narrow definition of a Christian and consider nominal adherents of other Christian faiths (especially Catholicism and Orthodoxy) candidates for evangelism. . . .

III. CONCILIAR ECUMENICAL

An Ecumenical Affirmation

The foremost document produced the by WCC and the CWME regarding mission and evangelism is a 1982 statement, *Ecumenical Affirmation: Mission and Evangelism*.[59] . . .

---

56. Lausanne Movement, *Manila Manifesto*, para. B9.
57. Lausanne Movement, *Manila Manifesto*, para. B9.
58. See Adeyemo, *Whatever Happened to Evangelism?*, 34; Oden, *How Should Evangelicals Be Ecumenical?*, 39; Packer, *Why I Left*, 33.
59. WCC, *Ecumenical Affirmation*. See also three "testimonies" (Orthodox, Roman

Since mission and evangelism are patterned after the ministry and teaching of Jesus, all people should hear the Gospel. Jesus spoke with people of every age, class, and ethnic group. In the same way, the Church must be committed to God's desire that every person have a chance to respond to the Good News of Christ. Jesus always acted in love and respect when dealing with people, even though he possessed the power and authority to act differently if he had chosen. Modeling our mission efforts after Christ, we are called to subordinate power to love, and authority to respect. *Ecumenical Affirmation* does not set forth a list of things in which churches may or may not engage when evangelizing, but it strongly asserts that whatever methodology is chosen for a given situation either "illustrates or betrays the Gospel we announce."[60] However individual churches or mission agencies choose to conduct their mission activities, all activities should be done in a spirit of love and respect. The document claims that "the sin of proselytism" is present even today among other Christian confessions, but it does not go on to spell this out in more detail at any point.[61] . . .

A similar problem recurs in the treatment of "nominal Christians." *Ecumenical Affirmation* uses something close to this phrase when it calls people who are "nominal in their commitment" back to their prior faith and enthusiasm.[62] Unfortunately, precisely who is a nominal Christian is undefined. One person's definition of a solid commitment to Jesus Christ may not be adequate for another person or church. Such situations lead to the latter feeling that the former is "nominal" and in need of evangelism. To brand a person a nominal Christian and evangelize him or her might well be perceived as proselytism.

Another problem is that the document never specifies who may or may not evangelize these persons who are nominal in their commitment to Christ. Are they the sole responsibility of the denominations to which they once belonged? What is the role of other Christian groups in response to these nominal Christians: are they merely to support the original churches or should they actively evangelize? Though *Ecumenical Affirmation* states that the churches everywhere are in missionary situations due to the growing

---

Catholic, and Protestant) that were given accompanying *Ecumenical Affirmation* when it was presented to the WCC Central Committee: Yannoulatos, "All of Us"; Meeking, "For Every Human Being in the World"; Miller, "Affluence and Privilege."

60. WCC, *Ecumenical Affirmation*, para. 28.
61. WCC, *Ecumenical Affirmation*, para. 39.
62. "In a world where so many Christians are nominal in their commitment to Jesus Christ, *how necessary it is to call them again to the fervor of their first love*" (WCC, *Ecumenical Affirmation*, para. 39).

secularism around the world,⁶³ it does not delineate who may (or should) evangelize in a given place. Can only "indigenous churches" evangelize (or reevangelize) in a given country, culture, or locale? If an area is truly secular, can other Christian groups evangelize there even if there is already a Christian church present that has been there longer? Do outside Christian groups have an obligation to help the existing group? What should the church look like in a given culture? . . .

B. Other Documentation

However, a few other statements by the WCC merit brief mention. . . . The CWME has convened two major conferences after the issuance of *Ecumenical Affirmation:* the first in San Antonio, Texas, in 1989,⁶⁴ the second in Salvador, Bahia, Brazil, in 1996.⁶⁵ . . . The theme of the San Antonio conference was "Your Will be Done: Mission in Christ's Way."

No formal document akin to *Ecumenical Affirmation* was adopted by the delegates. The report of Section I, though, entitled *Turning to the Living God*, picks up some of the themes of *Ecumenical Affirmation* and emphasizes solidarity and unity in mission. The report addresses the topic of proselytism, saying that evangelism should not turn into "programmes for denominational aggrandizement."⁶⁶ "We believe that any evangelism that does not promote good relationships with other Christians in the community must inevitably be called into question. . . . All unhealthy competition in mission work should be avoided as constituting a distorted form of mission."⁶⁷ The document further notes that "faith communities may become ingrown and stagnant."⁶⁸ In such settings, other Christians may play a "catalytic role," but they can only do so "if they identify with the local faith community and treat it with sensitivity, respect and integrity."⁶⁹ The document does not clearly delineate which faith groups are Christian and which are not, nor is "unhealthy competition in mission" further defined. But *Turning to the Living God* does not claim that some lands are already evangelized and in no need of mission. "Everywhere the churches are in

---

63. WCC, *Ecumenical Affirmation*, para. 37.

64. The official record of the conference is WCC, *San Antonio Report*.

65. Materials and reflections may be found in *International Review of Mission* 86.340-41 (1997) 3-197.

66. WCC, *San Antonio Report*, 29.

67. WCC, *San Antonio Report*, 29.

68. WCC, *San Antonio Report*, 29.

69. WCC, *San Antonio Report*, 29.

missionary situations," since secularism is dominant even in historically Christian countries.[70] . . .

The next CWME conference held in Salvador, Bahia, Brazil, focused on the theme "Called to One Hope—The Gospel in Diverse Cultures." The topic of proselytism was broached-and condemned.[71] The ensuing "Acts of Commitment" from the conference state:

> Unethical forms of coercion and proselytism which neither recognize the integrity of the local churches nor are sensitive to local cultures . . . run counter to God's reconciling love in Christ. *We therefore commit ourselves* to promote common witness and to renounce proselytism and all forms of mission which destroy the unity of the body of Christ.[72] . . .

The Conference Further Stated That "Competitiveness Is the Surest Way to Undermine Christian Mission."[73]

While these supplementary documents amplify, to some degree, *Ecumenical Affirmation*, they neither displace nor surpass it. Unfortunately, neither *Ecumenical Affirmation* nor any of the other documents deals with the problem of proselytism in a sufficiently in-depth fashion. Though the practice is decried by the WCC and all its members, some churches (particularly Orthodox Churches) do not think the WCC has done enough to stop the practice. One problem is that the WCC has yet to define exactly what proselytism is. While "unhealthy competition" is proclaimed as "distorting" . . . true witness, the limits of healthy versus unhealthy competition are not clearly demarcated.

The lack of definition of proselytism is exacerbated by the lack of definition of who is a Christian. As a body, the WCC adheres to broad definitions of who is a Christian (a person who is part of the larger Church) and a broad definition of evangelism. This dovetails into their overall emphasis on ecumenism and unity. . . . The difficulty arises when we try to determine how and by what means that evangelism should occur.

---

70. WCC, *San Antonio Report*, 29–31.

71. See the strong statements by Metropolitan Kirill in his address at Salvador below.

72. See "Acts of Commitment."

73. See "Conference Message."

IV. EASTERN ORTHODOXY

Like the Roman Catholic Church, Eastern Orthodoxy has a tradition that extends much farther back than any within Protestantism, whether evangelical or ecumenical. The Orthodox tradition is very important for Orthodox Christians and theologians. The sense of catholicity of the Orthodox Church is a stabilizing reference point, and the starting point, for Orthodox theology....

The Orthodox Primates occasionally issue joint statements or hold conferences at the request of the Ecumenical Patriarch of Constantinople (who is "first among equals"). Such joint statements obviously carry substantial weight, though they are still not binding on the Church in the way Catholic Conciliar statements are....

A. Theological Bases for Mission

Professor Ion Bria has collected and compiled essays from a number of... meetings of the Orthodox Advisory Group to the WCC-CWME. This compilation, *Go Forth in Peace: Orthodox Perspectives in Mission*, is a very useful and provocative resource on Orthodox missiology.[74] Although these essays and collected thoughts do not have authoritative value for the Orthodox churches, they are an accurate compilation and expression of recent Orthodox reflections on missions and evangelism.[75] ...

Proselytism is denounced as outside the bounds of true evangelistic witness. While evangelistic witness seeks to demonstrate to the world the Orthodox faith as an "active presence," proselytism is a corruption of Christian witness. In proclaiming the gospel, the priest must "have proper respect for others, possess an integrity of character, and allow others to use their free will in coming to the Orthodox faith."[76] This further strengthens claims against all forms of coercion in the name of Christ, which leads only to "a desire for spiritual aggressiveness" and not to true faith.[77] These documents

---

74. Bria, *Go Forth In Peace*. A number of the documents summarized in *Go Forth in Peace* can be found in Tsetsis, *Orthodox Thought*.

75. [Editor's note: Nichols gives an overview of Orthodox understandings of mission which I have omitted. He touches on the Trinitarian basis for mission and the importance of the Kingdom of God, the role of the Church, the centrality of the Eucharistic witness, and evangelistic witness: "The goal of proclamation of the gospel, then, is to establish eucharistic communities in every place, each within their own context, culture, and language."]

76. Bria, *Go Forth in Peace*, 32-33.

77. Bria, *Go Forth in Peace*, 33.

do not elaborate further on a definition of proselytism, nor do they state which groups under which circumstances they consider to be practicing proselytism rather than true evangelism....

An important area in the realm of evangelism and proselytism is a consideration of the target of the evangelistic witness. For the Orthodox authors of *Go Forth in Peace*, evangelistic witness is "directed toward all of the [created order] that groans and travails in search of adoption and redemption (Rom 8:22)."[78] This means, first of all, that the church's evangelistic witness is for "the Christian who is not a Christian."[79] The Orthodox define these people as those who have been baptized, but have not adhered to Christ, either deliberately or through indifference. Thus, the "re-Christianization of Christians" is an important part of the church's evangelistic witness. Linked with these nominal Christians is the direction of evangelistic witness to those who superficially identify Orthodox Christianity with their national culture. Such a witness should touch even the smallest part of the national life and culture.[80] The Orthodox Church acknowledges that nominal Christians exist in countries where Orthodoxy is the dominant religion, and asserts the need for evangelistic witness to these people. However, in this document, the Orthodox Church does not state its views on the role other Christian groups and churches can and should play in evangelistic witness to these nominal Christians. Other statements by Orthodox churches and the actions of various Orthodox churches clearly indicate that Orthodox Christians believe that the nominal Christians in Orthodox lands may only be evangelized by the Orthodox Church. However, if other Christian groups want to assist the Orthodox Church through prayers or financial support, that is welcomed. If other Christian groups offer "evangelistic witness" to these nominal Christians the Orthodox Church calls it proselytism....

The overall mission of the Church can be hindered in two ways, both of which relate to the influx of the world's values and systems into the Church. The first hindrance to the Church's missionary calling is a lack of connection to the trinitarian basis of communion. This occurs whenever a church is so divided or distorted that the true communal life that comes from God is no longer visible in the church. Lack of connection can also occur when mission efforts focus on individuals or "social realities of history" rather than using the Church as the reference point. Since the hall-mark of the Church, for the Orthodox believer, is that it is "one, holy, catholic, and apostolic," any division in the Church would detract from witness. Thus,

---

78. Bria, *Go Forth in Peace*, 34.
79. Bria, *Go Forth in Peace*, 34.
80. Bria, *Go Forth in Peace*, 34.

from an Orthodox perspective, Christian groups that are "competing" for potential adherents would undermine the entire basis for mission, as well as the basis for the Church. . . .

More recent Orthodox statements reveal changed attitudes toward other churches, but also confirmation of the theological framework established in *Go Forth in Peace*. The following is an analysis of (A) a statement by the Primates of the Orthodox Church in 1992, (B) Orthodox Consultations on Mission held at the WCC's request, culminating in (C) a speech delivered by Metropolitan Kirill of Smolensk and Kaliningrad at the WCC-CWME's Conference on World Mission and Evangelism in Salvador, Brazil in late 1996. This is followed by (D) a look at possible cracks in Orthodox involvement in the ecumenical movement,[81] and then (E) the recent position and statements of the Russian Orthodox Church, especially with regard to the new law "On Freedom of Conscience and on Religious Associations."

A. 1992 Pan-Orthodox Statement

On March 13-15, 1992, Patriarchs and Archbishops . . . convened at the headquarters of the Ecumenical Patriarchate in Istanbul, Turkey. . . . The Primates . . . issued a joint message . . . concerning a number of topics, including mission, evangelism, and proselytism. The Message carries substantial weight since it was signed by all of the fourteen Primates.

After an opening doxology and praise, the document addresses changes in the world and the response of the Church. These changes and their most distinct results are evident in the collapse of Communist systems in various countries. The Message claims that this collapse, coupled with the "failure of all anthropocentric ideologies," has led to an existential insecurity which, in turn, has led many people "to seek salvation in new religions and para-religious movements, sects or nearly idolatrous attachments to the material values of this world."[82] This has created a "deep crisis" in the contemporary world. Proselytism is a manifestation of this crisis, not a solution.[83]

The document next discusses the need for unity in the Church and the role the Orthodox Church has played in seeking and securing ecumenism in recent years. The Primates express their disbelief concerning the recent activities by both Catholics and "certain Protestant fundamentalists." The Orthodox Primates lament that these other "Christian" groups are not appropriately supporting the Orthodox Church in her important time. During

---

81. [Editor's note: This section will not be included here].
82. "Message of the Primates," para. 2.
83. "Message of the Primates," para. 2.

the atheistic regimes that formerly ruled in many countries, the Orthodox Churches were suppressed, tormented, and even persecuted. Now that the oppressive regimes have ended, the Primates had expected a favorable (*sic*) reaction from other Christian groups. Instead, "to the detriment of the desired journey towards Christian unity, the traditional Orthodox countries have been considered 'mission territories' and thus, missionary networks are set up in them and proselytism is practiced with all the methods which have been condemned and rejected for decades by all Christians."[84]

The Primates perceive the Roman Catholic Church as acting contrary to the spirit of love and dialogue established at many ecumenical meetings and bilateral theological discussions. The Uniate churches are a particularly sore subject for the Orthodox hierarchs.[85] The problem of Uniatism is so deep that any and all reconciliatory dialogue between the Catholics and the Orthodox is to remain focused on that single subject.

The document reserves a second diatribe for the "Protestant fundamentalists who are eager 'to preach' in Orthodox countries which were under Communist regimes."[86] These Protestant groups consider the former Communist countries as *terra missionis* (missionary lands). The Orthodox Church, comprising a clear majority in these countries, staunchly opposes consideration of their countries as *terra missionis* "since in these countries the Gospel has already been preached for many centuries."[87] True mission, in the Orthodox sense of the term, is "carried out in non-Christian countries and among non-Christian peoples."[88] This kind of mission is a sacred duty of the Church, and the Orthodox Church is involved in such mission activity in Asia and Africa (which must mean that the Primates consider those regions and peoples to be non-Christian).

Clearly, the Orthodox Church defines Christians very differently than the Protestants. For the Orthodox, the Church is community-centered, and Christians belong to the Church through baptism. For Protestants, Christians possess individual, personal relationships with God.[89] Further, Protestants would argue that it makes no sense to speak of a land as "already Christian."[90] These starkly different positions lead to problems of "proselytism."

84. "Message of the Primates," para. 4.
85. See also Kerr, "Mission and Proselytism," 12.
86. "Message of the Primates," para. 14.
87. "Message of the Primates," para. 14.
88. "Message of the Primates," para. 14.
89. See Volf, "Fishing in the Neighbor's Pond," 26.
90. See "From the Editor," 49, 50: "It no longer makes sense to speak of a Catholic

The Message of the Primates vigorously denounces all forms of proselytism, which it distinguishes from evangelization and mission. The Primates say that proselytism is practiced in many nations which are already Christian, including Orthodox nations. Proselytism sometimes occurs through material enticement and sometimes by various forms of violence. Such proselytism "poisons the relations among Christians and destroys the road towards their unity."[91] Since, for the Orthodox, true mission can occur only in non-Christian countries among non-Christians, the Orthodox definition of proselytism necessarily includes any "mission" effort to persons who are either already Christians or persons who are non-Christians but live in Christian countries. . . .

B. Orthodox Consultations on Mission

An ongoing series of consultations . . . have been held under the auspices of the WCC. The first of these meetings . . . was held at Chambesy, Switzerland, in February 1993. This gathering of fifteen, Orthodox, Roman Catholics, Protestants, and Evangelicals who met to discuss problems of proselytism produced a reflection paper: "Towards Responsible Relations in Mission: Some Reflections on Common Witness, Proselytism, and New Forms of Sharing."

The reflection paper affirms the importance of constructive dialogue among the Christian traditions regarding mission and proselytism. It yields a renewed recognition that "the commitment to evangelism is inseparable from the commitment to the unity of the Body of Christ."[92] While differences in perspectives and views on evangelism remain, the gathering affirmed some of the Orthodox Church's concerns as legitimate. The participants acknowledged that "mission activity from outside . . . invaded certain countries, particularly after the fall of communism."[93] While mission activity in itself is good, this particular "invasion" is wrong and harmful because the mission activity is occurring in places where the local church has existed for many centuries, namely in Orthodox countries.

Part of the increase in mission work in Orthodox countries stems from the new openness and religious freedom afforded by the new governments.

---

or Protestant or Orthodox nation, especially in light of Europe's growing secularism." See also the discussion of the secularism of the world and assertion that all churches are in missionary situations in WCC, *San Antonio Report* . . . and accompanying text.

91. "Message of the Primates," para. 4.
92. "Towards Responsible Relations in Mission," 235.
93. "Towards Responsible Relations in Mission," 236.

The participants acknowledged the freedom of persons to change their religion or belief, while simultaneously stressing the need for accountability among Christian churches so that there is not competition in mission. The document states bluntly: "Religious freedom must not become a license to disregard and marginalize local churches but should rather be used to promote common witness."[94] *The Message of the Primates* is affirmed in its condemnation of all forms of proselytism as outside the bounds of appropriate mission and evangelism.

Theologically, the document asserts the need for the communion of churches to correspond to the communion of the Triune God in diversity and unity.[95] This is firmly grounded in Orthodox trinitarian theology. Quoting the Second Vatican Council, the document asserts, "Another basis for our unity . . . is the recognition that all those who have received baptism in Christ are in real, though imperfect communion."[96] The participants committed themselves to the mutual sharing of information, accountability, and collaboration. Through this they hoped to avoid competition in mission activities, proselytism, and the creation of duplicative churches and structures in regions where the church is already present.[97] Finally, the assembly proposed a series of ten issues to the WCC for further reflection. The fifth issue was presented thus: "To ensure that no form of assistance to persons and churches is used to encourage a change in religious allegiance. Where such occurs, it must be condemned by all."[98]

Following the meeting at Chambesy, an Orthodox Consultation on Mission and Proselytism was held two years later in June 1995.[99] . . . The Consultation was attended by members of the Orthodox and Oriental Orthodox Churches, with representatives of the Roman Catholic Church and United Methodist Church in Russia in attendance as observers. The stated purpose of the meeting was "to formulate an Orthodox understanding of mission and of the phenomenon of proselytism and also to find ways and means to react against proselytism."[100] The Consultation produced a document that specifically dealt with defining mission and proselytism from an

---

94. "Towards Responsible Relations in Mission," 236.

95. "Towards Responsible Relations in Mission," 237.

96. Vatican II, *Unitatis Redintegratio* 3, cited in "Towards Responsible Relations in Mission," 238.

97. "Towards Responsible Relations in Mission," 238.

98. "Towards Responsible Relations in Mission," 239.

99. Organized by the World Council of Churches and took place at the Moscow Theological Academy in the Trinity-St. Sergius Monastery, Sergiev Posad, Russia.

100. Posad, *Final Document* [Editor's note: document unavailable for reference].

Orthodox perspective and the relationship of common witness and religious freedom to those concepts....

Proselytism is distinguished from true mission: "Proselytism is the conversion of Christians from one confession to another through methods and means that contradict the spirit of Christian love and violate the freedom of the human person."[101] The practice of proselytism uses many different means to accomplish its goal, including "open preaching of one's confession through mass media, public meetings in concert halls and stadiums, dissemination of literature, organizing print media, setting up parishes and dioceses, financing youth education, providing humanitarian aid accompanied by preaching one's own Church teaching, etc."[102] The Orthodox participants expressed that proselytizing often uses mis-information based on assumed cultural, social, economic, or political superiority. "[Proselytism] alienates people from their local ecclesial and cultural tradition, whereas true mission assures an integration of the gospel into the national culture, thus inspiring it."[103] Proselytism thus undermines ecumenism, particularly in Orthodox countries which have only recently been liberated from oppressive governments.

The participants at Sergiev Posad paid tribute to religious freedom, but insisted that it not be used as a legal justification for proselytism. Religious freedom is tied to respect for each person created by God. This respect carries over into relationships between Christians of different confessions. From the Orthodox perspective, freedom of religion necessarily means a view toward ecumenicity and excludes any Christian church from regarding traditionally Orthodox regions as *terra missionis*.[104] ...

Finally, the Orthodox Consultation on Mission and Proselytism submitted a list of recommendations, first to the Orthodox Churches, and then to the WCC. The Consultation recommended that the Orthodox Churches examine the causes for proselytism within their country, and eliminate those causes stemming from the weakness or ineffectiveness of the indigenous Orthodox church to minister effectively. Orthodox Churches were also urged to take a more active role in missions, both on a practical level and on a scholarly level. Finally, Orthodox Churches were encouraged to share information regarding proselytism, new religious movements, and sects.

The Consultation also proposed that the WCC continue to study proselytism and renounce it among member churches.... The Consultation

---

101. Posad, *Final Document*, para. 2.
102. Posad, *Final Document*, para. 2.
103. Posad, *Final Document*, para. 2.
104. Posad, *Final Document*, para. 3.

further urged the WCC to organize a consultation and comprehensive study concerning the proselytism of the "so-called new religious movements and destructive cults."[105]

In July 1996, the WCC organized another consultation, "Toward Common Witness" . . . for the purpose of producing a document for contribution to the [forthcoming] CWME conference.[106] Twenty-two representatives from sixteen countries attended this consultation. The representative from the Russian Orthodox Church (ROC)[107] . . . described the current situation in Russia and listed eight Christian groups which were "engaged in proselytism" in Russia: (1) the Roman Catholic Church; (2) major Protestant churches (Lutherans, Presbyterians, Methodists); (3) Korean churches from South Korea and the USA; (4) world and European missionary societies; (5) nondenominational missionary organizations (Campus Crusade for Christ, Ko-Mishn, etc.); (6) Pentecostal and charismatic movements; (7) free evangelists; and (8) electronic preachers.[108] She further asserted that religious freedom must not be used to justify proselytism.

Overall, the consultation did not come to any consensus regarding the following terms: mission, evangelism, proselytism, believer, inchurching, and other related terms.[109] Further study was recommended on these terms and issues. . . .

C. Speech by Metropolitan Kirill of Smolensk and Kaliningrad[110]

The speech by this prominent member of the Russian Orthodox Church hierarchy focused on three main subjects: one hope, the gospel in diverse cultures, and the problem of proselytism. The first two subjects of the speech are only tangentially related to the present inquiry. . . .

The last third of the speech is a bitter diatribe against incursions by foreign missionaries. Metropolitan Kirill characterizes all of the missionaries who entered Russia following the fall of the Soviet Union as engaging in "crusade . . . against the Russian Church," and states: "In most cases the intention [of the missionaries] was not to preach Christ and the gospel, but to

---

105. Posad, *Final Document*, para. 5.
106. Salvador, Brazil, November–December 1996.
107. Moscow Patriarchate, *Consultation on Proselytism*, 3.
108. Moscow Patriarchate, *Consultation on Proselytism*, 3.
109. Moscow Patriarchate, *Consultation on Proselytism*, 5.

110. Metropolitan Kirill of Smolensk and Kaliningrad, "Address at the Conference on World Mission and Evangelism in Salvador, Brazil, November 25, 1996," in Bordeaux and Witte Jr., *Soul Wars*.

tear our faithful away from their traditional churches and recruit them into their own communities."[111] Missionaries may at first have believed they were dealing with non-Christian or atheistic communist people, but foreign missionaries should have soon learned that "our culture was formed by Christianity and . . . our Christianity survived through the blood of martyrs and confessors, through the courage of bishops, theologians and laypeople asserting their faith. Metropolitan Kirill categorizes the activity of the foreign missionaries as "fighting with our church." He says the missionaries "came from abroad with dollars," buying time on radio and television and using "their financial resources to the utmost in order to buy people." From the perspective of the ROC, efforts by non-Orthodox missionaries to convert Russians via the medium of television or radio is proselytism, and, in effect, is an attempt to "buy people." Even humanitarian aid by foreign churches is suspect. "Proselytism is not some narrow religious activity generated by a wrong understanding of missionary tasks. Proselytism is the fact of invasion by another culture, even if Christian, but developing according to its own laws and having its own history and tradition."[112]

The actions by foreign missionaries, from the Russian Church's vantage point, undermine the very basis of ecumenism, because "ecumenism and proselytism are incompatible." "Incompatible also are mission and spiritual enslavement, the preaching of Christ and violence to one's conscience, the proclamation of the gospel and bribery." By making such a harsh statement, the Metropolitan implies that the non-Orthodox missionaries are performing all of the latter actions, and not the former. These statements from Metropolitan Kirill clearly point to an undermining of ecumenism, since the ROC views all foreign mission activity as competitive and parallel. Metropolitan Kirill does propose a number of solutions to these problems.

First, the WCC is called upon to take up the problem of proselytism and to help avoid all further problems. Second, and most importantly, the way out of the situation "lies in basing mission on the fundamental principle of early Christian ecclesiology: the principle of local church." Adopting this principle would cede all control and responsibility for the people in a given locale to the local church. The local church then would be fully responsible before God for its people. From the Orthodox view, this principle would mean that all foreign missionaries would abandon their independent efforts in Russia and

111. This quote and all following are from the speech unless otherwise specified.

112. Kirill in Bordeaux and Witte Jr., *Soul Wars*. See also Robeck Jr., "Mission and the Issue of Proselytism," 2, 4: "The Orthodox have essentially defined proselytism so broadly that any missionary or evangelistic activity undertaken by non-Orthodox within these countries is labeled illegitimate, and those who are active in such practices are frequently described as thieves."

instead focus any attention given to Russia on the Orthodox Church. Support and aid could be given to the ROC so that she could carry out the mission responsibilities (if any exist in Russia, which is unclear in the speech), but the Orthodox Church would never be threatened by competition.

This proposal is based on the assumption that non-Orthodox missionaries in Russia are "ignoring the local church." But if non-Orthodox Christians maintain a different definition of a Christian than the Orthodox Church holds, then the non-Orthodox missionaries can truthfully say that they are not ignoring the local church. By their definition, their activity would be appropriate mission activity provided they are not using truly forceful or coercive methods or inducements by promise of money or reward. Based upon a different definition of who is a Christian, non-Orthodox observers believe it is possible that Christian missions could occur in Russia (or other Orthodox countries) while the local church is still respected. So long as active members of the Orthodox Church are not being recruited and persuaded to change their religious affiliation, it is at least conceivable, on a theoretical level, that illegitimate proselytism is not occurring.

This is not to say that the Orthodox Church should sit passively by and allow anything to occur, or even that the Orthodox Church has weak arguments. The point is simply that the Orthodox Church and the non-Orthodox missionaries are not speaking about the same subject. Further dialogue on some deeper issues of Christianity is required. Diatribe and polemic from either side is not the solution. The Orthodox Church should not write off every mission activity in their country as proselytism and as a violation of religious freedom. Non-Orthodox missionaries should not condemn the Orthodox Church as being noncommitted to missions and should not unfairly characterize the Orthodox Church as being fundamentally opposed to religious freedom.[113] Accusations by either side are too often based on partial information and less than partial understanding.[114]

113. See Newbigin, "Dialogue of Gospel and Culture," 50, arguing that it is necessary to challenge the ROC to let go of the "old territorial principle that regards the presence on Russian soil of any form of Christianity other than its own as illegitimate," while at the same time contending that missionaries to Russia should learn from the ROC. and the long and costly history it endured under communism.

114. Editor's note: Nichols concludes his article with some paragraphs about the ROC and the Russian Law "On Freedom of Conscience and on Religious Associations." He argues that in supporting this law and the language that is used in the debate, "the Moscow Patriarchate has succeeded in vilifying all missionaries, not just illegitimate groups. However, from the view of the ROC, increasingly, all groups evangelizing in Russia are, by their very presence, engaging in proselytism and are thus illegitimate. Not only does this assertion run counter to international human rights norms, it runs counter to the theology of the ROC itself. This is a movement away from traditional Orthodox theology and toward a defensive, nationalistic stance."

3.5

Proselytism in a Central and Eastern European Perspective[1]

Journal of European Baptist Studies 8.2 (2008) 18–36

DARRELL JACKSON

INTRODUCTION

I AM A CONTEXTUAL missiologist, formerly employed by the Conference of European Churches (CEC) as a researcher in European Mission and Evangelism. The membership of CEC is both Protestant and Orthodox (Eastern and non-Chalcedonean). Given this constituency, CEC has been required to pay constant attention to issues of proselytism when discussing mission and evangelism.[2] These activities have often been characterized as obsessions of the western Protestant churches though in fact they are not absent from the Orthodox experience.[3] A further complicating factor in countries such as Russia is the fact that the charge of proselytism is often levelled at the Roman Catholic Church, in membership of neither CEC nor the World Council of Churches (WCC). This perception is fuelled by the observation that many Roman Catholic priests in Russia today are of Polish nationality. In the Ukraine, proselytizing activity is identified by the Ukrainian Orthodox

---

1. Used by permission.

2. See CEC and CCEE, *Charta Oecumenica*, a joint document of CEC and the Roman Catholic Bishop's conference of Europe (CCEE), signed by the Presidents of the two bodies on April 22, 2001, in Strasbourg.

3. For example, see Veronis, *Missionaries, Monks, and Martyrs*.

Church (Moscow Patriarchate) with both the Greek Catholic Church (or "Uniates") and the Ukrainian Orthodox Church (Kiev Patriarchate). In every majority Orthodox or Roman Catholic context the minority charismatic and Pentecostal churches suffer the strongest opprobrium, whilst in at least one majority Lutheran context the term has been used to describe the activity of local Baptist congregations.[4] It appears that the dynamic existing between majority and minority Christian traditions gains a dialectical, even conflictual, nature where the different religious traditions may at times seem little more than a veneer covering the more significant and underlying national realities and identities.

PROSELYTISM: A BRIEF HISTORY OF A CONCEPT

The use of the term "proselyte" became widespread during the late Hellenistic and Roman periods in Israel as a description of those who converted to Judaism. It is still used as such in contemporary Judaism.

> The word "proselyte" was originally used to designate in early Christian times . . . a person of another faith who converted to Christianity. . . . Proselytism in later centuries took on a negative connotation due to changes in the content, motivation, spirit, and methods of "evangelism."[5]

The term came to have negative connotations with the Enlightenment, where it was identified with fanaticism and intolerance (though not necessarily limited to religious usage).

In current ecumenical usage, the term is used to refer to a certain kind of evangelistic mission that is coercive rather than persuasive; typified by deception, distortion, manipulation and exploitation. So, for example, the WCC document "Towards Common Witness" (1997) states:

> "Proselytism" is now used to mean the encouragement of Christians who belong to a church to change their denominational allegiance, through ways and means that "contradict the spirit of Christian love, violate the freedom of the human person and diminish trust in the Christian witness of the church."[6]

---

4. Reported to the author in conversation with one of my MTh students from Norway.
5. Matthey, "Towards Common Witness," 49.
6. Matthey, "Towards Common Witness," 49.

The World Evangelical Alliance (WEA) felt the need to issue its own condemnation of proselytism in 2003. Attempting to distinguish between evangelism and proselytism, the text refers to the joint WCC and Roman Catholic text *Common Witness and Proselytism* (1970) and affirms:

> Proselytism takes place (1) whenever our motives are unworthy (when our concern is for our glory rather than God's); (2) whenever our methods are unworthy (when we resort to any kind of "physical coercion, moral constraint, or psychological pressure"); and (3) whenever our message is unworthy (whenever we deliberately misrepresent other people's beliefs).[7]

Although the WEA statement condemns unworthy motives, methods, and message, it nevertheless reserves space for an individual freely to choose their own religious beliefs, indeed to change those beliefs. However, it carefully avoids any suggestion that changing one's religious beliefs necessarily implies a change of institutional religious affiliation. By way of contrast, attempts to define proselytism, drawing upon the ecumenical "Towards Common Witness," have tended to decry activities that encourage others to join one's own church without addressing the extent or nature of existing institutional religious affiliation. The range of censured activities has typically included the following:

- Criticizing or caricaturing the beliefs and practices of another church without attempting to understand or enter into dialogue on those issues;
- Presenting one's own church as "the true church" in unique possession of an elevated moral and spiritual status, simultaneously highlighting the alleged weaknesses and problems of another's church;
- Offering financial, educational or humanitarian inducements in the hope of recruiting others to one's own church;
- Using political, economic, moral, psychological, cultural or ethnic pressure with the goal of recruiting others to one's own church;
- Exploiting inadequate education, Christian instruction or an ignorance of history in order to persuade another to change their church allegiance;

---

7. WEA, "Defining Evangelism versus Proselytism," Definition of Proselytism and Evangelism, 2003, www.wea.org. Accessed 20 November 2007. [Editor's note: the World Evangelical Alliance website is now: www.worldea.org; see also, https://worldreliefdurham.org/defining-evangelism-vs-proselytism (accessed 28.08.2017)].

- Threatening or deploying physical or emotional violence to induce people to change their church allegiance;
- Exploiting people's physical or mental illness, social isolation, emotional or psychological distress, offering "conversion" as a panacea.

Allegations of proselytism, the inappropriate use of manipulation, spiritual or mental, or inducement, financial and material, to persuade a member of one Christian tradition to join another,[8] bring to center stage the discussion about the nature of proselytizing Christian communities and those that resist their attempts at conversion and recruitment. At the heart of this discussion is a question of ethical behaviour. Put simply, the question may be formulated as, "What is the appropriate ethical way of life for a Christian community engaging in mission and evangelism?"

ETHICS AND MISSION

There is no mention of ethics as it relates to mission, evangelism, conversion or indeed proselytism in either *A New Dictionary of Christian Ethics*[9] or *The Cambridge Companion to Christian Ethics*.[10] If you were to search the internet and journal archives for the related terms, "conversion and ethics" or "mission and ethics," you would struggle to find much that is meaningful. Within the missiological corpus it is not much better. *The Dictionary of Mission*[11] contains a rather abstract article on ethics. *The Evangelical Dictionary of World Missions*[12] is only a little more useful, devoting two and a half pages to a discussion of mission, cross-cultural and contextual ethics. The failure of both dictionaries to address ethical questions raised by experiences and allegations of proselytism may seem an oversight, or it might suggest that both authors consider the proper place to discuss proselytism to fall within the theological domain, rather than that of ethics.

A notable exception is a chapter in Wilbert Shenk's *Anabaptism and Mission* which contains a useful discussion from the radical Reformation

---

8. I resist the tendency to label all Christian witness directed towards the conversion of individuals or communities as "proselytism." For an important discussion of the difference between conversion and assimilation and their respective usage with regards the discourse of proselytism, see Walls, "Converts or Proselytes?"
9. McQuarrie and Childress, *New Dictionary of Christian Ethics*.
10. Gill, *Cambridge Companion to Christian Ethics*.
11. Müller et al., *Dictionary of Mission*.
12. Moreau, *Evangelical Dictionary of World Missions*.

perspective.¹³ Gallardo's chapter emphasizes the need for integrity in communication, the avoidance of nationalism and cultural imperialism, and the necessity of obedient discipleship. It emphasizes the nature of the missionary church, and highlights other theological and ethical requirements that bear upon authentic witness.

However, it seems generally true that proselytism has been overlooked as an appropriate subject within the discourse of ethics. As an undergraduate I gained the view that ethics was the preoccupation of Christians concerned to develop the "right" understanding of a limited range of issues, including warfare, bioethics, family, and sexual ethics. The way in which ethics was taught as an issue-based subject seemed to confirm this understanding. In contrast to this approach (which admittedly contains an element of caricature) I intend to adopt an understanding of ethics developed by Anabaptist systematic theologian, James McClendon.

CONVICTIONAL COMMUNITIES IN THE DIALOGUE OF ENCOUNTER

McClendon begins his study of systematic theology with a discussion of ethics. Starting with the question, "What is theology?" he suggests that the answer, "Just a '*logos* of *Theos*,' merely ideas and discourse about God," is inadequate; instead, he offers the following definition:

> Theology [is] the discovery, understanding, and transformation of the convictions of a convictional community, including the discovery and critical revision of their relation to one another and to whatever else there is.¹⁴

As to ethics, McClendon continues,

> "Christian ethics" will refer to theories of the Christian way of life. These words can be used in other ways; this will be my way.¹⁵

I want to suggest that the "convictions" described by McClendon, in the sense that he frames them with reference to a "way of life," can only ever be embodied convictions, whether in community or individually. If, as a representative of such a convictional community, I am to maintain my integrity in order to convince others of the veracity of my convictions, McClendon's

---

13. Shenk, *Anabaptism and Mission*.
14. McClendon Jr., *Systematic Theology*, 23.
15. McClendon Jr., *Systematic Theology*, 47.

insight becomes particularly crucial. In addition we may extend this definition of ethics as a "way of life," being certain sets of actions appropriate to the Christian disciple and to the interior life of the disciple. We can then state that the attempt to embody a conviction is to self-reflexively address the question, "Who am I?"[16] Thereby Christian identity also falls within the domain of the ethical-theological life. When Jesus asks his disciples, "Who do people say that I am?" (Matt 13:13–16), we may understand him to be exploring with them the implication of the incarnation for his own sense of identity.

However, such a construction is problematized by the discourse of proselytism precisely when the transformation or critical revision of one's existing convictions prompts the need for the self-reflexive individual to address a further question, "Who am I becoming?" In the encounter of members or affiliates of two Christian traditions, the individual is likely to discover the extent to which he or she is embedded within the convictional communities of which they have hitherto been a part. The means by which such individuals are bound to those communities are likely to be a compelling amalgam, to a greater or lesser extent, of two clusters of theological-spiritual and historical-cultural factors. The manner in which these have been juxtaposed will be the test of either their resilience or their susceptibility. Understanding the juxtaposition is crucial to a proper appreciation of the issues that bear upon our discussion of mission and proselytism.

The classic dilemma for conversionist paradigms of mission is that they largely fail to adequately address the way in which cultural, ethnical and national identities bear upon questions of Christian identity; that is, upon the shared convictions of a convictional community. In the first volume of *The Information Age: Economy, Society, and Culture*, Manuel Castells[17] places technological revolution and restructured world capitalism in a dialectical relationship with the search for identity. Whilst the former tend towards a dislocation of former social and economic certainties and locate notions of time and place in a virtual realm, the search for identity is located within very concrete forms of communal expression. With an encyclopaedic presentation Castells illustrates its location variously within religious fundamentalism, nationalism, ethnicity and territory; locations for which one reviewer chooses the descriptive term, "treacherous slopes."[18]

---

16. I have found British sociologist Anthony Giddens helpful in understanding the inter-relation of the individuals who identify with an institution, particularly as each bears upon the other. See Giddens, *Constitution of Society*.

17. Castells, *Rise of the Network Society*.

18. Stern, "Back to the Future?"

In the encounter of two or more Christian traditions, particularly majority Christian traditions with minority Christian traditions, a tendency emerges that echoes the dialectic suggested by Castells. In Central and Eastern Europe, the minority Christian traditions typically share a Western Christian heritage, both Protestant and Roman Catholic. More specifically, however, they are usually of the Reformation, whether Methodist, Baptist, Reformed, Lutheran or charismatic. This tends to place them as the ready beneficiaries of technological revolution and renders them more amenable to restructured world capitalism.[19] They may be less committed to ecclesiastical expressions constructed upon fixed notions of time and place. In some instances there may be little confessional commitment either.[20] In contrast, the majority Orthodox traditions share a rather different historical and national experience. Time and place are essential components of Orthodox spirituality and self-understanding. The influence of national and territorial factors present within Orthodoxy remains ecclesiastically important, though becoming increasingly unfathomable to the other Christian traditions.[21]

As a consequence, majority and minority Christian traditions have tended to assume alternative versions of the discourse of mission and evangelism, each shaped by their respective historical and cultural experiences. The majority traditions, in the face of the perceived threat from more active minority traditions, adopt the discourse of proselytism as the preferred way of referring to mission and evangelism. Positively, this may be a valid attempt on the part of pastorally responsible church leaders to shore up the erosion of the religious and cultural identity of their church members when threatened by the mission activity of a minority church. It may, however, be used simply as a means of suppressing any mission activity by other historically present minority traditions. The minority traditions, in the face of perceived suppression and regulation, normally adopt the discourse of Human Rights as the preferred way of referring to mission and evangelism. Positively this may be a valid response to believing that basic human rights are being threatened. However, it may be little more than an attempt to justify

---

19. See, for example, Cox, *Fire from Heaven*, for a discussion of Pentecostalism as the example of globalized Christianity *par excellence*.

20. Global and regional evangelical bodies, for instance, will command the loyalties of members drawn from the widest possible range of Christian traditions.

21. These questions remain intractable beyond the traditional heartlands of the Orthodox Church. The claim of the Ecumenical Patriarch to jurisdictional authority over extra-territorial Orthodox communities is contested by some Orthodox. In practice, extra-territorial Orthodoxy has the appearance of being largely ethnically composed, and in the USA, it may at first appear somewhat "denominational."

aggressively expansionist plans in order to satisfy its existing members of spiritual vitality in the hope of their continued support and membership.

Consequently, rival forms of discourse for referring to mission and evangelism have made it very difficult for ecumenical discussion of mission and evangelism to proceed without allegations of deceptive expansionism by some and theological obscurantism by others. Even the task of finding and agreeing common language is a fraught exercise. Whilst "mission" for some Orthodox might be nothing more than a Protestant obsession, for others it can be readily understood as the equivalent of the "apostolic task" of the Church. Being of Latin origin rather hinders its adoption as a commonly taken description for what the Church is called to do. Where the two dialogue partners have not agreed on a common discourse accessible equally to both, the potential for mutual understanding is diminished and mutual suspicion is simultaneously heightened. With the passing of time, each respective discourse has gained respectability and validity through theological formulations, pastoral experience, and the continued phenomena of church members who switch their allegiance from one tradition to another.

Thus, what is often observed between majority churches and minority churches is a conflict fuelled by underlying convictions relating to mission and proselytism within a particular territory, in particular the potential consequence, destructive and constructive, of these activities upon the collective and individual identities and affiliation of existing church members. It may be that by focussing upon identity in this way we are in danger of overlooking issues of how and why power and control are wielded by Christian traditions. However, I would suggest that where identity is located primarily within one's understanding of nationality[22] then to focus upon identity is by extension to raise the issue of the appropriate national role that ought to be played by identity-forming Christian communities. The extent to which Christian identity and national identity inform and shape the other is likely to be a powerful predictor of the influence and control of a national Church.

In what follows I want to tentatively suggest that it is only possible to critique adequately the discourse of proselytism with reference to a theologically ethical community. Allegations of proselytism are best addressed through a dialogue that acknowledges the functional role of history and culture, carefully scrutinizes the phenomena being discussed, recognizes the distinctions in the discourses, and refocuses the discussion upon how

---

22. To be differentiated from identification with the Nation State, which, as Castells points out, is increasingly less likely to command our loyalty and provide the primary locale for our identity formation.

we are to nurture and witness to Christian identity from within our theologically formed ethical communities.

THE DISCOURSE OF PROSELYTISM AND THE EXAMPLE OF THE RUSSIAN ORTHODOX CHURCH

The theological vision of the Eastern Orthodox Churches emphasizes the visible unity of the Church.[23] One specific development of this theological vision is the concept of "canonical territory": "The concept of canonical territory denotes the inseparable identity of people, culture, land, and church."[24] Pre-empting the discussion of human rights below, we may say that this vision is collectivist and heteronomous (in contrast to autonomous). It is holistic, mystical, and arises from a profound reflection on incarnation and the indivisibility of the body of Christ. It privileges place and history as the appropriate locale within which the one Body of Christ can take shape. "People" and "nation" are thus to be understood as particular expressions of place and history, and therefore a theologically justified arena for the redemptive purposes of God. It is this vision that gives rise to the theological rationale for challenging the proselytizing of various missionary groups (usually though not exclusively from the West).

> The Russian Orthodox Church defines proselytism as the active or passive encouraging of members of a given ethnic or national group to join a religion, denomination, or sect that is not historically rooted in that ethnic group or nationality.[25]

We may, of course, note the difficulty of determining what is meant by "historically rooted." How historic is "historical"; fifteen years or fifty? Knowledge of certain groups that have been active and present can be forgotten, suppressed or ignored. History has proven highly vulnerable to officially sanctioned versions of it.[26] Properly approaching history and its interpretation requires an appropriate sensitivity to any interests that the history writer represents. It is hard to imagine the level of skill, patience and commitment to historical integrity that is required to sift through archival

---

23. Sometimes emphasized in contrast to the Protestant notion of the "invisible" unity of the church.

24. Kerr, "Christian Understandings of Proselytism," 9. See Moscow Patriarchate, "Relations of the Russian Orthodox Church." [Editor's note: see section 2.18 of this volume.]

25. Kerr, "Christian Understandings of Proselytism," 9.

26. See, for example, Byford, "Distinguishing Anti-Judaism from Antisemitism."

material drafted according to the canons of Soviet propaganda in order to discover fragments of truth regarding the history of the Christian traditions in the Former Soviet Union (or indeed in the Russian Empire of the Tsars).

However, the *Mission and Evangelism in Unity Today*[27] document illustrates well the position advanced by Castells. Ethnicity and nationality are given a functional value determinative of what may be considered proselytism. The definition allows for Christian mission activity to be considered appropriate in one particular ethnic and national context, whilst in another the same mission activity is inappropriate. With the demise in influence and function of the Nation State, according to Castells, the functional value of ethnicity and nationality will prove to be as contestable (and controversial) as claims to historicity. This is largely because these identifiers have become notoriously difficult terms to define with precision, a point underlined by Vera Tolz with her discussion of the (re)building of national identity in Russia and the five competing visions of the Russian nation available to those constructing the new nationalist discourse.[28]

In 1996 the Chairman of the External Relations Department of the Moscow Patriarchate, Metroplitan Kirill, addressed the Conference for World Mission and Evangelism of the World Council of Churches. In his speech he drew attention to a crisis of human civilization caused by the global crisis of human personality. He called for the privileging of Christian identity (through attention to spiritual renewal) over Christian activism (particularly of a socio-political type), implying that the ecumenical programmes of the WCC began in the wrong place. In the same speech, a full third of his text addressed issues of mission and proselytism. He began this section in the following way,

> Proselytism . . . is more than a purely theological issue. . . . It is primarily an expression of cultural and ideological clashes, as newcomers try to impose their own culturally conditioned form of Christianity on other Christians.[29]

In 2001, Patriarch Aleksii addressed, by letter, a mission consultation organized jointly in Moscow by the Anglican Church Mission Society and Orthodox Missiologists. He underlined the themes raised by Metropolitan Kirill: "Missionaries, not conscious of the values of the local culture, harm the spiritual wellbeing of society."[30] However, non-Orthodox writers are

---

27. WCC, *Mission and Evangelism in Unity Today*.
28. Tolz, "Forging the Nation."
29. Kirill, "Gospel and Culture," in Duraisingh, *Called to One Hope*, 89.
30. Aleksii, "Greeting," in Oxbrow, *Together in Mission*, 5.

also amongst those who are critical of the insensitive and aggressive efforts of some western missionaries, "Most of the time they were seen as ambassadors of their country's culture and ideology, and not of Jesus."[31] Such criticisms may be readily elicited from Baptists and other evangelical Christians in many parts of the former Soviet Union. Such judgements are reflected in the more sober response of senior theological educators in Russia, Poland, Hungary, the Czech Republic and Georgia who, reporting on the current challenges to theological education in their regions, point to the need to move away from the "off-the-shelf" theological programmes they were offered during the early 1990s and to adopt more contextually appropriate curricula.[32]

However, the discourse deployed above construes proselytism as principally a cross-cultural encounter in which existing ethnic and national identities are ignored and alternative forms of cultural Christianity are offered or imposed. In practice it has proven difficult for many Western newcomers and missionaries to understand, even imagine, how religiously and culturally homogenous cultures continue to survive, even flourish, in the globalizing world with which they are personally very familiar (and with which they may often be all too comfortable). Equally it has sometimes proven difficult for representatives of the indigenous churches in Central and Eastern Europe to imagine ways in which the impact of globalization upon local cultures can be evaluated beneficially. A typical response has been to simply dismiss it by characterizing globalization as little more than "secularization," "westernization," "democratization," or "late-capitalism." Individuals sensitive to the history of cultural exchange and interchange might suggest that the only cultures that have been resistant to change were either ossified or dead.

In the statements of Kirill and Aleksii, the agents of differently composed forms of cultural and ideological Christianity are construed as "the other." Romanian theologian Silvana Bunea has described how an encounter with the "other" by the Orthodox is frequently perceived as a threat to one's identity, typically resulting in the adoption of a defensive posture.[33] The demands placed upon attempts at authentic dialogue must therefore take seriously the reasons for this posture being so frequently adopted and seek to address the often genuine concerns that underlie it. The discourse deployed by the representatives of the Orthodox Church may be uncomfortable for Western Christians to read but it points to the instinctive

---

31. Gallardo, "Ethics and Mission," 138.
32. Reported to me on a number of occasions through personal conversations.
33. Bunea, "Reflections on the Encounter of Orthodoxy."

assumptions and attitudes that many western missionaries share and which inform their ecclesiology and theology more than they might care to admit. This can often appear to non-Westerners as little more than applying the techniques of the market-place to the religious domain. It is worth citing *Mission and Evangelism in Unity Today* in full on this point,

> Indeed, the highly competitive environment of the free market is reinforcing many churches and para-church movements in their perception of mission as the effort to attract and recruit new "customers," while retaining the old ones. Their programmes and doctrines are presented as "religious products," which must be appealing and attractive to potential new members. They evaluate the success of their mission in terms of growth, of numbers of converts or of newly planted churches. Unfortunately, very often their "new members" already belonged to other churches. Thus proselytism (as competition and "sheep-stealing") is one of the sharp contemporary issues facing the churches.[34]

The Orthodox Church in post-Soviet Russia understands herself to be threatened by active Protestant missionary groups offering an alternative identity-constituting discourse that is not always constructed with reference to ethnicity or nationality. Indeed in certain cases a universalizing form of evangelicalism is offered that in reality does reflect the cultural assumptions of the missionary. When one discusses the newer churches in Budapest, for example, a younger generation will readily talk excitedly about "Calvary Chapel," one of many similar congregations currently being "planted" in Central and Eastern Europe that has imported US-derived ecclesiastical values and guarantees these by conferring the quality assurance of its name as a "religious brand," wherever it plants congregations.

The response of the Russian Government to the rapid and widespread multiplication of this type of Christian group has been the September 1997 law "On Freedom of Conscience and Religious Associations," overturning many of the reformist principles of the 1990 "Law on Freedom of Worship" which guaranteed religious freedoms familiar to many in the western world. The attitude of the Christian community to this legislation is varied. Some express enthusiastic endorsement for the privileged status it confers upon the Orthodox Church as the historic Russian Church. Some find its restrictions objectionable and label it a return to Soviet-style legislation. Others express regret that such a measure should have been necessary yet hope that it will afford a measure of protection against the excesses of aggressive western missionary movements.

---

34. See WCC, *Mission and Evangelism in Unity Today*, para. 27.

In contemporary Russia, culture, ethnicity and nationality remain disputed notions and the controversy generated over discussions of the alternatives is likely to have its counterpart in Christian dialogue and ecumenical discussion of mission and evangelism for some time to come.

ECUMENICAL AND EVANGELICAL RESPONSES TO MISSION AND PROSELYTISM

It has been entirely appropriate that those Churches that have submitted themselves to an ecumenical discipline should make every effort to condemn what they sincerely and genuinely believe to be proselytism. Indeed, a number of these will themselves have suffered the loss of their own members to a variety of unaffiliated and vigorously active protestant churches and groups. However, their response has perhaps not always been as forthcoming as it might because of a deep commitment to notions of inalienable human rights, usually enshrined in various charters and declarations.[35]

As an example, the Conference of European Churches issued the widely adopted and consulted *Charta Oecumenica: A Text, a Process, and a Dream of the Churches in Europe*[36] in which the following statements with regards to mission and evangelism are included:

> We commit ourselves

- to discuss our plans for evangelization with other churches, entering into agreements with them and thus avoiding harmful competition and the risk of fresh divisions.
- to recognize that every person can freely choose his or her religious and church affiliation as a matter of conscience, which means not inducing anyone to convert through moral pressure or material incentive, but also not hindering anyone from entering into conversion of his or her own free will.

In 1997 the World Council of Churches issued an extensive treatment of these and related themes entitled "Towards Common Witness: A Call to Adopt Responsible Relationships in Mission and to Renounce

---

35. For example, one may consider *The Universal Declaration of Human Rights* (1948), *The European Convention for the Protection of Human Rights and Fundamental Freedoms* (1950), *The International Covenant on Civil and Political Rights* (1966), and *The Declaration on the Elimination of All Forms of Intolerance and Discrimination Based on Religion or Belief* (1981).

36. Ionita, *Charta Oecumenica*.

Proselytism."[37] In this document the WCC underlined, in very clear terms, its own commitment to the concept of Human Rights and Religious Liberty. The pertinent section is quoted here in full:

> 3. Mission in the context of religious freedom
>
> God's truth and love are given freely and call for a free response. Free will is one of the major gifts with which God has entrusted humans. God does not force anyone to accept God's revelation and does not save anyone by force. On the basis of this notion, the International Missionary Council and the World Council of Churches (in process of formation) developed a definition of religious freedom as a fundamental human right. This definition was adopted by the WCC First Assembly in Amsterdam (1948), and at the suggestion of the WCC's Commission of the Churches on International Affairs it was subsequently incorporated in the Universal Declaration of Human Rights: "Everyone has the right to freedom of thought, conscience and religion. This right includes the freedom to change his/her religion or belief, and freedom, either alone or in community with others, in public or in private, to manifest his/her religion or belief, in teaching, practice, worship and observance." The same principle is to be applied in mission work.
>
> The WCC Fifth Assembly (1975) reaffirmed the centrality of religious liberty, stating that "the right to religious freedom has been and continues to be a major concern of member churches and the WCC. However this right should never be seen as belonging exclusively to the church. . . . This right is inseparable from other fundamental human rights. No religious community should plead for its own religious liberty without active respect and reverence for the faith and basic rights of others. Religious liberty should never be used to claim privileges. For the church this right is essential so that it can fulfill its responsibilities which arise out of the Christian faith. Central to these responsibilities is the obligation to serve the whole community." One's own freedom must always respect, affirm and promote the freedom of others; it must not contravene the golden rule: "In everything do to others as you would have them do to you" (Matt 7:12).

Citing ecumenical and Roman Catholic texts, the WEA issued its own definition of proselytism and then condemned it in the following terms, in its document *Proselytism vs. Evangelism* (2003):

---

37. WCC, "Towards Common Witness."

> The World Evangelical Alliance strongly rejects proselytism but supports full religious freedom according to the United Nations declaration of Human Rights (art. 18–19). That freedom will give people of every religion the right to share their beliefs and allow everyone the freedom of conscience to believe as they choose.[38]

The WEA statement does not command equal respect amongst all evangelicals. "Some evangelicals have manifested a reluctance to entertain issues of . . . human rights for fear of diverting attention away from evangelism and church planting."[39]

Equally reluctantly, some Orthodox are cautious of the discourse of Universal Human Rights. Many of them might find themselves in the, perhaps surprising, company of one evangelical commentator on Human Rights legislation:

> Much modern rights-talk has connotations that are egoistic, licentious and antagonistic: in short, that are profoundly anti-Christian. For rights carry an inherent bias favoring individualism over collectivism, autonomy over heteronomy, and conflict over consensus.[40]

In each of the ecumenical and evangelical texts, appeal is made to the discourse of Human Rights. Significantly, the WCC statement draws attention to the inclusion of religious freedom clauses within the UN's Declaration at the suggestion of the WCC's own staff following the 1948 WCC Assembly. Minority Churches have been continuously represented within each of the constituencies responsible for these three documents. In many instances, membership of various regional and worldwide confessional or ecumenical bodies has been a means of ameliorating the perceived threat of the majority Churches to their minority counterparts, a means of seeking and securing some guarantee of basic freedoms of religious belief and practice in a majority context.

However, in addition to the evangelical cautions noted above, we may also note that the universal intention of the United Nations' Declaration is viewed with deep suspicion by some Orthodox who relativise its claims by arguing that it is an expression of western cultural aspirations and suggest alternative visions of freedom (from the Bible) might be prior to this.

---

38. Edmonds, *Proselytism vs. Evangelism*. [Editor: see footnote 7 above]
39. Carroll, "Ethics," 319–22.
40. Rivers, "Beyond Rights."

> The canons of the Orthodox Church help one understand the essence of Christian freedom as knowledge of the Truth (John 8:32). They protect the Christian from the secular understanding of freedom, based on the legal principle of the equality of all religions.[41]

Some highlight the abuses of freedoms implicit in the Universal Declaration, suggesting the triumph of license over liberty. The discourse of human rights has, in some instances, become little more than a means whereby, "fundamental interests," or, "forms of legitimate control over another—implying their duty to me" have been used viciously or virtuously. In some instances they have been extended to the point where they appear bizarre. Consequently their social utility has been brought into question. It might be worth noting at this point that the Islamic world has always been extremely cautious about using human rights discourse (obedience to the divine will of Allah is stressed over and against any notion of human autonomy).

ETHICS, THEOLOGY, AND IDENTITY IN THE LIGHT OF CHRISTIAN MISSION

In 1996, Metropolitan Kirill made his position very clear: mission, more accurately described as proselytism, was primarily an expression of cultural and ideological conflict in which the victims were Orthodox Christians.[42] By 2001, as seen in Patriarch Aleksii's letter, the deleterious effects of proselytism were considered to extend to the spiritual wellbeing of society as a whole.[43] At the 2002 consecration of an Orthodox Church at the Lubianka headquarters of the FSB (successor to the KGB), Patriarch Aleksii stressed the "need for concerted actions aimed at combating the current threats posed to Russia's 'spiritual security' . . . a concept that is very much on the public agenda in contemporary Russia."[44]

Removing the discourse of proselytism from the theological domain of mission and evangelism and re-locating it in the conceptual domain of culture, ethnicity and nationality has several implications. Firstly, this is conceptually slippery territory and therefore all the more difficult to navigate for ecumenical dialogue partners who do not understand contemporary Russia and its nation-building programmes (within which alternative

---

41. Ioann, "Ecclesiological and Canonical Foundations," 59.
42. Ioann, "Ecclesiological and Canonical Foundations," 89.
43. Ioann, "Ecclesiological and Canonical Foundations," 5.
44. Elkner, "Spiritual Security in Putin's Russia."

notions of ethnicity and nationality compete). Secondly, the discovery of a common language to discuss the issues of mission and proselytism becomes increasingly unlikely. Thirdly, it tends to overlook the legitimacy of indigenous Russian and Slavic forms of non-Orthodox Christianity that have existed on Russian territory for several centuries or more, in some cases.

However, a more adequate response to this conceptual shift is demanded of the non-Orthodox Churches than simply to adopt the discourse of Human Rights. Article 2 of the Universal Declaration of Human Rights asserts fundamental rights (including religious freedoms) "without distinction of . . . race . . . national or social origin."[45] It is self-evident that the adoption of universalized rights provides an alternative domain (particularly Article 18) in which to develop a discourse of mission and proselytism. However, the discourse of human rights appears to lack a fully adequate vocabulary to respond to questions of identity and culture, other than to reiterate that these cannot be used to justify discriminatory behaviour. Secondly, as we have seen above, the universality of human rights is not as widely accepted as might be assumed and has, in fact, been understood by some parts of the Christian Church (both Orthodox and non-Orthodox) as an alternative liberal and secular version of the Kingdom of God: and consequently the weaker for it.

What can be observed in the dialogue of minority and majority churches is a reliance on alternative discourses of mission and proselytism. One is located in the domain of "local" ethnic and nationality identity, the other in the domain of "universal" Human Rights. Both dialogue partners have abandoned the theological–ethical domain as the most appropriate for supplying a common language to discuss deeply divisive issues. The recovery of a common language, theological and ethical, is paramount if mutual understanding is genuinely to be sought. Petros Vassiliadis, a Greek Orthodox theologian, understands this point well as a consequence of his long experience as a dialogue partner within WCC ecumenical processes.[46]

A second reason for the failure to arrive at consensus about proselytizing activity is due in large part to the lack of a commonly understood theological vision and of the way of life that this implies. The failure is primarily a theological failure, it is not a failure of human rights. Theological vision is the central issue for our discussion as it relates to how particular theologically-formed communities understand themselves and establish their self-identity. This is of particular concern for Churches caught in the dialectic of minority Church-majority Church. If we can assume that

---

45. UN, *Universal Declaration of Human Rights*.
46. Vassiliadis, *Eucharist and Witness*.

Christian identity is constructed in community, then identity construction is a corporate undertaking shaped not only by perceptions of, and relationships to, the communal insider but also by perceptions of and relationships to the communal outsider. If the outsider is perceived as threatening then I am unlikely to leave little space in my theological self-identity for "the other." In fact I am likely to erect distinct theological and communal fences that enable me to minimise all encounter with the other.

In January 2004 I was introduced as an ecumenical guest from the Baptist Church to a class of Orthodox catechists in St. Petersburg. Of the thirty adults present, only two had ever met a Baptist before. I suspect that the same lack of encounter with the religious other might equally have been true if I were to have asked a similar-sized group of Baptist candidates for church membership about their close friendships with Orthodox Christians.

The lack of encounter with the other is at the heart of the current challenge facing the WCC as it struggles to create space for the vital and growing evangelical and pentecostal churches of the global South. Vassiliadis has been critical of the WCC in the past for its failure in bringing such dialogue partners to the ecumenical discussions of mission and proselytism.[47] The energy and mutual respect demonstrated by participants during their presentation of the Pentecostal-Orthodox dialogue to the WCC's World Mission Conference in Athens, May 2005, is an excellent example of what is possible when a new openness to the "other" is demonstrated; even where the missionary or regulatory activity of the "other" has traditionally been seen as mutually injurious.

The Pentecostal-Orthodox dialogue demonstrates that inter-confessional conflict, whether cultural, ideological or ethical, can only ever find its proper theological-ethical resolution through theological openness to the other. Only where one is able to locate the other in inter-relationship to one's own confessional community is it possible to begin to address the questions of ethnicity, nationality and identity together.

Rowan Williams, then Bishop of Monmouth, eloquently articulated the significance that the wellbeing of the Christian community has for the reduction and resolution of ethical conflict, in a series of questions he posed to the Lambeth Conference in 1998,

> Can we then begin thinking about our ethical conflicts in terms of our understanding of the Body of Christ? The first implication, as I have suggested, is to do with how we actually decide what we are to do, what standard we appeal to. An ethic of the Body of Christ asks that we first examine how any proposed

---

47. Personal conversation with the author, Athens, Greece, May 13, 2005.

action or any proposed style or policy of action measures up to two concerns: how does it manifest the selfless holiness of God in Christ? And how can it serve as a gift that builds up the community called to show that holiness in its corporate life?[48]

The theological vision of McClendon, mentioned at the outset of this paper, suggests the need for an appropriate spirituality of suffering in the face of (real or perceived) injustices. Simultaneously it would also point to the temptation for particular Christendom forms of the Church to disavow its role as servant in taking to itself the trappings of State privilege and power.

> Mission (or evangelism), *[is to be]* understood not as an attempt to control history for the ends we believe to be good, but as the responsibility to witness to Christ—and accept the suffering that witness entails.[49]

---

48. Williams, "On Making Moral Decisions," 12.
49. McClendon, *Ethics*, 28.

3.6

An Evangelical View of Proselytism

Elmer Thiessen and Thomas Schirrmacher

Prepared for and authorized by the Department for Theological Concerns of the World Evangelical Alliance, December 1, 2018

Elmer Thiessen taught at Medicine Hat College (Alberta, Canada) for thirty-six years and is currently adjunct professor of philosophy at Emmanuel Bible College in Kitchener (Ontario, Canada). He has published widely in the philosophy of religious education and religious schools, including two books, *Teaching for Commitment* and *In Defence of Religious Schools and Colleges* (1993, 2001). During the past decade he has been writing on evangelism, including *The Ethics of Evangelism: A Philosophical Defense of Proselytizing and Persuasion* (2011) and *The Scandal of Evangelism: A Biblical Study of the Ethics of Evangelism* (2018).

Thomas Schirrmacher is the World Evangelical Alliance's General Secretary. This paper was prepared for the WEA's Department of Theological Concerns.

Evangelical Christians have begun to pay attention, in the past decade, to an issue that was sadly often neglected in the past—the ethics of doing evangelism. For example, the World Evangelical Alliance joined the World Council of Churches and the Pontifical Council for Interreligious Dialogue to produce a joint statement entitled "Christian Witness in a Multi-Religious

World: Recommendations for Conduct."[1] This document spells out the ethics of mission, stressing that Christians are not only bound to the Great Commission but also to any other ethical command of Jesus, as is suggested in the Great Commission itself. This document is also our starting point for the following discussion.

The World Evangelical Alliance has also participated in discussions concerning a related issue—proselytism, understood as "sheep-stealing." Most recently, an international consultation of some thirty theologians and church leaders from a wide range of Christian traditions gathered in Accra, Ghana, to explore perceptions of proselytism in the exercise of the universal mandate to share the good news of Jesus Christ.[2] The issue of proselytism is best understood as a subset of the wider issue of evangelism. The following statement seeks to clarify the evangelical position on proselytism, as understood in the special and narrow sense of sheep-stealing.

I. EVANGELICALS, EVANGELISM, AND PROSELYTISM

Evangelism is part of the DNA of evangelicals. Evangelism is typically understood in terms of proclaiming the good news of Jesus Christ and his kingdom. Of course, there is more to the mandate of the church than evangelism. We are also called to demonstrate the good news of the kingdom. But the focus here is on evangelism as verbal proclamation of the gospel.

Concerns about proselytism often arise in connection with efforts at evangelism. Evangelical Christians are the group most often accused of proselytism, given their passion for evangelism.[3] Evangelicals believe in

---

1. WCC et al., "Christian Witness in a Multi-Religious World." See also Schirrmacher, "Christian Witness in a Multi-Religious World"; "Christian Witness in a Multi-Religious World—Three Years On"; "Code 'Christian Witness'"; "'But with Gentleness and Respect'"; Thiessen, *Ethics of Evangelism*; *Scandal of Evangelism*.

2. This gathering, held on June 8–11, 2017, was convened by the Global Christian Forum, whose purpose is to provide space for Christians from a wide variety of churches and traditions to meet, foster mutual respect and address common challenges. The planning and implementation of this consultation were undertaken by the Catholic Church's Pontifical Council for Promoting Christian Unity, the Pentecostal World Fellowship, the World Council of Churches, and the World Evangelical Alliance.

3. We use the word "evangelical" here to refer to those who are committed to the following theological tenets: a high view of the authority of the Bible, a belief in the historicity of the gospel accounts of Jesus, a belief in Jesus' death on the cross as the only sacrifice that could remove the penalty of sin, a commitment to Jesus as Savior and Lord, and a commitment to evangelism. We use the term in a broad sense, noting for example that most Pentecostals are evangelicals and are therefore included here as such. We distance ourselves from any political misuse of the term "evangelical," as occurs all too often in the USA today.

proclaiming the gospel to all who are lost. They believe in sowing the seed of the gospel everywhere and to everyone, even though they cannot know in advance how receptive people will be to the proclamation of the gospel.[4]

Evangelical efforts at evangelism could therefore include reaching out to people who were once Christians but who have strayed from the faith and who as a result are no longer attending church, though they might still be on a church membership list. Such evangelistic efforts (described in Orthodox and Catholic terminology as "re-evangelism") can lead to proselytism, because a recommitment to faith on the part of those being re-evangelized often results in a change in church affiliation.

Although most Christians agree with the mandate to evangelize those who have never heard of the gospel of Jesus Christ, there is strong disagreement about extending this mandate to lapsed or nominal Christians. Evangelicals are committed to both evangelism and re-evangelism. The key question here is whether re-evangelism that leads to proselytism can be done in an ethical manner.

II. DEFINITIONS

Much confusion surrounds the definition of the word *proselytism*. Historically, this word was understood in a positive sense, equivalent to evangelism—proclaiming the good news. Today, and especially in ecumenical circles, the term has acquired strongly negative connotations. For example, in a statement by the World Council of Churches (WCC), "Towards Common Witness," proselytism is defined as "the encouragement of Christians who belong to a church to change their denominational allegiance, through ways and means that contradict the spirit of Christian love, violate the freedom of the human person and diminish trust in the Christian witness of the church."[5] The WCC continues to be in dialogue with various Christian bodies regarding the definition of proselytism, but we use this text as a starting point as it describes a very common usage of the term. There are four problems with this and similar definitions of proselytism.

First, such definitions are confusing because they collapse into one concept two quite different meanings of proselytism: (a) unethical or unfaithful practices in evangelism that violate the freedom of the person, and (b) encouraging those who are already members of other churches to

---

4. Such indiscrimination would seem to be part of the thrust of the Parable of the Sower, especially when Jesus explains this parable to his own disciples (Matt 13:18–23).

5. WCC, "Towards Common Witness."

change their church affiliation. Clarity demands that we separate these two very different meanings.

Second, such definitions are arbitrary. Clearly, if proselytism is loaded with the negative implication of unethical practices, then all proselytism is unethical. But this is to make proselytism unethical by arbitrary definition. Again, we need to separate actions that might cause people who already belong to a church to change their denominational allegiance from adopting unethical means of doing so.

Third, such definitions are unfair when applied to evangelicals. Evangelicals are in principle strongly opposed to any forms of unethical evangelism, re-evangelism, or proselytism. They have joined other Christian denominations in condemning such activities, as noted above. Evangelism and re-evangelism must always be done in ways that are faithful to Jesus Christ and the norms of Scripture (see esp. Luke 9:51-55; 1 Cor 2:1-5; 2 Cor 4:1-2; 1 Thess 2:1-6; 1 Pet 3:13-17).

Fourth, such definitions can lead to dishonesty. Sadly, some opposition to proselytism as defined above is in fact rooted in opposition to evangelism in general.[6] It is a betrayal of forthrightness to hide one's opposition to evangelism behind objections to so-called proselytism.

Evangelicals are committed to evangelism, and therefore they reject any attempts to stop their evangelistic efforts under the guise of opposition to "proselytism" understood as evangelistic malpractice. At the same time, they are very much committed to following all biblical commands that concern presenting the gospel in an ethical manner.

III. EXAGGERATED CHARGES OF PROSELYTISM

Charges of unethical proselytism are often exaggerated in various ways, partly due to the vagueness surrounding terms specifically associated with proselytism. The WCC statement "Towards Common Witness," for example, associates proselytism with unfair criticism or caricaturing of the beliefs and practices of another church, offering humanitarian aid or educational opportunities as an inducement to join another church, using psychological pressure to induce people to change their church affiliation, or exploiting

---

6. This point is made in Uzzell, "Don't Call It Proselytizing." For a forthright claim that opposition to proselytism is really opposition to evangelism, see Vassiliadis, "Mission and Proselytism," esp. 260-61. Vassiliadis suggests that this assessment is common both in the Orthodox Church and in ecumenical circles.

people's loneliness, illness, distress or even disillusionment with their own church in order to "convert" them.[7]

The problem here is that many of the terms used to identify unethical means in proselytism are vague. When is the criticism of another church unfair? At what point does psychological pressure to change churches become excessive and unethical? Is offering humanitarian aid to someone in need always an inducement to join another church? What does exploitation of illness or loneliness mean? These questions are not easy to answer because of the vagueness of the descriptions of unethical methods. Critics of proselytism should spell out exactly what they find objectionable and then be prepared to defend their position that the practice is indeed unethical.

Many Christians today change their church affiliation entirely on their own, often after a long period of deliberation.[8] Here it is completely inappropriate to charge anyone with proselytism in the pejorative sense. Many people change their affiliation because they were not happy with their previous church. Surely it is unfair to charge a church that welcomes such people into its midst with unethical proselytism. (One could say that the best way to avoid losing members in this way is to make your own church vibrant and healthy.)

Other people leave a church because they experience love and caring from members of another church.[9] Surely it is not wrong to show love and caring to members of other churches. In such cases, the charge of unethical proselytism is quite inappropriate. Those making such allegations should show greater charity.

Many people change their church affiliation after moving to a new location.[10] The number of interconfessional marriages is also growing steadily. Theology students frequently spend a semester or two at seminaries of other confessions. In our globalized world, more Christians than ever are in contact with churches that have a different history and confession and, as a result of such contact, become interested in them.

All these trends are part of a broader international development: lifelong loyalty to institutions, including churches, is in decline worldwide. Globally, young people are increasingly leaving the religious affiliation of

---

7. WCC, "Towards Common Witness," 468.

8. This point is acknowledged in WCC, "Towards Common Witness," 468.

9. Evangelicals themselves often change churches because they find another church to be more attractive or even more faithful to Jesus Christ.

10. In Germany alone, about one hundred fifty thousand people a year switch between the two major faith traditions, Catholic and Protestant, without either side raising concerns or doing anything about it.

their parents in the same way in which they feel free to choose another profession, political party, music style or fashion.

One other caution is in order. It is incumbent on churches making the charge of proselytism to investigate carefully who is doing the proselytizing. All too often, accusations are made against evangelicals when the actual groups involved are Mormons, Jehovah's Witnesses or others who are not in fellowship with the global evangelical community and would not listen to us in any case.

We also urge all churches to make a distinction between active church members (who rarely change their affiliation anyway, even if approached to do it) and those Christians who are lapsed or who have never had any further contact with their original church beyond their infant baptism. We will return to this issue below.

The problems of definition and application discussed above suggest that should be very cautious about how we describe proselytism. Perhaps it would even be better to call a moratorium on the use of the word in Christian circles.

In the following discussion, we will continue using the word, since we are trying to an address an issue that is described in this way in ecumenical circles and that is creating problems in relationships between Christian communities. But henceforth, we will characterize proselytism, within a Christian context, in a morally neutral sense, as simply referring to *activities that contribute in any way to people's decision to change their church affiliation*. We are not arbitrarily loading the term with the additional assumption of unethical means. In other words, we are leaving open the possibility of an ethical form of proselytism.

IV. WHO IS A CHRISTIAN?

A basic question underlies the concerns about proselytism: who is a Christian? The WCC statement "Towards Common Witness" defines proselytism as "the encouragement of *Christians* who belong to a church to change their denominational allegiance" (emphasis added). For evangelicals, the reference to Christians in this definition can beg the question, leading once again to an arbitrary definition of proselytism.

Evangelicals take seriously the frequent biblical warnings about Christians losing the faith, forsaking their first love, being led astray, falling away or drifting from the faith (Amos 2:4-5; Hosea; Gal 1:6-9; 1 Tim 6:3-10; 2 Tim 4:3-4; Heb 2:1; 3:7-11; 5:11-6:6). Jesus told parables in Luke 15 to illustrate the possibility of God's people getting lost: sheep that were once part of the sheepfold wander away on their own, and a son leaves a loving household only to squander his life in wild living.

Jesus is the Good Shepherd who makes every effort to find lost sheep, the loving father who runs out to meet sons and daughters who have left the family and squandered their inheritance. Christians should follow the example of Jesus, the Good Shepherd, in caring about lost sheep and making every effort to bring them back to the sheepfold.

Accordingly, evangelicals are committed to proclaiming the gospel to all who are lost, including those who were once Christian but have strayed from the faith, those who have been baptized and might still be on church rosters but who never attend church, and those who are only nominal, lapsed or inactive Christians.[11] As such, evangelicals are committed to both evangelism and re-evangelism.

Evangelicals also interpret the return of the lost son or daughter as essentially a return to God the Father and to Jesus the Good Shepherd, not necessarily to a church or denomination. Our guiding motivation is to do what is best for the sheep, not for us. The goal of all churches should be to transform lives and see people become like Jesus. Indeed, this goal is expressed in different ways in different confessions: the Orthodox call it theosis, Catholics and Evangelicals call it holiness (with perhaps slightly different meanings), and Pentecostals call it a Spirit-filled life.

Beyond all theological differences, however, the DNA of Christianity is that the Father, Son and Holy Spirit want to transform lives and bring them into communion with other believers in the church. All churches should also agree that baptized "Christians" who do not confess their sins and live transformed Christian lives, and who have no communion with other Christians, are an anomaly. No church or confession should accept as normal a situation in which millions of baptized members have lost contact with their Christian communion and show no growth in faith and holiness. All should be happy if God uses other Christians to revive their nominal members.

Along with the issue of lapsed and nominal Christians, this serious theological question that merits further discussion. But regardless of how

---

11. Some of these church "members" do not even know that they were baptized as children; they only find out after their conversion to Christ and then have to wrestle with their status as Christians. If we would abstain from evangelizing these people, we would have to put a stop to public evangelism in countries like Germany or Russia altogether, because a majority of people belong to this category. It sometimes seems that these nominal church members are of interest to their established churches only after they have come to Christ and show interest in attending another church.

we address these theological questions, we need to treat each other in an ethical manner.

V. ETHICAL PROSELYTISM

Evangelical Christians maintain that ethical proselytism is possible, provided that it is consistent with biblical norms. Here it is helpful to focus on what is surely the paradigm case of proselytism: evangelism or re-evangelism of people who have drifted away from the church or have even rejected the faith they once espoused. What does ethical behaviour look like in this paradigm case?[12]

First, and of primary importance, the dignity and freedom of the individual must be respected (Gen 1:28; 2:15; Ps 8; Josh 24:15). Coercion must be avoided.[13] Any form of inducement to convert or to change churches is wrong. Exploitation of vulnerability must be scrupulously avoided.

Of course, as noted earlier, these general guidelines are somewhat vague, but the general principles still stand. God does not coerce, and we should not engage in coercion when interacting with someone considering a change in church affiliation.

Ethical re-evangelism and proselytism are always careful to speak the truth with love. Truthfulness is repeatedly held up as an ideal in the Scriptures.[14] Making false claims about other churches is unethical. It is wrong to misrepresent the doctrines of other churches when engaging in re-evangelism or proselytism.

Ethical re-evangelism and proselytism must also display tolerance. Although tolerance is not an explicitly biblical idea, the concept is certainly mandated in Scripture.[15] Tolerance, when properly defined, means treating

---

12. Here we need to distinguish between secular or legal rules and Christian ethics. The laws of the state, international law, and statements of human rights sometimes can allow or forbid certain actions that are contrary to Christian ethics. For example, freedom of speech might allow us to say things about other Christians that we would not say if we followed Christ's commands. In this discussion we are concerned with Christian ethics, or those things that bind us because we are followers of Jesus Christ, not because we are citizens of the state.

13. See where Jesus gives his disciples a "theology of failure" (Luke 9:51–55; Matt 10:12–15) and where evangelism follows an invitation to speak (1 Pet 3:13–17).

14. Jesus is the embodiment of truth (John 1:14; 14:6) and encourages truthfulness (Matt 5:37). Repeatedly, he introduces his teachings with "Truly, truly, I say to you" (Matt 5:18, 26; Mark 3:28; Luke 9:27; John 3:3, 5, 11). Paul also encourages us always to speak the truth in love (Eph 4:15).

15. The Old Testament contains calls to love one's neighbor, including the alien and the stranger (Exod 22:21; Lev 19:18, 33, 34; Deut 10:19). Paul introduces the notion of

persons who hold beliefs different from those of the evangelist with love and respect.[16] Ethical proselytism, while not precluding truthful and fair critical comments about the beliefs of other churches, makes such comments in a way that shows love and respect for people of other church traditions.

Attitudes and motivations are also important. Those engaged in evangelism or re-evangelism must display humility and a servant-like attitude.[17] Selfish motivation is ruled out for Christians, and thus preoccupation with growing one's own church is also inappropriate (Ps 119:36; Prov 18:1; Phil 1:17; 2:3). The fundamental motivation for re-evangelism and proselytizing is love for God and for neighbor (Deut 6:5; 10:12, 19; Matt 22:34–38; 2 Cor 5:14).

As should be evident, the guidelines for re-evangelism and proselytism are really the same as those for evangelism. We can generally describe them as specific applications of the Golden Rule (Matt 7:12; Gal 5:14). Put yourselves in the other person's shoes and try to imagine someone trying to persuade you to change churches. What would you find acceptable? Do the same when you engage in re-evangelism and proselytism.

So far, we have been looking at the re-evangelism of lapsed or nominal Christians. But another scenario deserves attention. Suppose that we are dealing with a genuine Christian who is deeply committed to and active in his or her church. Is it wrong to try to persuade such a person to change churches? This clearly violates the spirit of ecumenism, and such proselytism should not be a priority for any Christian.

However, one can easily imagine a scenario where this form of engagement might come about quite naturally. For example, friendly exchanges between two Christian friends might include frank discussions about the theological differences between their churches. One friend might even suggest to the other that his or her church is more faithful to Jesus Christ. This might result in the exploration of each other's churches, and in the end someone might change churches. Surely nothing inherently unethical

---

forbearance, which is closely related to tolerance (Col 3:12–14; Rom 2:2–4; 15:1–2).

16. Paul and his co-workers, facing the outbreak of a riot in Ephesus, were defended by a city clerk who said that "they have neither robbed temples nor blasphemed our goddess" (Acts 19:37). Peter, too, exhorts us to "show proper respect to everyone." This exhortation appears in an epistle that teaches Christians to respond to hostility with love and gentleness when defending their faith (1 Pet 2:17; 3:15–16).

17. The Bible frequently applies humility to our interpersonal relationships (Matt 18:2–4; John 13:1–17; Phil 2:3–11; Col 3:12). Jesus objects to "lording" it over others and admonishes us to be a servant as he was (Matt 20:24–28). Peter specifically talks about meekness, gentleness, and humility with regard to evangelism (1 Pet 3:15–16; cf. 5:5–6).

is occurring in this scenario. However, once again, the ethical guidelines discussed earlier in this section would apply.

VI. PROSELYTISM AND RELIGIOUS FREEDOM

Evangelical Christians are committed to respecting, affirming and promoting the religious freedom of all people.[18] This is not just a positive legal or political concept for evangelicals, but part of their theological DNA.[19] Men and women were created in the image of God, but with the freedom to obey or disobey him. God does not force anyone to accept his revelation or his offer of salvation. Jesus and the apostles always allowed people to reject the good news they were proclaiming.[20]

Religious freedom is central to human dignity. Therefore evangelical Christians support the definition of religious freedom as found in the Universal Declaration of Human Rights:

Everyone has the right to freedom of thought, conscience and religion. This right includes the freedom to change his/her religion or belief, and freedom, either alone or in community with others, in public or in private, to manifest his/her religion or belief, in teaching, practice, worship and observance.[21]

Religious freedom also entails that Christians should be free to change church affiliation. We thus need to be careful about language suggesting that church members are somehow owned by their churches. From this viewpoint, there is something odd about understanding proselytism in terms of stealing sheep from another church. Jesus bought every believer with his blood, and ultimately we belong to the church through the blood of Jesus, not by anything a church or other Christians have done.

---

18. See IIRF, "Resolution on Religious Freedom."
19. See Schirrmacher and Howell, "Freedom of Religion or Belief."
20. See, for example, Jesus' response to his disciples when they wanted to call down fire from heaven on those who rejected his message (Luke 9:51–55). Often we read of two quite different responses to the proclamation of the gospel in Acts: some believed and some did not (Acts 2:13, 41; 14:1–7; 17:32–34; 18:8, 12; 19:9, 19).
21. WCC, "Towards Common Witness," 467. For a review of international covenants regarding liberty of conscience, religious pluralism and equality, free exercise of religion, nondiscrimination on religious grounds, and autonomy for religious groups, see Lerner, "Proselytism, Change of Religion." See also Schirrmacher and Chaplin, "European Religious Freedom and the EU"; Schirrmacher, "Mission und Religionsfreiheit."

VII. SOME PRACTICAL SUGGESTIONS

1. Evangelism or re-evangelism cannot avoid the issue of church membership for the newly converted or re-committed, because being a committed Christian entails belonging to a church. If, upon conversion or re-commitment, persons indicate that they were once baptized or previously members of another church, ethical proselytism will first encourage these persons to reconnect with their original church. If there are major theological differences between the churches, these should be explained in a fair and open manner that helps persons to make their own decision on church affiliation. If such persons indicate that they do not want to return to their original church, great care must be taken to proceed in an ethical manner in advising these persons with regard to church membership. Everything possible should be done to ensure a peaceful relation with the original church (see the prior section, "Ethical Proselytism," especially the guidelines on truth and tolerance).

2. When someone changes church affiliation as a result of evangelism or re-evangelism, every effort should be made to notify the pastor or the priest at the person's original church of the person's desire to change church affiliation, thereby also giving the pastor or priest a chance to contact this person if he or she wishes. We should not be afraid that such contacts might lead people to change their minds. The aim is to help people to make a considered and mature decision that they will not regret in the future. We should also help people to maintain peace with relatives and friends from the original church, rather than creating unnecessary tensions in existing social relationships.

3. It is of utmost importance that the conscience and decision of the person changing church affiliation be respected. All too often, discussions of proselytism focus on the two churches involved, and the person involved becomes merely a pawn in the conflict. In reality, it should be the other way around: the person's wish or decision should be respected, and if we want to respect the dignity of this person, then we need to keep uppermost in our minds what is best for this individual person.

4. Evangelical Christians at local, national and international levels should develop a code of conduct regarding how pastors, priests and leaders

of various church communities will handle individuals who want to change their church affiliation.

5. Evangelical Christians will be sensitive to the problem of encroaching on someone else's territory in the task of evangelism, especially if an established church is actively engaged in programs of evangelism or re-evangelism. Here we follow the example of the apostle Paul, who in his letter to the saints in Rome wrote that his ambition was always "to preach the gospel where Christ was not known, so that I would not be building on someone else's foundation" (Rom 15:20; see also 2 Cor 10:12–18). We must be careful, however, not to overextend this principle of sensitivity to the problem of encroaching on someone else's territory. For example, the notion of canonical territory to which the Orthodox Church appeals is not only difficult to define but flies in the face of Orthodox principles of catholicity and unity, as well as the globalization of the modern human community. Where there is great need, and where the Orthodox Church is not evangelizing in its own country (which might be largely secularized), evangelical Christians will not be bound by the notion of canonical territory, which effectively exists only within the canon law of the Orthodox Church.[22]

6. Wherever possible, evangelicals will seek to cooperate with other churches in the task of evangelism or re-evangelism.

7. We must be very cautious about charging proselytism when clergy or other leaders or theologians change from one church or confession to another. With rare exceptions, such changes are not the result of any immoral offers or even activities by the receiving church, but of a long process of deliberation by the clergy themselves. Where the people involved have studied the matter thoroughly, we need to respect the theological reasoning behind their decision.

---

22. We humbly request that churches with a concept of canonical territory apply it only to their own church—i.e., a Catholic bishop may not act in the diocese of another Catholic bishop without his consent, and an autocephalous Orthodox Church may not become active in the territory of another autocephalous church without permission. But why should this bind other confessions? If it did, then it would also apply to the Orthodox Church's evangelistic activities in countries that are not Orthodox, such as Italy. This inconsistency suggests again that in a globalized world, the very notion of canonical territory should be re-evaluated.

VIII. COMMON WITNESS

Many of the concerns surrounding proselytism center on the need for the church to bear common witness to the world. Though sympathetic to this need, evangelicals also caution against an over-emphasis on common witness. In a post-Babel world, complete unity is impossible and perhaps even undesirable. There is something healthy about diverse theological emphases among differing Christian communions. We can learn from each other as we seek to serve and also to proclaim the good news of our common Lord and Saviour. Re-evangelism and proselytism can be conducted in "the spirit of Christian love" and in such a way as to enhance "trust in the Christian witness of the church."[23]

---

23. WCC, "Towards Common Witness," 467.

3.7

Christian Witness and Proselytism (Some Initial Thoughts After the Panorthodox Council)[1]

PETROS VASSILIADIS

Editor's Introduction

THIS IS A RECENT *paper which reflects upon the 2016 Holy and Great Council of the Orthodox Church, and the mission statement adopted thereat, "The Mission of the Orthodox Church in Today's World." Vassiliadis, however, also reflects on other recent mission texts from the WCC, the Roman Catholic Church and the Lausanne Movement, and notes that there are some positive signs of convergence among them. As such, not only does his paper bring a personal and Orthodox perspective, he also considers proselytism within a wider ecumenical context and, as such, it is a fitting paper with which to finish this Reader.*

Participating in the Holy Eucharist and praying for the whole world, we must continue the "liturgy after the Divine Liturgy" and give the witness of faith to those near and those far off, in accordance with the Lord's clear command before His ascension, "And you shall be my witnesses in Jerusalem and in all Judea and Samaria and to the end of the earth" (Acts 1:8). The re-evangelization of God's people in modern, secularized

---

1. Reproduced with the kind permission of the author

societies and the evangelization of those who have still not come to know Christ remain an unceasing obligation for the Church.

WITH THESE WORDS, ADDRESSED to all the Orthodox faithful and to all people of good will, the Holy Fathers of the recent Panorthodox Council, which was convened in Crete (June 19–26, 2016), underlined the importance of Christian witness in today's world,[2] which also attached "great importance to dialogue, primarily with non-Orthodox Christians,"[3] acknowledging, in addition, that "sober inter-religious dialogue helps significantly to promote mutual trust, peace and reconciliation."[4]

This importance to dialogue is stated in a more emphatic way in the ecclesiological document of this council:

> The Orthodox Church has a common awareness of the necessity for conducting inter-Christian theological dialogue. It therefore believes that this dialogue should always be accompanied by witness to the world through acts expressing mutual understanding and love, which express the "ineffable joy" of the Gospel (1 Pet 1:8), eschewing every act of proselytism, uniatism, or other provocative act of inter-confessional competition. In this spirit, the Orthodox Church deems it important for all Christians, inspired by common fundamental principles of the Gospel, to attempt to offer with eagerness and solidarity a response to the thorny problems of the contemporary world, based on the prototype of the new man in Christ.[5]

Proselytism as such was also addressed in the missiological document:

> The conveyance of the Gospel message according to the last commandant of Christ, *Go therefore and make disciples of all nations, baptizing them in the name of the Father and of the Son and the of the Holy Spirit, teaching them to observe all that I have commanded you* (Matt 28:19) is the diachronic mission of the Church. This mission must be carried out not aggressively or by different forms of proselytism, but in love, humility and respect towards the identity of each person and the cultural particularity of each people. All the Orthodox Church have an obligation to contribute to this missionary endeavor.[6]

2. HGCOC, "Message," 2.
3. HGCOC, "Message," 3.
4. HGCOC, "Message," 4.
5. HGCOC, "Relations of the Orthodox Church with the Rest of the Christian World," 23.
6. HGCOC, "Mission of the Orthodox Church," preamble.

With these fresh affirmations on delicate issues, such as proselytism, invested with the highest conciliar authority, I was invited to an ordinary meeting of the Global Christian Forum. What follow are my preliminary remarks to an inter-Christian journey towards reconciliation, which is hoped to have a binding significance to the entire Christian world, including not only Catholics, Orthodox, Eastern and Oriental, mainstream Protestants represented in the World Council of Churches, and other ecumenical bodies and missionary agents, but also the World Evangelical Alliance and the Pentecostal World Fellowship.

Proselytism as a dividing issue among Eastern and Oriental Orthodox Churches on the one hand, and western Christian missionary agencies—mainly from the Evangelical and Pentecostal world—on the other, is to some extent due to a variety of reasons, at the heart of which was, and still is, their diametrical views with regard to the values of modernity. The former take as a legitimate (and ethical?) view to have proselytism criminalized by law (in some Orthodox "countries") and their majority (Orthodox) Churches consider their jurisdiction as a closed canonical territory. The latter always argue on the basis of the human rights and the religious liberty. The former understand their missional responsibility mainly as a *Liturgy after the liturgy*, whereas the latter mostly as a *proselytizing mission*.

In order to properly tackle the issue one needs to seriously consider: (a) the present stage of the ecumenical movement; (b) the latest developments on the understanding of mission, with the variety of terms and notions involved in current ecumenical discussions; and (c) the fundamental biblical and theological parameters of an authentic mission.

(a) The present stage of the ecumenical movement is definitely characterized by a widely accepted new mission statement, the *TTL* (2012),[7] the heart of which is that it conceives of Christian mission, not only as an exclusive proclamation of the Good News (which traditionally had unavoidably also used proselytizing technics), but mainly as an address to the structural sin, expressed in the intertwined contemporary crises, the economic and environmental included, from the perspective of the marginalized: "Christians are called to acknowledge the sinful nature of all forms of discrimination and transform unjust structures,"[8] and that "all missional activity must . . . safeguard the sacred worth of every human being and of the earth."[9] This statement could not have any positive universal effect, if it was not followed by similar missiological affirmations by the wider Christian community.

---

7. See Keum, *Together Towards Life*.
8. Keum, *Together Towards Life*, §49.
9. Keum, *Together Towards Life*, §42.

And by God's providence, just one year later, in 2013, another mission statement of much greater magnitude was released: the first personal encyclical of Pope Francis *Evangeli Gaudium*, that has completely changed the older view of the Church as a fortress to be defended and promoted her missional responsibility; and just [last year] the Holy and Great Council of the Orthodox Church (the first ever after twelve centuries, i.e., since the seventh Ecumenical Council), adopted a similar Orthodox missiological document, entitled *The Mission of the Orthodox Church in Today's World*, which also reaffirmed a forgotten view that the Church exists not for herself but for the world. And there is also a fourth mission document produced in the same period (coming from the Lausanne movement), entitled *Cape Town Commitment* (2010), which although remains within the old mission paradigm it acknowledges the need for a spiritual change to meet the rapidly changing situation, as it is recognized by J. Stott, one of its leading members.

Assessing all these Mission Statements we notice three very important focuses: (a) the necessity of the inter-faith dialogue, i.e., an understanding of mission that conceives of the evangelized not as an object but as a real partner, although there is still an unresolved tension with regard to their views about the other religions; (b) the straightforward condemnation of the present economic system; and (c) the concern for the integrity of creation, as experienced in the contemporary ecological crisis.

If Christians now in this very positive environment fail to solve their differences regarding Proselytism, I am afraid they will never do!

(b) Diachronically mission was expressed by such words as *conversion, evangelism, evangelization, Christianization, witness* or *martyria*. Of these terms only the last one has been widely adopted in "ecumenical" circles as the more appropriate for a genuine and authentic Christian mission, whereas the imperative validity of all the other are still retained as the *sine qua non* of the Christian identity of those belonging to the "evangelical" stream of our Christian tradition. One very positive development towards this different and conflicting views I consider the attempt by TTL to consider "evangelism" within the above mentioned (a) new mission paradigm, although we need further in-depth analysis.

(c) Through a theological reflection on the basic biblical and theological foundations the understanding of mission in the ecumenical movement there is much optimism that we can move away from a "universal proselytizing mission" concept. And this not only because of the failure to convert the entire inhabited world, or the disillusion and disappointment caused by the end of the China mission, the most ambitious missionary enterprise in modern Christian missionary history. There are positive signs that world Christian mission is slowly but steadily rediscovering our authentic

Christian identity through the invaluable help of the theological treasures of the early undivided Church. More particularly the rediscovery of the Trinitarian basis of our mission (*missio dei*) by a conscious reinforcement of Pneumatology into our ecumenical reflections.

There is still, of course, a growing reaction to the "openness" of the Church to the outside world, especially after the latest developments in the ecumenical movement by the more "traditional"—some may label them even "fundamentalist"—segments of Christianity. These segments may belong to Protestantism, but they can also be found in Catholicism (see, e.g., the issue of Uniatism), although Pope Francis has now corrected the earlier very narrow interpretation by the Bishops' earlier appeal for "re-evangelization of Europe, and undoubtedly even within Orthodoxy (and certainly not limited to Old Calendarists), where an "exclusivist ecclesiology" is still in force within certain traditional groups who are the most active in proselytizing among western Christian Churches and denominations, and who also react against the inter-faith dialogue. This became quite evident during the deliberations; both before and during, the Holy and Great Council of the Orthodox Church, despite an "almost" inclusive ecclesiology that was finally adopted.

In view of this short and very sketchy consideration, I consider as *sine qua non* the following:

(i) Orthodoxy must reaffirm its commitment to ecumenism, and to a "common Christian witness," if it expects a lasting solution to this most painful in present circumstances issue of Proselytism. I stress this, because it is a widespread conviction that until the 2016 Panorthodox Council ecumenism was a controversial issue, with clearly evident the signs of a decline. The tragic events we experienced since the great changes in Europe—with Churches not in solidarity with, but fighting or undermining, each other especially in the mission field; and with the nations and the peoples not desiring to live peacefully with the "others," but wishing to distance themselves from other Christians, or in some cases to cleanse them—are just a few indications that the titanic ecumenical efforts of the past definitely need re-orientation.

(ii) The thorny issue of Proselytism can only be solved with a profound theological reconsideration of the notion of Christian mission combined with ecclesiology (unity) and social ethics (costly unity), with the involvement and active participation of all mission-oriented Christian groups (Evangelical and Pentecostal), and not just the "ecumenical WCC member Churches." Gospel, evangelism, mission are not for inner consumption of the Church. They are primarily aimed at the world. Theology in the Church has always tried to have common language with the world, in order to explain the Gospel in terms of a given culture. The problem in today's "post-Christian era" lies on the fact that there is no more common language, not only with the outside world, but also among the Christians themselves.

(iii) The reasons of not solving this problem, even within the ecumenical movement, after so many efforts and joint statements are to be traced in some inherent unresolved problems in the ecumenical movement. These are: (a) The Toronto Statement (1950) with its neutral ecclesiology which allows every member Church to have their basic beliefs (and for some Protestant groups universal proselytizing mission constitutes the core of their doctrine); (b) The consideration of the issue of proselytism always in relation to—in fact as the unquestionable consequence of—the "religious liberty," which is in fact a by-product of the western ideal of human rights, and above all of individualism, which is incompatible with *communion* (*koinonia*), the heart of Orthodoxy, and I now believe of nearly the entire Christianity.

(iv) Orthodoxy to be consistent with its outright condemnation of proselytism, should abandon also any kind of similar activities in the West. There was a fine ethos, which is now fading away, not to consecrate for the diaspora Orthodox communities any Bishop to a place belonging to the West (mainly giving them the names of cities shepherded in the past, e.g., *Thyatira* and *Great Britain*), thus respecting the jurisdiction of the Church of Rome, and consequently of western Christianity, of the ancient undivided Holy Catholic Church.

And finally, and most importantly, (v) any missionary activity in non-western mission fields must be conducted in a sister/ brotherly spirit and in co-operation of the living there traditional Christian institutional Churches, which in return will acknowledge the religious liberty and the human rights, and abandon any idea of the non-attested in the tradition canonical territory (which is still in force only among the Churches confessing the exactly the same faith). This, of course, will entail abandoning any publicly expressed demonizing any "other" Christian culture. All these, especially the human rights, are still contested by the Orthodox, most strongly by the Russians; the Orthodox have started insisting that human rights are awfully ineffective, if they are not accompanied by "human responsibilities." All Christians, together with people of other faiths—need not only struggle for, and publicly declare, the human responsibilities (side by side, or in addition to, the human rights); a *Universal Declaration of Human Responsibilities* also require an international (UN) legal endorsement.

Bibliography

Abbott, Walter M, ed. *The Documents of Vatican II*. New York: Guild, 1966.
"Acts of Commitment." *International Review of Mission* 86.340–41 (1997) 13–14.
Adeyemo, Tokunboh. "Whatever Happened to Evangelism?" *Christianity Today* 37 (1993).
Aleksii, Patriarch. "Greeting." In *Together in Mission*, edited by M. Oxbrow, 5. London: CMS, 2001.
Alta/Baja California Bishops. "Dimensions of a Response to Proselytism." *Origins* 19.41 (1990) 666–69.
Anastasios (Yannoulatos). *Facing the World: Orthodox Christian Essays on Global Concerns*. Translated by Pavlos Gottfried. Crestwood, NY: St. Vladmimir's Seminary, 2003.
Anderson, Rufus. *History of the Missions of the American Board of Commissioners for Foreign Missions to the Oriental Churches*. 2 vols. Boston: Congregational, 1872.
An-Na'im, Abdallahi Ahmed. "Qur'an, Shari'a and Human Rights: Foundations, Deficiencies and Prospects." In *The Ethics of World Religions and Human Rights*, edited by Hans Küng and Jürgen Moltmann. London: SCM, 1990.
Arberry, A. J., ed. *Judaism and Christianity*. Vol. 1 of *Religion in the Middle East: Three Religions in Concord and Conflict*. Cambridge: Cambridge University Press, 1969.
"Archbishop Calls Pentecostals Non-Christian." *Christianity Today* 39.1 (1995) 42.
"At Thy Word: Mission and Evangelization in Europe Today, Message of the Fifth European Ecumenical Encounter, Santiago de Compostela, November 13–17, 1991." *Catholic International* 3.2 (1991) 88–92.
Atiyah, Aziz. *A History of Eastern Christianity*. London: Methuen, 1968.
Badr, Habib. "Mission to 'Nominal Christians': The Policy and Practice of the American Board of Commissioners for Foreign Missions and Its Missionaries." PhD diss., Princeton University, 1992.
Barnea, Ioan. "Romanity and the Christianity of the Daco-Romanians." In *Autocephaly and Patriarchate*, edited by Biblical Institute. Bucharest: Biblical Institute, 1995.
Barrington-Ward, Simon. "Proselytism." In *A New Dictionary of Christian Theology*, edited by Alan Richardson and John Bowden. Paperback ed. London: SCM, 1989.
Barth, Karl. "Theological Declaration of Barmen." In *The Church's Confession Under Hitler*, by Arthur C. Cochrane, 237–42. Philadelphia: Westminster, 1962. Online. https://www.sacred-texts.com/chr/barmen.htm.

Beek, Huibert van, and Larry Miller, eds. *Discrimination, Persecution, Martyrdom: Following Christ Together. Report of the Global Consultation, Tirana, Albania, 2–4 November 2015*. Bonn: VKW, 2018.

Berman, Harold. "Religious Rights in Russia at a Time of Tumultuous Change." In *Religious Human Rights In Global Perspective: Religious Perspectives*, edited by John Witte Jr. and Johan D. van der Vyver. The Hague: Martinus Nijhoff, 1996.

Bermudez, Alejandro. "Evangelizing All Over Again." *Our Sunday Visitor*, June 11, 1995. 12.

Betts, Robert. *Christians in the Arab East: A Political Study*. Rev. ed. Atlanta: John Knox Press, 1978.

Bevans, Stephen B. "Mission at the Second Vatican Council, 1962–1965." *New Theology Review* 25.2 (2013), 101–11.

Bevans, Stephen B., and Roger P. Schroeder, eds. *Constants in Context: A Theology of Mission for Today*. Maryknoll, NY: Orbis, 2004.

Billington, James H. "Orthodoxy: Has Communism Found its Replacement?" *New Republic*, May 30, 1944.

Bird, Isaac. *Martyr of Lebanon*. Boston: American Tract Society, 1864.

Blauw, Johannes. *The Missionary Nature of the Church*. Grand Rapids: Eerdmans, 1962.

Block, Daniel I. *Judges, Ruth: An Exegetical and Theological Exposition of Holy Scripture*. New American Commentary 6. Nashville: Broadman and Holman, 1999.

Bosch, David J. *Transforming Mission: Paradigm Shifts in Theology of Mission*. Maryknoll, NY: Orbis, 1991.

Bradbury, Steve. "The Micah Mandate: An Evangelical View." In *Mission and Development: God's Work or Good Works*, edited by Matthew Clarke, 103–22. London: Continuum, 2012.

Braude, William G. *Jewish Proselytizing in the First Five Centuries in the Common Era* Providence, RI: Brown University Press, 1940.

Bria, Ion. "Dynamic of Liturgy in Mission." *International Review of Mission* 82.327 (1993) 317–25.

———. "Ecclesiology and Sociology." In *Le defi de l'Europe post-communiste et l'enseignement social chretien*, edited by Francis Frost. Fribourg: Editions Universitaires, 1994.

———. *Go Forth in Peace: Orthodox Perspectives on Mission*. Geneva: WCC Mission Series, 1986.

———. *Liturghia dupa Liturghie* [*The Liturgy after the Liturgy*]. Bucharest: Athena, 1997.

———, ed. *Martyria/Mission: The Witness of the Orthodox Church*. Geneva: WCC Commission on World Mission and Evangelism, 1980.

———. "A New Typology of Mission: From an Eastern Orthodox Perspective." *International Review of Mission* 84 (1995) 173–83.

———. *Ortodoxia in Europa: Locul spiritualiitaþii române*. Iasi: Trinitas, 1995.

———. *Proclaiming Christ Today: Report of an Orthodox-Evangelical Consultation, Alexandria, Egypt*. Geneva: WCC, 1996.

———. "Renewal of the Tradition through Pastoral Witness." *International Review of Mission* 65 (1976) 182–85.

———. *Romania: Orthodox Identity at a Crossroads of Europe*. Geneva: AC, 1995.

———. "Romanian Orthodox Theological Education: 1948 to the Present." *The Catholic World* 237 (1994).

Bruce, F. F. *New Testament History*. Garden City, NY: Doubleday, 1972.
Bruggemann, Walter. *Tradition for Crisis*. Richmond, VA: John Knox, 1968.
Bunea, S. "Reflections on the Encounter of Orthodoxy with Cultural Differences." *Connections* 7.1 (2003) 200.
Burke, Edmond. *Reflections on the Revolution in France: And on the Proceedings in Certain Societies in London Relative to that Event, in a Letter Intended to Have Been Sent to a Gentleman in Paris*. London: J. Doddsley, 1741.
Burrows William R., ed. *Redemption and Dialogue: Reading Redemptoris Missio and Dialogue and Proclamation*. Eugene, OR: Wipf and Stock, 1993.
Byford, Jovan. "Distinguishing Anti-Judaism from Antisemitism: Recent Championing of Serbian Bishop Nikolaj Velimirović." *Religion, State & Society* 34.1 (2006) 7–31.
Calian, Carnegie Samuel. *Theology without Boundaries: Encounters of Eastern Orthodoxy and Western Tradition*. Louisville, KY: Westminster John Knox, 1992.
Candea, Virgil. "The Gospel in the Romanian Tradition." In *Orthodoxy and Cultures*, edited by Ioan Sauca. Geneva: WCC 1996.
Carroll, M. D. "Ethics." In *Evangelical Dictionary of World Missions*, 319–22. Grand Rapids: Baker, 2000.
Carson, D. A. *Matthew*. Expositor's Bible Commentary 8. Grand Rapids: Zondervan, 1984.
Cassidy, Edward Idris. "Prolusio. Meeting of Representatives of the National Episcopal Commissions for Ecumenism, Rome, May 5–10, 1993." *Information Service* 84 (1993) 122.
Castells, Manuel. *The Rise of the Network Society*. Vol. 1 of *The Information Age: Economy, Society, and Culture*. Oxford: Blackwell, 2000.
Chichetto, James. "Dubious Tactics." *Commonweal* 120.2 (1993) 2.
Chrysostom, Konstantinidis. "Proselytism, the Ecumenical Movement, and the Orthodox Church." In *Orthodoxoi Katopseis IV*, 45–134. Katerini, 1991.
Ciachir, Dan "Biserica si societatea contemporana (Church and Contemporary Society)." In *Almanah bisericesc* 1997.
Ciurea, Alexandru I. "Patterns in Early Romanian Christianity." In *The Altar Almanah: 1971–1972*. London: Romanian Orthodox Parish, 1972.
Cleary, Edward L. "El maltrato de la jerarquia catolica a los pentecostales." *Pastoral Popular* 44.226 (1993) 15–17.
———. "John Paul Cries 'Wolf': Misreading the Pentecostals." *Commonweal* 119.20 (1992) 7–8.
Clifford, Catherine E. "The Ecumenical Context of *Dignitatis Humanae*: Forty Years After Vatican II." *Science et Esprit* 59.2–3 (2007) 387–403.
Conference of European Churches (CEC). "God Unites: In Christ a New Creation, Report of the 10th Assembly of CEC, Prague, September 1–11, 1992" by Mary Tanner. In *Final Report of the Policy Reference Committee*, 182–83. Geneva.
Conference of European Churches (CEC) and Roman Catholic Bishop's Conference of Europe (CCEE). *Charta Oecumenica*. Strasbourg, April 22, 2001. Online. http://www.cec-kek.org/content/charta.shtml.
"Conference Message." *International Review of Mission* 86.340–41 (1997) 7–11.
Constantineanu, Corneliu, et al. *Mission in Central and Eastern Europe: Realities, Perspectives, Trends*. Regnum Edinburgh Centenary Series 34. Oxford: Regnum, 2016.

"Constitution on the Sacred Liturgy/*Sacrosanctum Concilium*." In *The Documents of Vatican II*, edited by Walter Abbott. New York: Guild, 1966.

Cooney, Monica. "Towards Common Witness: A Call to Adopt Responsible Relationships in Mission and to Avoid Proselytism." *International Review of Mission* 85.337 (1996) 283–89.

Corley, Felix. *Religion In The Soviet Union: An Archival Reader*. London: MacMillan, 1996.

Corneanu, Nicolae, ed. *Ortodoxia Romaneasea*. Bucharest: Biblical Institute, 1992.

Cox, Harvey. *Fire from Heaven: The Rise of Pentecostal Spirituality and the Reshaping of Religion in the Twenty-First Century*. New York: De Capo, 1996.

Dahlburg, John-Thor. "Russian Law Curbs Foreigner Preaching, Seeking of Converts." *Los Angeles Times*, July 14, 1993. A4.

Danchin, Peter G., and Elizabeth A. Cole, eds. *Protecting the Human Rights of Religious Minorities in Eastern Europe*. New York: Columbia University Press, 2002.

Danker, Frederick W. "Proselyte, Proselytism." In *Baker's Dictionary of Theology*, edited by Everett F. Harrison. Grand Rapids: Baker, 1975.

Dellinger, R. W. "Evangelicals View Hispanic Evangelization Differently." *Tidings*, July 8, 1994. 10–11.

DeRidder, Richard R. *Discipling the Nations*. 1971. Reprint, Grand Rapids: Baker, 1979.

Dickson, Brice. "The United Nations and the Freedom of Religion." *International and Comparative Law Quarterly* 44.2 (1995) 327–57.

Douglas, J. D., ed. *Let the Earth Hear His Voice: International Congress on World Evangelization, Lausanne, Switzerland*. Minneapolis: World Wide, 1975.

Dowsett, Rose, et al., eds. *Evangelism and Diakonia in Context*. Regnum Edinburgh Centenary Series 32. Oxford: Regnum, 2016.

Duraisingh, Christopher, ed. *Called to One Hope—The Gospel in Diverse Cultures*. Geneva: WCC, 1997.

Dutch Reformed Mission Church (DRMC). "The Belhar Confession." 1982. Online. https://www.rca.org/about/theology/creeds-and-confessions/the-belhar-confession.

"Ecu News." *Ecumenical Trends* 24.2 (1995) 16.

Eliade, Mircea. *The Fate of Romania Culture*. Bucharest: Editura Athena, 1995.

Elkner, Julie. "Spiritual Security in Putin's Russia." *History and Policy*, January 1, 2005. Online. http://www.historyandpolicy.org/policy-papers/papers/spiritual-security-in-putins-russia.

Ellis, Jane. *The Russian Orthodox Church*. Oxford: Oxford University Press, 1996.

El-Zahlaoui, Joseph. "Witnessing in the Islamic Context." In *Your Will Be Done: Orthodoxy in Mission*, edited by George Lemopoulos, 95–104. Geneva: WCC Commission on World Mission and Evangelism, 1989.

Enchiridion vaticanum 10 (1989) 252–81.

"Evangelical Catholic Statement Criticized." *Christian Century* 111.17 (1994) 520–21.

"The Evangelical-Roman Catholic Dialogue on Mission, 1977–1984: A Report." *Information Service* 60 (1986) 71–97.

"Evangelicals and Catholics Together: The Christian Mission in the Third Millennium." *First Things* 43 (1994) 15–22.

"Evangelizing Mission of the Church in Africa." *Origins* 22.39 (1993).

Evans, G. R. *The Church and the Churches: Toward an Ecumenical Ecclesiology*. Cambridge: Cambridge University Press, 1994.

Farr, Thomas. *Historical Perspectives on Proselytism, Humanitarianism, and Development.* Washington, DC: Berkeley Centre for Religion, Peace, and World Affairs, Georgetown University, 2015. Online. https://s3.amazonaws.com/berkley-center/150304RFPSharingMessageProselytismDevelopmentPluralisticSocieties.pdf.

Federov, Vladimir. "New Religious Movements: An Orthodox Perspective." Paper presented to the Tantur Conference on Religious Freedom and Proselytism, 1998. Online. http://www.wcc-coe.org/wcc/what/interreligious/cd31-02.html.

Feinberg, C. L. "Proselyte." In vol. 4 of *The Zondervan Pictorial Encyclopedia of the Bible,* edited by Merrill C. Tenney. Grand Rapids: Zondervan, 1977.

Finnegan, David. "Armenian Pope Delights Faithful, Audiences During Valley Visit." *San Gabriel Valley News,* January 15, 1994. A8.

Flannery, Austin, ed. *Missions and Religions: A Commentary on the Second Vatican Council's Decree on the Church's Missionary Activity and Declaration on the Relations of the Church to Non-Christian Religions.* Translated by Redmond Fitzmaurice. Dublin: Scepter, 1968. Online. https://trove.nla.gov.au/version/25160349.

———. *Vatican Council II: The Conciliar and Post Conciliar Documents.* Rev ed. Grand Rapids: Eerdmans, 1988.

Foldesi, Tamas. "Les droits religieux de l'homme en l'Europe de l'Est." *Conscience et Liberte* 51 (1996).

Francis, and Tawadros II. "Common Declaration of His Holiness Francis and His Holiness Tawadros II." Address delivered April 28, 2017. Online. http://w2.vatican.va/content/francesco/en/speeches/2017/april/documents/papa-francesco_20170428_egitto-tawadros-ii.html#Common_Declaration.

"From the Editor." *Ecumenical Trends* 21 (1992) 49–50.

Frost, Francis, ed. *Le defi de l'Europe post-communiste et l'enseignement social chretien.* Fribourg: Editions Universitaires, 1994.

Fung, Raymond. *Evangelistically Yours: Ecumenical Letters on Contemporary Evangelism.* Geneva: WCC, 1992.

Gaal, Botond. "Religious Minorities in Central Europe and Their Relationship to the Nation-State." *Reformed World* 47 (1997) 72.

Gallardo, José. "Ethics and Mission." In *Anabaptism and Mission,* edited by Wilbert R. Shenk. Eugene, OR: Wipf and Stock, 1984.

Garaudy, Roger. "Human Rights and Islam: Foundation, Tradition, Violation." In *The Ethics of World Religions and Human Rights,* edited by Hans Küng and Jürgen Moltmann, 46–60. London: SCM, 1990.

Garner, Bryan A., ed. *A Dictionary Of Modern Legal Use.* Oxford: Oxford University Press, 1987.

Giddens, Anthony. *The Constitution of Society: Outline of the Theory of Structuration.* Cambridge: Polity, 1984.

Gill, Robin. *The Cambridge Companion to Christian Ethics.* Cambridge: Cambridge University Press, 2000.

Glanzer, Perry. "Teaching Christian Ethics in Russian Public Schools: The Testing of Russia's Church-State Boundaries." *Journal of Church and State* 41.2 (1999) 285–306.

———. *The Quest for Russia's Soul: Evangelicals and Moral Education in Post-Commmunist Russia.* Waco, TX: Baylor University Press, 2002.

Glendon, Mary Ann, and Hans F. Zacher, eds. *Universal Rights in a World of Diversity: The Case of Religious Freedom—The Proceedings of the 17th Plenary Session on 29*

April–3 May 2011. Acta 17. Vatican City: Pontifical Academy of Social Sciences, 2011.

Global Christian Forum. "*Call to Mission and Perceptions of Proselytism*": A Global Conversation. 2015.

Griffith, Sydney. "Faith and Reason in Christian Kalam: Theodore Abu Qurrah on Discerning the True Religion." In *Christian Arabic Apologists During the Abbasid Period (750–1258)*, edited by Samir Khalil and Jorgen Nielsen, 2–43. Leiden: Brill, 1994.

Guroian, Vigen. *Ethics After Christendom: Toward an Ecclesial Christian Ethic*. Grand Rapids: Eerdmans, 1994.

———. "Evangelism and Mission in the Orthodox Tradition." In *Sharing the Book: Religious Perspectives on the Rights and Wrongs of Proselytism*, edited by John Witte and Richard Martin, 231–44. Maryknoll, NY: Orbis, 1999.

Habib, Gabriel. "Renewal, Unity, and Witness in the Middle East: An Open Letter to Evangelicals." *Evangelical Missions Quarterly* 26 (1990) 256–62.

Habib, Samuel. "Mission in the Twenty-First Century: Impulses from Salvador." *International Review of Mission* 86.340–41 (1997) 119–24.

Hackett, Rosalind I. J., ed. *Proselytization Revisited: Rights Talk, Free Markets, and Culture Wars*. Abingdon: Routledge, 2014.

Haddad, Robert. *Syrian Christians in Muslim Society*. Princeton: Princeton University Press, 1970.

Harrington, Daniel. *The Gospel of Matthew*. Collegeville, MN: Liturgical, 1991.

Haughey, John C. "The Complex Accusation of Sheep-Stealing: Proselytism and Ethics." *Journal of Ecumenical Studies* 35.2 (1998). Online. https://www.questia.com/read/1G1-53590334/the-complex-accusation-of-sheep-stealing-proselytism.

Hayes, Stephen Tromp Wynn. "Orthodox Mission Methods: A Comparative Study." DTh thesis, University of South Africa, 1998. Online. http://uir.unisa.ac.za/bitstream/handle/10500/16924/thesis_hayes_stw.pdf?sequence=1&isAllowed=y.

Haynes, Gary. "Brazil's Catholics Launch 'Holy War.'" *Charisma* 19.10 (1994) 74–75.

Heideman, Eugene P. "Proselytism, Mission, and the Bible." *International Bulletin of Missionary Research* 20.1 (1996) 10–12.

Hirsch, Moshe. "The Freedom of Proselytism Under International and Israeli Law." *The Ecumenical Review* 50.4 (1998) 441–48.

Holy and Great Council of the Orthodox Church (HGCOC). "Message of the Holy and Great Council of the Orthodox Church." Online: https://www.holycouncil.org/-/message.

———. "Mission of the Orthodox Church in Today's World." Online: https://www.holycouncil.org/-/mission-orthodox-church-todays-world.

———. "Relations of the Orthodox Church with the Rest of the Christian World." Online: https://www.holycouncil.org/-/rest-of-christian-world.

The Holy Qur'an: Text, Translation, and Commentary. Translated by Yusuf Ali. New ed. Tahrike Tarsile Qur'an: New York, 2002.

Horner, Norman. *Guide to Christian Churches in the Middle East: Present-Day Christianity in the Middle East and North Africa*. Elkhart, IN: Mission Focus, 1989.

———. "The Problem of Intra-Christian Proselytism." *International Review of Mission* 70 (1981) 314–15.

Huber, Wolfgang. "Christianity and Democracy in Europe." *Emory International Law Review* 6 (1992) 35–53.

Hultgren, Gunnar. "Pullach Report." April 1972. Online. http://www.anglicancommunion.org/media/102169/the_pullach_report.pdf.
"Human Rights: The Unfinished Task." *The UNESCO Courier*, March 1994.
Hume, David. *From the Invasion of Julius Caesar to the Revolution in 1688*. Vol. 7 of *The History of England*. Philadelphia: Levis and Weaver, 1810.
Huntington, Samuel P. *The Clash of Civilizations and the Remaking of World Order*. New York: Simon and Schuster, 1996.
Iloaie, Stefan, ed. *Confessors Beyond the Bars*. Cluj-Napoca: Renasterea, 1995.
International Consultation between the Catholic Church and the World Evangelical Alliance 1993–2002 (ICCCWEA). "Church, Evangelization, and the Bonds of Koinonia." *Evangelical Review of Theology* 29.5 (2005) 100–130. Online. http://www.worldevangelicals.org/tc/pdf/CT-koinonia-statement.pdf.
International Federation of Red Cross (IFRC), et al. "Code of Conduct for the International Red Cross and Red Crescent Movement and Non-Governmental Organizations (NGOs) in Disaster Relief." *International Committee of the Red Cross*, December 31, 1992. Online. https://www.icrc.org/en/doc/assets/files/publications/icrc-002-1067.pdf.
International Institute for Religious Freedom (IIRF). "Resolution on Religious Freedom and Solidarity with the Persecuted Church." Developed at the 2008 General Assembly of the World Evangelical Alliance in Pattaya, Thailand. Online. https://www.iirf.eu/site/assets/files/112304/wea_res_eng-1.pdf.
International Religious Liberty Association. *FIDES ET LIBERTAS: The Journal of the International Religious Liberty Association 2000*. Maryland.
———. *FIDES ET LIBERTAS: The Journal of the International Religious Liberty Association 2001*. Maryland.
Ioann. "Ecclesiological and Canonical Foundations of Orthodox Mission." In *Together in Mission*, edited by Mark Oxbrow. London: CMS, 2001.
Ionita, Viorel, ed. *Charta Oecumenica: A Text, a Process, and a Dream of the Churches in Europe*. Geneva: Conference of European Churches, 2003.
Jackson, Darrell R. *Canonical Territory and National Security: Patriarch, President, and Proselytism in the Russian Federation: A Comparative and Contextual Study of Canonical Territory & Proselytism*. Prague: IBTS, 2009.
———. "Proselytism in a Central and Eastern European Perspective." *Journal of European Baptist Studies* 8.2 (2007) 18–36.
Jeremias, Joachim. *Jesus' Promise to the Nations*. London: SCM, 1967.
Jessup, Henry. *The Greek Church and Protestant Missions; or, Missions to the Oriental Churches*. New York: Christian Literature Company, 1891. Online. https://archive.org/stream/greekchurchproteoojess/greekchurchproteoojess_djvu.txt.
John XXIII. *Pacem in terris*. 1963. Rome: Libreria Editrice Vaticana, 1991.
John Paul II. "Letter to Bishops of Europe on Relations Between Catholics and Orthodox in the New Situation of Central and Eastern Europe (May 31, 1991)." *Information Service* 81 (1992) 101–3.
———. "Opening Address to the Fourth General Conference of the Latin American Episcopate." *Origins* 22.19 (1992).
———. "*Redemptoris Missio* [On The Permanent Validity Of The Church's Missionary Mandate]." Encyclical Letter, December 7, 1990. In *Redemption and Dialogue: Reading Redemptoris Missio and Dialogue and Proclamation*, edited by William R. Burrows, 5–55. Maryknoll, NY: Orbis, 1993.

———. "Tertio Millennio Adveniente." Apostolic Letter delivered November 10, 1994. Online. http://www.vatican.va/content/john-paul-ii/en/apost_letters/1994/documents/hf_jp-ii_apl_19941110_tertio-millennio-adveniente.html.

Joint International Commission for Theological Dialogue Between the Catholic Church and the Orthodox Church (JIC). "Seventh Plenary Session." Balamand School of Theology (Lebanon) June 17–24, 1993. Online. http://www.vatican.va/roman_curia/pontifical_councils/chrstuni/ch_orthodox_docs/rc_pc_chrstuni_doc_19930624_lebanon_en.html.

"Uniatism, Method of Union of the Past, and the Present Search for Full Communion." *Journal of the Moscow Patriarchate* 10 (1991) 60–62.

———. "Uniatism, Method of Union of the Past, and the Present Search for Full Communion." *Ecumenical Trends* 22.8 (1993) 4–7.

———. "Uniatism, Method of Union of the Past, and the Present Search for Full Communion." *Eastern Churches Journal* 1.1 (1994) 17–27.

Joint Working Group of the Roman Catholic Church and the World Council of Churches (JWG). "The Challenge of Proselytism and the Calling to Common Witness." *The Ecumenical Review* 48.2 (1996) 212–21.

———. "Common Witness and Proselytism: A Study Document." *The Ecumenical Review* 23.1 (1971) 9–20.

———. *Common Witness: A Study Document of the Joint Working Group of the Roman Catholic Church and the World Council of Churches*. CWME Series 1. Geneva: WCC/CWME, 1982.

———. *Seventh Report, Geneva-Rome 1998*. Geneva: WCC, 1998.

———. "Third Offical Report." January 1, 1971. Online. https://www.oikoumene.org/en/resources/documents/commissions/jwg-rcc-wcc/third-report-of-the-joint-working-group.

Josephus, Flavius. *The Life and Works of Flavius Josephus*. Translated by William Whiston. Philadelphia: John C. Winston, 1950.

Kaiser, Walter G. "Israel's Missionary Call." In *Perspectives on the World Christian Movement*, edited by Ralph Winter and Steven C. Hawthorne. 3rd ed. Pasadena, CA: William Carey; Carlisle, UK: Paternoster, 1999.

Kärkkäinen, Velli-Matti. *Ad ultimum terrae: Evangelization, Proselytism, and Common Witness in the Roman Catholic Pentecostal Dialogue 1990–1997*. Frankfurt: Peter Lang, 1999.

Kazmina, Olga. "Negotiating Proselytism in Twenty-First-Century Russia." In *Proselytization Revisited: Rights Talk, Free Markets, and Culture Wars*, edited by Rosalind I. J. Hackett. Abingdon, UK: Routledge, 2014.

Keil, C. F., and F. Delitzsch. *The Pentateuch*. Vol. 1 of *Commentary on the Old Testament in Ten Volumes*. Grand Rapids: Eerdmans, 1980.

Kerr, David A. "Mission and Proselytism: A Middle East Perspective." *International Bulletin of Missionary Research* 20.1 (1996) 12–22.

Keum, Jooseop, ed. *Together Towards Life: Mission and Evangelism in Changing Landscapes (with a Practical Guide)*. Geneva: WCC, 2013. Online. https://www.oikoumene.org/en/resources/publications/TogethertowardsLife_MissionandEvangelism.pdf.

Khalil, Samir, and Jorgen Nielsen, eds. *Christian Arabic Apologists During the Abbasid Period (750–1258)*. Leiden: Brill, 1994.

Khodr, Georges. "Christianity in a Pluralistic World: The Economy of the Holy Spirit." *Ecumenical Review* 23 (1971) 118–28.

Khouri, Milia. "The Mission of the Orthodox Youth in Lebanon." In *Your Will Be Done: Orthodoxy in Mission*, edited by George Lemopoulos. Geneva: WCC Commission on World Mission and Evangelism, 1989.

Kinnamon, Michael, and Brian Cope, eds. *The Ecumenical Movement: An Anthology of Key Texts and Voices*. Grand Rapids: Eerdmans, 1997.

Kishkovsky, Leonid. "Orthodoxy at a Crossroads." *Catholic World* 237.1417 (1994) 15–16.

Kozhuharov, Valentin. "Eastern Europe: Evangelism and Proselytism." In *Evangelism and Diakonia in Context*, edited by Rose Dowsett et al., 352–62 Regnum Edinburgh Centenary Series 32. Oxford: Regnum, 2016.

Küng, Hans, and Jürgen Moltmann, eds. *The Ethics of World Religions and Human Rights*. London: SCM, 1990.

Lausanne Movement. *The Cape Town Commitment*. 2011. Online. https://www.lausanne.org/content/ctc/ctcommitment#capetown.

———. *Christian Witness to Nominal Christians among the Orthodox*. Lausanne Occasional Paper 19. 1980. Online. https://www.lausanne.org/content/lop/lop-19.

———. *Christian Witness to Nominal Christians among Roman Catholics*. Lausanne Occasional Paper 10. 1980. Online. https://www.lausanne.org/content/lop/lop-10.

———. "Content Library." Online. https://www.lausanne.org/category/lop.

———. *The Lausanne Covenant*. 1974. Published by the Lausanne Movement at https://lausanne.org/content/twg-three-wholes-condensed.

———. "Legacy of the Lausanne Movement." Online. https://www.lausanne.org/our-legacy.

———. *The Manila Manifesto*. 1989. Online. https://www.lausanne.org/content/manifesto/the-manila-manifesto.

———. "South Asia Consultation, Sri Lanka, November 15–17, 2012." Online. https://www.lausanne.org/wp-content/uploads/2013/02/2012SouthAsiaConsultation.pdf.

———. "Statement to the Churches on Nominality." Statement from the Lausanne International Consultation on Nominalism, High Leigh, Hoddesdon, UK, December 1998. Online. https://www.lausanne.org/content/statement/statement-to-the-churches-on-nominality.

———. *The Whole Church*. Lausanne Occasional Paper 64. Published by the Lausanne Movement. 2009.

———. *The Whole Church Taking the Whole Gospel to the Whole World*. Theology Working Group Summary. Published by the Lausanne Movement. 2010

———. *The Whole Gospel*. Lausanne Occasional Paper 63. Published by the Lausanne Movement. 2008.

———. *The Whole World*. Lausanne Occasional Paper 65. Published by the Lausanne Movement. 2010.

The Law Library of Congress. "State Anti-Conversion Laws in India." *Library of Congress*, October 11, 2018. Online. https://www.loc.gov/law/help/anti-conversion-laws/india.php.

Lawton, Kim. "The Other Peace Conference: Middle Eastern and Western Christians Hold a Summit Meeting of Their Own to Resolve Long-Standing Tensions." *Christianity Today*, November 11, 1991.

"Lebanon Meeting Statement Rejects Proselytism." *Origins* 23.10 (1993) 166–69.

Lemopoulos, George, ed. *Your Will Be Done: Orthodoxy in Mission*. Geneva: WCC, 1989.

Lerner, Natan. "The Final Text of the UN Declaration Against Intolerance and Discrimination Based on Religion or Belief." Edited by Yoram Dinstein. *Israel Yearbook on Human Rights* 12 (1982) 185–89. Netherlands: Brill, 2020.

———. "Proselytism, Change of Religion, and International Human Rights." *Emory International Law Review* 12 (1998) 477.

Liennemann-Perrin, Christine, et al., eds. *Contextuality in Reformed Europe: The Mission of the Church in the Transformation of European Culture*. Currents of Encounter. Amsterdam; New York: Rodopi, 2004.

Lodwick, Robert C., ed. *Remembering the Future: The Challenges to the Churches of Europe*. New York: Friendship 1995.

Loffler, Paul. "Proselytism." In *Dictionary of the Ecumenical Movement*, edited by Nicholas Lossky et al., 829. Geneva: WCC; Grand Rapids: Eerdmans, 1991.

Lossky, Nicholas, et al., eds. *Dictionary of the Ecumenical Movement*. Geneva: WCC; Grand Rapids: Eerdmans, 1991.

Loya, Joseph. "Uniatism in Current Ecumenical Dialogue." *Ecumenical Trends: Graymoor Ecumenical and Interreligious Institute* 21.6 (1992).

Luchterhandt, Otto. "Religous Freedom and Proselytism in Russia and Eastern Europe." Paper presented to the Tantur Conference on Religious Freedom and Proselytism. 1998.

Ma, Wonsuk, and Robert P. Menzies, eds. *Pentecostalism in Context: Essays in Honor of William W Menzies*. JPT Supplement Series 11. Sheffield: Sheffield Academic, 1997.

Macquarrie, John, and James F. Childress. *A New Dictionary of Christian Ethics*. London: SCM, 1990.

Major, Blair. "Religious Proselytism in Global Perspective: A Critical Examination of International and Regional Human Rights Law." LLM thesis, McGill University, 2012.

Margolis, Mac. "A Wave of Religious Revival Splits Brazil." *Los Angeles Times*, July 6, 1993. H6.

Martin, Larry. *The Complete Azusa Street Library*. 12 vols. Joplin: Christian Life, 2014.

Marx, Karl, and Friedrich Engels. *Werke*. Berlin: Dietz Verlag, 1978.

Matthey, Jacques. "Editorial." *International Review of Mission* 90.358 (2001) 227–31. Online. https://www.questia.com/read/1g1-75479500/editorial.

———. "Towards Common Witness: A Call to Adopt Responsible Relationships in Mission and to Renounce Proselytism." In *You Are the Light of the World: Statements on Mission by the World Council of Churches 1980–2005*, edited by Jacques Matthey, 39–67. Geneva: WCC, 2005.

Mayer, Ann. *Islam and Human Rights*. Boulder: Westview, 1995.

Mazawi, Andre. "Palestinian Local Theology and the Issue of Islamo-Christian Dialogue: An Appraisal." *Islamochristiana* 19 (1993) 93–115.

McClendon, James Wm., Jr. *Systematic Theology: Ethics*. Nashville: Abingdon, 1986.

Mclintock, John, and James Strong. "Proselyte." In vol. 8 of *Cyclopedia of Biblical, Theological, and Ecclesiastical Literature*, edited by John Mclintock and James Strong, 658–64. Grand Rapids: Baker, 1981.

Medgyessy, László. "Mission or Proselytism? Temptations, Tensions, and Missiological Perspectives in Eastern European Christianity: A Case Study of Hungary." In

Contextuality in Reformed Europe: The Mission of the Church in the Transformation of European Culture, edited by Christine Liennemann-Perrin et al., 99–120. Currents of Encounter. Amsterdam; New York: Rodopi, 2004.

Meeking, Basil. "For Every Human Being in the World." *International Review of Mission* 71.284 (1982) 454.

Meeking, Basil, and John Stott, eds. *The Evangelical-Roman Catholic Dialogue on Mission, 1977–1984*. Grand Rapids: Eerdmans; Exeter, Devon: Paternoster, 1986.

"Message of the Primates of the Most Holy Orthodox Churches." *Ecumenical Trends* 21.4 (1992) 57–60.

Meyer, Harding, et al., eds. *Dokumente wachsender Übereinstimmung* [*Documents of Growing Consensus*]. 4 vols. Bonifatius: 1983–2012.

Micah Network Disaster Management Working Group, South Asia. "Proselytism Policy Statement." 2007. Online. https://www.micahnetwork.org/sites/default/files/doc/library/proselytism_policy_statement.pdf.

Middle East Council of Churches (MECC). *Proselytism, Sects, and Pastoral Challenges: Working Document of the Commission of Faith and Unity*. Beirut: Middle East Council of Churches, 1989.

———. "Who Are the Christians of the Middle East?" In *MECC Perspectives*, L. J. Niilus. Limassol: Middle East Council of Churches, 1986.

Mill, John Stuart. *On Liberty*. 1859. Reprint, Indianapolis: Hackett, 1978.

Miller, Lois. "Affluence and Privilege Are a Stumbling Block." *International Review of Mission* 71.284 (1982) 456.

Minnerath, Roland. "An Ethical/Catholic Perspective of Proselytism." In *FIDES ET LIBERTAS: The Journal of the International Religious Liberty Association 2000*, 42–51. International Religious Liberty Association.

Moreau, A. Scott, ed. *Evangelical Dictionary of World Missions*. Grand Rapids: Baker, 2000.

Moreno, Pedro C. "Rapture and Renewal in Latin America." *First Things* 74 (June/July 1997) 31–34.

Moscow Patriarchate. *Consultation on Proselytism*. 4 Information Bulletin, Department of External Church Relations: 3 (1996).

———. "Relations of the Russian Orthodox Church with the Non-Orthodox on Her Canonical Territory." Online. https://mospat.ru/en/documents/attitude-to-the-non-orthodox/vi.

Müller, Karl, et al., ed. *Dictionary of Mission*. Maryknoll, NY: Orbis, 1997.

Mycio, Mary. "America Losing Luster in Ukraine." *Los Angeles Times*, June 1, 1993. H2.

National Conference of Catholic Bishops (NCCB). *Celebrating "To The Ends Of The Earth": An Anniversary Statement On World Mission*. Washington, DC: United States Conference of Catholic Bishops, 1996.

———. *To the Ends Of The Earth*. Washington, DC: United States Conference of Catholic Bishops, 1986. Online. http://www.internationalbulletin.org/issues/1987-02/1987-02-050-the.pdf.

Newbigin, Lesslie. "The Dialogue of Gospel and Culture: Reflections on the Conference on World Mission and Evangelism, Salvador, Bahia, Brazil." *International Bulletin of Missionary Research* 21 (1997) 50–52.

Nicastro, R. Vito, Jr. "Mission Volga: A Case Study in the Tensions Between Evangelizing and Proselytizing." *Journal of Ecumenical Studies* 31.3–4 (1994) 223–43.

Nichols, Joel A. "Mission, Evangelism, and Proselytism in Christianity: Mainline Conceptions as Reflected in Church Documents." *Emory International Law Review* 12 (1998) 563–650. Online. https://papers.ssrn.com/sol3/papers.cfm?abstract_id=762467.

O'Collins, Gerald, and Farrugia, Edward G., eds. *A Concise Dictionary Of Theology*. 3rd ed. Mahwah, NJ: Paulist, 2013.

Oden, Thomas C. "How Should Evangelicals Be Ecumenical?" *Christianity Today* 37.4 (1993) 39.

Office of the Panorthodox Secretariat. *News Bulletin* 1 (21 June 2016). Online: https://www.holycouncil.org/-/news-bulletin-number-1.

Office of the United Nations High Commissioner for Human Rights. (OHCHR). "Universal Declaration of Human Rights." Online. https://www.ohchr.org/EN/UDHR/Pages/UDHRIndex.aspx.

Olteanu, Liviu, editor. *Agents and Ambassadors for Peace: Protecting Freedom of Religion and Freedom of Expression Against Violence in the Name of Religion*. Special ed. Bern, Switzerland: International Association for the Defence of Religious Liberty, 2015.

On the Freedom of Conscience and Religious Associations. Federal Law No. 125-FZ. September 26, 1997. LEXIS, Intlaw Library, Rfarch File.

Otis, George, Jr. "The Holy Spirit Around the World." *Charisma* 18.6 (1993) 55–56, 58–59.

Oxbrow, Mark, ed. *Together in Mission*. London: CMS, 2001.

Oxbrow, Mark, and Tim Grass, eds. *The Mission of God: Studies in Orthodox and Evangelical Mission*. Oxford: Regnum, 2015.

Packer, J. I. "Why I Left." *Christianity Today* 37 (1993).

Parks, James W. *The Conflict of the Church and Synagogue*. London: Sociono; New York: World, 1961.

"Patriarchal and Synodical Encyclical of 1920." 1920. *Orthodox Voice* (blog), April 2011. Online. http://orthodox-voice.blogspot.com/2011/04/patriarchal-and-synodical-encyclical-of_26.html.

Paul VI. *Evangelii nuntiandi: On Evangelization in the Modern World*. Rome: Libreria Editrice Vaticana, 1975.

Paul VI, and Amba Shenouda III. "Common Declaration of His Holiness Paul VI and His Holiness Patriarch Amba Shenouda III." May 10, 1973. Online. http://w2.vatican.va/content/paul-vi/en/speeches/1973/may/documents/hf_p-vi_spe_19730510_dichiarazione-comune.html.

Penner, P. "Proselytism." In *Dictionary of Mission Theology: Evangelical Foundations*, edited by John Corrie, 321–22. Nottingham: IVP, 2007.

"Perspectives on Koinonia." *Pneuma: The Journal of the Society for Pentecostal Studies* 12.1 (1990) 125–31.

Peters, George. *A Biblical Theology of Missions*. Chicago: Moody, 1975.

Robeck, Cecil. "Specks and Logs, Catholics and Pentecostals." *Pneuma: The Journal of the Society for Pentecostal Studies* 12.1 (1990) 77–142.

Pontifical Council for Interreligious Dialogue (PCID). "The Attitude of the Church toward Followers of Other Religions: Reflections and Orientations on Dialogue and Mission." June 10, 1984. Online. https://www.pcinterreligious.org/the-attitudes-of-the-church-towards-the-followers-of-other-religions.

Pontifical Council for Promoting Christian Unity (PCPCU). *The Ecumenical Dimension in the Training of Pastoral Ministers*. 1997.

———. "Evangelization, Proselytism, and Common Witness: The Report from the Fourth Phase of the International Dialogue 1990–1997 between the Roman Catholic Church and Some Classical Pentecostal Churches and Leaders." Rome: Pontifical Council for Promoting Christian Unity, 1997. Online. http://www.vatican.va/roman_curia/pontifical_councils/chrstuni/pentecostals/rc_pc_chrstuni_doc_1990-1997_evangelization-proselytism-common-witness_en.html.

———. *Sects or New Religious Movements: Pastoral Challenge*. Rome: Secretariat for Promoting Christian Unity, 1986.

Pontifical Commission for Russia (PCR). *General Principles and Practical Norms for Coordinating the Evangelizing Activity and Ecumenical Commitment of the Catholic Church in Russia and in the Other Countries of the CIS*. Rome: Vatican, 1992.

———. "Principles and Norms: Evangelization and Ecumenism in Former Soviet Territories." *Origins* 22.5 (1993) 301–4.

Popescu, Teodor M. "De la Nero la Stalin." *Gandirea* 1 (1942). Online: https://www-fericiticeiprigoniti-net.translate.goog/sinteze/2165-de-la-nero-la-stalin?_x_tr_sl=ro&_x_tr_tl=en&_x_tr_hl=en&_x_tr_pto=nui,sc.

Posad, Sergiev. *Final Document: Orthodox Consultation on Mission and Proselytism*. June 26–29, 1995.

"Principles and Norms: Evangelization and Ecumenism in Former Soviet Territories." *Origins* 22.5 (1993) 301–4.

Quiet, Olivier. *Religion et nationalisme: L'ideologie dc L'Eglise Orthodoxe Roumaine sous le regime communiste*. Brussels: Editions de l'Universite de Bruxelles, 1997.

Raheb, Mitri. *I Am a Palestinian Christian*. Minneapolis: Fortress, 1995.

Ramirez, Ricardo. "The Crisis in Ecumenism Among Hispanic Christians." *Origins* 24.40 (1995) 663.

"Rapport de Balamand: Questions and Responses." *Le Courrier Oecumenique du Moyen Orient* 33.3 (1997).

"Revised Report of the Commission on 'Christian Witness, Proselytism, and Religious Liberty.'" *The Ecumenical Review* 13 (1961) 79–89.

Richards, Matthew K., et al. "Codes of Conduct for Religious Persuasion: The Legal Framework and Best Practices." *International Journal for Religious Freedom (IJRF)* 3.2 (2010) 65–104.

Richardson, Alan, and Bowden, John, eds. *The Westminster Dictionary Of Christian Theology*. Philadelphia: Westminster, 1983.

Richardson, Rick. "Emerging Missional Movements: and Overview and Assessment of Some Implications for Mission(s)." *International Bulletin of Missionary Research* 3 (2013) 131–36.

Rivers, J. "Beyond Rights: The Morality of Rights-Language." *Cambridge Papers* 6.3 (1997) 1–4. Online. http://jubilee-centre.org/wp-content/uploads/2014/03/06-3-Beyond-rights.pdf.

Robeck, Cecil M., Jr. "The Assemblies of God and Ecumenical Cooperation, 1920–1965." In *Pentecostalism in Context: Essays in Honor of William W Menzies*, edited by Wonsuk Ma and Robert P. Menzies, 107–50. JPT Supplement Series 11. Sheffield: Sheffield Academic, 1997.

———. "Evangelization or Proselytism of Hispanics? A Pentecostal Perspective." *Journal of Hispanic/Latin Theology* 4.4 (1997) 42–64.

———. "The Past: Historical Roots of Racial Unity and Division in American Pentecostalism." *Cyberjournal for Pentecostal-Charismatic Research* 14 (May 2004) Online: www.pctii.org/cyberj/cyberj14/robeck.html.

———. "Mission and the Issue of Proselytism." *International Bulletin of Missionary Research* 20.1 (1996) 2–9.

———. "What the Pope Said." *Commonweal* 119.22 (1992) 30–31.

Robeck, Cecil M., Jr., and Jerry L. Sandidge. "The Ecclesiology of Koinonia and Baptism: A Pentecostal Perspective." *Journal of Ecumenical Studies* 27.3 (1990) 504–34.

Roberston, Roland. "Contemporary Romanian Orthodox Ecclesiology: The Contribution of Dumitru Staniloae and Younger Colleagues." PhD diss., Pontifical Oriental Institute, Rome, 1988.

———. *The Eastern Christian Churches*. 3rd ed. Rome: Pont. Institutum Studiorum Orientalium, 1990.

———. *The Eastern Churches: A Brief Survey*. Rev. 3rd ed. Rome: Pont. Institutum Studiorum Orientalium, 1990.

Roman Catholic Church, Synod of Bishops. *De iustitia in mundo [Justice in the World]*. Pontificia Commissio Iustitia et Pax, 1971. Online: https://www.cctwincities.org/wp-content/uploads/2015/10/Justicia-in-Mundo.pdf.

Rossel, Jacques. *Aux racines de l'Europe Occidentale: Essai sur l'interpenetration des cultures aux neufs premiers siecles de notre ere*. Bale: Editions Basilei, 1995.

Russian Orthodox Church, Department for External Church Relations. "Basic Principles of Attitude to the Non-Orthodox." No date. Online: https://old.mospat.ru/en/documents/attitude-to-the-non-orthodox/.

Sabra, George. "Proselytism, Evangelism, and Ecumenism." *Theological Review: Near East School of Theology* 9.2 (1988) 23–36.

Sarkissian, Karekin. *The Witness of the Oriental Orthodox Churches*. Beirut: Mesrob, 1968.

Sauca, Ioan, ed. *Orthodoxy and Cultures*. Geneva: WCC, 1996.

Scherer, James A., and Stephen B. Bevans, eds. *Basic Statements 1974–1991*. Vol. 1 of *New Directions in Mission and Evangelization*. Maryknoll, NY: Orbis, 1992.

———. *Faith and Culture*. Vol. 3 of *New Directions in Mission and Evangelization*. Maryknoll, NY: Orbis, 1999.

———. *Theological Foundations*. Vol. 2 of *New Directions in Mission and Evangelization*. Maryknoll, NY: Orbis, 1994.

Schirrmacher, Thomas. "'But with Gentleness and Respect': Why Missions Should Be Ruled by Ethics—An Evangelical Perspective for a Code of Ethics of Christian Witness." *Current Dialogue* 50 (2008) 55–66.

———. "Christian Witness in a Multi-Religious World." In *Sharing of Faith Stories: A Methodology for Promoting Unity*, edited by Richard Howell, 345–70. New Delhi: Caleb, 2018.

———. "Christian Witness in a Multi-Religious World—Three Years On." *Current Dialogue* 56 (2014) 67–79. Online. www.oikoumene.org/en/what-we-do/current-dialogue-magazine/current-dialogue-56.

———. "The Code 'Christian Witness in a Multi-Religious World'—Its Significance and Reception." *Evangelical Review of Theology* 40 (2016) 82–89.

———. "Mission und Religionsfreiheit—eine evangelikale Perspektive." In *Religionen und Religionsfreiheit: Menschenrechtliche Perspektiven im Spannungsfeld von Mission und Konversion*, edited by Marianne Heimbach-Steins and Heiner Bielefeldt, 113–33. Würzburg: Ergon Verlag, 2010.

Schirrmacher, Thomas, and Jonathan Chaplin. "European Religious Freedom and the EU." In *God and the EU: Faith in the European Project*, edited by Jonathan Chaplin and Gary Wilton, 151–74. 2nd ed. London and New York: Routledge, 2017.

Schirrmacher, Thomas, and Richard Howell. "Freedom of Religion or Belief from a Biblical Perspective." In *Freedom of Belief and Christian Mission*, edited by Hans Aage Gravaas et al., 18–29. Oxford: Regnum, 2015.

Schreiter, Robert J. "Changes in Roman Catholic Attitudes toward Proselytism and Mission." In *New Directions in Mission and Evangelization 2: Theological Foundations*, edited by James A. Scherer and Stephen B. Bevans, 113–25. Maryknoll, NY: Orbis, 1994.

Second Vatican Council (Vatican II).

———. *Ad Gentes* [*Decree on the Church's Missionary Activity*]. 1965. Online: https://www.vatican.va/archive/hist_councils/ii_vatican_council/documents/vat-ii_decree_19651207_ad-gentes_en.html.

———. *Apostolicam Actuositatem* [*Decree on the Apostolate of Lay People*]. 1965. Online: https://www.vatican.va/archive/hist_councils/ii_vatican_council/documents/vat-ii_decree_19651118_apostolicam-actuositatem_en.html.

———. *Dignitatis Humanae* [*Declaration on Religious Liberty*]. 1965. Online: https://www.vatican.va/archive/hist_councils/ii_vatican_council/documents/vat-ii_decl_19651207_dignitatis-humanae_en.html.

———. *Gaudium et Spes* [*Pastoral Constitution on the Church in the Modern World*]. 1965. Online: https://www.vatican.va/archive/hist_councils/ii_vatican_council/documents/vat-ii_const_19651207_gaudium-et-spes_en.html.

———. *Lumen Gentium* [*Dogmatic Constitution on the Church*]. 1965. Online: https://www.vatican.va/archive/hist_councils/ii_vatican_council/documents/vat-ii_const_19641121_lumen-gentium_en.html.

———. *Nostra Aetate* [*Declaration on the Relation of the Church to Non-Christian Religions*]. 1965. Online: https://www.vatican.va/archive/hist_councils/ii_vatican_council/documents/vat-ii_decl_19651028_nostra-aetate_en.html.

———. *Orientalium Ecclesiarum* [*Decree on Eastern Catholic Churches*]. 1965. https://www.vatican.va/archive/hist_councils/ii_vatican_council/documents/vat-ii_decree_19641121_orientalium-ecclesiarum_en.html.

———. *Sacrosanctum Concilium* [*Constitution on the Liturgy*]. 1965. Online: https://www.vatican.va/archive/hist_councils/ii_vatican_council/documents/vat-ii_const_19631204_sacrosanctum-concilium_en.html.

———. *Unitatis Redintegratio* [*Decree on Ecumenism*]. 1965. Online: https://www.vatican.va/archive/hist_councils/ii_vatican_council/documents/vat-ii_decree_19641121_unitatis-redintegratio_en.html.

Secretariat for Non-Christians, Plenary Assembly. "The Attitude of the Church toward Followers of Other Religions: Reflections and Orientations on Dialogue and Mission." *The Furrow* 36.7 (1985) 453–57; 36.8 (1985) 519–24.

Semaan, Wanis. *Aliens at Home: A Socio-Religious Analysis of the Protestant Church in Lebanon and Its Backgrounds*. Beirut: Librarie du Liban/Longman, 1986.

Serbin, Ken. "Latin America's Catholics: Postliberationism?" *Christianity and Crisis* 52.18 (1992) 405–6.

Seventh-Day Adventist Church. "Religious Liberty, Evangelism, and Proselytism." June 29, 2000. Online. https://www.adventist.org/articles/religious-liberty-evangelism-and-proselytism.

Seymour, William J. *The Doctrines and Discipline of the Azusa Street Apostolic Faith Mission of Los Angeles, with Scripture Readings*. 1915. Complete Azusa Street Library. Joplin: Christian Life, 2014.

Shakespeare, William. *The Winter's Tale*. London: J. S. Virtue, 1770.

Shenk, Wilbert R. *Anabaptism and Mission*. Eugene, OR: Wipf & Stock, 1984.

Shupack, Martin. "The Churches and Human Rights: Catholic and Protestant Human Rights Views as Reflected in Church Statements." *The Harvard Human Rights Journal* 6 (1993) 127.

Sigmund, Paul E. "Religious Human Rights in Latin America." In *Religious Human Rights in Global Perspective: Religious Perspectives*, edited by John Witte Jr. and Johan D. van der Vyver, 467–82. The Hague: Martinus Nijhoff, 1996.

Signs of Hope in the Middle East. Cyprus: MECC/EMEU, 1992.

Simon, Marcel. *Verus Israel, Etude sur les relations entre Chrétiens et juifs dans l'empire romain (135–425 AD)*. Paris: E. De Boccard, 1948.

South Asia Human Rights Documentation Center. "Anti-Conversion Laws: Challenges to Secularism and Fundamental Rights." *Economic and Political Weekly* 43.2 (2008) 63–69, 71–73. Online. https://www.jstor.org/stable/40276904.

Stackhouse, John G., Jr. "Evangelicals Reconsider World Religions: Betraying or Affirming the Tradition?" *Christian Century* 110 (1993) 858–65.

Stahnke, Tad. "Proselytism and the Freedom to Change Religion in International Human Rights Law." *BYU Law Review* 1999.1 (1999) 251–354.

Stalnaker Cecil. "Proselytism or Evangelism?" *Evangelical Review of Theology* 26.4 (2002) 337–53.

Stamoolis, James J. *Eastern Orthodox Mission Theology Today*. Eugene, OR: Wipf & Stock, 2001.

Staniloae, Dumitru. "The Gate of Christendom." In *The Altar Almanah (1970)*. London: Romanian Orthodox Parish, 1970.

Stern, M. J. "Back to the Future? Manuell Castells's *The Information Age* and the Prospects for Social Welfare." *Cultural Studies (Routledge)* 14.1 (2000) 99–116.

Stockwell, Eugene L. "Conciliar Missions." In *Toward the Twenty-First Century in Christian Mission*, edited by James M. Phillips and Robert T. Coote, 21–29. Grand Rapids: Eerdmans, 1993.

Stott, John. *The Lausanne Covenant: An Exposition and Commentary*. Lausanne Occasional Paper 3. Wheaton: Lausanne Committee for World Evangelization, 1975. Online. https://www.lausanne.org/content/lop/lop-3#13.

Stransky, Thomas. "Common Witness." In *Dictionary of the Ecumenical Movement*, edited by Nicolas Lossky, José Míguez Bonino, John S. Pobee, Geoffrey Wainwright, Tom F. Stransky, and Pauline Webb, 197. Geneva: WCC, 1991.

"Summons to Witness to Christ in Today's World: A Report on the Baptist-Roman Catholic International Conversations, 1984–1988." *Information Service* 72 (1990) 5–14. Online: http://www.prounione.urbe.it/dia-int/b-rc/doc/e_b-rc_report1988_01.html.

Taylor, John G. "Catholic-Evangelical Agreement Criticized by Latino Baptists." *San Gabriel Valley News*, May 28, 1994.

Teague, David, ed. *Turning a New Leaf: Protestant Missions and the Orthodox Churches of the Middle East*. 2nd ed. London: Interserve; Lynnwood, WA: Middle East Media, 1992.

Thiessen, Elmer John. *The Ethics of Evangelism: A Philosophical Defence of Proselytizing and Persuasion.* Milton Keynes: Paternoster; Downers Grove, IL: IVP Academic, 2011.

———. *In Defense of Religious Schools and Colleges.* Montreal; Kingston: McGill-Queen's University Press, 2001.

———. *The Scandal of Evangelism: A Biblical Study of the Ethics of Evangelism.* Eugene, OR: Cascade, 2018.

———. *Teaching for Commitment: Liberal Education, Indoctrination, and Christian Nurture.* Montreal; Kingston: McGill-Queen's University Press, 1993.

Thual, Francois, ed. *Geopolitique et l'Orthodoxie.* Paris: Dunnond, 1993.

Tierney, Brian. "Religious Rights: An Historical Perspective." In *Religious Human Rights in Global Perspective: Religious Perspectives,* edited by John Witte Jr. and Johan D. van der Vyver, 17–45. The Hague: Martinus Nijhoff, 1996.

Todorović, Dragan, ed. *Evangelization Conversion Proselytism.* Niš: Yugoslav Society For The Scientific Study Of Religion Komren Sociological Encounters Punta, 2004.

Tokes, Laszlo. *In the Spirit of Timisoara: Ecumenism and Reconciliation.* Oradea, 1996.

Tolz, V. "Forging the Nation: National Identity and Nation Building in Post-Communist Russia." *Europe-Asia Studies* 50.6 (1998) 993–1022.

Tomkins, Oliver S., ed. *The Third World Conference on Faith and Order (Lund, August 15–25, 1952).* London: SCM, 1953.

"Towards Koinonia in Faith, Life, and Witness: Discussion Paper for the Fifth World Conference on Faith and Order, Santiago de Compostela, August 3–14, 1993." In *On the Way to Fuller Koinonia,* edited by T. F. Best and Günther Gassmann. Faith and Order Paper 166. Geneva: WCC, 1994.

"Towards Responsible Relations in Mission: Some Reflections on Common Witness, Proselytism, and New Forms of Sharing." *International Review of Mission* 82.326 (1993) 235–39. Online: http://www.jstor.org/stable/43052403.

Tsetsis, Georges, ed. *Orthodox Thought: Reports of Orthodox Consultations Organized by the World Council Of Churches, 1975–1982.* Geneva: WCC, 1983.

"Uniatism: Method of Union of the Past, and the Present Search for Full Communion: Report of the Joint International Commission for the Theological Dialogue between the Roman Catholic Church and the Orthodox Church—Balamand, June 17–24, 1993." *Information Service* 83 (1993) 96–99.

United Nations (UN). *Declaration on the Elimination of All Forms of Intolerance and of Discrimination Based on Religion or Belief.* 1981. Online: https://www.ohchr.org/en/professionalinterest/pages/religionorbelief.aspx.

———. *Universal Declaration of Human Rights.* 1948. Online. http://www.un.org/en/universal-declaration-human-rights.

United States Catholic Conference (USCC). *Go And Make Disciples: A National Plan and Strategy for Catholic Evangelization in the United States.* Washington, DC: United States Conference of Catholic Bishops, 1993.

"US Orthodox/Roman Catholic Consultation at the Holy Cross Orthodox School of Theology, Brookline, MA, May 26–28, 1992." *Origins* 22.5 (1992) 79–80.

Uzzell, L. *The Catholic World Report,* November 1997.

Vaporis, N. M., ed. *Orthodox Christians and Muslims.* Brookline, MA: Holy Cross Orthodox, 1986.

Vassiliadis, Petros. *Eucharist and Witness: Orthodox Perspectives on the Unity and Mission of the Church*. New York: Holy Cross Seminary, 2002.

———. "Mission and Proselytism: An Orthodox Understanding." *International Review of Mission* 85.337 (1995) 257–75.

———. "Mission, Proselytism and the Ecumenical Movement." In *Go Forth: Festschrift for the Archbishop of Albania, Anastasios Yannoulatos*, 77–97. Athens: 1997.

———. "An Orthodox Assessment of the New Mission Statement." *International Review of Mission* 102.2 (2013) 174–78.

"Vatican Reports on Sects, Cults, and New Religious Movements." *Origins* 16.1 (1986) 2–10.

Veronis, L. *Missionaries, Monks, and Martyrs: Making Disciples of All Nations*. Minneapolis: Light and Life, 1994.

Vignot, Bernard. *Les Eglises Parallèles*. Paris: Les Editions du Cerf, 1991.

Visser't Hooft, W. A. *No Other Name: The Choice Between Syncretism and Christian Universalism*. London: SCM, 1963.

Volf, Miroslav. "Exclusion and Embrace: Theological Reflections in the Wake of 'Ethnic Cleansing.'" *Journal of Ecumenical Studies* 29.2 (1992) 230–48.

———. "Fishing In The Neighbor's Pond: Mission And Proselytism In Eastern Europe." *International Bulletin of Missionary Research* 20.1 (1996) 26–31.

———. "A Vision of Embrace: Theological Perspectives on Cultural Identity and Conflict." *The Ecumenical Review* 48.2 (1995) 195–205.

———. "When the Unclean Spirit Leaves: Tasks of the Eastern European Churches After the 1989 Revolution." *Cross Currents* 41 (1991) 84–86.

Vyver, Johan van der. "Religious Freedom and Proselytism: Ethical, Political, and Legal Aspects." *Ecumenical Review* 50.4 (1998) 419–29.

Wagner, Donald. *Anxious for Armageddon: A Call to Partnership for Middle Eastern and Western Christians*. Scottdale, PA: Herald, 1994.

Walker, George. *History of the First Church in Hartford, 1633–1883*. Hartford, CT: Brown & Gross, 1884.

Walls, A. "Converts or Proselytes? The Crisis over Conversion in the Early Church." *International Bulletin of Missionary Research* 28.1 (2004) 2–6.

Webster, Alexander. *The Price of Prophecy: Orthodox Churches on Peace, Freedom, and Security*. Grand Rapids: Eerdmans, 1995.

Webster's Ninth New Collegiate Dictionary. Springfield, MA: Merriam-Webster, 1983.

Williams, Rowan. "On Making Moral Decisions." *Anglican Theological Review* 81.2 (1999) 295–308.

Witte, John, Jr. "Christianity and Democracy: Past Contributions and Future Challenges." *Emory International Law Review* 6 (1992) 68.

———. "Introduction: Soul Wars: the Problem and Promise of Proselytism in Russia." *Emory International Law Review* 12.1 (1998) 1–42.

———. "Law, Religion, and Human Rights." *Columbia Human Rights Law Review* 28 (1996) 1–17.

———. "A Primer on the Rights and Wrongs of Proselytism." In *FIDES ET LIBERTAS 2000: The Journal of the International Religious Liberty Association* (2000) 12–17.

Witte, John, Jr., and Michael Bourdeux. *Proselytism and Orthodoxy in Russia: The New War for Souls*. Maryknoll, NY: Orbis, 1999.

———. *Proselytism and Orthodoxy in Russia: The New War for Souls*. Eugene, OR: Wipf & Stock, 2009.

Witte, John, Jr., and Paul Mojzes. "Pluralism, Proselytism, and Nationalism in Eastern Europe." *Journal of Ecumenical Studies* 36.1-2 (1999) 1-286.

Witte, John, Jr., and Johan D. van der Vyver, eds. *Religious Human Rights in Global Perspective: Religious Perspectives*. The Hague: Martinus Nijhoff, 1996.

Wolterstorff, Nicholas. *Until Justice and Peace Embrace*. Grand Rapids: Eerdmans, 1983.

World Council of Churches (WCC). *Breaking Barriers: The Official Report of the Fifth Assembly of the World Council of Churches, Nairobi*. Edited by David M. Paton. Grand Rapids: Eerdmans, 1976.

———. "Christian Witness, Proselytism, and Religious Liberty in the Setting of the World Council of Churches." *Ecumenical Review* 9.1 (1956) 48-56.

———. *Church and World: The Unity of the Church and the Renewal of Human Community*. Faith and Order Paper 151. Geneva: WCC, 1990.

———. "Constitution and Rules of the World Council of Churches, amended by the Central Committee of the WCC in Geneva, Switzerland, 2018." Online: https://www.oikoumene.org/resources/documents/constitution-and-rules-of-the-world-council-of-churches.

———. *Dictionary of the Ecumenical Movement*. Geneva: WCC, 1991.

———. *Ecumenical Considerations on Christian-Muslim Relations*. Geneva: WCC, 1991. Online. https://www.oikoumene.org/en/resources/documents/wcc-programmes/interreligious-dialogue-and-cooperation/interreligious-trust-and-respect/issues-in-christian-muslim-relations-ecumenical-considerations.

———. *Ecumenical Considerations on Jewish-Christian Dialogue*. Geneva: WCC, 1982. Online. https://www.oikoumene.org/en/resources/documents/wcc-programmes/interreligious-dialogue-and-cooperation/interreligious-trust-and-respect/ecumenical-considerations-on-jewish-christian-dialogue.

———. *Evanston to New Delhi, 1954-1961: Report of the Central Committee to the Third Assembly of the World Council of Churches*. Geneva: WCC, 1961.

———. *Minutes and Reports of the Central Committee of the World Council of Churches, St. Andrews, Scotland, August 1960*. Geneva: WCC, 1960.

———. *Mission and Evangelism: An Ecumenical Affirmation*. Geneva: WCC, 1982.

———. *Mission and Evangelism in Unity Today*. Geneva: WCC, 2000.

———. *Mission from Three Perspectives*. Geneva: WCC-CWME, 1989.

———. *On the Way to Fuller Koinonia: Official Report of the Fifth World Conference on Faith and Order*. Edited by T. F. Best and Gunther Gassman. Faith and Order Paper 166. Geneva: WCC, 1994.

———. *Religious Liberty—Some Major Considerations in the Current Debate*. WCC/CCIA Background Information, 1987/1.

———. *San Antonio Report: Your Will Be Done—Mission in Christ's Way*. Edited by Frederick R. Wilson. Geneva: WCC, 1990.

———. *Signs of the Spirit—Official Report of the Seventh Assembly*. Edited by Michael Kinnamon. Geneva: WCC, 1991.

———. *Study Paper on Religious Liberty*, WCC/CCIA Background Information, 1980/1

———. *The Theology of the Churches and the Jewish People: Statements by the World Council of Churches and Its Member Churches*. Geneva: WCC, 1988.

———. "Towards Common Witness: A Call to Adopt Responsible Relationships in Mission and to Renounce Proselytism." September 19, 1997. Online. https://www.oikoumene.org/en/resources/documents/commissions/mission-and-evangelism/towards-common-witness.

———. *The Uppsala Report 1968: Official Report of the Fourth Assembly of the World Council of Churches, Uppsala, July 4–20, 1968*. Edited by Norman Goodall. Geneva: WCC, 1968.

———. "WCC Executive Committee Statement on Religious Liberty." September 1979.

World Council of Churches, et al. "Christian Witness in a Multi-Religious World: Recommendations for Conduct." 2011. Online. www.worldevangelicals.org/pdf/1106Christian_Witness_in_a_Multi-Religious_World.pdf.

World Evangelical Alliance (WEA). "Defining Evangelism versus Proselytism." *World Relief Triad*. Online. https://worldrelieftriad.org/defining-evangelism-v-proselytism.

Yannoulatos, Anastasios. "All of Us Are in a Missionary Situation." *International Review of Mission* 71.284 (1982) 452.

———. *Sharing the Good News in a Multi-Religious Country: Theological Reflections on Other Religions*. New York: Fordham University Press, 2014. Online. https://www.fordham.edu/download/downloads/id/2070/anastasios_lecture.pdf.

———. *Various Christian Approaches to the Other Religions (A Historical Outline)*. Athens: Porefthentes Editions, 1971.

Zander, Leon. "Ecumenism and Proselytism." *International Review of Mission* 3 (1951) 258–66.

Zissis, Theodore. "Uniatism: A Problem in the Dialogue Between Orthodox and Roman Catholics." *Greek Orthodox Theological Review* 35 (1990) 21–31.

Subject Index

Some words do not appear in this Index for they appear hundreds of times. These include evangelism and its derivatives; faith and its derivatives; free and freedom (except Religious freedom); God and derivatives; Gospel; individual and derivatives; Jesus, Jesus Christ, Christ; Love and derivatives; Mission and derivatives; Orthodox, Orthodox Church, but not all derivatives; proselytism, but not all derivatives; Religious and Religion and derivatives, excepting Religious Freedom; Social and its derivatives; theology and its derivatives; and, true and truth and their derivatives.

I have included footnotes in this Index.

Abraham, 15,
Abuse(s) (d), 10, 61, 73, 126, 178, 185, 190, 192, 214–15, 254, 304
Ad Gentes, 27, 51, 53–57, 69, 131, 248, 265–69, 272
Advocacy, 34, 175, 178, 184, 186
Affiliation(s), 5, 89, 105, 112, 114, 126, 140, 157, 239, 240, 258, 270, 288, 291, 296, 301, 313, 315, 317–19
Afghanistan, 157
Africa(n), 38, 123, 135, 174, 179, 187, 218, 220, 222–25, 227, 231–32, 236, 237, 240–42, 251, 282, 330
African-American, 123, 220
African Independent Churches, 38, 251
Aid, 55, 60, 70, 136, 140, 158–60, 197, 254, 285, 287–88, 311–12. *See also* Development
Albania, xi, 166, 193, 234

Alta/Baja Californian Bishops 243, 245, 250–51, 270
Alexandria, 19, 193, 199–200, 225–27
Allegiance, 5, 11–12, 23, 29, 75, 105, 122, 136, 139–40, 143, 152, 190, 219, 284, 290, 292, 296, 310–11, 313
Allurement, 184, 191
America(n), xiii, 15, 25, 83, 220–21, 230–31, 243–44, 247. *See also* Latin America, North America, South America, United States of America
American Board of Commissioners for Foreign Missions , 31, 229,
Anglican, 4, 31–32, 128, 230–31, 251, 298
Anti-conversion/proselytism laws, 5–6, 127, 256
Antioch, 22, 94, 177, 225–27
Antiochian, 237

Apostle(s), the, 21–22, 58, 62–64, 102, 129, 137, 161, 176, 198, 203, 225, 317, 319
Apostolic, 28, 30, 56–57, 64, 82, 98, 102, 123, 177, 201, 225, 267, 280, 296
Apostolic succession, 98, 102, 233
Arab, 223, 227, 237, 241–2
Arabic, 227, 241
Aramaic, 225, 241
Armenia, 225, 247
Armenian, 28–29, 32, 225–26, 228, 231, 241, 244
Asia/Asian, 19, 92, 135, 158, 162–63, 179, 181, 222–25, 227, 229–33, 237, 240–42, 282 *see also* West Asia(n)
Assyrian, 29, 223, 226, 228,
Atheist(ic)/atheism, 11, 209, 248, 282, 287
Athens, 234, 306
Authentic/authenticity, 33–34, 80, 85, 90, 97, 100, 102, 108, 121, 138–40, 144, 152, 156, 179, 191–92, 214, 224, 232, 293, 299, 323–24
Authority, 8–10, 28, 31, 49, 51, 55, 63–64, 74, 101, 104, 118, 141, 155, 160, 178, 185, 194, 225–26, 269, 273, 276, 295, 309, 323
Autocephalous, 28, 95, 103, 226, 319
Azusa Street, 123, 220

Balamand Declaration, 30, 93–103
Baptism, 10–11, 26, 53, 56, 76, 114, 117, 119, 129, 137, 139, 149, 200–203, 225, 235, 245, 250, 251, 270, 282, 284, 313
Baptist(s), 157, 210, 289–90, 295, 306
Baptized, 10, 22, 62, 76, 82, 111, 156, 165, 172, 211, 245, 260, 262–64, 266, 268–70, 280, 314, 318
Barmen Declaration, 218–19, 327
Barth, Karl, 218–19
Beirut, 94, 104, 229–30, 232
Benefits, 224, 260
   Temporal/material benefits, 33, 73, 100, 197

Bible, 15, 22, 26, 31, 109, 114, 124, 155, 160, 171, 177, 212, 221, 229, 245, 272–73, 304, 308, 309, 316. *See also* Scripture
Bilateral, 33, 106, 115, 123, 134, 232, 252, 282
Bishop, 135, 200, 249, 306, 319, 326
Bishops, 38, 98, 100–102, 106, 132, 236, 243, 245, 248–51, 267, 270, 305, 325
Body of Christ, 80, 85, 119, 121, 131, 136, 142–43, 171, 174–75, 178–79, 201, 203, 225, 234, 254, 278, 283, 297, 306, 307
Brazil, 135, 243, 277–78, 281, 286
Bria, Ion, 82, 234–36, 279–80
British Council of Churches, 166
Buddhist(m), 35, 168, 177, 246
Byzantium, 225. *See also* Constantinople

Cairo, 203, 231–32
Canon law. *See* Law, Canon law
Canonical territory, 11, 28, 141, 196, 297, 319, 323, 326
Cape Town Commitment, 162–63, 174–80, 181, 324
Capitalism(t), 191, 294–95, 299
Caricature(s), 38, 177, 234, 252, 293
Catechumenate/catechumens/catechetical, 56–57, 70, 202, 209
Catholicism, 120, 214, 227–28, 231–32, 251, 271, 275, 325
Catholic Church, xi, xii, 4, 29–30, 64, 76, 88, 94, 96–97, 99–100, 102, 120, 122, 128, 130, 154, 157, 200–201, 228–29, 250, 260–61, 266–72, 290, 326. *See also* Roman Catholic
Catholic-Evangelical relations, 155, 252
Catholic-Orthodox relations, 29–30, 232–23
   Eastern Catholic Churches, 29–31, 76, 93–94
   non-Catholic, 218, 249, 270, 272
Catholicos, 28–29, 244
Chaldean, 29, 226, 228

SUBJECT INDEX

Charismatic(s), 4, 38, 86, 91, 134, 210, 224, 246, 286, 290, 295
Charta Oecumenica, 289, 301
Christendom, 165, 307
Christian-Jewish relations, 34
Christian-Muslim relations, 24, 34
Christian Unity, 70. *See also* Pontifical Council for Promoting Christian Unity
Christian witness, 33-34, 53, 68, 73-74, 134, 139, 163-65, 237, 253, 309, 321
Christian Witness in a Multi-Religious World, 182-88, 191-92, 309
Christian Witness, Proselytism, and Religious Liberty, 33, 68, 134, 139, 253
Citizen(s), 5, 61, 65, 120-22, 128, 173-74, 178, 218, 315
Civil(c), 10, 27, 44, 59, 63, 65, 68, 74, 97, 102, 122, 127-28, 208, 239, 242
Collaboration, xi, 13, 54, 75, 112-15, 143, 150, 162, 186-87, 202, 284
Commission for Theological Dialogue RCC Coptic Orthodox, 93-95, 102, 201, 247
Commission for World Mission and Evangelism (CWME), 4, 79, 81, 84, 148, 151-53, 189, 275, 277-79, 281, 286
   San Antonio (World Mission Conference 1989), 79, 82, 84, 85, 191, 277-78, 283
Commission of the Churches on International Affairs (WCC), 138, 302
Common Witness (title), 33, 66, 66-77, 82, 106, 110, 114-15, 117, 117-32, 133, 133-45, 148, 148-53, 157, 190, 252-56, 283, 286, 290-91, 302, 310-13, 317, 320
Common witness (general), 137, 140, 150-51, 190,
Commonwealth of Independent States (CIS), 196-97, 208, 243, 246
Communion, 30, 87, 96, 117

Communist, 35, 207-9, 211, 214, 235, 248, 262, 281-82
Community, 68, 168, 188-9
Competition, 12, 83, 85, 105-8, 111, 136, 142, 151, 156, 179, 194, 211, 255, 261, 263, 277-78, 284, 288, 300-301, 322,
Competitive, 34, 75, 126, 135, 157, 189, 197, 232, 261, 287, 300
Conciliar, 258-59, 279
Conduct, code of/Recommendations for, 159-60, 192, 309,
Conference, 25, 146, 233, 243, 249, 271, 278, 306
   of African Bishops, 38
   of European Churches (CEC), 107, 134, 209, 289, 301
   of Latin American Bishops, 38, 249
   on Faith and Order, 106, 114, 134, 255
   on/for World Mission, 79, 135, 281, 286, 298, 306
   Pentecostal World, 124
Confession/confessional, 68, 145, 174, 176, 186, 194, 218-19, 241, 295, 303, 306, 322
Conflict(s), 6, 11, 31, 71, 83, 89, 97, 100-101, 105, 111, 120-22, 125, 129, 149-51, 156, 186-87, 208, 210, 212, 216, 217-19, 221, 296, 303-4, 306, 318
Conscience(s), 12, 26, 36, 40-41, 43, 45, 52, 58, 60, 62-64, 68, 71, 75, 91, 98, 100-101, 109-10, 128, 138, 161, 164, 177, 202, 221, 238, 268, 270-71, 287, 301-3, 317-18,
Constantinople, 28-29, 165-66, 202, 225-29
Constitutional/constitution(s), 35, 58-59, 65, 109, 241
Consultation(s), xi, xii, xv, 30, 90, 95, 100, 113, 121, 134, 139, 143, 148, 151, 154, 163, 181, 186-88, 199, 234-35, 283, 286, 298, 309
   CWME Consultation of Orthodox Churches, 82, **82-83**, 134
   International Consultation Roman Catholic and Evangelical, 154
   Stuttgart, 78, 78-80

Context(s), xiii, 4, 6–7, 10–12, 14, 52, 68, 71, 78, 99–101, 105, 108–9, 112, 114, 116, 122, 126, 141–43, 147–48, 150, 165, 181, 183–84, 186, 190–92, 197, 213–14, 218, 235, 237–40, 251, 267, 279, 290, 298, 302–3, 313, 321,
Contextual(ly)/contextualisation, 26, 90, 177, 212–13, 224, 238, 262, 289, 292, 299
Conversion, 26, 27, 147 see also Anti-Conversion
Cooperate/cooperation, 51, 70, 124, 170, 186
Copts/Coptic, 28–29, 32, 199–200, 225–26, 228, 231, 233, 241
Council(s), 28, 86, 165–66, 200, 202, 324
  British Council of Churches (see British Council of Churches)
  Holy and Great Council (see Holy and Great Council)
  International Missionary Council, 4, 138, 253, 302
  Middle East Council of Churches see Middle East Council of Churches
  of Chalcedon, 28, 166, 226
  of Constantinople, 165–66, 202
  of Ephesus, 28, 165, 202, 226
  of Ferrara-Florence, 29, 228
  of Nicaea/Nicea, 28, 166, 200, 202
  Pontifical Council (see Pontifical Council)
  Second Vatican (see Second Vatican Council)
  World Council of Churches (see World Council of Churches)
Cross-cultural, 236
Culture(s), 25, 118, 263, 278, 288, 294, 298
Cultural, 166, 168, 236, 241

Death, of Jesus, 55
Declaration on the Elimination of All Forms of Intolerance and Discrimination, 37, 39, 43–46, 127, 301

Declaration of Human Rights. See, Universal Declaration of Human Rights
Dialogue, 34, 93–95, 102, 104, 106, 110, 117–19, 123–27, 130, 157, 192, 196, 201, 232, 249, 252, 257, 263, 288
Dignitatis Humanae, 27, 51–52, 56, 58–65, 68, 127–28, 157, 248–49, 269–70
Disciples, 271–2
Discrimination, 11, 37, 39, 43, 195, 301
Division, 107, 220,

East, 20, 22, 29, 32, 92, 96–98, 180, 222–23, 225, 228, 231–32, 236, 247. See also Middle East, the
Eastern, 19, 28, 88, 135, 172, 222, 225, 227–28, 231–33, 237, 241, 289
Eastern Catholic Churches, 29–31, 76, 93, 94
Eastern Christian(s)/Christianity, 88, 223, 225, 233
Eastern Churches, 89, 222, 228, 267. See also Orthodox Church
Ecclesiology, ecclesiological, 82, 87, 95–96, 251, 304
Economic(s), 10, 12, 29, 32–33, 70, 74, 88, 110, 122, 114, 125, 140, 152, 155, 162, 175, 187, 192, 219, 224, 254, 285, 291, 294, 323–24
Economic life/sphere, 44, 54, 235
Ecumenical, 30, 33, 34, 90, 107, 124, 134, 232, 259, 261, 270
  Councils, 200, 202, 324 (see also Council[s])
  Patriarch, 28–29, 49, 76, 99, 133, 193, 279, 281, 295
Ecumenical Affirmation, 78–79, 148, 189, 275–78
Ecumenism, 32, 132, 224, 239–40, 242, 246, 250
Edinburgh World Mission Conference, 3, 50, 128, 174
Education, 32, 41, 44, 54, 70, 74, 88–89, 91–2, 100, 102, 110, 114, 140, 145, 149–50, 184, 197, 207, 217, 239, 285, 292, 299, 308

SUBJECT INDEX

Educational, educate, 29, 61, 83, 140, 144, 152, 169, 238, 291, 311
Egypt, 15, 19-20, 26, 31, 167, 200-202, 231, 233
Equality, 25, 61, 179, 304, 317
Etchmiadzin, 225-26,
Ethic(s), 7, 37, 71, 123, 205, 267, 292-94, 299, 303-4, 307-9, 315, 325
Ethical, 4, 10, 19, 36, 171, 176, 292-94, 296-97, 305-6, 309-11, 313, 315-18, 323
Ethnic, 10-12, 17, 28, 42, 105, 140, 179, 217-19, 221, 225-27, 233, 235, 237, 241, 276, 291, 297-99, 305
Ethnicity, 218, 240, 295, 298, 300-301, 304-6
Ethiopia(n), 22, 28-29, 167, 226, 254,,
Eucharist/Eucharistic, 70, 82, 94, 137, 195, 201, 233, 260, 262-64, 279, 305, 321
Europe/European, 4, 49, 106, 122, 207, 289, 325
  Central, 95, 105, 135, 207, 209, 214, **289-307**
  Eastern, 5, 35, 95, 99, 105, 135, 166-69, 205, **207-21**, 236, 244, 246, 250, **289-307**
  Western, 83, 167, 169
Evangel, the, 79
Evangelical(s) (general usage), 10, 31-33, 35, 78-79, 83, 86, 101, 108, 134, 149, 151, 155, 162-63, 166, 168, 170-71, 181, 207, 208-12, 214-15, 220-22, 229-33, 237, 244-45, 247, 249, 250-52, 256-58, 261-63, 273-75, 279, 295, 299, 303, 306, 309-11, 313-14, 317, 319-20, 323-5
Evangelical (proper noun), 14, 32, 106, 110, 123-24, 155, 157, 229, 231, 248, 252, 259, 261, 273, 292, 308-9, 315, 317-19 (*see also* World Evangelical Alliance)
Evangelii nuntiandi, 132, 267-68, 269, 272
Evanston General Assembly, 33, 133, 252-3

Exile, the, 15, 18-19, 23, 195,
Exilic, 14, 18-9
Exploit/exploiting *etc.*, 33, 74, 79, 110, 140, 147, 152, 159, 169, 184-85, 191, 254, 273, 290, 292, 311-12, 315

Faith and Order, 106, 114, 133-34, 148, 151, 255-6
False witness, 156, 185, 252-3
Family/families, 44, 61-62, 65, 71, 76, 83, 128, 135, 159, 165, 175-76, 186, 188, 200-202, 223, 226-27, 231, 293, 314
Force(s), 12, 20, 27, 37, 58-63, 68, 125, 136, 138, 147, 159, 166, 171, 173, 176, 178, 190, 208, 216, 218, 226, 237, 240, 248, 264-65, 268, 270, 274, 288, 302, 317, 325-6
Forgiven(ness), 30, 72, 113, 152, 175, 236
Fraternal/fraternity, 34, 54, 72, 75, 92, 102, 194, 196, 200-201
Freising Declaration, 96, 232
Free/freedom *see* Religious freedom
Fundamentalist(s)/fundamentalism, 38, 87, 91, 123-24, 136, 224, 247, 251, 281-82, 295, 325

Gaudium et Spes, 56, 132, 249
Ger, 15-18, 21, 26
German/Germany, 66, 78, 115, 148, 166, 231, 312, 314
Global, xi, xii, xiv, 4, 12, 25, 38, 50, 146, 162, 175, 179, 197, 226, 295, 298, 306, 313
Global Christian Forum, xi, xii, 4, 309, 323
Globalization, 12, 148, 201, 299, 319
Good News, 3, 7, 26, 68, 76, 79, 80, 83, 131-32, 146, 149, 156, 159, 176, 181, 183, 189, 190-91, 195, 208, 213, 271-72, 276, 309-10, 317, 320, 323
Government(s), 5-6, 55, 58, 60-61, 63, 65, 112, 160-61, 164-65, 168-69, 172-73, 178, 186, 208, 218, 283, 285, 300

Grace(s), 16, 55, 65, 69, 73, 130, 171, 173, 175–77, 179, 181, 184, 191, 195, 202, 232
Graham, Billy, 126, 162
Great Commission, the, 179, 256, 309
Greek/Greece, 19–21, 25–26, 29, 94, 167, 193, 195, 200, 219–20, 225, 227–28, 230, 234, 236, 241, 244–45, 290, 305, 306

Healing of memories, 113, 152, 186
Heal/healing, xii, 90, 94, 152, 185–86, 190–91, 228, 232
Health(y), 8, 41–43, 45, 70, 110, 151, 184, 278, 312, 320
Hegemony, 38, 248, 251
Hindu, 168, 172, 177, 221, 246
History/historical(ly), xii, 3, 11–12, 14, 21, 28–29, 31, 35, 39, 50, 64, 68, 87, 90, 95, 100, 102, 108–9, 113, 127, 137, 141, 152, 165, 169, 174, 187, 195, 199, 215, 223–24, 227, 229, 230–31, 236–37, 240, 244–45, 250, 262–64, 278, 280, 287–88, 290, 292, 295, 297–99, 307, 310, 312, 324
History of Israel, 18
Holistic/Wholistic, 10, 79, 111, 137, 297
Holocaust, 257
Holy and Great Council, 4, 8, 193–94, 321, 324–5
Holy See, 29, 186-7
Holy Spirit/Spirit, the, 7, 9–10, 20, 25, 33, 38, 53–56, 58, 65, 67–68, 72–3, 101, 117, 119, 123–24, 129, 130–31, 136–37, 143, 147, 149–50, 152, 159, 161, 170, 174, 176, 179, 183–84, 190–92, 196, 200, 202–3, 232, 234–35, 246, 265, 272, 314, 322
Human dignity, 43, 54, 58–60, 62, 64, 110–11, 126, 143, 147, 185, 191–92, 194, 197, 201–2, 249, 261, 273, 315, 317–8
Human rights, 5, 8, 12, 32, 37, 39, 40, 43, 44, 70, 138, 178, 259, 263–64, 270, 273, 289, 296–97, 301–5, 315, 323, 326

Humanitarian, 45, 114, 136, 140, 143, 147, 159, 285, 287, 291, 311–2
Humility, 131, 147, 174, 178, 181, 184, 190–91, 196–97, 217, 221, 316

Identity/identities, 5, 8, 11, 22, 28, 34, 80, 152, 179, 190, 196–97, 208, 224, 227–28, 233, 235, 239–41, 261, 290, 294–300, 304–6, 322
  Christian identity, 90, 160, 186, 239–40, 294, 297–98, 324–5
Ignorance, 54, 65, 88, 125, 143, 152, 156, 168, 169, 224, 245, 292
Ignore(s) *etc.*, 19, 31, 49, 85, 90, 101, 110, 129, 168–69, 209, 230, 235, 244, 288, 297, 299
Immigrant, 15, 136
Incarnation, 53, 238, 294, 297
India(n), 6, 19, 28, 167, 181, 226
Indigenous/indigenized, 28, 31, 38, 123, 172, 217, 223–25, 227, 229, 230, 232, 233–36, 240–42, 277, 285, 299, 305
Inducement(s), 12, 25, 36, 110, 140, 147, 197, 248, 254, 288, 291–92, 311–12, 315
Initiation, 56, 117
Injustice(s), 70, 164, 237, 307
Inter-Christian, 187–88, 194, 196, 322–3
Interfaith, 110, 192, 210
International Covenant on Civil and Political Rights , 36, 39, 41–42, 161, 301
International Dialogue – Roman Catholic and Pentecostal, 117, 118–32, 157
International Law, 4, 36–37, 259, 315
International Missionary Council, 4, 138, 253, 302
International Review of Mission, 148, 277
Interreligious, 27, 33–34, 36, 38, 184–87, 256, 261–63, 274–5
Intolerance, 25, 37, 39, 43–46, 109, 127–28, 136, 290, 301
Intra-Christian, 6, 8, 33–34, 36, 38, 163, 224, 231–32, 239, 242, 246, 253–4

Islam/Islamic, 24, 34–37, 166, 172, 200, 225–27, 236–38, 240–42, 256, 304
Israel/Israelites, 15–21, 23, 26, 36, 124, 155, 175, 219–20, 245, 257, 290
Italy, 115, 127, 187, 319

Jerusalem, 10, 18, 21–22, 25, 29, 32, 125, 137, 193, 225–28, 231–33, 321
Joint Working Group, RCC and WCC, 33, 66–77, 87, 104–16, 123, 128, 134–35, 157, 253, 256
Joy/joyful, 7, 56, 65, 143, 146, 149–52, 183, 194, 197–200, 322
Judaism, 16–23, 26, 35, 143, 155, 223, 290, 297
Justice, 16, 58, 99–100, 118, 132, 164, 184–86, 194, 195, 202, 218, 249, 261, 271–3

Kerala, 226
Kingdom of God/God's Kingdom, 7, 16, 22, 54, 149, 151, 159, 176–78, 183, 195, 271, 279, 305, 309
Kirill, 35, 197, 278, 281, 286–87, 298–99, 304
Koinonia, 105–8, 114, 117, 119, 129, 133, 137, 140, 154, 154–57, 190, 232–34, 250--1, 255, 326

Laity, 72, 236, 239
Language(s), xiii, 7–8, 20, 24–25, 42, 51, 68, 131, 172, 174, 213, 219, 225, 241, 249–50, 254, 279, 288, 296, 305, 317, 325–6
Lapsed, 156, 252, 310, 313–14, 316
Latin America, 38, 122–23, 127, 135, 179, 248–51, 266, 270
Latin (church/rite), 32, 93, 99, 102, 202, 222, 228, 231–32, 241, 296
Latin (language), 25, 27, 51, 234, 241
Latinization, 29, 228
Latino, 252
Lausanne Committee for World Evangelization 4, 162
Lausanne Movement, 4, 49, 162–81, 162, 261, 273–75, 321, 324,

Lausanne Covenant, 162, **163–64**, 169, 176, 273
Lausanne Theology Working Group, 174
Second Lausanne Congress Manila 1989, 78, 170 *see also* Manila Manifesto, the
Third Lausanne Congress Cape Town 2010, 174 *see also* Cape Town Commitment, the
Law(s), 5, 6, 17, 21, 23, 26, 35–37, 41, 43, 52, 59, 61, 109, 112, 122, 127–28, 139, 155, 217, 220–21, 228, 239, 243, 256, 262–64, 281, 287–88, 315, 323
  Anti-conversion laws (*see* anti conversion laws)
  Canon law, 29, 57, 226, 319
  Divine law, 59, 60
  Emory International Law Review, 4, 259
  International (*see* International Law)
  of Freedom of Conscience and Religious Organizations 1997, 35, 262, 288, 300
  on Freedom of Worship 1990, 35, 300
Learn(ed)/learning, 12, 16, 32, 54, 56, 90, 122, 125, 129, 143, 176, 179, 185, 198, 213, 232–33, 238, 263, 287–88, 320,
Lebanon, 30–32, 93–94, 103, 226–27, 229–31, 237–38, 241, 243
Legal, 4–6, 8, 33, 35–36, 39, 41, 44, 61, 74, 205, 239, 241, 259–60, 263–64, 267, 285, 304, 315, 317, 326
Legislation, 5, 17–18, 36–7, 44–45, 127, 210, 243, 300, 303
Liberal, 220, 305
Liberation, 137, 189, 234–35
Liberty, 41, 164, 216, 249, 273, 304, 317 (*see also* Religious freedom/liberty)
Linguistic, 25, 42, 68, 226, 241

SUBJECT INDEX

Listen(ed)/listening, 32, 37, 62, 142–43, 150, 152, 156, 177, 185, 216–17, 219, 238, 331
Liturgy/liturgical, 26, 29–30, 32, 56, 101, 126, 135, 149, 196, 200, 225–27, 233–35, 240, 267, 321, 323
Liturgy after the Liturgy, 234, 321, 323
Lutheran(s), 31–32, 231, 286, 290, 295
LXX. *See* Septuagint

Majority/majorities, 74–75, 112, 141, 170, 192, 222, 227, 231, 256, 271, 282, 290, 295–96, 303, 305–6, 314, 323
Majority world, 4, 179
Manila Manifesto, 162–63, 170–73, 176, 273–75
Manipulate(d)/manipulation/manipulative, 27, 108–10, 126, 128, 140, 143, 159, 161, 163, 255, 258, 264, 272–73, 290, 292
Margin(s)/marginalized, 79, 105, 114, 156, 189–90, 284, 323
Maronite Church/Maronites, 31, 227–30, 240
Marriage, 173, 187, 201
  Mixed marriages, 32, 76, 89, 91, 239, 312
Martyr(s)/martyria/martyrdom, 11, 38, 63, 120, 165, 172–73, 200, 202, 230, 234–36, 264, 287, 289, 324
Media, 40–41, 70, 83, 140, 158, 177, 285
Mass media, 102, 106, 110, 126, 285
Marx, Karl, 215
Marxist, 217
Melkites, 227
Messiah, 21–22, 62, 215, 221
McClendon, James, 293, 294, 307
Middle East, the, 5, 31–33, 49, 107, 167, 202, 205, 222–23, 231–33, 238, 246–47, 254 *see also* West Asia
Middle East Council of Churches (MECC), 32, 86, 91, 107, 134, 223–24, 227, 231–33, 238–39, 246

Migration(s), 12, 105
Minority/minorities, 6, 33–34, 42, 74–75, 83, 89, 112, 121, 127, 136, 141, 173, 192, 208, 215, 218, 222, 225, 231, 237, 241–42, 254, 271, 290, 295–96, 303, 305–6
Missio Dei, 8, 136, 150, 325
Missiology and derivatives, 7, 12, 51, 81–82, 87, 111, 134–35, 148, 153, 155, 234–35, 254, 260, 263, 265–66, 279, 289, 292, 298, 322–4
Mission agencies, 134, 136, 170, 183, 276
Mistrust, 49, 94, 99, 223
Monastery, 94, 284,
Monastic/monasticism, 83, 134, 200, 202, 236, 240
Moral, 8–9, 11, 20, 27, 33, 41, 44, 55, 59, 64, 73, 110, 125, 128, 139–40, 197, 217, 253, 291, 301, 307
Multi-religious, 182–83, 191–92, 308–9
Muslim(s), 24, 34, 37, 122, 168, 177, 202, 225, 227, 229, 231, 237–38, 241–42, 246
Mutual respect, 90, 98–99, 109, 129, 151, 185, 197–99, 306, 309

Nation(s), 9, 15–20, 23, 28, 44, 51, 53–54, 58, 62, 64–65, 71, 105, 109, 137, 141, 147, 164, 172–74, 176, 178–79, 181, 196, 202, 208, 218–20, 235, 263, 283, 296–98, 305, 322, 325
United Nations/UN, 6, 12, 36–37, 39, 40–46, 50, 68, 127, 303, 305, 326
National, 18, 21, 28, 36, 42, 45, 54, 91, 144, 167, 186, 218, 239, 247, 262, 290, 295–96, 297–98, 305, 318,
Nationalism/nationalist(ic), 9, 35, 167, 218, 227, 262, 289, 293, 295, 298
National church, 5, 11, 28, 32, 170, 225, 228, 231, 247, 296
National culture/identity, 5, 11, 235, 280, 285, 294, 296, 298–99

SUBJECT INDEX

Neighbor(s)/neighbour(s), 33, 55, 67, 73, 130, 156, 176, 183–84, 187, 219, 315–16. *See also* 207–21
Nestorian, 223, 226
New Delhi, 33, 69, 134, 253
New Religious Movements, 35, 106, 113, 136, 224, 246, 249–51, 255, 285–6
New Testament, 21–22, 26, 33, 80, 125, 159, 170, 245
Nominal, 11, 31, 75, 80, 82, 91, 141–42, 156, 163, 164–69, 171, 229–30, 239, 252, 258, 260–64, 266–70, 275–76, 280, 310, 314, 316
Non-Christian(s), 27, 55, 69, 173, 208–10, 245, 247, 253, 262, 265–66, 274, 282–83, 287
Non-Western, 24, 38, 170, 326
North, 4, 179
North Africa(n), 222–25, 227, 231–32, 237, 240–42, 244–5
North America(n), 4, 32–33, 35, 169
Nostra Aetate , 27

Old Testament, 15–16, 18–9, 124, 219, 245, 315
Oppress(ed) *etc.*, 5, 11, 79, 93, 190, 216, 236, 248, 258, 260, 262, 282, 285
Oriental Catholic Churches. *See* Eastern Catholic Church
Orthodox *see also* Copt, Holy and Great Council, Russian Orthodox Church, Ecumenical Patriarch
  Advisory Group to the WCC, **81–8**3, 279
  Eastern, 28–29, 32, 81, **82–**83, 222–23, 227–28, 232, 244, 262, 279, 297
  Non-Orthodox, 28, 35, 193, 196–97, 218, 248, 262–63, 287–88, 299, 305, 322
  Oriental, 28–29, 81, **82–8**3, 201, 223, 226–29, 240, 284, 323
  Panorthodox, 97, 193, 227, 281, 321–22, 325
  Ottoman, 89, 230, 241

Palestine/Palestinian, 14, 19, 21, 31, 223, 231, 238
Parachurch, 87, 208, 245–6
Partner(s), 27, 33, 37, 112, 174, 178, 180, 232, 270, 296, 305–6, 324
Partnership, 142–43, 175, 178–79, 190,
Pastoral, 11, 32, 76, 83, 85, 87, 91–92, 100, 105–6, 110–11, 125–26, 131–32, 135, 144, 188, 202, 238–39, 296
  Pastoral activity, 30, 95, 99, 101, 114, 121
  Pastoral care, 92, 112–13, 239
  Pastoral challenge(s), 32, **86-92**, 107, 223–24, 238, 239, 246
Patient/patience, xvi, 54, 62, 65, 72, 131, 171, 175, 178, 195, 298
Patriarch(s), 16, 23, 28, 30–31, 94, 197, 200, 209–10, 281, 227, 229–30, 298, 304 *see also* Ecumenical Patriarch
Patriarchate(s), 28, 35, 94, 133, 193, 225–28, 241, 281, 286, 288, 290, 297–98
Peace/peaceful, 40, 44, 49, 54, 65, 70, 81–82, 100, 109, 124, 129, 131, 149, 152, 164, 174, 177–79, 185–86, 194–98, 200, 202–3, 208–19, 233–34, 238, 271, 273, 279, 280–81, 318, 322, 325
Pejorative(ly), 7, 11, 68–69, 147, 155, 312
Pentecostal, xi, xii, 4, 10, 38, 117–32, 134, 157, 186, 210, 220, 239, 286, 290, 306, 323, 325
Pentecostal World Fellowship/Conference, xi, xii, 4, 124, 309, 323
People of God/God's people, 3, 16, 18, 55–56, 64, 99, 114, 170, 174–75, 217, 235, 313, 321
Persecution(s), xi, 11–12, 20, 31, 100, 102, 119–21, 127, 163–65, 172, 178, 185, 209, 226, 230, 236, 247, 263–65
Pluralism/pluralistic, 82, 174, 181, 183, 211–12, 238, 248, 257, 317
Pneumatology, 325

Polemic(s)/polemical, 102, 108, 143, 288

Politics, political, 4–5, 10–12, 16, 24, 32–34, 36, 39, 41–42, 44, 62, 71, 74, 88–89, 96, 110–11, 122, 125, 127, 140, 155, 159, 160–62, 166–67, 171, 175, 177, 185, 187–88, 207–8, 210–11, 218–19, 223–25, 233, 235–37, 239, 241–42, 247, 254, 285, 291, 298, 301, 309, 313, 317

Prayer(s)/pray, xiii, 13, 22, 64, 70, 80, 82, 98, 102, 107, 111–14, 122, 129, 131, 137, 139, 142, 145, 149, 159–61, 163–64, 170–73, 175, 177–78, 181, 187, 200–202, 236, 280

Pre-exilic, 14, 18

Prejudice, 102, 113, 143, 156, 168, 177, 221

Presbyterian, 31–32, 229, 231, 257, 286

privilege(d)(s), 17–18, 34, 59, 69, 75, 85, 89, 138, 175, 179, 183, 200, 218, 275, 297, 300, 302, 307

Prophet(s)/prophetic, 18–19, 112, 175, 185

Protestant, 28, 32–33, 38, 123, 128, 186, 210, 212–13, 215–16, 219, 222–24, 231, 240, 246–47, 251, 259–60, 266, 273, 276, 281–83, 286, 289, 295–97, 301, 312, 326

Protestant mission(s), 28, 31, 128, 167, 230, 233, 246, 266, 300

Protestant-Orthodox relations, 30–31, 231, 233, 289

Pontifical Council for Interreligious Dialogue (PCID), 182–83, 186–87, 308

Pontifical Council for Promoting Christian Unity PCPCU, xi, xii, 4, 66, 93, 104, 117–18, 157, 199, 249, 251, 309

Poor, the, 54, 61, 79–80, 98, 136, 160, 161, 199, 209, 214, 220, 236, 252, 260–61

Pope(s), 29, 38, 59, 76, 93, 98–99, 101, 132, 197, 199–202, 229, 244, 249–50, 267–71, 324–25

Pope Francis, 197, 199–200, 202, 324–25

Pope John Paul II, 38, 98–99, 101, 106, 157, 201, 243, 249, 269–71

Pope Paul VI, 29–30, 47, 76, 98, 132, 199–200, 267–69, 272

Pope Shenouda, 199–201

Pope Tawadros II, 199–202

Post-exilic, 19

Poverty, 105, 176, 184

Power(s)/powerfully, xi, 4–5, 8–10, 12, 16, 20, 25, 27, 29, 34, 38, 53, 56, 58–60, 63, 65, 68–69, 75, 83, 110, 119, 126, 130, 149, 161, 163, 167, 170, 175, 178–79, 181, 183–85, 190, 192, 208, 210, 215, 223, 225, 228, 234, 235–36, 238, 270, 272, 276, 296, 325

Preaching, 36, 55, 67, 121, 126, 128, 131, 147, 149, 190–91, 209, 243, 254, 285, 287

Primates, 81, 193, 209, 246–47, 279, 281, 283–84,

Private(ly), 12, 27, 36, 40–41, 43, 55, 59–60, 65, 109, 138, 160–61, 270, 302, 317

Priest(s)/priesthood, 16–18, 31, 56, 98, 101–2, 168, 194, 215, 218, 232, 245, 262, 267, 279, 290, 318

Proclamation/proclaim(ing), 18, 22, 55, 64, 68–71, 75, 78, 88, 107, 119, 126, 129–31, 142, 144, 146, 149, 182–83, 191, 198, 208, 212–14, 218, 221, 251, 253, 260–64, 268, 271, 279, 287, 309–10, 314, 317, 320, 323

Prophet(s)/prophetic, 18–19, 112, 175, 185

Proselyte(s), 15–23, 25–26, 38, 109, 124–25, 139, 152, 155, 241, 245, 255, 290, 292

Proselytism, Biblical and historical perspectives, 14–23, 26, 88–89, 109, 224, 225–31,

Proselytism Definition(s), 7–8, 26–28, 87–8, 122, 158–59, 223–24, 253–54, 268, 278, 280, 283, 291, 298, 303, 310–11, 313
Protestant(s)/Protestantism, 28, 30–33, 35, 38, 123–24, 128, 165, 167, 169, 186, 207–17, 219–24, 230–31, 233, 240, 245–47, 249, 251, 254, 259–61, 266, 273, 276, 279, 281–83, 286, 289, 295–97, 300–301, 312, 323, 325–26
Psychology/psychological(ly), 32–33, 59, 73, 92, 110, 125, 140, 152, 185, 215, 224, 241, 253, 291–92, 311–12
Public, 10, 12, 27, 40–43, 54–5, 60–61, 65, 109, 120–21, 123, 138, 159, 161, 177, 185, 192, 209, 218, 230, 241, 251, 258, 270, 285, 302, 304, 314, 317, 326
Public order, 42, 59, 60–1

Rabbi(s), 15, 23
Racist/racial, 70, 177, 194, 218, 220–1
Rebaptized, 97, 139
Re-Christianization, 82, 280
Reconcile(d)/reconciling, 35, 80, 106–8, 119, 129, 136, 176, 179, 278
Reconciliation, 30, 70, 80, 101, 107, 113, 129, 142, 144, 152, 170, 178–79, 186, 191, 196, 197, 201–2, 217, 221, 223, 233, 244, 322–23
Redeem/redemption, 19, 22, 62–63, 219, 280, 297
Redemptoris Missio, 269–72
Re-evangelization, 102, 111, 141, 321, 277, 325
Reformation, 88, 166, 251, 293, 295
Reformed, 31–32, 231, 295
Relationship, 19, 27, 30, 55, 78, 80, 86, 97, 117–19, 123, 129–30, 156, 161, 165, 197, 200, 225, 233, 238, 239–41, 250, 253, 255, 257, 285, 294, 306
Relationship(s), 65, 80, 85, 107–8, 110–12, 114, 119, 127, 129, 130–31, 133–36, 140–41, 144, 163, 170, 186, 192, 199, 215, 231, 253, 277, 282, 285, 302, 306, 313, 316, 318
Religious freedom, liberty, 12, 25, 27, 33, 36–37, 51–52, 58–65, 68, 70–72, 74, 87–88, 91, 97, 100, 105, 109, 115, 122, 127–28, 129, 136–39, 158, 170, 172, 178, 185, 192, 198, 200, 202, 238, 253, 260, 265, 270–71, 273–74, 283–86, 288, 302–3, 317
Renewal, 32, 72, 74, 78, 82–83, 85, 88, 91–92, 99, 108, 143, 215, 223–24, 233, 236, 238–40, 242, 298
Repent/repentance, 8, 22, 26, 82, 108, 117, 130, 142, 156–57, 175, 177, 184, 191, 273
Respect. *See* Mutual respect
Resurrection, 7, 9, 55–56, 149, 159
Rights *see* Human rights
Rival/rivalry(ies), 13, 67, 71, 101, 108, 142, 145, 150–51, 170, 251, 296,
Robeck Jr., Cecil M, 86, 124, 220, 243–58, 263, 287,
Roman Catholic, 25–26, 157, 245, 249–52, 256, 259, 265, 271, 289–91, 295, 303
Roman Catholicism, 231–32, 251, 265–72
Roman Catholics, 28, 119, 154, 156, 163–65, 248, 250–51, 257, 283
Roman Catholic Church, 33, 51–65, 66–77, 87, 93–103, 104–16, 117–32, 134–35, 156–57, 171, 247–48, 251–53, 260, 272, 275, 279, 282, 284, 286, 289, 321
Roman Church, 28
Romania(n), 29, 166, 193, 207–8, 213, 217, 234, 247, 299
Rome, xii, 20, 23, 29–30, 88, 95, 97–98, 135, 200–201, 225–28, 319, 326
Russia, 11, 35–36, 106, 134, 166, 197, 209, 213–14, 236, 247–48, 262–63, 284, 286, 288–90, 298–301, 304–5, 314
Russian, 35–36, 217–18, 243, 247, 262–63, 288, 298, 300, 305

Russian Duma, 35
Russian Federation, 35
Russian Orthodox Church/ROC, 28, 35, 193, 196–98, 245, 248, 262–63, 281, 286–98, 297, 300

Sacrament(s)/sacramental, 10–11, 56, 82, 92–93, 98, 101–2, 141, 165, 201, 236
Salvation, 7, 10–11, 17, 19, 22, 26, 53, 55–56, 63, 69, 71–73, 80, 83, 97–98, 101, 107, 111, 130, 137, 139, 140–42, 146, 149, 155, 165, 213–14, 221, 233, 240, 255–56, 261, 268–69, 274, 281, 317
School, 93–94, 259,
Schools, 54, 89, 144, 168, 213, 251, 308,
Scripture, 9, 26, 31, 69,70–1, 92, 117, 129–30, 137, 163, 171, 202, 212, 229, 238, 311, 315. See also the Bible
Second Vatican Council, 27, 29, 51–65, 97–98, 132, 228, 265, 267, 270, 284
Sectarian/sectarianism, 72, 242, 249, 254
Sect(s), 6, 25, 28, 32, 72, 83, 86–92, 106–7, 113, 119, 122, 136, 197, 210, 215, 223–24, 233, 238–39, 246, 249–51, 255, 262, 270, 281, 285, 297
Secular, 4, 26, 82, 84, 127, 185, 239, 241, 277, 304–5, 315
Secularism, 163, 277–78, 283
See of Rome, 97–8
Septuagint/LXX, 15, 20, 26
Service(s), 16, 18, 44, 54–55, 63, 67–68, 70, 85, 88, 108, 113–14, 151, 157, 173, 175, 183–84, 191, 195, 217, 222, 238
Shakespeare, William, 25, 38
Sheep-stealing, xi, 7, 156, 242, 254, 300, 309
Sin(s)/sinful, 3, 55, 176, 196, 216, 234, 235, 273, 276, 309, 314, 323
Sinners, 211
Sister Church(es), 30, 95, 97–98, 101, 232,

Slavorum Apostoli , 98
Slovakia(n), 193, 214, 247
Solidarity, 150, 175, 183, 185–86, 191, 194, 209, 237, 260–61, 271, 277, 322, 325
Soteriology, 7–8, 11
South, 136, 158, 162–63, 174, 180–81, 218, 244–45, 286, 306
Soviet (Union)/USSR, 5, 11, 35, 66, 166, 172, 218, 236, 244, 246–47, 256, 262, 286, 298–300
Spirit. See Holy Spirit
Spiritual/spirituality, 9, 16, 27–28, 30, 35, 55, 72, 80, 83, 89, 92, 96, 99, 101, 107–8, 111–12, 114, 126, 139–40, 143, 152, 156, 163–64, 168, 179, 195, 202, 210, 212, 215, 224–26, 230, 233, 237–38, 240, 247, 255, 262, 268, 274, 279, 287, 291–92, 294–96, 298–99, 304, 307, 324
Spirit of God. See Holy Spirit
Stott, John, 78, 155, 157, 162–63, 249, 252, 324
Suffer(ed)/suffering(s), 20, 49, 54, 84, 89, 97, 100, 102, 119, 121, 152, 164, 172–73, 175–76, 178, 181, 184, 195, 202, 215, 238, 290, 301, 307,
Suspicion, 74, 99, 100–101, 121, 124, 126, 155, 170, 179, 186, 231, 237, 241, 254, 296, 303
Syncretism, 90–91, 177
Syria, 17, 20, 28–29, 31–2, 226, 228, 231, 237
Syriac, 225, 228, 241

Territory/territories *see also* Canonical territory, 11, 28, 93–94, 101, 209, 247, 266, 282, 295, 296, 304–5, 319
Tolerate/tolerant(ce), 25, 44, 122, 161, 172, 210, 273, 316, 318
Totalitarian/Totalitarianism, 166, 208–9, 218
Trinity/Trinitarian, 10, 197, 216, 262, 279, 280, 284, 325,
Turkey, 31, 231, 281

SUBJECT INDEX

Two-Thirds World. *See also* Majority World 170, 213

Ukraine/Ukrainian, 29, 243, 247, 290
Uniate(s)/Uniatism, 29–30, 93–103, 106, 110, 113, 123, 194, 228–29, 231–32, 247, 267, 282, 290, 322, 325
Unilateral/unilaterally, 119, 254–55, 258, 263
United Nations, UN, 6, 12, 36–37, 39–46, 50, 68, 127, 303, 305, 326
United States/US/USA, 30, 106, 113, 167, 220–21, 244, 251, 254, 257, 271–72, 286, 295, 300, 309
Universal Declaration of Human Rights, 12, 36, 39, 40, 44, 46, 138, 164, 173, 273–74, 301–2, 305, 317
Unity, xi, 4, 32, 67, 70, 78, 80, 82, 84, 86, 118, 128–30, 137–38, 155, 157, 178–80, 189–90, 220, 223, 238, 249, 251, 262, 298, 300, 309
Unworthy, 27, 61, 63, 79, 110, 155, 157, 173, 176, 181, 248, 251–52, 258, 265, 269, 274, 291
USSR. *See* Soviet (Union)/USSR

Vassiliadis, Petros, 81, 138, 139, 305–6, 311, 321–6
Vatican, 228, 249–50, 253, 264
Vatican II, 26–27, 29, 49–51, 56, 68, 69, 107, 121–22, 127–28, 130, 157, 228, 232, 248–49, 252–53, 265–70, 284. *See also* Second Vatican Council

WCC. *See* World Council of Churches
West Asia(n), 222–25, 227, 229–33, 237, 240–2
West Bank, 232

Western, the West, 9, 11, 20, 22, 26, 32, 38, 81, 89, 91–93, 96–8, 122, 161, 166–67, 169–70, 179–80, 208–9, 211, 213, 222, 224–28, 231–34, 236–37, 239–41, 244, 247, 263, 295, 297, 299–300, 326
Wholistic. *See* Holistic
Witness. *See* Christian witness, Common witness, False witness
Word, of God/God's word, 59, 62–64, 174, 182, 216, 220–21, 273
World Council of Churches/WCC, xi, xii, 4, 33–34, 50, 66–77, 78–80, 81–82, 84, 87, 104–16, 123, 128, 133–45, 148–53, 157, 171, 182–88, 189–92, 197, 234, 248, 252–57, 261, 264, 275–79, 281–87, 290–91, 298, 300, 302–3, 305–6, 309–13, 317, 320–21, 323, 325
WCC Assembly, 33, 69, 115, 134, 136, 138, 189, 252–53, 256, 302–3
Central Committee, 115, 133–34, 144, 148–49, 189, 252–53, 276
World Evangelical Alliance, xi, xii, 4, 14, 50, 154–57, 162, 182–88, 291, 303, 308–20, 323
World Evangelical Fellowship, 154, 162
World Missionary Conference. *See* Edinburgh World Missionary Conference

Yahweh, 16–19, 109, 124, 139, 155, 219
Young people/youth, 54, 75, 83, 89, 236, 238, 285, 312
Younger churches, 10, 246, 258

Zeal/zealous/zealots, 7, 17, 20, 23, 25, 38, 49, 68, 83, 161, 168, 208–9, 213, 247

Scripture Index

GENESIS
15, 185, 192, 315

EXODUS
15, 16, 124, 155, 156, 178, 245, 315

LEVITICUS
15, 16, 73, 130, 315

NUMBERS
15, 16,

DEUTERONOMY
15, 16, 26, 73, 130, 240, 315, 316

JOSHUA
16, 17, 315

RUTH
17

2 KINGS
17

1 CHRONICLES
16, 17,

2 CHRONICLES
16, 18

PSALMS
17, 315, 316

PROVERBS
316

ISAIAH
15, 16, 200

JEREMIAH
15, 173, 178

EZEKIEL
15

DANIEL
178

AMOS
313

HOSEA
313

MICAH

184

ZECHARIAH

15

MALACHI

15

MATTHEW

5	53, 164, 173, 315
7	139, 302, 316
9	54
10	315
12	63
13	294, 310
18	316
20	316
22	63, 73, 130, 184, 316
20	55
23	21. 26, 245,
25	184, 191
28	9, 58, 64, 67, 146, 184, 196, 256, 322

MARK

3	315
9	129
10	63, 191
16	55, 56, 62, 137, 171, 184

LUKE

2	56
4	164, 183
7	264
9	311, 315, 317
15	313
24	137, 184

JOHN

1	214, 315
3	184, 190, 195, 315
7	216
8	304
10	137
11	195
12	173, 195
13	67, 175, 191, 316
14	55, 184, 315
15	115, 164, 173
16	184
17	67, 68, 80, 102, 107, 113, 122, 123, 129, 137, 142, 144, 164, 171, 175, 195, 201
18	183, 216
20	184

ACTS

	9, 21, 317
1	10, 67, 137, 184, 321
2	21, 22, 26, 125, 245, 317
3	22, 178
4	55, 63, 69, 131, 164, 173
5	63, 164, 173, 178
6	5, 26, 125, 245
8	22, 56
9	55
10	54, 184
11	177
13	22, 26, 55, 245
14	22, 55, 317
15	177
16	55
17	5, 55, 131, 183, 192, 317
18	317
19	55, 177, 316, 317
20	171
21	22
26	55
28	55

ROMANS

1	131, 256
2	316
3	184
6	56
8	65, 68, 280
10	22, 55, 190

12	108
13	63, 173, 178
14	63, 171, 178
15	101, 126, 171, 195, 198, 316, 319

1 CORINTHIANS

1	55, 80, 173, 191
2	173, 311
6	102, 130
9	55, 79
11	195
12	142, 175, 201–2
13	126, 130, 244

2 CORINTHIANS

2	164
3	55
4	79, 164, 173, 190, 311
5	80, 129, 195, 316
6	64, 173
7	55
10	123, 164, 319
12	54

GALATIANS

55, 100, 164, 184, 195, 219, 313, 316

EPHESIANS

	129
1	68, 77, 107, 136, 142
2	171
3	55, 77
4	55, 108, 124, 129, 131, 132, 138, 142, 157, 171, 203, 315
5	175
6	55, 131, 164

PHILIPPIANS

5, 55, 170, 171, 173, 196, 316

COLOSSIANS

55, 56, 68, 77, 164, 195, 316

1 THESSALONIANS

22, 55, 56, 175, 190, 311

2 THESSALONIANS

64, 175

1 TIMOTHY

63, 64, 164, 173, 178, 313,

2 TIMOTHY

313

HEBREWS

164, 175, 195, 313

1 PETER

	215
1	194, 322
2	178, 215, 316
3	56, 177, 183, 215, 311, 315, 316
5	316

2 PETER

195

1 JOHN

54, 107, 164, 175

REVELATION

77, 147, 173, 175, 195, 219,

www.ingramcontent.com/pod-product-compliance
Lightning Source LLC
Chambersburg PA
CBHW071145300426
44113CB00009B/1094